D1553791

ECOLOGY AND NATURAL RESOURCE MANAGEMENT

ECOLOGY AND NATURAL RESOURCE MANAGEMENT
Systems Analysis and Simulation

WILLIAM E. GRANT
Texas A&M University, College Station, Texas

ELLEN K. PEDERSEN
Texas A&M University, College Station, Texas

SANDRA L. MARÍN
Universidad de Magallanes, Punta Arenas, Chile

JOHN WILEY & SONS, INC.
New York / Chichester / Weinheim / Brisbane / Singapore / Toronto

Copyright © 1997 by John Wiley & Sons, Inc.

All rights reserved. Published simultaneously in Canada.

Reproduction or translation of any part of this work beyond
that permitted by Section 107 or 108 of the 1976 United
States Copyright Act without the permission of the copyright
owner is unlawful. Requests for permission or further
information should be addressed to the Permissions Department,
John Wiley & Sons, Inc., 605 Third Avenue, New York, NY
10158-0012.

Library of Congress Cataloging in Publication Data:
Grant, William E. (William Edward), 1947–
    Ecology and natural resource management: systems analysis and
simulation / William E. Grant, Ellen K. Pedersen, Sandra L. Marín.
        p.   cm.
    Includes bibliographical references.
    ISBN 0-471-13786-3 (cloth : alk. paper)
    1. Ecology—Computer simulation.   2. Natural resources—
Management—Computer simulation.   3. System analysis.
    I. Pedersen, Ellen K.   II. Marín, Sandra L.   III. Title.
    QH541.15.S5G73   1997
    333.7′2′0113—dc20   96-28354

Printed in the United States of America

10 9 8 7 6 5 4 3 2

CONTENTS

PART II   THEORETICAL FRAMEWORK: FOUR PHASES OF SYSTEMS ANALYSIS

3   CONCEPTUAL-MODEL FORMULATION   31

4   QUANTITATIVE-MODEL SPECIFICATION   44

PREFACE

Throughout the world, both in developed and developing nations, we face complex natural resource management problems related to our attempt to achieve economic growth without destroying the ecological systems that ultimately form the basis of human existence. This book introduces the use of systems analysis and simulation to university students, faculty, and professionals interested in solving such problems. Systems analysis refers both to a general problem-solving philosophy and to a collection of quantitative techniques, including simulation, developed specifically to address problems related to the functioning of complex systems. Formal exposure to systems analysis should be an integral part of the training of all professionals and academicians who make or influence decisions affecting the well being of our natural resources.

The material contained in the current text has evolved over roughly two decades through experiences in a graduate course in the Department of Wildlife and Fisheries Sciences at Texas A&M University and, over the past several years, through experiences in a series of short courses at various universities in Latin America. In 1986, the senior author published a textbook titled *Systems Analysis and Simulation in Wildlife and Fisheries Sciences*, and the theoretical section of the current text draws heavily on this earlier work. Our motivation for developing a new text resulted from the need to reconsider selected theoretical aspects of the topic in view of current ecological applications, the possibility of providing readers direct access to computerized versions of the models used in the text, and the desire to have a single textbook to support all of our teaching activities (the text is available both in English and Spanish). We hope that the book will provide a practical introduction to the systems approach to problem solving and the use of simulation within a familiar subject-matter context, not only for our own students, but for all those interested in ecology and natural resource management.

The text is divided into five parts. Part I presents the philosophical basis for use of systems analysis and simulation in ecology and natural resource management. Important systems concepts are described, an overview of systems analysis is presented, and the systems approach is compared with other methods of problem solving. Part II presents the theoretical framework for development, evaluation, and use of simulation models, formally describing each of the four phases of systems analysis: conceptual model formulation, quantitative model specification, model evaluation, and model use. Part III provides a practical guide for application of the systems approach in ecology and natural resource management. Useful "building blocks" for constructing systems models are presented, the flow of ideas that pass through an experienced modeler's mind during model development is described, an annotated example of model development and use is presented, and a format for reporting the development and use of simulation models is suggested. Parts IV and V provide examples of use of simulation models to address a variety of questions in ecology and natural resource management, respectively. Each example briefly introduces an ecological or natural resource management topic, states objectives of the model, and provides background information on the problem. This is followed by a description of the model, results of selected simulations addressing initial objectives, and suggestions concerning further questions that could be addressed using the model.

The usefulness of systems analysis and simulation results as much from the process (problem specification and model development and evaluation) as the product (the final model). Skill in the process of "modeling" is gained through practice, ideally under the supervision of an experienced modeler. Obviously, this dynamic dialogue between apprentice and master cannot be captured in a book. However, we are particularly pleased to provide readers the opportunity to practice with fully operational computerized versions of all models presented in the text. Using programs on the enclosed CD ROM, readers can modify the models as described in the text and also can experiment with their own modifications within a flexible, user-friendly simulation environment (STELLA®II) developed for personal computers by High Performance Systems, Inc. However, we want to emphasize that the objective of examples provided in the text is to demonstrate use of simulation models to address realistic questions in ecology and natural resource management, not to promote specific ecological theories nor to suggest particular solutions to natural resource management problems. Nor are the computerized models intended for use outside the hypothetical context in which they were developed.

Finally, we would like to acknowledge our indebtedness to Bill Neill and Michael Corson for their thorough and thoughtful critiques of the manuscript. The book is much improved thanks to their efforts—we simply could not have had better reviewers. We also would like to thank Mort Kothmann and Dick Fisher for their advice on the models presented in chapters 19 and 20, respectively, our colleagues at High Performance Systems and at John Wiley for their flexibility in working with us to provide computerized versions of models found in the text, and Rosemary Payton and Vivian Gonzales for help with preparation of the manuscript.

WILLIAM E. GRANT, ELLEN K. PEDERSEN, AND SANDRA L. MARÍN

PART I

THE SYSTEMS PERSPECTIVE

Part I presents the philosophical basis for use of systems analysis and simulation in ecology and natural resource management and introduces basic systems concepts. Chapter 1 provides a brief example of the systems approach to problem solving in ecology and natural resource management and compares the systems approach with other methods of problem solving. Chapter 2 describes important concepts implied by the terms system, systems analysis, model, and simulation, and presents an overview of the four phases of systems analysis: conceptual-model formulation, quantitative-model specification, model evaluation, and model use. Computerized (STELLA®II) versions of the models presented in this part can be found in the "nrm" folder on the enclosed CD ROM. Names of particular models appear in the right-hand margin of the text.

CHAPTER 1

THE SYSTEMS APPROACH TO PROBLEM SOLVING

1.1 INTRODUCTION

Consider the following situation. A group of landowners has petitioned the government to obtain a permit that would allow them to divert water from a river to irrigate their crops. Currently, water diversion is prohibited. Downstream from the landowners' land, the river flows into a wildlife refuge in which an endangered animal species lives. The government has hired you to provide an assessment of the likely impact of water diversion on the endangered species. Almost surely the permit will be granted; thus, your charge is to provide guidelines concerning the relative impacts of diverting different quantities of water during different seasons. The landowners propose to plant 100 kg/ha of crops each January, harvest each December, and divert 15% of the river flow for irrigation during the entire year. The government has provided the following information.

1.1.1 General Background Information About the Wildlife Refuge

During the past decade, habitat improvement efforts within the refuge appear to have stabilized population levels of the endangered animal species. These efforts have focused primarily on encouraging production of a particular native plant species that serves both as food and cover for the endangered species. Standing biomass of this native plant and population size of the endangered animal have been monitored closely over the last 5 years (Table 1.1).

TABLE 1.1 **Estimates of the Standing Biomass of the Native Plant Species and the Population Size of the Endangered Animal Species Based on Field Data Collected at 3-Month Intervals over the Last 5 Years**

Year	Month	Standing Biomass of Native Plants (kg/ha)	Population Size of Endangered Animal (Animals/ha)
1	1	90	2.0
	4	8	1.5
	7	115	1.6
	10	231	1.9
2	1	93	2.2
	4	60	1.6
	7	117	1.7
	10	236	2.0
3	1	95	2.3
	4	61	1.7
	7	120	1.7
	10	242	2.0
4	1	97	2.3
	4	62	1.7
	7	123	1.8
	10	248	2.0
5	1	99	2.4
	4	64	1.7
	7	126	1.8
	10	253	2.1

1.1.2 Information About the Endangered Animal Species

Population density, as measured in January, is 2.5 animals per hectare. Per capita natality rate of the animal population is 0.1 animal per month. That is, for each animal in the population, 0.1 animal is born each month. Mortality rate depends on the per capita availability of a native species that provides both food and cover for the animals (Table 1.2). Each animal consumes 1 kilogram of plant biomass each month.

1.1.3 Information About the Native Plant Species

Standing biomass of native plants, as measured in January, is 100 kilograms per hectare. The plant species grows from the beginning of March through the end of September, during which time its growth rate depends on soil water content, which in turn depends directly on river flow. In fact, for every unit of river flow during each month of the growing season, each kilogram of plant biomass produces 0.05 kilogram on net growth. During the nongrowing

TABLE 1.2 Proportion of the Animal Population Dying Each Month as a Function of the Per Capita Availability of Native Plants

Proportion of Population Dying	Kilograms of Plants per Animal
0.95	0
0.68	5
0.53	10
0.435	15
0.345	20
0.27	25
0.21	30
0.165	35
0.115	40
0.075	45
0.05	50

season, from the beginning of October through the end of February, 25% of the standing crop of plant biomass is lost each month via decomposition.

1.1.4 Information About River Flow and the Crop That Landowners Propose to Irrigate

The river normally flows at a rate of 5.5 units per month as it passes the landowners' land and enters the wildlife refuge. The relationship among the growth rate of the crop, the standing crop biomass, and the rate of irrigation is shown in Table 1.3.

What guidelines concerning water diversion would you suggest? Can the landowners divert 15% of the river flow for irrigation during the entire year without negatively affecting the endangered animal species in the refuge? What are the relative impacts, both on the endangered species and on crop production, of diverting different quantities of water during different seasons? And, even more important, on what type of analysis would you base your recommendations? We will return to these questions at the end of the chapter; however, we encourage you to take a few minutes right now to write down your responses.

We begin with this example to emphasize that predicting the dynamics of even relatively simple ecological systems for which we have a solid database is not a trivial matter. An understanding of the behavior of each part of the system does not guarantee an understanding of the behavior of the system. We need an effective way of dealing with the complexity generated by inter-action among the parts.

TABLE 1.3 Growth Rate of the Crop Per Unit of Standing Crop Biomass Present That Results from Each Unit of Irrigation Water Received During the Month

Growth Rate of Crop (kg/ha-mo of Growth per kg/ha of Standing Crop Biomass per Unit of Irrigation Water per Month)	Standing Crop Biomass of Crop (kg/ha)
0.08	100
0.07	150
0.06	200
0.05	250
0.04	300
0.03	350
0.02	400
0.01	450
0.00	500

The most interesting and critical questions that we face as ecologists and natural resource managers deal with inherently complex systems. In addition to considering interactions among many physical, biological, and ecological factors, we also may need to consider economic, cultural, and legal factors when addressing a given issue. Attempts to deal with such complex problems in a narrow or fragmentary way often lead to poor research design and ultimately to poor management decisions. Management plans based on sound biological information fail when unforeseen economic factors shift demand for a natural resource. Apparently sound economic policies fail when unforeseen biological limits are exceeded.

Systems analysis is both a philosophical approach and a collection of techniques, including simulation, developed explicitly to address problems dealing with complex systems. Systems analysis emphasizes a holistic approach to problem solving and the use of mathematical models to identify and simulate important characteristics of complex systems. In the simplest sense, a system is any set of objects that interact. A mathematical model is a set of equations that describes the interrelationships among these objects. By solving the equations comprising a mathematical model, we can mimic, or simulate, the dynamic (time-varying) behavior of the system.

The origins of systems analysis can be traced to attempts by the military to deal with complex logistical problems during World War II. Subsequently, the systems approach to problem solving has been applied successfully in a variety of fields in engineering, industrial dynamics, business management, and economics, and since the late 1960s has found increasing application in the fields of biology, ecology, and natural resource management. The goal of the systems approach within the context of ecology and natural resource management is quite simply to provide a useful perspective on complex systems that promotes good research design and wise resource management decisions.

1.2 THE SYSTEMS APPROACH COMPARED TO OTHER METHODS OF PROBLEM SOLVING

The systems approach certainly is not the only useful approach to problem solving. Throughout the history of mankind, trial and error has been by far the most widespread and useful method. Unfortunately, for some problems, the appropriate trials are too long and the possible errors are too costly. The scientific method of solving problems emphasizes more disciplined observation and perhaps manipulation of particularly interesting parts of the world. Scientists formally interpret these observations in a variety of qualitative (description and classification) and quantitative (mathematical and statistical analyses) ways, depending on the type of problem, or type of system, with which they are dealing. Scientists and other problem solvers use the systems approach to integrate relevant information gained from trial and error or expert opinion and from the scientific method in a form that facilitates formal description of the structure and dynamics of complex systems.

Precise definition of a "complex system" is neither possible nor necessary. However, it is possible and useful to relate types of systems to formal methods of problem solving in a very general way. For example, we might characterize systems in terms of number of components and degree of interrelatedness of components (Figure 1.1). Problems related to systems with relatively few, highly interrelated components can be addressed in analytical form mathematically. Physicists deal with mechanical systems in this manner—Newton's laws of motion are an example. Problems related to systems with relatively many, loosely related components can be addressed statistically. For example, the movement of gas molecules inside a closed, expandable container can be viewed as random, and interesting system relationships can be described in terms of average temperature, pressure, and volume. But problems related to systems with relatively many, closely interrelated components cannot be addressed effectively by either of these two problem-solving methods. On the one hand, such systems usually cannot be solved mathematically because an analytical solution to the set of equations describing the system does not exist. On the other hand, dynamics of these systems cannot be represented statistically as average tendencies because interrelatedness of components, or system structure, causes markedly nonrandom behavior. Systems analysis and simulation focus specifically on these "intermediate" systems characterized by "organized complexity" in which system structure both controls and is changed by system dynamics.

From a slightly different perspective, we might compare methods of problem solving in terms of the relative level of understanding and the amount of data available on the system in which we are interested (Figure 1.2). As used

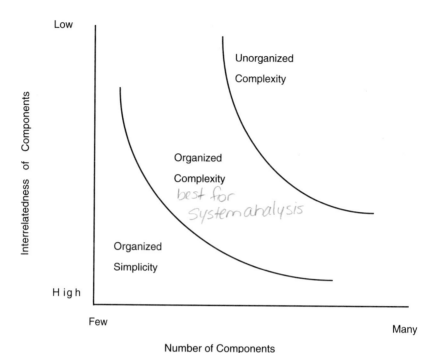

Figure 1.1   General characterization of different types of systems in terms of the number of components and the degree of interrelatedness of components (modified from Weinberg, 1975).

def.

here, understanding refers to the informal integration of all that we have learned about the system by any means. The amount of data refers to the degree to which we have good data on all relevant aspects of the system. If we understand the structure and general dynamics of the system and have good data on all important processes occurring within the system, we often can develop mathematical models and solve them analytically. If we have good data but lack understanding of the underlying system processes that generated them, we often can use statistical analyses to search for patterns in the data that will help us hypothesize the nature of these underlying processes. If we have relatively few data but at least some understanding of system structure and general dynamics, we often can use systems analysis and simulation to investigate our hypotheses about how the system works. Obviously, if we can not formulate useful hypotheses concerning system structure and function based on our current understanding, we should focus our efforts on further observation of the system.

Of course, in practice, domains of the various methods of problem solving overlap broadly. The most useful method for a given problem at a particular time depends on our conceptualization of the problem itself, which places us in one of the regions in Figure 1.1, and on the current state of knowledge

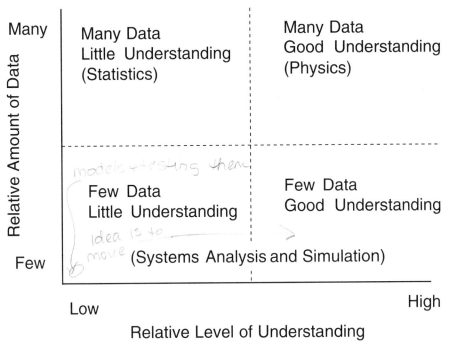

Figure 1.2 Comparison of methods of problem solving in terms of the relative level of understanding and the relative amount of data available on the system (modified from Holling, 1978, and Starfield and Bleloch, 1986).

about the problem within this conceptual framework, which places us in one of the regions of Figure 1.2. Relative usefulness of the various methods also changes as we continue to work on a given problem, that is, as we increase understanding and accumulate data. We might imagine a scenario in which we start with few data and little understanding. We first integrate existing knowledge via systems analysis and the use of simulation models to generate hypotheses about how the system works. This model-building process increases our understanding of the system and identifies specific areas in which important data are lacking. As we accumulate more relevant data, we use statistical analyses to interpret these data, thus generating further hypotheses concerning system structure and function that can be incorporated into our simulation models. Further simulation increases understanding and identifies more data needs, and so on. Theoretically, as we continue to accumulate relevant data and increase our knowledge of the system, we eventually achieve complete understanding of the system and the definitive solution of our problem.

As ecologists and natural resource managers, we deal primarily with systems characterized by "organized complexity" for which we have relatively few data and little hope of ever accumulating a "complete" data set. That is, we find ourselves dealing with exactly those sorts of systems for which systems analysis and simulation were developed. The systems approach does not replace other methods of problem solving but, rather, provides a framework that allows effective integration of knowledge gained from description, classification, and mathematical and statistical analysis of our observations of the world.

1.3   A BRIEF EXAMPLE OF THE SYSTEMS APPROACH

We now reconsider, using the systems approach, the natural resource management problem with which we began the chapter. That is, we describe development and use of a simulation model to evaluate impact of the proposed water diversion for agriculture on the endangered animal species in the wildlife refuge. The basic approach is to (1) develop a conceptual model (box-and-arrow diagram) identifying specific cause-effect relationships among important components of the system in which we are interested, (2) quantify (write mathematical equations for) these relationships based on the analysis of the best information available, (3) evaluate the usefulness of the model ("validate" model) in terms of its ability to simulate known system behavior, and (4) use the model (conduct simulated experiments) to address our questions concerning unknown system behavior. We emphasize that our objective is to provide a general overview of "what the modeling process is" without concerning ourselves at this point with details of "how modeling is done."

Conceptually, relative to our present interests, there appear to be two principal parts of the system: the cropland and the wildlife refuge (Figure 1.3). In the cropland, the main component is the CROP, although we also are interested in TOTAL HARVEST accumulated over the years. In the refuge, the main components are native PLANTS and endangered ANIMALS. Important processes in the system include RIVER FLOW and WATER DIVERSION for IRRIGATION of the cropland, which reduces river flow in the refuge (RIVER REFUGE); the PLANTING, GROWTH, and HARVEST of the crop; the PRODUCTION, GRAZING LOSS, and DECOMPOSITION of native plants; and the NATALITY and MORTALITY of animals. Crop GROWTH is a function of the standing biomass of the CROP (via the GROWTH INDEX) and the amount of IRRIGATION. The amount of WATER DIVERSION and both PLANTING MONTH and HARVEST MONTH are controlled by landowners. Native plant PRODUCTION is a function of the standing biomass of native PLANTS and the amount of river water entering the refuge (RIVER REFUGE). GRAZING LOSS depends on the amount of biomass of native PLANTS and the number of ANIMALS, and DECOMPOSITION depends only on the biomass of native PLANTS. Animal NATALITY and MORTALITY both depend on the number of ANIMALS in the population, with MORTALITY also depending on FORAGE AVAILABILITY (via the MORTALITY INDEX). (PROD RATE, DECOMP RATE, CON RATE and NATALITY RATE are constants used in calculation of rates associated with the indicated processes.)

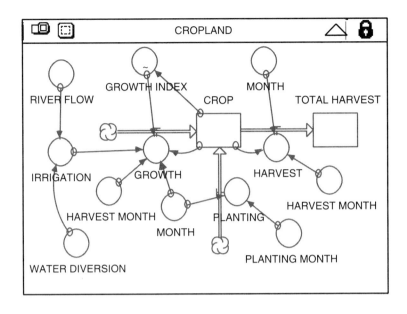

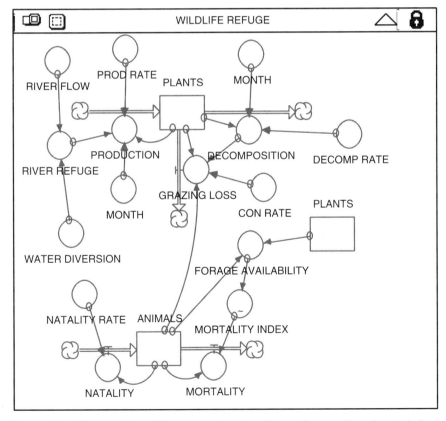

Figure 1.3   Conceptual model representing the effects of water diversion to irrigate crops on population dynamics of an endangered animal species in a downstream wildlife refuge.

We can quantify this qualitative description, or conceptual model, of the system based on information provided by the government (Section 1.1). We know how much water normally flows in the river and how much water landowners propose to divert. We know when and how much landowners plant and when they harvest and we have information on crop growth. We also have information on native plant production, decomposition, and grazing loss, and on animal natality and mortality. Finally, we know the current (January) standing biomass of crops and native plants and number of animals in the system.

We can evaluate how well the quantitative model represents the real system by simulating system behavior over the 5-year period for which field observations are available. The fact that predicted dynamics of both native plant biomass and animal population size correspond closely with observed plant and animal fluctuations (Figure 1.4) increases our confidence that the model is a useful tool to address our initial questions. Our confidence also is based on the reliability of the information we used to quantify important ecological processes represented in the model.

To provide an initial assessment of the impact of water diversion on the endangered animal species, we will run two 10-year simulations representing (1) the proposed 15% diversion scheme and (2) no diversion. Simulation results indicate drastic declines in both native plant biomass and animal population size under the proposed 15% diversion scheme (Figure 1.5a), whereas both native plants and the endangered animal population continue their slow recovery with no water diversion (Figure 1.5b). Simulated crop production is approximately 100kg/ha-yr under the 15% diversion scheme (Figure 1.5a), whereas crops cannot grow without irrigation (Figure 1.5b).

We can simulate impacts of alternative water diversion schemes by changing the representation of the water diversion variable in the model. For example, we might change the numerical value of WATER DIVERSION (Figure 1.3) to 0.10 to 0.05 to simulate continuous diversion of 10 or 5% of river flow. Or we might represent WATER DIVERSION as a variable that changes from month to month, for example, allowing 15% diversion during June and July, but only 5% diversion during other months (IF (MONTH=6) OR (MONTH=7) THEN 0.15 ELSE 0.05).

The basic idea is that we conduct experiments with the model exactly as we would conduct experiments in the field or laboratory (Figure 1.6—modified from Van Dyne, 1969). Just as we "abstract" particular parts of the world to permit more detailed studies in the field or laboratory, we abstract important real-system components and processes in the form of a simulation model to allow more controlled observation and experimentation. We develop an experimental design for simulations in exactly the same manner that we do for field experiments. Likewise, we analyze simulation results using the same qualitative, quantitative, and/or statistical methods that we use to analyze results from field experiments.

We encourage you to take a few minutes right now to experiment with the simulation model and reconsider our original question: What are the relative

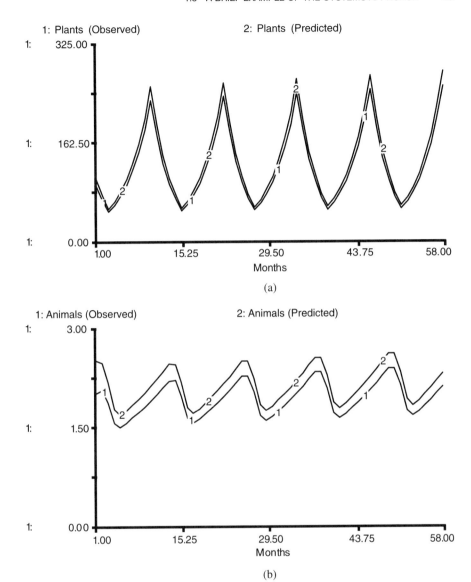

Figure 1.4   Comparison of (1) observed and (2) predicted (a) biomass dynamics of native plants (kg/ha) and (b) the population dynamics of the endangered wildlife species (animals/ha) over a 5-year period for which field data are available.

impacts, both on the endangered species and on crop production, of diverting different quantities of water during different seasons? Based on these simulation results, would you change the water diversion guidelines that you recommend to the government? And, even more importantly, would you consider modifying the type of analysis on which you based your recommendations?

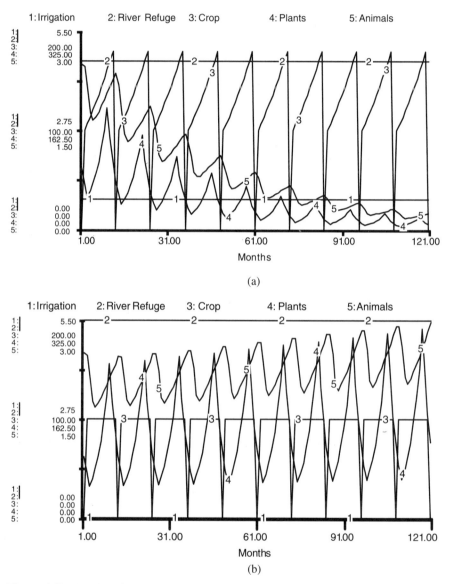

Figure 1.5 Results of two 10-year simulations representing (1) the amount of water diverted for irrigation (units/mo), (2) the amount of water entering the wildlife refuge (units/mo), (3) the biomass of crops (kg/ha), (4) the biomass dynamics of native plants (kg/ha), and (5) the population dynamics of the endangered wildlife species (animals/ha) with (a) 15% water diversion and (b) no water diversion.

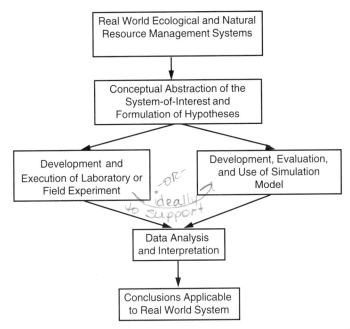

Figure 1.6   Comparison of simulation to laboratory and field experimentation as alternative methods of approaching ecological and natural resource management problems (modified from Van Dyne, 1969).

CHAPTER 2

BASIC CONCEPTS OF SYSTEMS ANALYSIS AND SIMULATION

2.1 INTRODUCTION

In this chapter, we describe important concepts implied by terms such as system, systems analysis, model, and simulation, and provide an overview of the four theoretical phases of systems analysis. The primary objective is to begin to develop the conceptual framework that will facilitate a working knowledge of systems analysis and simulation. First, we consider the idea of a system from a rather philosophical perspective and propose the concept of a "system-of-interest" as the cornerstone of the modeling process. Next, we briefly define the terms system, systems analysis, and model, and offer a simple scheme for classifying different types of models. Then, we take a practical look at simulation model development and use by working through a simple numerical example. Finally, we present a brief overview of the four theoretical phases of systems analysis, which will provide the framework for the more detailed presentation of the theory of Part II.

2.2 SOME BASIC CONCEPTS

2.2.1 System

Like many words for which we have an intuitive understanding, "system" is difficult to define precisely. In relation to the physical or biological sciences, a system is an organized collection of interrelated physical components characterized by a boundary and functional unity. A system is a collection of "communicating" materials and processes that together perform some set of functions. A system is an interlocking complex of processes characterized by many reciprocal cause-effect pathways.

Clearly, any collection of interacting objects can be viewed as a system. The principal attribute of a system is that we can understand it only by viewing it as a whole. Another important attribute of a system, or more strictly speaking, of our conceptualization of a particular system, is that it is chosen for a particular purpose: to answer a question, to demonstrate a theory, or to classify part of the natural world. Common examples of ecological systems include ecosystems, communities, populations, and individuals. But the rumen of a deer may be viewed as a system, as can the planet earth.

We may view, or conceptualize, the same real-world system in different ways depending on our particular interests. This idea can be demonstrated nicely using the analogy of a movie camera with an adjustable focus. Suppose that we begin filming with the camera focused on a 10-m^2 area from a height of 10 meters. From this perspective, we see that the camera is centered on a man standing in a meadow. As the film proceeds, we adjust the focus so that the field of vision increases by an order of magnitude every 5 seconds. After 5 seconds, we are viewing an area of 100 m^2 from a height of 100 m, after 10 seconds an area of 1,000 m^2 from a height of 1,000 m, and so on. As the perspective changes, we see that the man is in a small meadow surrounded by a large forest, that the forest is in a vast mountain range, and that the mountain range is bordered on the eastern side by a vast prairie. As the perspective changes further, we see that the man must be in a mountain meadow near the eastern edge of the Rocky Mountains as the outline of North America becomes clear. Soon we are viewing the entire western hemisphere, then the entire solar system, and so it goes until we behold the Milky Way!

Of course, none of these views of the real world is any more valid or real than any other view. But we would all agree that for any particular set of interests, some views would be more appropriate and enlightening than others. If our primary interest is in the movements of the man in the meadow, we would be ill-advised to worry about the stars in the Milky Way. Likewise, we would be ill-advised to confine our attention solely to the original view of the man in the 10-m^2 area. The system that would be most appropriately analyzed to obtain results relevant to our primary interest lies in between these two extremes.

Summarizing these ideas more formally, systems have two properties that are most useful. First, systems may be nested: An individual is part of a population, a population is part of a community, and so on. But systems at any scale, including any level of detail, can be studied using a common set of principles and techniques often referred to as general systems theory (von Bertalanffy, 1969). Second, systems at the same scale and level of detail may overlap: The system that we define to study population dynamics of species A will overlap with the system that we define to study population dynamics of species B if the two species are competitors. For our purposes, it is useful to think in terms of a subjective "system-of-interest" that is defined arbitrarily relative to a specific problem. This is not to imply that the systems we study can be defined capriciously. We must take great care to define the boundaries of the system-of-interest appropriately for the problem at hand. As we shall see shortly, this is the first step in systems analysis and definitely is not a trivial task.

2.2.2 Systems Analysis

Perhaps systems analysis can be defined most directly as application of the scientific method to problems involving complex systems. It is a body of theory and techniques for studying, describing, and making predictions about complex systems, which often is characterized by use of advanced mathematical and statistical procedures and by use of computers. However, the essence of systems analysis is not found in a collection of quantitative techniques, but rather in a broad problem-solving strategy.

2.2.3 Model

A model is an abstraction of reality. It is a formal description of the essential elements of a problem. Because the essential elements of a problem are exactly those that we define to be in our system-of-interest, we can think of a model as a formal description of the system-of-interest. The description can be physical, mathematical, or verbal, although some modelers object to the idea of "word models" because language can be so ambiguous (Jeffers, 1978).

Models can be classified in a variety of ways (e.g., see Forrester, 1961; Gold, 1977; Jeffers, 1978). Some of the more relevant dichotomies for our purposes include (1) physical versus abstract, (2) dynamic versus static, (3) empirical (correlative) versus mechanistic (explanatory), (4) deterministic versus stochastic, and (5) simulation versus analytical.

Physical versus Abstract. Physical models usually are physical replicas on a reduced scale of objects under study. A scaled-down architectural model used to help us visualize floor plans and space relationships is an example. Of course, even physical models still are abstractions of reality in the sense of our original definition of a model. Abstract models use symbols rather than physical devices to represent the system being studied. The symbolism used can be a written language, a verbal description, or a thought process. A mathematical model is a special type of abstract model written in the language of mathematics. It is fundamentally the same as other abstract models in that it describes the system that it represents. But because mathematical notation is more specific than language, a mathematical model is less ambiguous than most word models. The process of converting a word model to a mathematical model is not inherently difficult. The word model "energy requirements of individual A are 100 kcal/day when the ambient temperature is 0°C and increase by 20 kcal/day with each 10°C decrease in ambient temperature" can be translated easily into the mathematical model "$Y = 100 - 2X$," where Y represents the energy requirements (kcal/day), and X represents the ambient temperature (°C). But difficulties arise when the word model is not an adequate description of the system, as often is the case with complex models.

Dynamic versus Static. Models may or may not represent systems that change with time. A static model describes a relationship or set of relationships that do not change with time. Common examples include regression models that do not have time as an independent variable. A dynamic model describes a time-varying relationship. Examples include simulation models, which we will discuss further in a moment, and regression models that do include time as an independent variable.

eye of the beholder

Empirical (*Correlative*) versus Mechanistic (*Explanatory*). Empirical, or correlative, models are developed primarily to describe and summarize a set of relationships, without regard for the appropriate representation of processes or mechanisms that operate in the real system. The goal is prediction, not explanation. A model predicting metabolic rate of an animal solely as a function of body size is an example. Mechanistic, or explanatory, models are developed primarily to represent the internal dynamics of the system-of-interest appropriately. The goal is explanation through representation of the causal mechanisms underlying system behavior. A model representing the metabolic rate of an animal as a function of body size, level of activity, environmental temperature, wind, and length of exposure to ambient conditions is an example. Solely mechanistic models and solely empirical models form two ends of a continuum, and classification relative to this dichotomy is based more on the intent of the modeler than on the structure of the model. A model that we view as explanatory at one level of detail we might view as correlative at a finer level of detail. A model representing the annual population recruitment as a function of population size appears explanatory compared to a model representing the annual recruitment simply as a constant determined by averaging historical data. But this same model appears correlative compared to a model that calculates recruitment based on age-specific natality rates of individuals within the population, which, in turn, are based on the individuals' social rank and nutritional status during the breeding season.

Deterministic versus Stochastic. A model is deterministic if it contains no random variables. Deterministic-model predictions under a specific set of conditions are always exactly the same. The simple model that we developed relating energy requirements of an individual (Y, in kcal/day) to ambient temperature (X, in °C).

$$Y = 100 - 2X$$

is a deterministic model. When the ambient temperature is 0°C, the model always predicts that energy requirements are 100 kcal/day. When the temperature is −10°C, requirements always are 120 kcal/day, and so on. A model is stochastic if it contains one or more random variables. Stochastic-model predictions under a specified set of conditions are not always exactly the same, because random variables within the model potentially can take on different values each time the model is solved. Our deterministic energy requirements model has the general form

$$Y = a - bX$$

where a and b are constants ($a = 100$, $b = 2$). We can change this into a stochastic model by representing either a or b as a random variable. Suppose we represent b as a random variable that can take on values of 2.0 or 2.5 with equal probability. Now each time we compute a model prediction, we must randomly choose a value for b from the distribution of b values that we have specified. We could flip a coin: heads means $b = 2.0$; tails means $b = 2.5$. Model predictions of energy requirements when the ambient temperature is −10°C (or any other temperature except 0°C) no longer remain the same. If the coin lands heads-up, we compute

$$Y = 100 - 2.0(-10) = 120$$

If the coin lands tails-up, we compute

$$Y = 100 - 2.5(-10) = 125$$

Of course, random variables in most stochastic models are chosen from more "sophisticated" distributions (uniform, normal, negative binomial, and so on), but the general procedure is exactly the same.

The choice between using a deterministic or a stochastic model depends on the specific objectives of the modeling project. Deterministic models generally are easier to build because they require only point estimation of constants, rather than the specification of complete distributions for random variables, as is the case for stochastic models. They also are easier to use because predictions for a given situation need be made only once (because they always are the same), whereas stochastic-model predictions must be replicated an appropriate number of times to obtain the average response for a given situation. However, if project objectives require explicit representation of variability, either the variability associated with the estimates of system parameters or the inherent variability of the system itself, we must use a stochastic model. Likewise, if we wish to make statistical comparisons of model predictions for different situations, we must use a stochastic model.

Simulation versus Analytical. Models that can be solved in closed form mathematically are analytical models. Regression models, models of standard theoretical statistical distributions, and some simple differential equation models are examples. For such models, a general solution can be obtained that applies to all situations the model can represent. A simple analytical model of population growth in an unlimited environment (exponential growth) is

$$N_t = N_0 e^{rt}$$

where

N_t = population size at time t
N_0 = initial population size
r = intrinsic rate of population increase
t = time

We can solve this model for population size (N_t) at any time (t) by substituting the desired value for t into the model, assuming that we have defined the initial population size (N_0) and the intrinsic rate of population increase (r). If the initial population size is 100 individuals and the intrinsic rate of increase is 0.1, the population size at time 5 is

$$N_5 = 100e^{0.1(5)} = 164.9$$

at time 8 is

$$N_8 = 100e^{0.1(8)} = 222.6$$

and so on. Models that have no general analytical solution must be solved numerically using a specified set of arithmetic operations for each particular situation the model can represent. These are simulation models. Many ecological models are of this type. For example, models representing population dynamics in response to density-dependent, competitive relationships, which, in turn, are influenced by changing environmental conditions, might be summarized in general form as

$$N_{t+1} = f(N_t, E_t)$$

where

N_{t+1} = population size at time $t + 1$
$f(N_t, E_t)$ = some complex function of population size and environmental conditions at time t

Often, we cannot solve such models analytically because the function, or set of equations, comprising $f(N_t, E_t)$ is too complex. The model must be solved numerically for each successive time step. We will take a more detailed look at simulation (including a numerical example) in the next section. Philosophically, the choice between analytical and simulation models involves deciding whether we sacrifice ecological realism to obtain an analytical model or sacrifice mathematical power to include more ecological realism. From a more practical standpoint, these considerations are no less interesting and are influenced primarily by objectives of the modeling project. If the level of detail at which the system-of-interest must be represented to meet our objectives permits use of an analytical model, then we should use an analytical model. However, if the appropriate level of detail requires a model too complex to be represented in an analytically tractable form, then we should use a simulation model. In most cases in ecology and natural resource management, we will need to represent the system-of-interest in a manner too complex for analytical treatment.

2.2.4 Simulation

Simulation is the process of using a model to mimic, or trace through step by step, the behavior of the system we are studying. Simulation models are composed of a series of arithmetic and logical operations that together represent the structure (state) and behavior (change of state) of the system-of-interest. These two very simple yet powerful concepts of the state of the system and the change of state of the system are fundamental to simulation (Patten, 1971). The system-of-interest exists in different states at different points in time and rules govern the manner in which the state of the system changes as time passes. The rules governing change also may change from time to time, because they are themselves a function of the state of the system. If we choose appropriate variables to describe the system and appropriately represent the rules governing change, then we should be able to trace the state of the system through time, which is to say we can simulate behavior of the system.

Suppose that we wish to simulate fluctuations in weight (in g) of an animal over time. Conceptually, our system-of-interest includes the amount of biomass contained in the individual animal, which varies over time as a function of the amount of food consumed and the amount of energy respired. Assume that assimilation efficiency is 100%. We might choose the number of g in the animal at any time t (WEIGHT$_t$) as the variable describing the state of the system. Further, suppose we know that the rate of consumption of food (in g/day) is a function of the weight of the animal and that the respiration rate (in g/day) is a function of the weight of the animal and the environmental temperature (Figure 2.1). (The symbols used in Figure 2.1 have specific meanings that we will define formally in Chapter 3. For now, note only that the figure is a simple diagrammatic representation of the weight fluctuation model just described.) We might appropriately represent the rules governing changes in the state of the system using two equations, one representing CONSUMPTION as a function of animal WEIGHT and one representing RESPIRATION as a func-

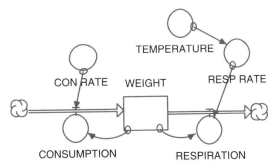

Figure 2.1 Diagram of a simulation model predicting fluctuations in weight (g) of an animal over time. The rate of consumption is affected by the weight of the animal and a consumption rate constant, and the respiration rate is affected by the weight of the animal, a respiration rate variable, and the environmental temperature.

tion of environmental TEMPERATURE and WEIGHT. (CON RATE and RESP RATE are numbers that we will use in a moment to quantify the model.)

We now can construct a simulation model predicting fluctuations in weight of the animal under a specific set of environmental temperatures, given that we know the initial WEIGHT. Mathematical representation of simulation models may take a variety of forms. One useful format involves use of difference equations. We might construct a simulation model for our example using difference equations as follows.[1]

$$\mathrm{WEIGHT}_{t+1} = \mathrm{WEIGHT}_t + \Delta\mathrm{WEIGHT}_{t,\,t+1} \qquad (1.1)$$

where

$$\Delta\mathrm{WEIGHT}_{t,\,t+1} = \mathrm{CONSUMPTION}_{t,\,t+1} - \mathrm{RESPIRATION}_{t,\,t+1} \quad (1.2)$$

$$\mathrm{CONSUMPTION}_{t,\,t+1} = f(\mathrm{WEIGHT}_t) \qquad (1.3)$$

$$\mathrm{RESPIRATION}_{t,\,t+1} = f(\mathrm{TEMPERATURE}_t,\ \mathrm{WEIGHT}_t) \qquad (1.4)$$

Equation (1.1) states that the number of g in the animal at one time unit into the future—at time $(t + 1)$(WEIGHT$_{t+1}$)—is equal to the number of g in the animal now—at time t(WEIGHT$_t$)—plus the net change in the number of g in the animal over the next time unit—from t to $(t + 1)$(ΔWEIGHT$_{t,t+1}$).

Equation (1.2), which is the difference equation from which this mathematical format takes its name, states that the net change in the number of g

---

[1]Difference equations also are written in the slightly different but equivalent form: WEIGHT$_t$ = WEIGHT$_{t-1}$ + ΔWEIGHT$_{t,t+1}$. We always will define $\Delta t = 1$ time unit: 1 week, 1 month, or 1 year, and so on, depending on the temporal resolution required in the model.

in the animal over the next time unit (ΔWEIGHT$_{t,t+1}$) is equal to the number of g consumed over the next time unit (CONSUMPTION$_{t,t+1}$) minus the number of g respired over the next time unit (RESPIRATION$_{t,t+1}$).

Equation (1.3) states that the number of g consumed over the next time unit (CONSUMPTION$_{t,t+1}$) is equal to a function (f) of animal weight at the beginning of the time unit (WEIGHT$_t$).

Equation (1.4) states that the number of g respired over the next time unit (RESPIRATION$_{t,t+1}$) is equal to a function (f) of environmental temperature at the beginning of the time unit (TEMPERATURE$_t$) and animal weight at time t (WEIGHT$_t$). Of course, f(WEIGHT$_t$) and f(TEMPERATURE$_t$, WEIGHT$_t$) need to be made explicit. For example, if CONSUMPTION is a linear function of WEIGHT, we might write

$$\text{CONSUMPTION}_{t,t+1} = f(\text{WEIGHT}_t) = \text{CON RATE} * \text{WEIGHT}_t$$

where CON RATE is a constant equal to, say, 0.05 g/g-day. Likewise, for RESPIRATION, we might write

$$\text{RESPIRATION}_{t,t+1} = f(\text{TEMPERATURE}_t, \text{WEIGHT}_t)$$
$$= \text{RESP RATE} * \text{WEIGHT}_t$$

where RESP RATE is a function of environmental temperature equal to, say, $0.0025 * $ TEMPERATURE, in g/g-day, and TEMPERATURE is in °C. If we assume that the initial weight of the animal is 100 g and the environmental temperature is 20°C and 19°C on two consecutive days, we can simulate weight fluctuations of the animal over this 2-day period as follows:

$$\text{CONSUMPTION}_{0,1} = \text{CON RATE} * \text{WEIGHT}_0$$
$$= 0.05(100) = 5$$

$$\text{RESPIRATION}_{0,1} = \text{RESP RATE} * \text{WEIGHT}_0$$
$$= 0.0025(20)(100) = 5$$

$$\Delta\text{WEIGHT}_{0,1} = \text{CONSUMPTION}_{0,1} - \text{RESPIRATION}_{0,1}$$
$$= 5-5 = 0$$

$$\text{WEIGHT}_1 = \text{WEIGHT}_0 + \Delta\text{WEIGHT}_{0,1}$$
$$= 100+0 = 100$$

and

$$\text{CONSUMPTION}_{1,2} = \text{CON RATE} * \text{WEIGHT}_1$$
$$= 0.05(100) = 5$$

$$\text{RESPIRATION}_{1,2} \ = \ \text{RESP RATE} \ * \ \text{WEIGHT}_1$$

$$= \ 0.0025(19)(100) \ = \ 4.75$$

$$\Delta\text{WEIGHT}_{1,2} \ = \ \text{CONSUMPTION}_{1,2} \ - \ \text{RESPIRATION}_{1,2}$$

$$= \ 5-4.75 \ = \ 0.25$$

$$\text{WEIGHT}_2 \ = \ \text{WEIGHT}_1 \ + \ \Delta\text{WEIGHT}_{1,2}$$

$$= \ 100+0.25 \ = \ 100.25$$

Our simulation model predicts that a 100-g animal weighs 100.25 g after 2 days given that environmental temperatures are 20°C and 19°C on days 0 and 1, respectively.   C02MOD01

2.3 THEORETICAL PHASES OF SYSTEMS ANALYSIS

A variety of schemes for applying the systems approach in biology and ecology has been suggested (Gold, 1977; Jeffers, 1978; Innis, 1979; Kitching, 1983). These schemes differ with regard to details (number of steps, names of steps), but all are based on the same underlying general systems theory. Our preference, which has been shaped by application of systems analysis and simulation to a variety of problems in ecology and natural resource management over the past two decades, is to identify four fundamental phases in the process of developing and using a systems model: (1) conceptual-model formulation, (2) quantitative-model specification, (3) model evaluation, and (4) model use (Figure 2.2). The remainder of this chapter provides a general overview of these four theoretical phases, each of which will be examined in more detail in Part II.

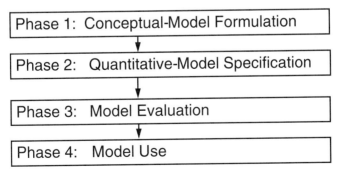

Figure 2.2   Four phases of systems analysis.

2.3.1 Phase 1: Conceptual-Model Formulation

The goal of the first phase of systems analysis is to develop a conceptual, or qualitative, model of the system-of-interest (Figure 2.2). Based on the objectives of the modeling project, we decide which components in the real-world system should be included in our system-of-interest and how they should be related to one another. We represent these components and their relationships, which collectively form our conceptual model, diagrammatically using symbols that indicate the specific nature of the relationships. We also sketch patterns of behavior that we expect our model will exhibit, often in terms of the general temporal dynamics of key system components.

Reexamining the diagrammatic representation of the weight fluctuation model introduced in the previous section, we note that the conceptual model includes the weight of the animal, consumption, consumption rate, respiration, respiration rate, and environmental temperature (Figure 2.1). It does not include, for example, the amount of food available or the number of other animals present. Our objective must be to simulate weight fluctuations of an animal that has unlimited access to food. We further note that factors in the conceptual model represented by different symbols play different roles in the system. The weight of the animal represents material (g) that has accumulated up to the present moment within the system (within the animal). This accumulation can continue to change as the result of the net difference between consumption and respiration, which represent processes occurring within the system over time (g/day). Consumption and respiration rates are numbers that represent consumption and respiration per unit body weight of the animal (g/g-day). Environmental temperature represents a factor affecting respiration, whose value (in °C) is not controlled by anything else in the system. In terms of expected behavior of this model, assuming that the animal is an adult, we expect the animal to maintain a relatively constant weight under normal environmental temperatures.

2.3.2 Phase 2: Quantitative-Model Specification

The goal of the second phase of systems analysis is to develop a quantitative model of the system-of-interest (Figure 2.2). This basically involves translating our conceptual model, which is represented diagrammatically and using words, into a series of mathematical equations that collectively form the quantitative model. This translation, or quantification, is based on the consideration of various types of information about the real system. We then solve all of the model equations, or instruct a computer to solve them, each time step over the entire period of simulated time in which we are interested. That is, we run the baseline simulation.

We illustrated mechanical aspects of writing and numerically solving equations for the weight fluctuation model in the previous section. We might estimate the respiration equation by analyzing data collected in the laboratory relating respiration of an adult of this species to environmental temperature. We might write the consumption equation based on an empirical relationship between food requirements and body weight that generally applies to a broad group of species to which our species belongs, assuming that no information on our particular species is available. We directly assign values to environmental temperature to represent the conditions we wish to simulate.

2.3.3 Phase 3: Model Evaluation

The goal of the third phase of systems analysis is to evaluate the usefulness of the model in meeting our objectives (Figure 2.2). This process, which is the subject of much debate, commonly is referred to as "model validation" and often erroneously focuses on comparison of model predictions with real-system observations as the only validation criterion. We prefer the concept of "model evaluation" based on consideration of a broad array of different aspects of model structure and behavior that make it potentially useful. We may place more emphasis on interpretability of relationships among components within the model or on predictive capabilities of the model, depending on our objectives. Often we are interested in determining how sensitive model predictions are to the uncertainties with which we have represented certain aspects of the model.

Suppose the primary objective of our weight fluctuation model is to simulate the effect of environmental temperature on weight resulting from the temperature dependency of respiration. A useful model not only needs to predict weight fluctuations well as temperatures change, it also needs to exhibit the correct relationships between temperature and respiration and between respiration and consumption over the range of environmental temperatures in which we are interested. We might be particularly interested in determining the sensitivity of model predictions of weight fluctuations to possible errors in our representation of the consumption equation, which is based on a general empirical relationship for a broad group of species.

2.3.4 Phase 4: Model Use

The goal of the final phase of systems analysis is to answer the questions that were identified at the beginning of the modeling project (Figure 2.2). This involves designing and simulating the same experiments with the model that we would conduct in the real system to answer our questions. We also analyze, interpret, and communicate simulation results using the same general procedures that we would use for real-world results.

The experimental design for our weight fluctuation model might include three simulations in which environmental temperatures are normal (the baseline simulation with environmental temperatures equal to 20°C and 19°C on days 0 and 1, respectively), warmer (perhaps 21°C and 20°C), and colder (perhaps 19°C and 18°C). If we had a stochastic version of the model (which we will develop in a later chapter), we could run an appropriate number of replicate simulations and compare the final mean weights predicted under each temperature regime using an analysis of variance.

2.3.5 Iteration of Phases

The four phases of systems analysis are highly interconnected. Although theoretically we may think of the process as proceeding sequentially in the indicated order (Figure 2.2), in practice, we may cycle through several phases more than once. During any phase, we may find that we have overlooked or misrepresented an important system component or process and need to return to an earlier phase, often to conceptual-model formulation or quantitative-model specification.

During model evaluation in particular, we examine the model to detect any inadequacies that may require us to cycle back to earlier phases. Discovery of such inadequacies in the model during its development usually provides additional insight into the dynamics of the system-of-interest and is an important benefit of modeling. We will demonstrate this iterative nature of model development in more detail in Chapter 8.

PART II

THEORETICAL FRAMEWORK: FOUR PHASES OF SYSTEMS ANALYSIS

Part II presents the theoretical framework for development, evaluation, and use of simulation models in ecology and natural resource management, formally describing each of the four phases of systems analysis. Chapter 3 presents the conceptual-model formulation (Phase 1), which is the process of abstracting from the real system for inclusion in a model only those factors and processes that are relevant to our specific objectives. Chapter 4 describes the quantitative-model specification (Phase 2), or the quantification of all relationships among model components that were identified in a qualitative manner during the conceptual-model formulation. Chapter 5 focuses on model evaluation (Phase 3), which is the process of determining the relative usefulness of a model for meeting our specific objectives. Chapter 6 describes model use (Phase 4) to meet objectives of the modeling project. Computerized (STELLA® II) versions of models presented in this part can be found in the "nrm" folder on the enclosed CD ROM. Names of particular models appear in the right-hand margin of the text.

CHAPTER 3

CONCEPTUAL-MODEL FORMULATION

3.1 INTRODUCTION

The goal of the first phase of systems analysis is to develop a conceptual, or qualitative, model of the system-of-interest (Figure 3.1). Based on a clear statement of the objectives of the modeling project, we abstract from the real system those components that must be considered to address our questions. By including these components within our model and excluding all others, we bound the system-of-interest. Next, we categorize model components depending on their specific roles in describing system structure and identify specific relationships among components that generate system dynamics. We then formally represent the resulting conceptual model, usually as a box-and-arrow diagram indicating points of accumulation of material (boxes), such as individuals, energy, biomass, nutrients, or dollars, and routes by which the material flows within the system (arrows). Finally, we describe expected patterns of model behavior, most often as graphs representing changes in values of important variables within the system over time.

In many respects, conceptual-model formulation is the most intellectually challenging phase of systems analysis. The best basis for the many difficult, and often highly subjective, decisions that must be made regarding choice of model components is a thorough familiarity with the real system. Prior modeling experience also is an asset. There are two general approaches to identifying model components. One makes the initial choice of components as simple as possible and subsequently adds critical components that were overlooked; the other includes initially all components that possibly could have any importance and then deletes superfluous ones. Theoretically, the end prod-

Phase 1: Conceptual-Model Formulation

1. State the model objectives
2. Bound the system-of-interest
3. Categorize the components within the system-of-interest
4. Identify the relationships among the components of interest
5. Represent the conceptual model
6. Describe the expected patterns of model behavior.

Figure 3.1 Steps within Phase 1 of systems analysis: conceptual-model formulation.

uct of either approach should be a conceptual model that is no more complex than is absolutely necessary to address our interests. In practice, it is better to begin with the simplest model possible.

3.2 STATE THE MODEL OBJECTIVES

We begin with a clear statement of our interests in terms of a problem to be solved or a question to be answered. Questions may arise from general observations of a system, as is the usual case in scientific inquiry, or may be imposed by the practical necessity of evaluating proposed management schemes. Because model objectives provide the framework for model development, the standard for model evaluation, and the context within which simulation results will be interpreted, this is arguably the most crucial step in the entire modeling process. Yet, surprisingly, this step often receives far less attention than its importance warrants.

Often, our initial formulation of an objective is too broad to address directly and thus is of little use in guiding model development. For example, recalling the weight fluctuation model of Chapter 2, the objective "to understand the effect of temperature on weight fluctuations of an animal" might be stated more clearly "to determine the effect of temperature-induced changes in respiration on weight fluctuations of an animal." The first form of the objective does not indicate our interest in representing the physiological effect of temperature on respiration and thus provides no guidance in terms of the level of detail to include in the model. As a general rule, objectives that begin with "to understand—" need to be stated more specifically.

3.3 BOUND THE SYSTEM-OF-INTEREST

Bounding the system-of-interest consists of separating those components that should be included within the system-of-interest from those that should be excluded. We do not want an unnecessarily complex model, but likewise we do not want to exclude components that might be critical to the solution of our problem. From the simple simulation model presented in Figure 2.1, the only components included within the system-of-interest were weight of the animal, consumption, consumption rate, respiration, respiration rate, and environmental temperature. Other potential system components such as rainfall, weight of available food, and the number of animals in the population were excluded because they were considered unimportant in predicting fluctuations in weight of the animal.

Obviously, this step in conceptual-model formulation is highly subjective. Often difficult decisions arise regarding the need to include certain components. Our prior modeling experience helps us make such decisions, but ultimately we must base our decisions on the best information available about the system in question. Again returning to the example in Figure 2.1, rainfall clearly may have been irrelevant. But perhaps the decision to exclude the amount of available food and the number of animals in the population was based not on clear evidence that they were unimportant, but rather on the more tenuous assumption that they would have a negligible effect over the range of conditions that we wished to simulate.

Suppose that after reconsidering the problem of predicting fluctuations in animal weight, we decided that the amount of available food was an important factor affecting animal consumption after all, and that we should represent variability of both the amount of available food and the temperature in the model as functions of season. We then would bound the system differently by including available food as a system component affecting transfer of material from the food source to the animal and by indicating the influence of season on both availability of food and environmental temperature (Figure 3.2). (As we mentioned in Chapter 2, the symbols that we are using to diagrammatically represent conceptual models have specific meanings. We will define them formally in a later section, but figures presented in this section [Figures 3.2 to 3.4] can be interpreted informally without losing meaning for our present purpose.) Further suppose that we could not predict fluctuations in the weight of individual animals without considering the number of animals in the population because population density affected availability of food to individuals. The number of individuals in the population was of course a function of natality and mortality rates, which, let us suppose, were both density-dependent. We would change again our bounding of the system by including the number of individuals in the population as a system component affecting availability of food, and, in turn, affected by density-dependent natality and mortality rates (Figure 3.3).

Another aspect of bounding the system-of-interest involves identifying particular attributes or units of measure of system components that are of interest. In some cases, we may be interested in only a single attribute throughout the entire system. Consider the problem of predicting harvest of a migratory game fish population from specific fishing grounds as fish return from the ocean en route to freshwater spawning grounds. Suppose that for our purposes, we can

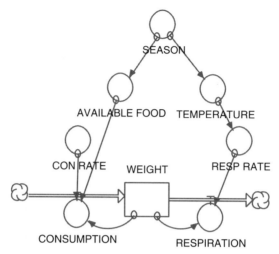

Figure 3.2   The weight fluctuation model (Figure 2.1) modified to represent available food and season as system components affecting weight fluctuations.

assume that fish are all the same size when they pass through the fishing grounds and that natural mortality is zero during the several weeks of their passage. We might bound the system, as indicated in Figure 3.4. We are interested only in the number of fish on the fishing grounds and in the number of fish harvested, perhaps under a variety of management schemes. The rate of recruitment of fish to the fishing grounds is a function of season. The rate of emigration of fish to the spawning grounds is a function of season and the number of fish on the grounds. The rate of fishing mortality is a function of the number of fish on the grounds and restrictions on harvest imposed by management. Thus, our description of the system is univariate: We are interested only in the number of fish passing through the system.

In some cases, we may wish to monitor several attributes of a system simultaneously. For example, we may be interested in population dynamics of a particular species. But we can represent those dynamics in terms of several attributes of the population: numbers of individuals, total biomass, or total energy content. It also is possible that different system components may have different attributes in which we are interested. In Figure 3.2, our interest in the animal component of the model was in terms of number of g, but temperature was monitored in terms of °C. In our later extension of this model to include representation of the number of individuals in the animal population (Figure 3.3), we further increased dimensionality of our description of the system. Thus, system descriptions can be multivariate.

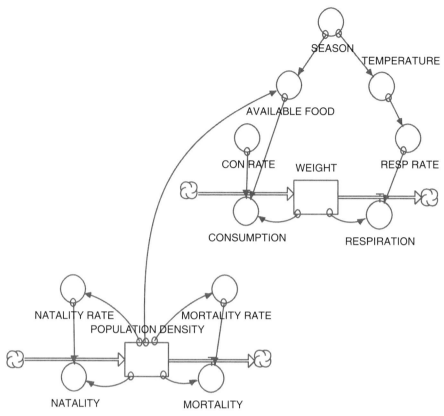

Figure 3.3   The weight fluctuation model (Figure 3.2 and Figure 2.1) modified to represent the number of individuals in the population as a system component affecting the availability of food and affected by density-dependent natality and mortality rates.

3.4   CATEGORIZE THE COMPONENTS WITHIN THE SYSTEM-OF-INTEREST

Once the system-of-interest has been bounded by separating those compo-nents that should be included within the system from those that should be excluded and by identifying particular attributes of system components that are of interest, we proceed to step 3 of conceptual-model formulation, cate-gorizing components within the system-of-interest. System components may not all serve the same purpose in a model. Certainly, they all represent im-portant aspects of the system-of-interest, but there may be as many as seven fundamentally different categories of system components: (1) state variables, (2) driving variables, (3) constants, (4) auxiliary variables, (5) material trans-fers, (6) information transfers, and (7) sources and sinks (Forrester, 1961; Innis, 1979; Grant, 1986).

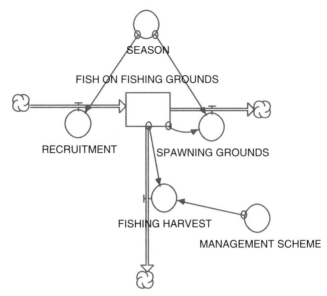

Figure 3.4   A model predicting harvest of migratory game fish from a specific fishing grounds under different management schemes.

3.4.1   State Variables

State variables (Figure 3.5) represent points of accumulation of material within the system. If we are interested in energy flow through an ecosystem, energy contained in plants, energy contained in herbivores, and energy contained in carnivores might be three state variables in the model (Figure 3.6). In the version of our weight fluctuation model described in Figure 3.2, the weight of the animal (measured as number of g) is a state variable. We later expanded this model to include population density of animals (measured as number of individuals/ha) (Figure 3.3), which also is a state variable. In our model predicting the harvest of migratory game fish (Figure 3.4), the number of fish on the fishing grounds is the only state variable, representing the single point of accumulation of "material" in the system.

3.4.2   Driving Variables

Driving variables (Figure 3.5) affect but are not affected by the rest of the system. For example, we may wish to represent the transfer of energy from the sun to plants as a function of the amount of rainfall (Figure 3.6). But, of course, the amount of rainfall is not affected by plants or by another system component. The season is a driving variable in both our weight fluctuation model (Figures 3.2 and 3.3) and our migratory fish model (Figure 3.4). In the fish model, season affects rates of recruitment to and emigration from the

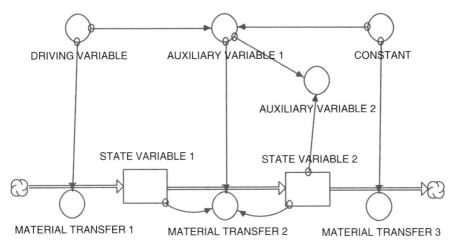

Figure 3.5   Symbols used to construct conceptual-model diagrams indicating all permissible connections (High Performance Systems, Inc., 1994).

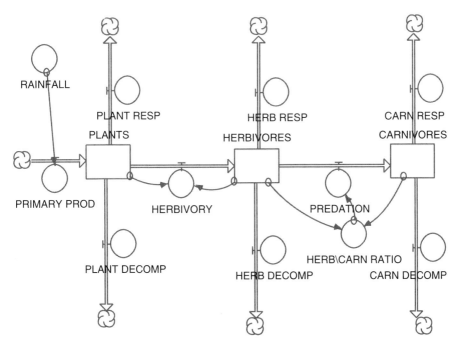

Figure 3.6   Conceptual-model diagram representing energy flow through an ecosystem.

fishing grounds. Obviously, these rates do not affect season. In the weight model, season affects the rates of consumption and respiration (indirectly through available food and environmental temperature—both auxiliary variables that we will define shortly). Whereas we associate some driving variables with specific units of measure, such as the rainfall (mm) driving variable in Figure 3.6, others can be unitless. Season, for example, often is described as taking on values of 1, 2, 3, and so on, to represent January, February, March, or first quarter, second quarter, third quarter of the year. (The way this technique works will become clear when we discuss quantitative specification of the model in Chapter 4.)

3.4.3   Constants

Constants (Figure 3.5) are numerical values describing characteristics of a system that do not change, or that can be represented as unchanging, under all of the conditions simulated by the model. Coefficients appearing as part of rate equations, such as the consumption coefficient in the original weight fluctuation model (Figure 3.2), are common examples of constants. Factors such as environmental temperature and rainfall, which more commonly are represented as driving variables, also are represented as constants, by definition, if they do not change under the conditions simulated.

3.4.4   Auxiliary Variables

Auxiliary variables (Figure 3.5) arise as part of calculations determining a rate of material transfer or the value of another variable, but represent concepts that we wish to indicate explicitly in the model. Auxiliary variables also may represent an end product of calculations that is of particular interest to us. For example, we may wish to represent the transfer of energy from herbivores to carnivores as a function of both the number of herbivores and the number of carnivores. Further, the ratio of herbivores to carnivores may have a special meaning for us over and above the fact that it is an intermediate step in calculations determining the transfer of energy from herbivores to carnivores. Thus, we represent the herbivore/carnivore ratio as an auxiliary variable (Figure 3.6).

In our weight fluctuation model (Figures 3.2 and 3.3), available food and environmental temperature are auxiliary variables (as is resp rate). Both consumption and respiration by the animal ultimately are a function of season (driving variable). But the effect of season on consumption results from changes in available food, whereas the effect of season on respiration results from changes in environmental temperature. We call attention to this difference by creating auxiliary variables (available food and environmental temperature) mediating the effects of season on consumption and respiration. As an alternative version of the model in Figure 3.2, had we not wanted to call attention to the fact that available food and environmental temperature vary seasonally, we might have omitted season completely and represented both food and temperature as driving variables because neither is affected by the rest of the system. The model in Figure 3.3 also might be modified to represent temperature as a driving variable (with no link to season), but available food cannot be represented as a driving variable because it is affected by another system component (the population-density state variable).

3.4.5 Material and Information Transfers

A material transfer (Figure 3.5) represents physical transfer of material over a specific period of time: (1) between two state variables, (2) between a source and a state variable, or (3) between a state variable and a sink. As energy flows (in kcal/week) through the grazing food chain within an ecosystem, it is transferred from plants to herbivores to carnivores (Figure 3.6). As an animal gains weight (in g/day), biomass is transferred from a food source to the animal to a respiration sink (Figure 3.2). As fish enter and leave fishing grounds (in number of individuals/month), individuals are transferred from a recruitment source to the fishing grounds to a spawning grounds sink (Figure 3.4). Note that units of measure associated with material transfers always include a time dimension such as per hour or per year.

Information transfers (Figure 3.5) represent the use of information about the state of the system to control the change of state of the system. We may wish to represent the material transfer of energy from plants to herbivores as a function of both the number of herbivores and the amount of plants (Figure 3.6). Or, more strictly speaking, to calculate the rate of energy transfer from the plant state variable to the herbivore state variable, we need information about the number of kcal of herbivores and number of kcal of plants in the system. Likewise, to calculate harvest in our fish migration model (the material transfer of individuals from the fish on fishing grounds state variable to the fishing harvest sink), we need information about the number of fish on the fishing grounds and the management scheme (driving variable) (Figure 3.4).

3.4.6 Sources and Sinks

Sources and sinks (Figure 3.5) represent origination and termination points, respectively, of material transfers into and out of the system. By definition, we are not interested in the level of accumulation of material within sources or sinks. For example, we may note that energy enters an ecosystem by being transferred from sun to plants, but we may have no interest in the amount of energy in the sun (solar energy source) (Figure 3.6). Likewise, we may note that energy is lost from the grazing food chain both through respiration of plants, herbivores, and carnivores, and as plants, herbivores, and carnivores are eaten by decomposer organisms. But we may not be interested in the level of accumulation of respired energy (respiration sink) or of energy in decomposers (decomposition sink) (Figure 3.6).

3.5   IDENTIFY THE RELATIONSHIPS AMONG THE COMPONENTS THAT ARE OF INTEREST

Step 4 of conceptual-model formulation consists of identifying relationships among system components that are of interest. There are two ways that system components may be related: by material transfers or by information transfers (Figure 3.5). Material transfers can leave sources and state variables and enter state variables or sinks. Units of measure of state variables, sources, and sinks connected by material transfers must be the same. "Information" transferred within the system refers to information about current values of state variables, driving variables, constants, and derived auxiliary variables. This information is "transferred" for use in determining the rate at which specific material transfers occur or for calculating specific results, or "output," required of the model. Information transfers can leave state variables, driving variables, constants, and auxiliary variables and can enter material transfers and auxiliary variables. Units of measure of variables affecting a given material transfer or auxiliary variable need not be the same. Respiration rate in our weight fluctuation model (the material transfer from animal state variable to respiration sink) is determined by information about weight of the animal in g and environmental temperature in °C.

3.5.1   Submodels

We have seen that the system-of-interest may be described by more than one attribute, but that material transfers can occur only among state variables, sources, and sinks described by the same attribute. This brings us to the concept of submodels within a model.

   If we wish to represent the transfer of different materials within a system, we must represent each set of transfers associated with a given material in a separate submodel. Various submodels, or sets of material transfers, may be connected by information transfers but not by material transfers. Material transfers in Figure 3.3 include both biomass and individuals, but they follow different routes within the model. They are in different submodels connected only by an information transfer from the population-density state variable to the available food auxiliary variable.

   As another example of use of submodels, suppose that we wish to modify our weight fluctuation model (as conceptualized in Figure 3.2) to simulate nitrogen balance as well as weight fluctuations. Further suppose that nitrogen intake is a function of the nitrogen content of available food and the food consumption rate, which we already know is a function of animal weight, a consumption rate constant, and the amount of available food. Nitrogen output is a function of animal weight and nitrogen content of the animal.

We might model this new system by adding a new submodel consisting of a state variable representing g of nitrogen in the animal, a constant representing the nitrogen content of available food, and material transfers representing nitrogen consumption and loss (Figure 3.7). We then would use information on the weight of animal state variable, consumption rate constant, available food auxiliary variable, and the nitrogen content of available food constant to determine the material (nitrogen) transfer from the nitrogen source to the nitrogen in the animal state variable. We would use information on the weight of the animal state variable and nitrogen in the animal state variable to determine the material (nitrogen) transfer from the nitrogen in the animal state variable to nitrogen sink (Figure 3.7). Our model now has a weight submodel and a nitrogen submodel, each representing dynamics of a different

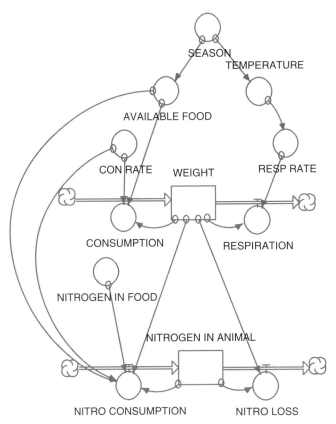

Figure 3.7 Conceptual-model diagram of the weight fluctuation model (Figure 3.2) modified to include nitrogen balance as well as weight fluctuation submodels.

attribute of the system-of-interest, connected only by information transfers or by the "information network."

3.6   REPRESENT THE CONCEPTUAL MODEL

3.6.1   Conceptual-Model Diagrams

Formal representation of the conceptual model most commonly takes the form of a box-and-arrow diagram such as those we have been using to illustrate our example models thus far. As we have seen, such diagrams play an important role in modeling by helping us visualize the "big picture" and by facilitating communication between different people who are interested in a particular system. Although we present this as the fifth step in conceptual-model formulation, and indeed the conceptual-model diagram might be thought of as the end product of the first phase of systems analysis, diagrammatic representation of the conceptual model usually is concurrent with the earlier steps and aids them greatly. Conceptual-model diagrams also provide a framework that facilitates subsequent quantification of the model because equations can be related directly to specific parts of the conceptual model.

A variety of schemes exists for formal representation of the conceptual model. Diagrams based on symbols introduced in Figure 3.5 are particularly useful because they are simple, flexible, and defined in terms identical to those that we have chosen to describe components and relationships within the system-of-interest. These particular symbols are those used in the simulation program STELLA® II (High Performance Systems, Inc., 1994). They are similar to those suggested by Forrester (1961) for modeling dynamics of industrial systems, although the driving variable concept was added by Innis (1979) for modeling ecological systems. We will use these symbols to represent models throughout the text.

3.7   DESCRIBE THE EXPECTED PATTERNS OF MODEL BEHAVIOR

We usually have some expectations concerning patterns of model behavior before ever running the first simulation. These expectations are based on the same a priori knowledge that we draw on to formulate the conceptual model as well as what we have learned about the system-of-interest during the process of conceptual-model formulation. We formalize these expectations, most often as graphs representing changes in values of important variables over time, to (1) use as points of reference during model evaluation and (2) ensure that the model provides the type of predictions that allows us to address our questions directly.

During model evaluation, we will compare model behavior and the expected patterns of model behavior before more formally comparing model

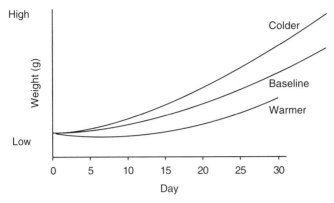

Figure 3.8 Expected patterns of animal weight fluctuations (g) under baseline, warmer, and colder temperature regimes.

predictions to data from the real system. Most often, we know more about relationships among variables within the system-of-interest than can be documented in a rigorous way by data. We want to describe the expected behavior of those variables that most effectively represent this broader knowledge, thus allowing a more extensive evaluation of model behavior than would be possible based solely on data. For example, recalling what we know about the relationship between environmental temperature and respiration in our weight fluctuation model, although we may not be confident about the exact form of the curve, we expect animal weight to decrease monotonically as temperature increases.

During model use, we will analyze and interpret patterns of behavior of selected variables under different management policies or environmental situations to meet our objectives. We want to describe the expected behavior of those variables that most directly represent hypotheses that we want to test. In this sense, expected patterns of model behavior often are a graphical representation of model objectives. For example, recalling the objective of our weight fluctuation model "to determine the effect of temperature-induced changes in respiration on weight fluctuations of an animal," we might graph a series of curves representing weight fluctuations under several different temperature regimes (Figure 3.8).

CHAPTER 4

QUANTITATIVE-MODEL SPECIFICATION

4.1 INTRODUCTION

The goal of Phase 2 of systems analysis is to develop a quantitative model of the system-of-interest (Figure 4.1). Using the conceptual model as a template for this quantitative development, we describe the rules governing the flow of materials in the model (the dynamics of the system) using mathematical equations. The first step is to choose a general quantitative structure for the model. Perhaps the simplest, most flexible general structure consists of modules containing two model components connected by a flow of material (in terms of our conceptual model, two boxes connected by an arrow). This general compartmental structure lends itself well to the description of complex models, because it facilitates decomposition of complex interrelations into simpler cause-effect pathways.

Having decided on the general quantitative structure form of the model, we next must develop the specific equations that collectively comprise the model. This consists of choosing the basic time unit for the solution of model equations (1 day, 1 week, 1 year, and so on), the functional form (linear, exponential, sigmoid, sinusoidal, and so on) of model equations, and estimating the parameters of model equations. The best type of information that we can use to develop model equations is data from the real system. Available data often can be analyzed using standard statistical procedures to quantify various aspects of the model. However, most commonly, there will be some aspects of the model for which no data are available and for which we cannot collect new data at the present time. In such cases, we may be able to use information based on theoretical or generally applicable empirical relation-

Phase 2: Quantitative-Model Specification

1. Select the general quantitative structure for the model
2. Choose the basic time unit for the simulations
3. Identify the functional forms of the model equations
4. Estimate the parameters of the model equations
5. Code the model equations for the computer
6. Execute the baseline simulation
7. Present the model equations

Figure 4.1 Steps within Phase 2 of systems analysis: quantitative-model specification.

ships. Alternatively, we may be able to convert qualitative information, either from the technical literature or from "expert opinion," into a quantitative form. Finally, after the model is fairly well developed, we may be able to use information generated from experimentation with the model itself to gain insight into the quantification of a certain relationship.

The final steps in the quantitative specification of the model involve computer coding of the model, which consists of translating model equations from the language of mathematics to a language that digital computers understand, executing the baseline simulation, and formally presenting model equations. Baseline simulation refers to solving the model, or simulating behavior of the system-of-interest, under a specific set of conditions that usually represent the "normal" or "status quo" situation for the system. Model equations are presented formally by listing them sequentially in some logical order that unambiguously describes how to solve the model.

4.2 SELECT THE GENERAL QUANTITATIVE STRUCTURE FOR THE MODEL

There are different types of mathematical formats suitable for representing models of dynamic ecological systems: matrix algebra, differential equations, and difference equations are examples. However, most formats represent a general compartment-model structure in which the basic unit, or module, consists of two state variables connected by a material transfer. Material transfer is controlled by information about other parts of the system, including information about state variables, driving variables, constants, and/or auxiliary variables. Of course, this is exactly the framework that we used in Chapter 3 to represent qualitatively the conceptual model of a system-of-interest.

4.2.1   Difference Equations

Difference equations provide the most flexibility for representing dynamic systems in terms of a general compartment-model structure. The price paid for this flexibility is that analytical solutions usually are not possible and therefore models based on difference equations must be solved numerically by simulation. However, it is likely that few systems of direct interest to us can be represented adequately by either matrix models or differential equation models simple enough for analytical solution. Thus, it appears that in most cases, little is lost, because analytical solutions are at best a remote possibility, and much is gained through use of difference equations. Models presented in remaining chapters will follow the general compartment-model structure based on a difference equation format.

4.2.2   General Compartment-Model Structure

The general compartment-model structure is appealing because it is simple and yet can represent large complex models. The strategy is to write an equation or set of equations determining at selected points in time the value of each driving variable, each auxiliary variable, each material transfer (called rate equations), and each state variable. Collectively, these equations completely describe the model. They completely describe the behavior of the system-of-interest.

The computing sequence for model equations each time unit is as follows:

1. driving variable equations
2. auxiliary variable equations (if present)
3. rate equations
4. state variable equations

The initial conditions of the model, including constants and initial values of all state variables, must be specified at time zero. To simulate behavior of the system-of-interest, we "solve" the model by calculating equations in sequence for each unit of simulated time (Figure 4.2).

Recall our model predicting fluctuations in weight of an animal over time first presented in Chapter 2 (Figure 2.1). In Chapter 2, we simulated consumption and respiration of an animal for 2 consecutive days assuming that environmental temperatures are 20°C and 19°C, respectively. Initial weight of the animal is 100 g and a constant (CON RATE = 0.05) represents consumption rate per gram of body weight per day. Environmental temperature is a driving variable that simply is assigned a specific value each day:

$$\text{If } t=0 \text{ THEN TEMPERATURE} = 20$$

$$\text{If } t=1 \text{ THEN TEMPERATURE} = 19$$

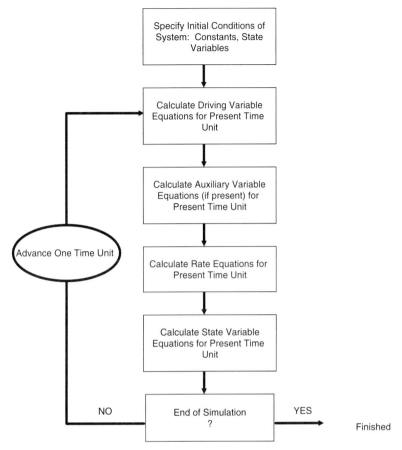

Figure 4.2 Computing sequence for the model equations within the general compartment-model structure.

These are driving variable equations. An auxiliary variable represents respiration rate per gram of body weight per day as a function of environmental temperature:

$$\texttt{RESP RATE = 0.0025 * TEMPERATURE}_t$$

This is an auxiliary variable equation. The consumption equation,

$$\texttt{CONSUMPTION}_{t,t+1} \texttt{ = CON RATE * WEIGHT}_t$$

and the respiration equation,

$$\text{RESPIRATION}_{t, t+1} = \text{RESP RATE} * \text{WEIGHT}_t$$

are rate equations. Finally,

$$\text{WEIGHT}_{t+1} = \text{WEIGHT}_t + \Delta\text{WEIGHT}_{t, t+1}$$

is the state variable equation, where

$$\Delta\text{WEIGHT}_{t, t+1} = \text{CONSUMPTION}_{t, t+1} - \text{RESPIRATION}_{t, t+1}$$

(remember that we assumed assimilation efficiency equals 100%). For each day of simulated time, we first evaluate the driving variable equation, next the auxiliary variable equation, next the two rate equations, and finally the state variable equation.

4.3 CHOOSE THE BASIC TIME UNIT FOR THE SIMULATIONS

After the general quantitative structure is decided, the next step in quantitative specification of the model is to choose the basic time unit for simulations. The basic time unit for simulations is the time interval (Δt) between iterative solutions of model equations. The basic time unit for simulations in our weight fluctuation model as presented in Chapter 2 was 1 day. We solved model equations for each day of simulated time.

Choice of the basic time unit depends on the level of resolution in time needed (1) for the model to address our questions of interest, (2) to represent appropriately temporal changes in rates at which processes within the system-of-interest occur, (3) to facilitate parameterization of model equations in view of the temporal resolution of available data or other information, and (4) to make computing costs reasonable in terms of both time and money.

If in our weight fluctuation model we had been interested in questions concerning diurnal fluctuations in consumption and respiration of the animal, those questions would have dictated a basic time interval less than 1 day. We might have chosen $\Delta t = 1$ h or $\Delta t = 6$ h, depending on the resolution required to answer our questions concerning diurnal fluctuations. If we had known or suspected that consumption or respiration rates fluctuated through the day in a manner that made us uneasy about representing them as average daily rates, we might have chosen Δt smaller than 1 day. Implicit in choice of the basic time unit is the assumption that all rates within the system remain constant over any given Δt. If all data and other information that we used to parameterize model equations were based on a temporal resolution of 1 h, we might have chosen $\Delta t = 1$ h simply to facilitate parameterization of model equations, although this third consideration is not as important as the first two. Finally, computing costs can become a very real consideration in the choice of Δt for some models. Obviously, as the number of time steps in a simulation increases, so does computing time and associated dollar costs if one is using a mainframe computer. If one is using a microcomputer, dollar costs are not a concern, but computing time can become a limiting factor.

4.4   IDENTIFY THE FUNCTIONAL FORMS OF THE MODEL EQUATIONS

The next step in quantitative specification of the model is to choose the functional forms of the model equations. We now specify whether the general forms of equations representing specific relationships within the model are linear, sigmoidal, exponential, and so on.

In our model predicting the fluctuations in the weight of an animal (Figure 2.1), we stated in Chapter 2 that material transfer from the food source to the animal component (CONSUMPTION) was an increasing linear function of the value of the animal state variable (WEIGHT). We chose the functional form of the rate equation representing consumption to be linear. We might indicate the functional form of the consumption equation as

$$\text{CONSUMPTION} \;=\; f(\text{WEIGHT}) \;=\; \beta_0 \,+\, \beta_1 \,{}^*\, \text{WEIGHT}$$

which is the equation for a linear relationship. Parameters of this equation, β_0 and β_1, must be estimated, but we defer parameter estimation for the moment and concentrate only on the specification of the functional forms of equations. The functional form of the other rate equation (RESPIRATION) was of the form

$$\text{RESPIRATION} \;=\; f(\text{TEMPERATURE, WEIGHT})$$
$$=\; \beta_0 \,{}^*\, \text{TEMPERATURE} \,{}^*\, \text{WEIGHT}$$

where once again β_0 is a parameter to be estimated. We will look at this equation more closely a bit later. The driving variable equations simply equated environmental temperature with an input datum at each time unit. It is common practice to equate driving variables directly with input data, although they also can be explicit functions of time. The general functional form of state variable equations is the same for all discrete-time compartment models, because these equations are essentially bookkeeping functions to update the state of the system at each time unit. The general form is

$$(\text{state variable})_{t+1} = (\text{state variable})_t + (\text{transfers into state variable})_{t,t+1}$$
$$-\, (\text{transfers out of state variable})_{t,t+1}$$

For our weight fluctuation model, the state variable equation is

$$WEIGHT_{t+1} = WEIGHT_t + CONSUMPTION_{t,t+1} - RESPIRATION_{t,t+1}$$

4.4.1   Information on Which to Base the Choice of Functional Forms

Information on which to base the choice of functional forms of model equations is of four general types: (1) quantitative data from direct observation or experimentation with the real system, either collected firsthand or from literature; (2) information based on theoretical relationships or generally applicable empirical relationships that are appropriate for the situation being modeled; (3) qualitative information based on expert opinion or on the literature; and (4) information gained from experimenting with the model itself.

Quantitative Data. The best information comes from quantitative experimentation with the real system. If we had data for our weight fluctuation model relating consumption to the weight of the animal that appeared as plotted in Figure 4.3, we would feel secure in choosing a linear form for the consumption-weight relationship.

Theoretical or Generally Applicable Empirical Relationships. Sometimes theoretical relationships or generally applicable empirical relationships exist that suggest the functional form of a particular relationship. Suppose with regard to our weight fluctuation model that a general empirical relationship existed relating respiration to environmental temperature that had been established for a variety of animal species closely related to the animal in our model. This relationship suggested that respiration equaled consumption at 20°C but decreased by 5% relative to consumption for every 1°C below 20°C and increased by 5% relative to consumption for every 1°C above 20°C. Thus, at 19°C, respiration would be 95% of consumption, at 21°C, it would be 105% of consumption, and so on. Then we might represent the functional form of

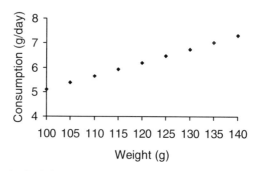

Figure 4.3   Hypothetical data for the weight fluctuation model (Figure 2.1) relating CONSUMPTION to WEIGHT of an animal.

the respiration relationship, or the material transfer from the animal state variable to the respiration sink, as

$$\mathrm{RESPIRATION} = \beta_0 * \mathrm{TEMPERATURE} * \mathrm{WEIGHT}$$

Qualitative Information. In some cases, there may be no quantitative data or theoretical relationships available on which to base the choice of functional forms. In such situations, we may rely on qualitative information from the literature or on opinions of experts in the field to establish assumptions on which to base the choice of functional forms of some model equations. Without the consumption data in Figure 4.3, we might have based the choice of a linear relationship between consumption and the weight of the animal on the opinion of a person with extensive experience in feeding such animals, even though written records concerning the rate of consumption never were maintained.

Information from Experimentation with the Model. In some cases, there may be little known in even a qualitative sense on which to base our choice of functional forms. In such situations, we may be able to gain insight into possible functional forms of a model equation by hypothesizing different functional forms and observing model behavior in response to each. Through such experimentation with the model, we may narrow possible choices by excluding those functional forms that produce unreasonable model behavior. Without specific information about the relationship between consumption and the weight of the animal in our weight fluctuation model, we might have hypothesized an exponential and a sigmoidal as well as a linear relationship. However, after parameterizing each equation (as discussed in what follows) and running test simulations, we may have found that, of these three choices, only the linear relationship produced reasonable predictions of animal weight changes in view of what we know about weight changes of animals in the real system. Obviously, the number of equations that can be specified in this manner within any single model necessarily is small. The more equations specified by this trial-and-error method, the higher the likelihood that we will obtain apparently reasonable model behavior purely by chance.

4.4.2   Selecting Types of Equations to Represent the Chosen Functional Forms

When we choose the functional form for a relationship in our model, we often can find a single equation that can be parameterized to represent the appropriate curve. This is not always the case, but knowledge of the types of equations associated with different types of curves is most helpful. Although we probably remember that a straight line can be represented by the equation

$$y = \beta_0 + \beta_1 X$$

and perhaps that an exponential curve can be represented by the equation

$$y = \beta_0 e^{\beta_1 X}$$

numerous other useful types of equations exist. There is no need to commit a large number of equations to memory, but we should be aware that there are logical approaches to selecting appropriate equations (e.g., Spain 1982, pp. 47 and 341). Figure 4.4 presents several particularly useful equation types.

4.5 ESTIMATE THE PARAMETERS OF THE MODEL EQUATIONS

Information on which to base parameterization of model equations is of the same four general types used to choose functional forms of model equations, namely: (1) quantitative data, (2) information based on theoretical or generally applicable empirical relationships, (3) qualitative information, and (4) information gained from experimenting with the model itself.

In fact, the choice of functional forms and the parameterization of model equations for any given model are based most commonly on the same information, and the entire process often is an iterative one. Nonetheless, from a theoretical standpoint, we should view the choice of functional forms and the parameterization of model equations as two distinct steps because the former usually has more profound implications concerning ecological interpretations of model structure than does the latter.

4.5.1 Information on Which to Base the Estimation of the Model Equations

Quantitative Data. Specific techniques available to estimate parameters of model equations based on quantitative data are diverse, and a substantive discussion covering the spectrum of available techniques is beyond the scope of this text. Problems that arise within the framework of model parameter estimation are identical to those encountered in analysis of data in general, and modelers are well advised to consult with professional statisticians during this step in quantitative specification of the model. Nonetheless, the role of the various techniques of data analysis often employed during this step of model development should be clear: They serve as tools allowing us to interpret appropriately quantitative information about important relationships within our system-of-interest. Among the techniques more widely applicable for our purposes is regression analysis. As an example of parameterization of model equations based on quantitative data, we return again to our weight fluctuation model (Figure 2.1). Parameterization of the consumption equation, the functional form of which is

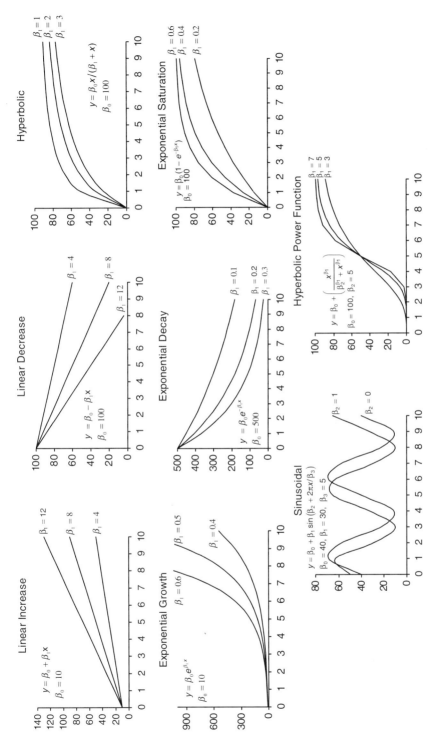

Figure 4.4 Selected types of equations that are particularly useful in representing a variety of functional relationships.

$$\text{CONSUMPTION} = \beta_0 + \beta_1 * \text{WEIGHT}$$

involves estimation of β_0 and β_1. If the data plotted in Figure 4.3 relating consumption to animal weight were available to us, we might run a simple linear regression analysis with consumption as the dependent variable and weight as the independent variable to estimate β_0 and β_1. In this particular case, we have specified hypothetical data such that all data points lie exactly on the line

$$\text{CONSUMPTION} = 0.05 * \text{WEIGHT}$$

Thus, $b_0 = 0$, $b_1 = 0.05$ (where b_0 and b_1 represent our estimates of parameters β_0 and β_1, respectively, and β_1 will become CON RATE in our weight fluctuation model), and the proportion of the variability in consumption accounted for by variability in weight equals 1 ($r^2 = 1.0$). Of course, the r^2 of regressions based on real data will always be less than 1.0, even if the true relationship is perfectly linear, due to error in data measurements.

Theoretical or Generally Applicable Empirical Relationships. In cases where data describing a relationship within our system-of-interest are not available, we may be able to rely on theoretical or generally applicable empirical relationships established based on information about similar relationships in other systems. Earlier, we assumed the respiration relationship in our weight fluctuation model was based on a general empirical relationship that suggested respiration equaled consumption at 20°C but decreased by 5% relative to consumption for every 1°C below 20°C and increased by 5% for every 1°C above 20°C. The functional form of the equation was specified as

$$\text{RESPIRATION} = \beta_0 * \text{TEMPERATURE} * \text{WEIGHT}$$

where β_0 must be estimated such that b_0 * TEMPERATURE * WEIGHT causes respiration to equal consumption at 20°C and makes respiration 5% larger or smaller than consumption as environmental temperatures either rise or fall 1°C above or below 20°C. Thus, b_0 must equal 0.0025 because this causes the appropriate shifts in respiration as temperature varies. Thus,

$$\text{RESPIRATION} = 0.0025 * \text{TEMPERATURE} * \text{WEIGHT}$$

where the term 0.0025 * TEMPERATURE is represented as the auxiliary variable RESP RATE (Figure 2.1).

Qualitative Information. In cases where no quantitative data are available, we may be able to rely on qualitative information from the literature or on opinions of experts to establish assumptions on which to base our estimates of model parameters. Without the consumption data in Figure 4.3, we might have based our estimates of parameters of the consumption equation on the opinion of an expert on animal consumption. We may have been given approximate consumption estimates for both relatively light and relatively heavy animals, thus providing two points through which we could fit a straight line and estimate β_0 and β_1.

Information from Experimentation with the Model. In cases where little is known even in a qualitative sense on which to base our parameter estimates, we may be able to bound the range of reasonable parameter estimates by hypothesizing different estimates and observing model behavior in response to each. Those parameter estimates resulting in unreasonable model behavior can be excluded from further consideration. Suppose that we lacked both consumption data and expert opinion concerning consumption of light and heavy animals for our weight fluctuation model. However, we did know that consumption was some linear function of weight and we knew the relationship of respiration to consumption at different environmental temperatures. Given this information, we could bound our parameter estimates for the consumption equation simply through trial-and-error experimentation with the model itself. As with the choice of functional forms, the number of parameters in any single model estimated by this trial-and-error method must be relatively small or we run the risk of obtaining apparently reasonable model predictions purely by chance.

4.5.2   Deterministic- versus Stochastic-Model Parameterization

One final consideration regarding model parameterization is whether the model is deterministic or stochastic. So far, we have talked in terms of point estimates of variables and transfer rates within models, thus implying that we are dealing with deterministic models. However, the same parameterization procedures just presented are equally applicable to stochastic models except that some additional information is needed to represent inherent randomness of variables or transfer rates occurring within the model.

Representation of a random variable or transfer rate in a stochastic model requires specification of either a statistical distribution or an empirical frequency distribution from which values of the variable or transfer rate are selected randomly, rather than specification of a single-point estimate such as is required for deterministic models. As before, information on which to base specification of the statistical or empirical distributions can be (1) quantitative data, (2) information based on theoretical relationships or generally applicable empirical relationships, (3) qualitative information, or (4) information gained from experimenting with the model itself.

To illustrate the differences in information required to parameterize deterministic versus stochastic models, consider possible representations of the environmental temperature driving variable in our weight fluctuation model. Recall that initially we equated temperature directly with an input datum for each of 2 days that were simulated: TEMPERATURE = 20°C if t = 0 and TEMPERATURE = 19°C if t = 1. This representation is deterministic. If we wish to represent environmental temperature as a stochastic (random) variable, there are at least three alternatives. We can select random temperature variables from (1) a frequency distribution of historical data, (2) a statistical distribution fitted to historical data, or (3) a set of statistical distributions generated from regression of temperature on the day of the year.

Frequency Distribution of Historical Data. If temperature data from the real system are available from several years, we might use all historical temperatures available for a given date to construct a frequency distribution of temperatures for that date (Figure 4.5a). We then randomly select temperature for the first day of simulated time (t = 0) from the day-0 frequency distribution rather than simply specifying it to be 20°C, as in the deterministic model, and we select temperature for the second day of simulated time (t = 1) from the day-1 frequency distribution rather than specifying it to be 19°C as before.

To select temperature randomly from the frequency distributions in Figure 4.5a, we first construct the associated cumulative frequency distributions (Figure 4.5b). The height of each bar in the cumulative frequency distributions represents the proportion of observed temperatures less than the value indicated beneath the bar. Thus, for day 0, one-tenth of the observed temperatures were less than 18°C, three-tenths were less than 19°C, and so on (Figure 4.5b). Next, we select a uniform random variate on the interval zero to one (a random number between zero and one) from a table of random numbers (Rohlf and Sokal, 1969, p. 152). Or we might obtain a uniform random variate from a random-number generator on a computer. We then find the temperature in the appropriate cumulative frequency distribution corresponding to the frequency whose value equaled the selected random number. If we were using the day-0 distribution and if the random number selected were 0.1, the corresponding temperature would be 18°C (Figure 4.5b). If the random number were 0.3, the corresponding temperature would be 19°C, and so on.

Statistical Distribution Fitted to Historical Data. An alternative way to represent environmental temperature as a random variable is to fit a statistical distribution to historical real-system temperature data. We might find that temperatures for each date are approximately normally distributed. We then might fit a normal distribution to temperatures for each date by estimating the parameters of a normal distribution (mean μ and standard deviation σ) based on temperatures for each date (Figure 4.6). Next, we randomly select temperature for the first day of simulated time (t = 0) from the day-0 normal distribution and temperature for the second day of simulated time (t = 1), from the day-1 normal distribution.

Of course, there are numerous statistical distributions other than the normal that might be fitted to historical data. The uniform and Poisson, for example,

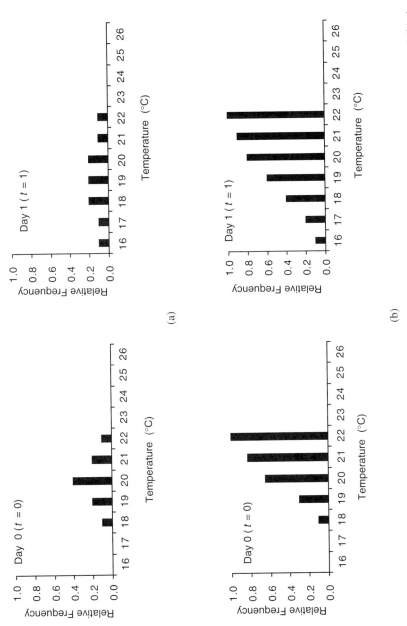

Figure 4.5 (a) Frequency distributions of hypothetical environmental temperature data for two days ($t = 0$ and $t = 1$) and (b) the associated cumulative frequency distributions.

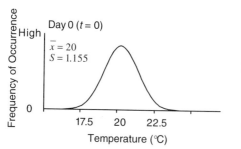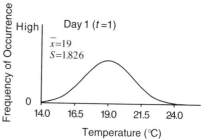

Figure 4.6 Normal distributions fitted to the hypothetical environmental temperature data in Figure 4.5a.

are two distributions that find wide application in ecology. The degree to which a data set resembles a particular statistical distribution, or the goodness of fit to that distribution, can be evaluated using standard statistical procedures (Johnson and Kotz, 1969). Algorithms for generating random variates from a variety of statistical distributions that we might wish to use in stochastic simulation models are readily available (Hastings and Peacock, 1975).

Statistical Distributions Generated from Regression. Yet another way to represent environmental temperature as a random variable is to generate the required statistical distributions from a regression of temperature on the day of the year. Suppose that we are interested in simulating animal weight fluctuations for a particular 30-day period and that real-system data suggest environmental temperatures decrease linearly during this period from 20°C to 15°C (Figure 4.7a). We could calculate a regression of temperature on the day and use the mean squared error of regression (MSE) to generate a normal distribution about the temperature predicted for each day. Because the MSE is an unbiased predictor of variance (σ^2), the normal distribution associated with each predicted daily temperature has the temperature predicted by regression as its mean and a variance equal to the MSE. For this example, the regression equation is temperature $= 20 - 0.167t$ and the MSE $= 2.0006$ (Figure 4.7a). As before, we randomly select temperature each day from the normal distribution for the day. The normal distribution of temperature generated for day 15 ($t = 15$) based on the MSE is shown in Figure 4.7b. Actually, if we do not know the slope of the regression line exactly, the variance about predicted temperatures will increase with increasing distance from the overall mean. It is possible to obtain the variance associated with each predicted temperature (Snedecor and Cochran, 1967, p. 154) and these separate variances could be used instead of the MSE to specify the temperature distributions. However, assuming that our intent is to represent the general variability of temperature, rather than the variability associated with temperatures predicted from a particular data set, the MSE probably is the better choice.

Note in the preceding discussion the relationship between statistical analyses, or statistical models, and simulation models. We commonly employ

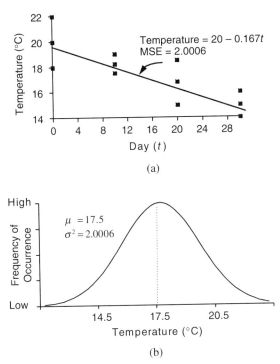

Figure 4.7   (a) Regression of temperature on day of the year based on hypothetical data over a 30-day period, and (b) the normal distribution of temperatures predicted for day 15 using $\mu = \hat{y}$ for day 15 and σ^2 as the mean squared error of regression (MSE).

statistical techniques to help us determine appropriate quantitative representations for particular relationships in simulation models when data pertaining to those relationships are available. Often, the statistical models used to analyze the data, or, more strictly speaking, results of the statistical analyses, actually become a part of the simulation model. If, for example, we use a linear regression model to correlate consumption with animal weight based on the data in Figure 4.3, the right-hand side of the regression equation (of the form $\beta_0 + \beta_1$ WEIGHT) becomes the right-hand side of the material-transfer equation describing consumption in our weight fluctuation model (CONSUMPTION $= \beta_0 + \beta_1$ WEIGHT).

4.6   CODE THE MODEL EQUATIONS FOR THE COMPUTER

Coding model equations for solution on a digital computer can be done in a variety of computer languages or simulation programs. If a computer language is used, the general strategy for programming a simulation model on a digital computer involves (1) constructing a flow diagram indicating the steps involved in solving model equations and simulating model behavior, (2) writing computer code in the chosen language to accomplish those steps, (3) debugging the computer program, or correcting the syntax or logical errors that prevent the program from compiling, and (4) verifying that the program is doing what the modeler intended. If a simulation program is used, the steps followed vary depending on the particular program. We have used one particularly useful simulation program (STELLA® II, High Performance System, Inc., 1994) to develop all of the models presented in this text.

4.7 EXECUTE THE BASELINE SIMULATION

The baseline simulation represents the behavior of the system-of-interest, or the solution of the model, under the particular set of conditions that we wish to use as a benchmark or standard against which to compare changes in system behavior resulting from other sets of conditions of interest to us. The baseline simulation is the end product of the second phase of systems analysis just as the conceptual-model diagram is the end product of the first phase of systems analysis. As we will see in Chapter 5, model evaluation involves close examination of the baseline simulation and comparisons of baseline simulation predictions of various system attributes with corresponding attributes observed in the real system. As we will see in Chapter 6, model use involves comparison of baseline simulation results with results of simulations representing management policies or environmental situations that we wish to evaluate.

Suppose that the normal, or baseline, situation that we wish to simulate with our weight fluctuation model consists of the 30-day period for which we have data from the real system and during which temperatures decreased linearly from 20°C to 15°C (Figure 4.7a). Recall that the regression equation representing temperature as a function of day during this period was

$$\text{TEMPERATURE}(^\circ\text{C}) = 20 - 0.167t$$

where $0 \leq t < 30$ represented day. We modify our weight fluctuation model by using this new equation to calculate the environmental temperature driving variable:

$$\text{TEMPERATURE} = 20 - 0.167t$$

The results of the baseline simulation indicate that the animal gains weight throughout the 30-day period, but that the rate of weight gain, both in absolute terms (g/day) and as a proportion of animal weight (g/g-day), increases as the environmental temperature decreases (Figure 4.8).

C04M

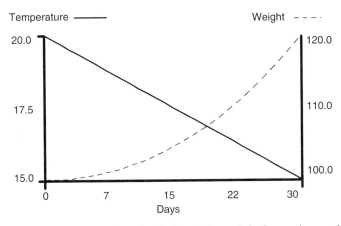

Figure 4.8 Results of the baseline simulation of the weight fluctuation model (Figure 2.1).

4.7.1 Baseline Simulations for Stochastic Models

Whereas there is only one baseline simulation for deterministic models, baseline simulation for stochastic models actually consists of a set of replicate simulations, each representing baseline conditions. Thus, for stochastic models, an additional consideration arises at this point, namely, how many replicate simulations should be run. This question is directly analogous to the question of how many samples should be obtained in an experiment in the real world.

There is no simple answer to this sample size question, but perhaps one of the most useful answers can be found if we consider the framework within which the model ultimately will be used and rephrase the question as follows: How large a sample must we obtain in order to show that a true difference of magnitude δ between alternative management policies or environmental situations is statistically significant at a significance level α with a probability P that the difference will be detected if it exists (Sokal and Rohlf, 1969, p. 246)?

We can answer this question if we know two things: (1) inherent variability of items that we are sampling and (2) magnitude of difference between different samples of items (representing different management policies or different environmental situations) that we consider practically significant relative to the problem at hand.

We can obtain an estimate of the variability of items that we are sampling by running relatively many stochastic simulations of baseline conditions and calculating the variance of the model output in which we are interested. Although it is difficult to define "relatively many," as we increase the number of these initial simulations, the estimate of variance should reach a stable level. We must determine the magnitude of differences between samples that we consider practically important independent of the model based on our knowledge of what size differences are relevant in the real system.

The formula for calculating the number of samples needed to detect a given true difference between sample means, assuming that we have an estimate of variability within samples, is

$$n \geq 2 \left(\frac{\sigma}{\delta}\right)^2 [t_{\alpha,\gamma} + t_{2(1-P),\gamma}]^2$$

(Sokal and Rohlf, 1969, p. 247)

where

n = number of samples

σ = true standard deviation, which we estimate as the square root of the estimated variance within samples

δ = smallest true difference that we desire to detect

γ = degrees of freedom of the sample standard deviation with b groups of samples and n samples per group, or $\gamma = b(n-1)$

α = significance level

P = desired probability that a difference will be found to be significant if it is as small as δ

$t_{\alpha,\gamma}$ and $t_{2(1-P),\gamma}$ = values from a two-tailed t-table with γ degrees of freedom and corresponding to probabilities of α and $2(1 - P)$, respectively

We cannot solve for n directly because we do not know γ, which is a function of n. Therefore, we

1. guess a value for n
2. calculate γ
3. solve the equation for n

We then compare the calculated n with our guess of n. If the calculated n rounded to the nearest whole number is not equal to the guessed n, we adjust our guess for n accordingly and repeat the procedure.

Suppose that we wish to represent temperature as a random variable in our weight fluctuation model and use the stochastic version to simulate the same baseline situation that we simulated previously using the deterministic version (Figure 4.8). We modify the calculation of the temperature driving variable such that we now randomly choose temperature for each day from a normal distribution with a mean equal to the temperature predicted by the regression equation representing temperature as a function of day and a variance equal to the MSE of that regression (Figure 4.7). Further suppose that our primary use of the model is to compare the weight of an initially 100-g animal after a 30-day exposure to baseline conditions with the weight of an initially 100-g animal after a 30-day exposure to a warmer temperature regimen. We want to detect a true difference in weight of 3 g (δ) at a statistical significance level of $\alpha = 0.05$ with probability $P = 0.80$ that the difference will be detected if it exists. Fifty preliminary stochastic baseline simulations suggest that 7.14 g is a good estimate of the inherent variability (σ^2) of weight after a 30-day exposure to baseline conditions. Assuming that this also is a good estimate of the inherent variability of weight after a 30-day exposure to the warmer temperature regime, we can estimate the appropriate number of stochastic simulations to run as

$$n \geq 2 \left(\frac{\sigma}{\delta}\right)^2 [t_{\alpha,\gamma} + t_{2(1-P),\gamma}]^2$$

If we estimate $n = 14$, then

$$\sigma = \sqrt{7.14} = 2.67$$
$$\delta = 3$$
$$\gamma = 2(14 - 1) = 26$$
$$\alpha = 0.05$$
$$P = 0.80$$
$$t_{\alpha,\gamma} = t_{0.05,26} = 2.056$$

and

$$t_{2(1-P),\gamma} = t_{0.40,26} = 0.856$$

Therefore, the formula becomes

$$14 \geq 2(2.67/3)^2(2.056 + 0.856)^2$$

or

$$14 \geq 13.43$$

and we should run 14 replicate stochastic simulations.

For practical purposes, the improvement in our estimate of n gained by iteration is often unimportant. Usually, we arbitrarily set $\gamma = \infty$ and use the initial calculated value of n as our estimate of the required sample size, realizing that it is a slight underestimate. Had we done this for the preceding

C04MOD02

Table 4.1 Formal Presentation of the Weight Fluctuation Model Equations Written to Correspond to Variable Designations in Figure 2.1 and Organized by the Computing Sequence of Equation Types

Inital Conditions of State Variables	`WEIGHT`$_0$`=100`
Values of Constants	`CON RATE=0.05`
Driving Variable Equations	`TEMPERATURE=20 if `t`=0` `TEMPERATURE=19 if `t`=1`
Auxiliary Variable Equations	`RESP RATE=0.0025*TEMPERATURE`
Rate Equations	`CONSUMPTION=CON RATE*WEIGHT` `RESPIRATION=RESP RATE*WEIGHT`
State Variable Equations	`WEIGHT`$_{t+1}$`=WEIGHT`$_t$`+CONSUMPTION-RESPIRATION`

example, we would have calculated $n \geq 12.44$, and probably would have chosen a sample size of 13 or 14.

4.8 PRESENT THE MODEL EQUATIONS

Formal presentation of model equations aids in ultimately solving the model and also facilitates the unambiguous description of model structure to others. An effective manner in which to present model equations formally is in a table organized by the computing sequence of equation types. Driving variable equations are presented first, followed by auxiliary variable equations, rate equations, and state variable equations. Initial conditions of state variables and constants of the model also must be identified. Our weight fluctuation model equations are represented formally in Table 4.1. This set of equations uniquely describes the model and also relates model equations to the conceptual-model diagram (Figure 2.1). C02

CHAPTER 5

MODEL EVALUATION

5.1 INTRODUCTION

The goal of Phase 3 of systems analysis is to evaluate the model in terms of its relative usefulness for a specific purpose. A model that is very useful for one purpose might be useless or, worse, misleading for another purpose. Most commonly, this process is referred to as "model validation," erroneously suggesting that a "valid" or "correct" model exists for any given system-of-interest. Holling (1978), among others, recognized that this was an unfortunate choice of terms and suggested that we might better refer to the process of "model invalidation," making an analogy between the process of attempting to invalidate a model and the process of attempting to reject a hypothesis via the scientific method. This analogy has merit in that a model can be viewed as a collection of hypotheses that represents our current understanding of the structure and function of the system-of-interest. However, it tends to overemphasize the role of quantitative, often statistical, comparisons of model predictions with selected observations from the real system as the sole criterion for evaluation.

Rykiel (1996) argues that different validation criteria are appropriate for different types of models and suggests that validation should mean simply that a model is acceptable for its intended use. Rykiel also emphasizes that no generally accepted standards currently exist for the validation of ecological models and provides an excellent discussion of the semantic and philosophical debate concerning validation in which ecological modelers still are involved. Although the details of the debate may seem quite confusing, we believe that the basic ideas involved in evaluating the usefulness of a model are easy to understand. Thus, we prefer to refer simply to the process of "model evaluation" and to focus our attention on examination of the various characteristics of a model that make it a potentially useful tool.

During model evaluation, we should examine a broad array of qualitative as well as quantitative aspects of model structure and behavior (Figure 5.1). We begin by assessing reasonableness of model structure and interpretability of functional relationships within the model. Reasonableness and interpretability are defined relative to the ecological, economic, or other subject-matter context of the model. Next, we evaluate correspondence between model behavior and the expected patterns of model behavior that we described during conceptual-model formulation. We then examine more formally the correspondence between model predictions and real-system data. These comparisons may or may not involve the use of statistical tests of significance. Finally, we conduct a sensitivity analysis of the model, which usually consists of sequentially varying one model parameter (or set of parameters) at a time and monitoring the subsequent effects on model behavior. By identifying those parameters that most affect model behavior, sensitivity analysis provides valuable insight into the functioning of the model and also suggests the level of confidence we should have in model predictions.

Relative importance of these various steps for any given model depends on the specific objectives of the modeling project. If we are dissatisfied with the model during any of these steps, we return to an earlier step in systems analysis to make appropriate modifications to the model. The step to which we return depends on the reasons for which we are dissatisfied (Figure 5.2).

5.2 ASSESS THE REASONABLENESS OF THE MODEL STRUCTURE AND THE INTERPRETABILITY OF FUNCTIONAL RELATIONSHIPS WITHIN THE MODEL

This first step involves attempting to refute aspects of model structure and functional relationships within the model based on their lack of correspondence with the real system. Thus, this step receives particular emphasis with mechanistic, or explanatory, models and might be omitted for strictly empirical, or correlative, models. The procedure is exactly the same as scientific hypothesis testing. The hypotheses tested are our hypotheses about how functional relationships within the model work and about structural connections among individual parts of the model. Hypothesis tests are based on the best information available about the corresponding aspects of the real system, viewed at the appropriate level of detail. If any aspect of model structure or any functional relationship within the model can be shown to be an inadequate representation of the corresponding aspect of the real system, then that particular portion of the model is refuted. Criteria for failing hypothesis tests

---

Phase 3: Model Evaluation

1. Assess the reasonableness of the model structure and the interpretability of functional relationships within the model
2. Evaluate the correspondence between model behavior and the expected patterns of model behavior
3. Examine the correspondence between model predictions and the data from the real system
4. Determine the sensitivity of model predictions to changes in the values of important parameters

---

Figure 5.1   Steps within Phase 3 of systems analysis: model evaluation.

may be qualitative or quantitative, depending on objectives of the modeling project and the type of information available from the real system.

If the model fails to pass this step in our evaluation, we first should reconsider steps 3 and 4 of conceptual-model formulation, categorizing components within the system-of-interest and identifying relationships among components that are of interest. Then, we should reconsider step 3 in the quantitative-model specification, identifying the functional forms of the model equations (Figure 5.2).

Recalling our weight fluctuation model (Figure 2.1), we initially represented consumption as a linear function of weight of the animal. Presumably, this representation was consistent with available information when we first included it in the model. But suppose that subsequently during model evaluation, we discover new information, based on data collected over a wider range of animal weights than had been examined previously, suggesting that consumption per unit body weight actually is a decreasing function of animal weight. Thus, consumption is some curvilinear function of weight and we reject the hypothesis of a linear relationship. In this case, our conceptual model of the system still appears adequate, but we must return to step 3 of quantitative-model specification and identify a new functional form for the consumption equation.

5.3   EVALUATE THE CORRESPONDENCE BETWEEN MODEL BEHAVIOR AND THE EXPECTED PATTERNS OF MODEL BEHAVIOR

During the second step in model evaluation, we compare model behavior to our a priori expectations, which we described during the final step in conceptual-model formulation. We look for obvious impossibilities or implausibilities in the baseline simulation, such as negative values for state variables

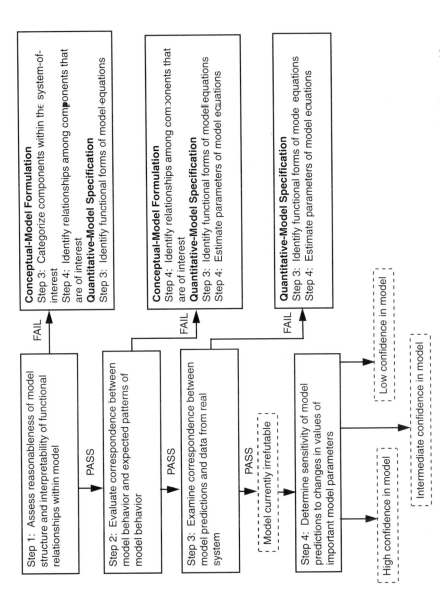

Figure 5.2 Steps in model evaluation and the steps of systems analysis to which we should return if our model fails to pass a given evaluation step.

or transfer rates that by definition must be positive, or impossibly high or low values for state variables or material transfers. In addition to examining the baseline simulation for unreasonable behavior, we might also examine model behavior over a wide range of input conditions (wide range of values for driving variables) to attempt to expose additional inadequacies in the model. It may seem strange to mention such obvious shortcomings in model behavior, but models that initially show gross inconsistencies with our expectations based on general knowledge about the real system are common. At this point, these gross inconsistencies may result from a fundamental misconception about the nature of relationships within the system-of-interest, in which case changes in the conceptual model are required. Presumably, errors in coding the model or errors in model logic already have been corrected during the quantitative-model specification.

When a model no longer exhibits obviously implausible behavior, we turn our attention to a closer examination of model components: state, driving, and auxiliary variables; constants; and material transfer rates. General dynamics of each component should be reasonable in terms of the timing of maximum and minimum values, the relative amplitude and periodicity of fluctuations, and its relationship to dynamics of other components. Both state variables and material transfers should vary in the right direction and by the right order of magnitude in response to changes in the values of driving variables. Inadequacies detected as a result of this closer examination of model components still may be caused by a fundamental misconception about the nature of relationships within the system-of-interest, but at this stage, it is likely that inadequacies are caused by inclusion of erroneous parameter estimates or perhaps by inclusion of incorrect functional forms of equations.

Recalling our weight fluctuation model (Figure 2.1), suppose that in addition to simulating animal growth under laboratory conditions with food provided ad libitum, we want to simulate weight fluctuations under food-limited field conditions. Further, suppose that the expected pattern of model behavior, based on our general field observations, indicates relatively rapid growth during part of the year and essentially no growth during part of the year. Comparing model behavior to this expected pattern, we discover that our simulated animals gain weight throughout the year. In this case, inadequacies in our model cannot be remedied by modification of parameter estimates or functional forms of equations. We must correct a fundamental error in our conceptual model of the system-of-interest.

5.3.1 Tuning the Model

At this point, assuming that no gross inadequacies in model behavior remain, it may be possible to further improve correspondence with expected patterns of model behavior by adjusting some parameter values or by altering functional forms of some equations. This general procedure is referred to as "tuning the model." It is a legitimate activity during this step of model evaluation, but is an activity that must be confined strictly in terms of (1) choosing parameters or functional forms to be altered, (2) determining when to end tuning activities, and (3) limiting the number of parameters or functional forms tuned.

5.3.2 Choosing Parameters or Functional Forms to be Altered

Discretion must be used in choosing the parameters or functional forms to be altered and in choosing the types of alterations to be made. Alterations will be arbitrary because no new information external to the model is being drawn on to make them, although the nature of differences between model behavior and expected patterns of behavior may suggest specific alterations. But we must alter only those parameters or functional forms that we have specified in a tentative fashion, and the type of alteration made must not result in a parameter value or functional form that could have been refuted in the previous model-evaluation step.

For example, suppose that we have estimated two parameters in a given model. For one parameter, we have strong evidence that the value must be 8. For the other parameter, we have information suggesting only that the value probably lies between 10 and 20; perhaps we have chosen a value of 15 for inclusion in the model. Because we have strong evidence supporting our estimate of the first parameter, we should not "tune" or alter that parameter. But because our current estimate of the second parameter (15) was chosen over other possible estimates between 10 and 20 based on little or no information, we might legitimately tune or alter this parameter within the range of 10 to 20 in order to improve correspondence with expected patterns of model behavior.

Likewise, suppose that we have specified functional forms of two material-transfer equations within a given model. For one transfer, we have strong evidence that the functional form is linear. For the other transfer, we have information suggesting only that the curve relating rate of transfer (Y) to the variable governing the transfer (X) passes through points (X_1, Y_1) and (X_2, Y_2). Perhaps we have chosen a linear relationship passing through these two points for inclusion in the model. Because we have strong evidence supporting our choice of a linear functional form for the first transfer, it should not be altered. But because our current functional form of the equation representing the second transfer was chosen over other possible functional forms that pass through (X_1, Y_1) and (X_2, Y_2) based on little or no information, we might legitimately tune this transfer by specifying another functional form for the equation. We might see if an exponential functional form of the equation improves correspondence with expected patterns of model behavior.

5.3.3 Determining When to End Tuning Activities

All tuning of the model must be completed before proceeding to the next model-evaluation step, which is the examination of the correspondence between model predictions and data from the real system. If statistical comparisons are made between model predictions and real-system data, then clearly tuning must be completed before statistical tests are performed. If comparisons between model predictions and real-system data are nonstatistical, tuning still must be completed before the final round of "formal" quantitative comparisons are performed.

5.3.4 Limiting Number of Parameters or Functional Forms Tuned

We must limit the number of parameter values or functional forms of equations that we tune in any given model. Although there is no set limit, obviously, as the number of components that are tuned increases, so does the number of possible combinations of alterations and, hence, the possibility that any improvement in model behavior will result solely from a fortuitous combination of alterations.

In practice, it is more common to tune parameter values than functional forms of equations. This is understandable because the choice of functional forms usually has more profound implications concerning ecological interpretations of model structure than does the choice of parameter values. We are likely to have based our original choice of general functional forms on a relatively sound understanding of the nature of relationships in the real system, whereas we are less likely to have based our original choice of specific parameter values on an equally sound basis.

If the model fails to pass this second evaluation step, we should reconsider steps 3 and 4 of the quantitative-model specification, identifying the functional forms of the model equations and estimating the parameters of the model equations, and perhaps even reconsider step 4 of the conceptual-model formulation, identifying the relationships among components that are of interest (Figure 5.2).

At this point in model development, there is an interesting philosophical consideration with regard to whether we are tuning an existing model or developing a new model after having completely rejected the old model. Perhaps the most practical distinction is based on the degree of our dissatisfaction with model behavior. If our dissatisfaction is relatively minor, we may tune the model as just described without use of new information external to the model. If our dissatisfaction is major, we may decide that the model is fatally flawed and begin developing a new model by drawing on new information about the system-of-interest or by changing basic assumptions about the structure or function of the system.

Suppose that initial predictions of our weight fluctuation model indicated that respiration exceeds consumption at all environmental temperatures and thus weight changes are always negative. Because animals in the real system do gain weight, we conclude that model behavior is unreasonable. This unreasonable behavior might be remedied by arbitrarily adjusting, or tuning, parameters of the consumption or respiration equations, or perhaps by arbitrarily altering their functional forms, assuming that this is appropriate. However, it may be that such tuning, within constraints imposed by our current knowledge about the real system, does not improve model behavior. In the latter case, we might completely refute the model and begin development of a new model based on new information or insights about the system-of-interest.

5.4 EXAMINE THE CORRESPONDENCE BETWEEN MODEL PREDICTIONS AND THE DATA FROM THE REAL SYSTEM

The third step in model evaluation focuses more specifically on the correspondence between model predictions and real-system data. This step receives particular emphasis with empirical, or correlative, models and theoretically might be omitted for strictly mechanistic, or explanatory, models, although in practice, we almost always are interested to some extent in a model's predictive abilities. Strictly speaking, data from the real system that are used in model evaluation must be independent of data used to develop the model. If the same data used in the quantitative-model specification are used in model evaluation, we can hardly expect to reject the model, because we would have examined already and failed to reject any aspects of the model that were quantified based on those data. The situation is directly analogous to quantifying a regression model using a given data set, concluding that we will tentatively accept the regression model because it has an r^2 of 0.90 and then "evaluating" the model simply by observing that it does indeed predict values in that given data set well. The appropriate evaluation for the regression model is to use the model, as parameterized based on the first data set, to predict values of the dependent variable in a new data set based on values of the independent variables in that new data set. Likewise, for this step in the simulation-model evaluation to be meaningful, model predictions must be compared to real-system data that were not used directly to quantify model equations.

The manner in which we examine correspondence between model predictions and data from the real system depends on (1) the type of model predictions in which we are interested, single-value or time-series; (2) the type of model, deterministic or stochastic; and (3) the type of data available from the real system, replicated or nonreplicated (Table 5.1).

Single-value model predictions of interest often are summary statistics from an entire simulation, although they can be any single prediction from a simulation. In our weight fluctuation model, the weight of an animal on day 30 of simulated time and total consumption of an animal over a 30-day period both are single-value predictions. We would calculate total consumption by summing daily material transfers from the food source to the weight of animal state variable (Figure 2.1) for each of the 30 days of simulated time. Time-series predictions of interest often consist of sequential values of state variables or material transfers over the course of an entire simulation. The 30

TABLE 5.1 Summary of Appropriate Quantitative Comparisons of Model Predictions to Real-System Data and Associated Procedures, Depending on (1) the Type of Model Predictions, (2) the Type of Model, and (3) the Type of Data Available From the Real System

Type of Predictions	Type of Model	Type of Real-System Data	Appropriate Comparison	Appropriate Procedure — Statistical: Hypothesis Tested	Appropriate Procedure — Statistical: Test Statistic	Appropriate Procedure: Nonstatistical
Single-value	Stochastic	Replicated	Compare mean of model predictions (μ_{MP}) to mean of real-system data (μ_{RSD})	$\mu_{MP} = \mu_{RSD}$ See Table 5.2 for example calculations and symbol definitions	$t = (\bar{X}_{MP} - \bar{X}_{RSD})/\sqrt{(S^2_{MP} + S^2_{RSD})/n}$	
		Nonreplicated	Compare mean of model predictions to single real-system datum (which represents μ_{RSD})	$\mu_{MP} = \mu_{RSD}$ See Table 5.3 for example calculations and symbol definitions	$t = (\bar{X}_{MP} - X_{RSD})/(s_{MP}/\sqrt{n})$	
	Deterministic	Replicated	Compare single model prediction (which represents μ_{MP}) to mean of real-system data	$\mu_{MP} = \mu_{RSD}$ See Table 5.3 for example calculations and symbol definitions	$t = (X_{MP} - \bar{X}_{RSD})/(s_{RSD}/\sqrt{n})$	
		Nonreplicated	Compare single-model prediction to single real-system datum			X

TABLE 5.1 (Continued)

Type of Predictions	Type of Model	Type of Real-System Data	Appropriate Comparison	Appropriate Procedure		
				Statistical		Nonstatistical
				Hypothesis Tested	Test Statistic	
Time-series	Stochastic	Replicated	Compare mean curve predicted by model to mean curve based on real-system data with regard to timing of maximum and minimum values and amplitude and periodicity of fluctuations	Statistical procedures may be possible to apply in specific cases, but are beyond the scope of this book		
		Nonreplicated	Compare mean curve predicted by model to single curve based on real-system data	Statistical procedures may be possible to apply in specific cases, but are beyond the scope of this book		
	Deterministic	Replicated	Compare single curve predicted by model to mean curve based on real-system data	Statistical procedures may be possible to apply in specific cases, but are beyond the scope of this book		
		Nonreplicated	Compare single curve predicted by model to single curve based on real-system data			X

sequential daily weights and the 30 sequential values of daily consumption from the model mentioned before both comprise time-series predictions.

5.4.1 Comparison of Single-Value Predictions

Replication in Both Model Predictions and Real-System Data. If we are interested in comparing a single-value prediction from a stochastic model to replicated data from the real system, we can use a two-sample t-test to test the hypothesis that the mean of model predictions equals the mean of real-system data (Table 5.1). Suppose that we run 14 replicate simulations of our weight fluctuation model (with the sample size of 14 based on appropriate considerations as presented in the previous chapter) and record the weight of an initially 100-g animal on day 30 of simulated time for each. Assuming that we use a different set of random numbers in each replicate simulation to generate the random environmental temperature driving variable, the 14 predictions of weight on day 30 form a set of independent, identically distributed, random variates. If we also have 14 independent replicate observations of weight on day 30 of initially 100-g animals from the real system, we can compare the 14 replicate model predictions to the 14 replicate estimates from the real system using a t-test, as shown in Table 5.2

C04MOD02

TABLE 5.2 **Example Comparing 14 Replicate Predictions of Weight of an Initially 100-g Animal on Day 30 of Simulated Time from the Weight Fluctuation Model (Figure 2.1) to 14 Replicate Estimates of the Weight on Day 30 of Initially 100-g Animals from the Real System Using a Two-Sample t-Test**

Model Predictions (X_{MP}) of Weight (g) on Day 30	Real-System Estimates (X_{RSD}) of Weight (g) on Day 30
122.3	177.5
122.6	116.0
120.6	122.5
123.4	117.1
121.1	126.6
120.2	116.9
120.4	118.0
114.8	119.6
119.1	121.5
119.4	118.8
119.3	114.9
118.4	121.2
119.1	117.4
117.4	120.1

Degrees of freedom, df $= 26$
Test statistic, $t = 0.703$
Significance level, $\alpha > 0.05$

There are other statistical tests that also can be used to compare model predictions to real-system data when we have replication in both. If the values we wish to compare are not normally distributed (normality is an assumption of the *t*-test), we might use a nonparametric procedure such as a Wilcoxon signed-rank test (Snedecor and Cochran, 1967, p. 130) or a Kolmogorov-Smirnov test (Sokal and Rohlf, 1969, p. 571) to compare the frequency distributions of predicted and observed values. However, the *t*-test is quite robust to departures from normality and can be used in most cases.

Replication in Either Model Predictions or Real-System Data. If we are interested in comparing a single-value prediction from a stochastic model to nonreplicated data from the real system, or a single-value prediction from a deterministic model to replicated data from the real system, we can use a modified two-sample *t*-test to test the hypothesis that the mean of model predictions (or the mean of real system data) equals the single real-system datum (or the single deterministic-model prediction) (Table 5.1). We assume that the single datum is a sample from a population, but because the population is represented by a single variate, the sample does not contribute to the degrees of freedom or to the within-group variance calculated as part of the *t*-test. An example comparing the 14 replicate model predictions of weight of an initially 100-g animal on day 30 of simulated time used in Table 5.2 to a single real-system estimate of weight on day 30 of an initially 100-g animal is shown in Table 5.3. The procedure for comparing a single model prediction to replicated real-system estimates is directly analogous.

No Replication in Model Predictions or Real-System Data. If we are interested in comparing a single-value prediction from a deterministic model to nonreplicated data from the real system, our comparison is nonstatistical (Table 5.1). We must base our comparison solely on the practical significance of the difference between model prediction and the real-system estimate.

5.4.2 Comparison of Time-Series Predictions

Comparisons of time-series model predictions to time-series data from the real system follow the same general scheme just presented for comparisons of single-value predictions and data with regard to stochastic versus deterministic models and replicated versus nonreplicated real-system data (Table 5. 1). The question concerning model evaluation is whether or not the curve based on the time-series of model predictions resembles the curve based on the real-system time series closely enough. Criteria defining "closely enough" will vary depending on model objectives, but in general, they will be more specific quantitative versions of the general criteria used to evaluate correspondence between model behavior and expected patterns of model behavior. We quantitatively examine the timing of maximum and minimum values and the amplitude and periodicity of fluctuations within the time series.

TABLE 5.3 Example Comparing 14 Replicate Predictions of Weight of an Initially 100-g Animal on Day 30 of Simulated Time from the Weight Fluctuation Model (Figure 2.1) to a Single Estimate of the Weight on Day 30 of an Initially 100-g Animal from the Real System Using a Modified Two-Sample t-Test

Model Predictions (X_{MP}) of Weight (g) on Day 30	Real-System Estimate (X_{RSD}) of Weight (g) on Day 30
122.3	122.5
122.6	
120.6	
123.4	
121.1	
120.2	
120.4	
114.8	
119.1	
119.4	
119.3	
118.4	
119.1	
117.4	

Degrees of freedom, df $= 13$
Test statistic, $t = -1.148$
Significance level, $\alpha > 0.05$

Suppose that evaluation of our deterministic weight fluctuation model includes comparison of 30 sequential daily predictions of animal weight to sequential daily estimates of animal weight based on nonreplicated real-system data. If the curves representing these two time series are as shown in Figure 5.3a, we see that although general shapes of the curves are similar, the model underestimates daily weights by 0.5 g to almost 8 g. On closer examination, we also note that real-system data suggest a decrease in rate of growth at heavier weights, which is not reflected in model predictions, particularly during the last 8 days when real-system data suggest a 5 1/2% increase in weight, whereas the model predicts a 9 1/2% increase. Whether these quantitative differences are sufficient grounds for refuting the model depends again on modeling objectives.

Use of statistical tests to compare time-series model predictions to time-series data from the real system is more complicated than is the case for single-value predictions and data. Complications arise because of auto-correlation between values within each time series; because often variances increase from beginning to end of simulations, particularly for state variables; and because for many of the situations of interest to us, we have relatively few (less than 50) values within each time series. Exploration of these problems and presentation of possible ways to overcome them in specific situa-

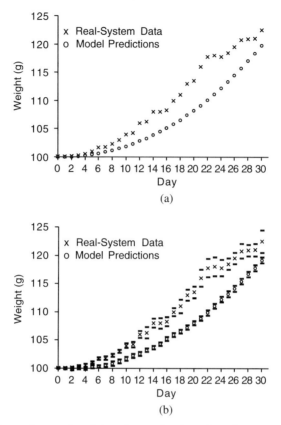

Figure 5.3 Comparisons of weight of an animal (a) based on deterministic-model predictions and nonreplicated real-system data, and (b) based on stochastic-model predictions and replicated real-system data. Horizontal bars represent ± 1 standard error of the mean.

tions are beyond the scope of this book. One useful procedure when examining replicated time-series data is to represent the variance (or standard error) around each mean value in the two time series that we wish to compare, as illustrated for our weight fluctuation model (Figure 5.3b). In Figure 5.3b, we note that variation in real-system data on daily weights is noticeably larger than variation in model predictions. We also can examine the relative distance between mean observed and predicted values compared to the widths of bars representing variability within observed and predicted values (standard errors of the mean in Figure 5.3b). The general interpretation is that if the bars are broadly overlapping, such as occurs for days 1 through 5, there is no "significant" difference between observed and predicted values. If the bars do not overlap (days 6 through 30), the difference may well be "significant." Note that this procedure does not imply a formal statistical comparison of the two curves. We can compare observed and predicted values statistically for any single day, for example, the final day, on the curves by treating the problem as a single-value comparison. Thus, we can use a t-test to compare observed and predicted animal weights on day 10, for example, but having conducted this single test, we cannot repeat the procedure for other days because our data are not independent from day to day; in fact, they are autocorrelated. The weight predicted on day 10 depends on the weights predicted on preceding days and affects the weights predicted on subsequent days.

Practical versus Statistical Significance. We should consider for a moment the distinction between practical significance and statistical significance within the framework of model evaluation. Theoretically, there are four possible combinations of practical and statistical significance that we might encounter when comparing model predictions to real-system data. Differences may be (1) both statistically significant and of practical significance to the modeler or resource manager, (2) both statistically nonsignificant and of no practical significance, (3) statistically significant but of no practical significance, or (4) statistically nonsignificant but of practical significance (Table 5.4).

Ideally, we would encounter only the first two of these cases, in which practical significance and statistical significance are synonymous. If we have designed our evaluation tests well, if we have selected sample sizes capable of showing that a true difference of a practically significant magnitude between model predictions and real-system data is statistically significant at the desired significance level (α) and probability level (P) (as described in the previous chapter), then this will be the case. Interpretation of such results is clear. If the differences are practically/statistically significant, we conclude

TABLE 5.4 Interpretations of the Four Possible Combinations of Practical and Statistical Significance That Might Be Encountered When Comparing Model Predictions to Real-System Data

Statistically	Practically	
	Significant	Nonsignificant
Significant	Modeler/manager considers differences important, rejects model as not useful; statistical design of evaluation appropriate	Modeler/manager considers differences unimportant, fails to reject model as not useful; statistical design of evaluation overdesigned
Nonsignificant	Modeler/manager provided with no additional information from statistics; statistical design of evaluation underdesigned	Modeler/manager considers differences unimportant, fails to reject model as not useful; statistical design of evaluation appropriate

that the model is not useful in meeting the objectives that we stated during the conceptual-model formulation. If the differences are practically/statistically nonsignificant, we conclude that the model passes this step in the evaluation procedure (Table 5.4).

However, if we have overdesigned or underdesigned our evaluation experiment, we may encounter cases in which there is a discrepancy between practical and statistical significance. If our sample size is too large (overdesign), we may have enough statistical power to declare relatively small differences between model predictions and real-system data, which are of no practical significance, statistically significant at the chosen α and P levels. But the interpretation of such results also is clear. We do not refute the model, because we have not detected practically significant differences (Table 5.4). Statistical significance alone is not relevant and we have wasted resources by overdesigning the experiment. If our sample size is too small (underdesign), we may not have enough statistical power to declare even practically significant differences statistically significant. Such results are not interpretable, or at least the statistical test provides no useful information. In fact, because we can identify statistical tests that have insufficient power to detect practically significant differences a priori, such statistical tests should not be conducted (Table 5.4).

As an example of overdesigned and underdesigned experiments, consider the following situation. Suppose that we want to detect a true difference of 10 units between the mean of model predictions and the mean of real-system data for a particular variable of interest. The level of practical significance is 10 units. Further, suppose that based on initial estimates of the variability of our variable of interest, we determine the appropriate sample size needed to detect a true difference of 10 units at the desired α and P levels is 50. If we run 500 replicate stochastic simulations, assuming that we also have 500 replicate observations available from the real system, our experiment is overdesigned. Not only can we detect a difference of 10 units at the desired α and P levels, we can detect smaller differences if they truly exist. We might declare a difference of one unit statistically significant. But such a small difference has no practical significance for us. We care only that the difference is less than 10 units and we could have obtained this information from 50 samples. If we run five replicate stochastic simulations, assuming that we also have five replicate observations available from the real system, our experiment is underdesigned. Even if our predicted mean differs from the observed mean by more than 10 units, we still lack the confidence that the difference is not due purely to chance.

Quantitative versus Qualitative Model Evaluation. At this point, we also should consider the relative merits of qualitative as opposed to quantitative methods of model evaluation. The tendency is to think of quantitative methods, particularly those involving statistical tests, as being more rigorous and definitive than qualitative methods. We should use quantitative methods of evaluation whenever appropriate. However, we also should keep in mind that objective quantitative methods ultimately rest on subjective judgments relative to the appropriateness of their use in the evaluation procedure. Even statistical hypothesis tests rely on subjective judgment to determine appropriate significance levels for a given problem. Quantitative methods are not inherently better than qualitative methods and both should be viewed within a framework that emphasizes evaluation of the ability of the model to meet project objectives.

If the model fails to pass this third step in model evaluation, we should reconsider steps 3 and 4 of the quantitative-model specification, identifying functional forms of model equations and estimating parameters of model equations (Figure 5.2).

5.5 DETERMINE THE SENSITIVITY OF MODEL PREDICTIONS TO CHANGES IN THE VALUES OF IMPORTANT PARAMETERS

Step 4 in model evaluation is to perform a sensitivity analysis on the model. The objective is to determine the degree of response, or sensitivity, of model behavior to changes in various model components (Smith, 1973; Steinhorst, 1979). The basic procedure is to alter the value of one parameter at a time by a specified amount throughout an entire simulation and observe the subsequent effect on model behavior. This procedure may be modified to include varying sets of parameters at the same time and also may include varying the functional form of relationships within the model. By identifying those parameters or relationships to which model behavior is most responsive, or sensitive, sensitivity analysis provides an indication of the relative accuracy with which each parameter or relationship ideally should be estimated. This information is useful in determining the degree of confidence that should be placed in the model based on the confidence with which the most influential parameters or relationships have been estimated, and also is useful in establishing future research priorities.

Determination of the effect of parameter or relationship changes on model behavior requires specification of procedures for assessing model behavior. These procedures depend on objectives of the modeling project, but most commonly include monitoring selected state variables and material transfers and the calculation of selected summary statistics. In our weight fluctuation model (Figure 2.1), we might choose to monitor CONSUMPTION (material transfer) and WEIGHT (state variable), and also calculate total consumption over a 30-day simulation, as indicators of model behavior.

Design of the sensitivity analysis, that is, specification of the parameters or relationships to be varied and the manner in which they are to be varied, likewise depends on objectives of the modeling project. A possibility with relatively small models is to vary each parameter and each combination of parameters over a selected range of values. However, simulating all possible combinations of even relatively few levels of relatively few parameters becomes an overwhelming task. Thus, most commonly, sensitivity analysis is designed to address a limited number of questions concerning model sensitivity that are suggested by prior knowledge that the modeler has about system structure. Sensitivity analysis of our weight fluctuation model might consist of noting changes in model behavior, based on the three criteria mentioned before, as we vary the coefficient of the consumption equation (CONSUMP- C04 TION = 0.05 * WEIGHT) from 0.04 to 0.06 in increments of 0.005. Our choice of this design for sensitivity analysis might be based on the lack of confidence in our point estimate (0.05) for this coefficient, but confidence that the true value lies somewhere in the range 0.04 to 0.06.

The manner in which we compare model sensitivity to changes in one parameter with model sensitivity to changes in another parameter follows the same general scheme described for comparison of model predictions to real-system data (Table 5.1). It depends on the type of model predictions that we are monitoring, single-value or time-series, and whether the model is deterministic or stochastic. If the model is stochastic, statistical comparisons are possible; if the model is deterministic, statistical comparisons are not possible. In practice, sensitivity analysis of stochastic models of even moderate size usually is conducted using a deterministic version of the model, a version in which all random variables are arbitrarily assigned their mean values. This is done to reduce the number of simulations required and is justified in that initially we are more interested in getting a general feel for the relative magnitude of changes in model behavior caused by various alterations than in statistical comparisons of the changes. If after initial examination of sensitivity analysis results based on the deterministic version of the model, we decide that statistical comparisons of certain changes in model behavior are necessary, we then can run the appropriate number of replicate stochastic simulations and conduct the appropriate statistical tests of the specific model alterations in which we are interested.

Interpreting Sensitivity Analysis within Model Evaluation Framework.

Interpretation of sensitivity analysis results differs somewhat from interpretation of results obtained in earlier steps of model evaluation. In earlier steps, we attempt to refute the model as being useless. Through sensitivity analysis, we attempt to evaluate more clearly our level of confidence in the ability of the model to address our questions (Figure 5.2). If we have failed to refute the model during the first three steps of the evaluation procedure, we must consider the model irrefutable based on current knowledge about the real system. However, this does not necessarily mean that we have great confidence in the model's ability to answer our questions. Model behavior may be sensitive to changes in some parameters or functional forms of equations that we have estimated based on inadequate information. Our lack of confidence in estimates of these influential parameters or functional forms translates into a lack of confidence in model predictions.

If sensitivity analysis results for our weight fluctuation model, in which we varied the coefficient of the consumption equation from 0.04 to 0.06, indicate that model behavior is not sensitive to changes in the coefficient within this range, then our confidence in the ability of the model to address our questions remains unaffected by our lack of confidence in the coefficient estimate. If, however, changes in the coefficient noticeably change model behavior, then we become less certain about the model's ability to address our questions, and subsequent interpretations of model behavior should reflect this uncertainty.

CHAPTER 6

MODEL USE

6.1 INTRODUCTION

The goal of the final phase of systems analysis is to meet the objectives that were identified at the beginning of the modeling project (Figure 6.1). Most often, we wish to use the model to simulate system dynamics under alternative management policies or environmental situations. The general scheme for model use follows exactly the steps involved in addressing a question through experimentation in the real world. We first develop and execute the experimental design for simulations. We must avoid the temptation to abandon a well-planned experimental design in favor of the apparent expediency of a "shotgun" approach made possible by the tremendous computing capabilities of modern computers. The ability to generate voluminous results does not preclude the need for a logical approach to the problem.

Next, we analyze and interpret simulation results. For stochastic models, this often includes the use of statistical procedures such as analysis of variance to compare model predictions under different circumstances. Because results of our initial simulations invariably raise new questions, we almost always run additional simulations, further examining selected types of management policies or environmental situations. These results will raise more questions, which will suggest more simulations, which will raise more questions, and so on. At some point, we will need to modify the model to address these new questions, which brings us full circle to the formulation of a new conceptual model. However, before continuing development of more models, we must complete the last step of model use that is to communicate results to the appropriate audience.

Phase 4: Model Use

1. Develop and execute the experimental design for the simulations
2. Analyze and interpret the simulation results
3. Examine additional types of management policies or environmental situations
4. Communicate the simulation results

Figure 6.1 Steps within Phase 4 of systems analysis: model use.

6.2 DEVELOP AND EXECUTE THE EXPERIMENTAL DESIGN FOR THE SIMULATIONS

The same principles that apply to the design of experiments conducted in the real world (Cochran and Cox, 1957) apply to experiments conducted, or simulated, on the computer. A primary consideration is whether the model is deterministic or stochastic. If the model is deterministic, comparison of system behavior in response to alternative management policies or environmental situations is nonstatistical and is based on one simulation of each alternative.

If the model is stochastic, comparison of system behavior in response to alternative management policies or environmental situations is based on statistical analysis of a set of replicate simulations of each alternative. The question of how many replicate simulations of each alternative to run is directly analogous to the real-world question of how large a sample is needed. We discussed a method for determining the appropriate sample size in Chapter 4 when considering stochastic baseline simulations. In practice, the number of replicate simulations needed for comparisons of alternatives usually is established when running the baseline simulations during the sixth step of quantitative model specification.

As an example of developing the experimental design for model use, we will return again to our weight fluctuation model (Figure 2.1). Suppose we wish to use the stochastic version of this model to compare animal weights on day 30 under baseline, warmer, and colder conditions. Recall that baseline conditions represent a 30-day period during which environmental temperatures decrease linearly from 20°C to 15°C. We will define warmer and colder conditions as 30-day periods during which temperatures decrease linearly from 21°C to 16°C and from 19°C to 14°C, respectively. These alternative environmental situations are represented by modifying the driving variable equation representing temperature. For the baseline situation,

$$\text{TEMPERATURE} = \text{RV}$$

where RV is a normal random variate from a distribution with mean

$$\mu = 20 - 0.167t$$

and variance

$$\sigma^2 = 2.0006$$

(2.0006 is the MSE of the regression of temperature on day; Figure 4.7)
For the warmer situation,

$$\mu = 21 - 0.167t \qquad \text{and} \qquad \sigma^2 = 2.0006$$

For the colder situation,

$$\mu = 19 - 0.167t \qquad \text{and} \qquad \mu^2 = 2.0006$$

We determine the number of replicate simulations to run (n) using the sample size formula presented in Chapter 4:

$$n \geq 2 \left(\frac{\sigma}{\delta} \right)^2 [t_{\alpha,\gamma} + t_{2(1-P),\gamma}]^2$$

If we want to detect a true difference of $\delta = 3$ g between weights on day 30 resulting from alternative environmental situations at a statistical significance level $\alpha = 0.05$ with probability $P = 0.80$ that the difference will be detected if it exists, we find that 14 replicate simulations are needed:

$$14 \geq 2 \left(\frac{2.67}{3} \right)^2 [t_{0.05,39} + t_{2(1-0.80),39}]^2$$

$$14 \geq 2 \left(\frac{2.67}{3} \right)^2 (2.021 + 0.851)^2$$

$$14 \geq 13.07$$

Recall that the inherent variance (σ^2) of weight on day 30 under baseline conditions is 7.14 and therefore $\sigma = 2.67$. Also recall that $\gamma = b(n - 1)$, where b is the number of situations compared (Section 4.7.1); in the present case, $\gamma = 3(14 - 1) = 39$. Thus, for our weight fluctuation model, we need the same number of replicate simulations to compare three alternative environmental situations that we need to compare model predictions to real-world data during model evaluation. Note, however, that the sample size needed for model evaluation may differ from that needed for model use.

6.3 ANALYZE AND INTERPRET THE SIMULATION RESULTS

As was the case with the development of the experimental design for simulations, the same principles that apply to analysis of real-world experimental data apply to analysis of simulated data. Again, a primary consideration is whether the model is deterministic or stochastic. Analyses appropriate for deterministic versus stochastic models resemble those discussed in the previous chapter on model evaluation.

If the model is deterministic, the analysis of system behavior in response to management policies or environmental situations is nonstatistical. Comparison of single-value model predictions consists of ordinating alternative predictions and assessing the practical significance of differences between them. Comparison of times-series predictions consists of assessing the practical significance of differences with regard to the timing of maximum and minimum values and the amplitude and periodicity of fluctuations within the time series. Interpretation of results is solely in terms of the magnitude of practically significant differences established within the context of the particular problem.

If the model is stochastic, analysis of system behavior in response to alternative management policies or environmental situations is statistical. Comparison of single-value model predictions consists of analysis of variance testing the hypothesis that the mean of model predictions generated under each alternative is the same. If the analysis of variance indicates statistically significant differences among alternatives, a multiple comparison (Snedecor and Cochran, 1967, p. 271), such as a Duncan's Multiple Range Test (Ott, 1984, p. 376), is used to identify statistically significant differences among specific alternatives. This assumes that more than two alternatives are compared. If only two are compared, a two-sample t-test is used, as described in Chapter 5. The results are interpreted both in terms of the magnitude and the statistical significance of differences in model predictions among alternatives.

From our stochastic weight fluctuation model, the analysis of variance of predicted animal weights on day 30 of simulated time under baseline, warmer, and colder environmental situations indicates statistically significant ($P <$ 0.001) differences among alternative environmental situations (Table 6.1). The results of Duncan's Multiple Range Test indicate that animal weights on C04MOD02 day 30 predicted under each alternative environmental situation are statistically significantly ($P < 0.05$) different from weights predicted under each of the other alternatives.

The statistical comparison of times-series model predictions is more complicated than is the case for single-value predictions. As discussed in Chapter 5, exploration of problems associated with the analysis of time-series and the presentation of possible ways to overcome them in specific situations are beyond the scope of this book. The procedure suggested as useful during model evaluation—graphically representing the variance around each mean

TABLE 6.1   Analysis of Variance of Animal Weights on Day 30 of Simulated Time Predicted by the Weight Fluctuation Model (Figure 2.1) Under Baseline, Warmer, and Colder Environmental Situations

Model Predictions (X) of Weight (g) on Day 30		
Baseline Simulation	Warmer Situation	Colder Situation
122.3	107.9	125.6
122.6	111.4	129.8
120.6	112.2	132.2
123.4	106.2	135.8
121.1	107.2	129.8
120.2	113.1	133.0
120.4	110.5	131.8
114.8	109.1	132.6
119.1	114.0	127.2
119.4	110.4	131.6
119.3	115.2	126.6
118.4	110.7	128.8
119.1	114.4	128.6
117.4	110.4	133.0

Analysis of Variance Table			
Source of Variation	Degrees of Freedom (df)	Sum of Squares (SS)	Mean Square (MS)
Between classes	2	2681.7	1340.85
Within classes	39	268.2	6.88
Total	41	2949.9	

Test statistic, F = 194.89
Significance level, $\alpha < 0.001$

value in each time series that we wish to compare—is equally useful during model use. But, again, such representation does not imply a statistical test.

6.4   EXAMINE ADDITIONAL TYPES OF MANAGEMENT POLICIES OR ENVIRONMENTAL SITUATIONS

The next step in model use involves further examination of additional types of management policies or environmental situations found most interesting based on results of initial model-use simulations. At this point, we should have answers to initial questions specified during conceptual-model formulation. However, initial simulations often raise as many questions as they answer. We may learn something new about the behavior of the system-of-interest through simulation that suggests a new line of questions relevant to our interests or allows us to refine our original questions to obtain more precise answers. This is exactly the iterative procedure of analysis and redesign on which all scientific experimentation is based. The new set of questions that we wish to address may necessitate fundamental changes in our model or may even suggest that we must redefine our system-of-interest. In such cases, we return to Phase 1 of systems analysis—conceptual-model formulation—and repeat the entire model-building procedure. But often our new questions can be addressed using essentially the same model slightly modified to represent a new variant of the management policies or environmental situations that we represented in our original model-use simulations.

For example, the results of initial simulations with our weight fluctuation model, in addition to answering our initial question concerning possible differences in weights of animals exposed to three different environmental situations for 30 days, may raise a new question concerning identification of temperature regimes required for animals to reach various weights after 30 days. This type of question can be addressed with only minor modification of our present model. We need only modify the driving variable equation for temperature to represent the new temperature regimes that we wish to simulate.

Often, this step in model use consists of two parts: (1) an exploratory examination of system behavior under relatively many variants of a few original management policies or environmental situations and (2) detailed description and/or formal comparison of system behavior under selected new variants.

During exploratory simulations, we are interested primarily in identifying trends in system behavior and not in detailed description or formal comparison of system behavior under all the management or environmental variants simulated. If we have a stochastic model, it is more efficient to conduct these exploratory simulations using a deterministic version of the model in which all random variables are assigned their mean values. Trends are clearer without the inherent variability of the stochastic model and fewer simulations are required.

After examining the results of exploratory simulations, we may identify certain new management policies or environmental situations that we wish to describe in detail and/or compare formally. Formal comparison requires the development of a new experimental design for simulations. For deterministic models, we may have run most or all simulations required by the new experimental design as part of the exploratory analysis. But for stochastic models, we must recalculate the sample size, or the number of replicate stochastic simulations, required by the new experimental design, run replicate stochastic simulations, and conduct appropriate statistical analyses, as described in the previous section.

Returning one final time to our weight fluctuation model (Figure 2.1), suppose that as a result of initial simulations, we become interested in establishing the relationship between temperature on day 0 and animal weight on day 30, assuming that the rate of temperature decline over the 30-day period remains the same as in initial simulations. We establish this relationship by using the deterministic version of our model to simulate a series of temperature regimes. In each of these exploratory simulations, we change only the intercept on the temperature driving variable equation, which represents temperature on day 0, and record animal weight on day 30. Results of such simulations indicate that the weight on day 30 decreases almost linearly (actually exponentially) as the temperature on day 0 increases linearly. If we want to describe system behavior under some of the new temperature regimes in more detail or formally compare system behavior under certain new regimes, we develop the appropriate experimental design and run the needed stochastic simulations.

6.5 COMMUNICATE THE SIMULATION RESULTS

The final step in model use involves communication of simulation results. Within a research setting, this usually means publication in an appropriate scientific journal. We will suggest a format for reporting development and use of a simulation model that differs somewhat from the traditional format for scientific articles in Chapter 10. Within a management framework, this implies effective communication of model results to those managers and policy makers whose decisions ultimately impact natural resources. As with the design, analysis, and interpretation of simulated experiments, the communication of simulation results to decision makers is no different than communication of results of real-world experiments. We must describe the database, the technical method used to analyze the data (i.e., to develop the model), the results of evaluation procedures and simulated experiments, and our conclusions. Communication with potential users of the model is facilitated greatly by their early involvement in the modeling project. Model development usually requires many subjective decisions that, when viewed en masse by users for the first time only after completion of the model, can be quite difficult to explain. User confidence in the model, as well as the overall quality of the model, almost always is higher as the result of early and continued dialogue with potential users. Communication also is easier if emphasis is placed on interpreting general trends in model behavior in ecological terms. General trends usually are of more relevance in a management context than are specific numerical values of model predictions. Users and modelers also have more confidence in the model's ability to predict trends and feel less comfortable with any given single numerical prediction. However, for most modelers, there is a tendency even with relatively simple models to become preoccupied with presenting detailed results at the expense of a clear overview. This tendency is ironic considering that an underlying rationale for use of a modeling approach is to attain a holistic view of our problem.

PART III

PRACTICAL GUIDE TO SIMULATION-MODEL DEVELOPMENT AND USE

Part III provides a practical guide for application of the systems approach in ecology and natural resource management. Chapter 7 describes the mechanics of constructing a systems model and presents several modules, composed of simple combinations of basic systems components introduced in Part II, that provide useful "building blocks" for representing structure and dynamics of a wide variety of systems. Chapter 8 focuses on the process of developing a systems model, describing a practical synthesis of the four theoretical phases of systems analysis that represents the flow of ideas passing through an experienced modeler's mind during model development. Chapter 9 presents a detailed example of model development and use, dealing with aquaculture pond management, annotated to correspond to the practical guide of Chapter 8. Chapter 10 suggests a format for technical articles reporting the development and use of simulation models within the context of ecology and natural resource management, using the aquaculture model of Chapter 9 as an example. Computerized (STELLA® II) versions of models presented in this part can be found in the "nrm" folder on the enclosed CD ROM. Names of particular models appear in the right-hand margin of the text.

CHAPTER 7

MODULAR REPRESENTATION OF SYSTEM STRUCTURE AND DYNAMICS

7.1 INTRODUCTION

In this chapter, we focus on the practical mechanics of constructing a systems model by presenting several modules composed of simple combinations of the basic systems components introduced in Chapter 3 (Figure 3.5). These modules provide useful building blocks for constructing a wide variety of system structures that represent a variety of basic processes such as positive and negative feedback, thresholds, and time lags that control system dynamics. The intent is not to be exhaustive, but rather to present a relatively few basic building blocks that in our experience have proven useful as a point of departure for modeling many systems. We describe representation of (1) linear growth and decline, (2) exponential growth and decline, (3) sigmoid growth, (4) overgrowth and collapse, (5) oscillations, and (6) time lags. Table 7.1 presents equations for each module.

7.2 LINEAR GROWTH AND DECLINE

7.2.1 Linear Growth

This module consists of one state variable and one material transfer that enters the state variable from a source (Figure 7.1a). The rate of material transfer is constant and, thus, does not depend on the level of accumulation in the state variable. The state variable increases at a constant rate forever.

TABLE 7.1   Equations for Each Module Described in Figures 7.1 through 7.6

EXPONENTIAL GROWTH AND DECLINE

☐ SV4(t)=SV4(t−dt)+(I4)*dt
  INIT SV4=10
  INFLOWS:
    ⏀ I4=0.05*SV4

☐ SV5(t)=SV5(t−dt)+(−O5)*dt
  INIT SV5=10
  OUTFLOWS:
    ⏀ O5=0.05*SV5

☐ SV6(t)=SV6(t−dt)+(I6−O6)*dt
  INIT SV6=10
  INFLOWS:
    ⏀ I6=0.05*SV6
  OUTFLOWS:
    ⏀ O6=0.04*SV6

LINEAR GROWTH AND DECLINE

☐ SV1(t)=SV1(t−dt)+(I1)*dt
  INIT SV1=10
  INFLOWS:
    ⏀ I1=0.5

☐ SV2(t)=SV2(t−dt)+(−O2)*dt
  INIT SV2=10
  OUTFLOWS:
    ⏀ O2=0.5

☐ SV3(t)=SV3(t−dt)+(I3−O3)*dt
  INIT SV3=10
  INFLOWS:
    ⏀ I3=0.5
  OUTFLOWS:
    ⏀ O3=0.4

OSCILLATIONS

☐ SV13(t)=SV13(t−dt)+(I13−O13)*dt
  INIT SV13=100
  INFLOWS:
    ⏀ I13=0.2*SV13*(200−SV13)/200
  OUTFLOWS:
    ⏀ O13=0.02*SV13*SV14

☐ SV14(t)=SV14(t−dt)+(I14−O14)*dt
  INIT SV14=10
  INFLOWS:
    ⏀ I14=0.0065*SV13*SV14
  OUTFLOWS:
    ⏀ O14=0.2*SV14

TABLE 7.1 *(Continued)*

☐ SV15(t)=SV15(t−dt)+(I15−O15)*dt
   INIT SV15=5
   INFLOWS:
     ⟳ I15=DV15
OUTFLOWS:
     ⟳ O15=SV15
○ DV15=SINWAVE(5,50)+5

OVERGROWTH AND COLLAPSE

☐ SV11(t)=SV11(t−dt)+(I11−O11)*dt
   INIT SV11=10
   INFLOWS:
     ⟳ I11=0.05*SV11
   OUTFLOWS:
     ⟳ O11=MIN(0.07*SV12,SV11)
☐ SV12(t)=SV12(t−dt)+(I12−O12)*dt
   INIT SV12=6
   INFLOWS:
     ⟳ I12=0.005*SV12*SV11
   OUTFLOWS:
     ⟳ O12=0.04*SV12

SIGMOID GROWTH

☐ SV10(t)=SV10(t−dt)+(I10−O10)*dt
   INIT SV10=10
   INFLOWS:
     ⟳ I10=IF10*SV10
   OUTFLOWS:
     ⟳ O10=OF10*SV10
☐ SV7(t)=SV7(t−dt)+(I7)*dt
   INIT SV7=10
   INFLOWS
     ⟳ I7=IF7*SV7
☐ SV8(t)=SV8(t−dt)+(I8−O8)*dt
   INIT SV8=10
   INFLOWS:
     ⟳ I8=IF8*SV8
   OUTFLOWS:
   ⟳ O8=0.01*SV8
☐ SV9(t)=SV9(t−dt)+(I9−O9)*dt
   INIT SV9=10
   INFLOWS:
     ⟳ I9=0.05*SV9
   OUTFLOWS:
     ⟳ O9=OF9*SV9

TABLE 7.1 *(Continued)*

⊘ IF10=GRAPH(SV10)
  (0.00,0.05),(10.0,0.045),(20.0,0.04),(30.0,0.035),
  (40.0,0.03),(50.0,0.025),(60.0,0.02),(70.0,0.015),
  (80.0,0.01),(90.0,0.005),(100,0.00)

⊘ IF7=GRAPH(SV7)
  (0.00,0.05),(10.0,0.045),(20.0,0.04),(30.0,0.035),
  (40.0,0.03,)(50.0,0.025),(60.0,0.02),(70,0,0.015),
  (80.0,0.01),(90.0,0.00525),(100,0.00)

⊘ IF8=GRAPH(SV8)
  (0.00,0.0488),(10.0,0.045),(20.0,0.04),(30.0,0.035),
  (40.0,0.03),(50.0,0.025),(60.0,0.02),(70.0,0.015),
  (80.0,0.00975),(90.0,0.00475),(100,0.00)

⊘ OF10=GRAPH(SV10)
  (0.00,0.00),(10.0,0.005),(20.0,0.01),(30.0,0.015),
  (40.0,0.02),(50.0,0.025),(60.0,0.03),(70.0,0.035),
  (80.0,0.04),(90.0,0.045),(100,0.05)

⊘ OF9=GRAPH(SV9)
  (0.00,0.00),(10.0,0.005),(20.0,0.01),(30.0,0.015),
  (40.0,0.02),(50.0,0.025),(60.0,0.03),(70.0,0.035),
  (80.0,0.04),(90.0,0.045),(100,0.05)

TIME LAG

☐ SV16(t)=SV16(t−dt)+(I16−O16)*dt
  INIT SV16=5
  INFLOWS:
    ⇒ I16−DV16
  OUTFLOWS:
  ⇒ O16=SV16

☐ SV17(t)=SV17(t−dt)+(O16−O17)*dt
  INIT SV17=5
  INFLOWS:
    ⇒ O16=SV16
  OUTFLOWS:
    ⇒ O17=SV17

☐ SV18(t)=SV18(t−dt)+(O17−O18)*dt
  INIT SV18=5
  INFLOWS:
    ⇒ O17=SV17
  OUTFLOWS:
    ⇒ O18−SV18

☐SV19(t)=SV19(t−dt)+(O18−O19)*dt
  INIT SV19=5
  INFLOWS:
    ⇒ O18=SV18
  OUTFLOWS:
    ⇒ O19=SV19

○ DV16=SINWAVE(5,50)+5

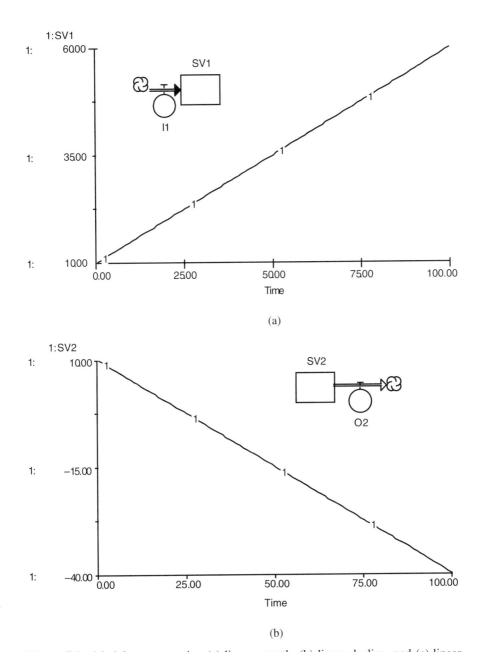

Figure 7.1 Modules representing (a) linear growth, (b) linear decline, and (c) linear growth/decline. Differences among the three curves in part (c) result from differences in values of constants in material-transfer equations.

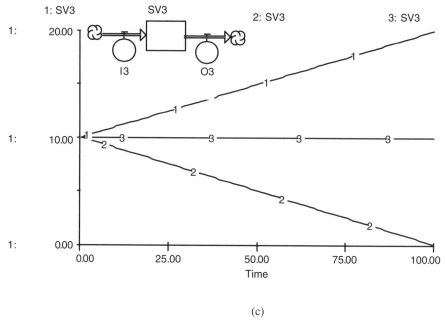

(c)

Figure 7.1 (*Continued*).

7.2.2 Linear Decline

This module consists of one state variable and one material transfer that leaves the state variable to a sink (Figure 7.1b). As before, the rate of material transfer is constant and, thus, does not depend on the level of accumulation in the state variable. The state variable decreases linearly at a constant rate forever, obviously resulting in negative values for the state variable at some point in time.

7.2.3 Linear Growth/Decline

This module is a simple combination of the previous two modules. Because both material transfers are constant, the state variable will increase linearly, decrease linearly, or remain in equilibrium forever depending on the relative sizes of the two material transfers (Figure 7.1c).

7.3 EXPONENTIAL GROWTH AND DECLINE

7.3.1 Exponential Growth

This module is the same as the linear increase module except that the rate of material transfer is a constant proportion of the level of the state variable

(Figure 7.2a). This results in a positive feedback loop and both the level of the state variable and the rate of material transfer increase exponentially forever.

7.3.2 Exponential Decline

This module is the same as the linear decrease module except that the rate of material transfer is a constant proportion of the level of the state variable (Figure 7.2b). This results in a positive feedback loop and both level of the state variable and the rate of material transfer decrease exponentially forever. Note that the term positive feedback refers to the nature of the change, that is, increasing at an increasing rate or decreasing at a decreasing rate, not to the direction of the change.

7.3.3 Exponential Growth/Decline

This module is a simple combination of the previous two modules and results in another positive feedback loop (Figure 7.2c). Because both material transfers are constant proportions of the level of the state variable, the state variable will increase exponentially, decrease exponentially, or remain in equilibrium forever depending on the relative sizes of the two proportions controlling the two material transfers.

7.4 SIGMOID GROWTH

There are a variety of modules that produce sigmoid growth. One option is a module consisting of a single material transfer entering the state variable, with the rate of material transfer represented as a decreasing proportion (calculated in the auxiliary variable) of the level of the state variable (Figure 7.3a). Other options include modules consisting of one material transfer entering and one material transfer leaving the state variable, in which case, as the level of the state variable increases, inflow is represented as a decreasing proportion of the level of the state variable (Figure 7.3b), outflow is represented as an increasing proportion of the level of the state variable (Figure 7.3c), or both (Figure 7.3d). The common characteristic of these modules is the negative feedback loop from the state variable to rate of growth. Thus, as the level of the state variable increases, the rate of growth decreases directly (Figure 7.3a) or indirectly through proportionally decreasing the rates of inflow (Figure 7.3b), proportionally increasing the rates of outflow (Figure 7.3c), or both (Figure 7.3d).

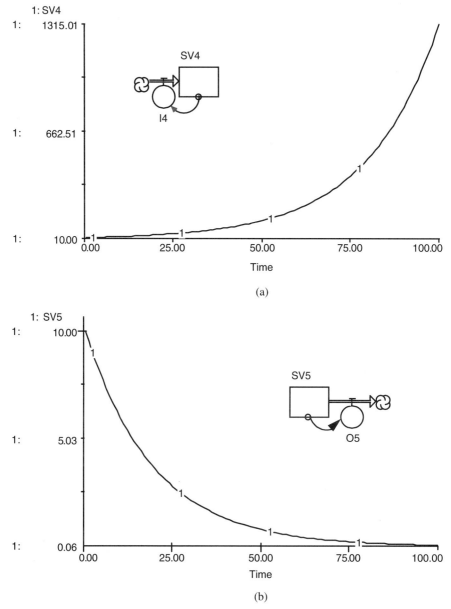

Figure 7.2   Modules representing (a) exponential growth, (b) exponential decline, and (c) exponential growth/decline. Differences among the three curves in part (c) result from differences in values of constants in material-transfer equations.

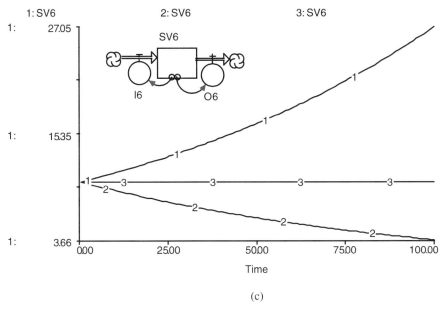

SV6

(c)

Figure 7.2 (*Continued*).

7.5 OVERGROWTH AND COLLAPSE

This module consists of a pair of state variables that affect one another. Each state variable has one material transfer entering from a source and one material transfer leaving to a sink (Figure 7.4). The rates of inflow and outflow of each state variable depend on the level of the state variable to which they are attached, with the outflow of the first state variable also depending on the level of the second state variable, and the inflow of the second state variable depending on the level of the first state variable. In this particular example, the inflow of the first state variable is represented as exponential growth and the outflow of the second state variable is represented as exponential decline. The outflow of the first state variable is calculated as a proportion of the level of the second state variable, with the restriction that outflow cannot exceed the level of the first state variable. The inflow of the second state variable is calculated as a proportion of the product of the levels of the two state variables. The levels of both state variables increase at first, but as the level of the second state variable passes a threshold, the level of the first state variable decreases abruptly. Then, as the level of the first state variable decreases, the level of the second state variable increases beyond a sustainable level and subsequently decreases abruptly.

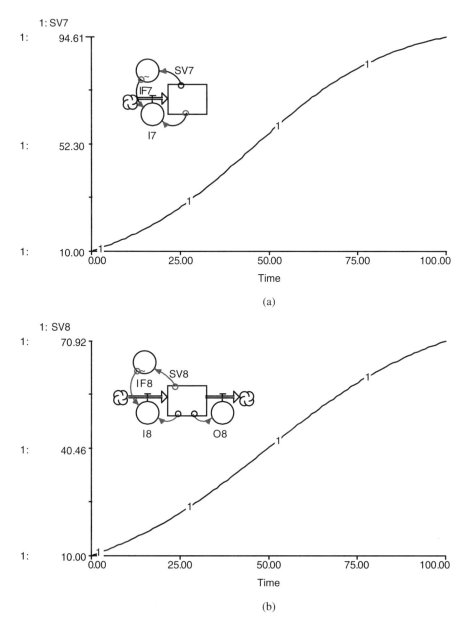

Figure 7.3 Various modules representing sigmoid growth. Differences among the four curves result from differences in structure of the modules and values of constants in material-transfer equations.

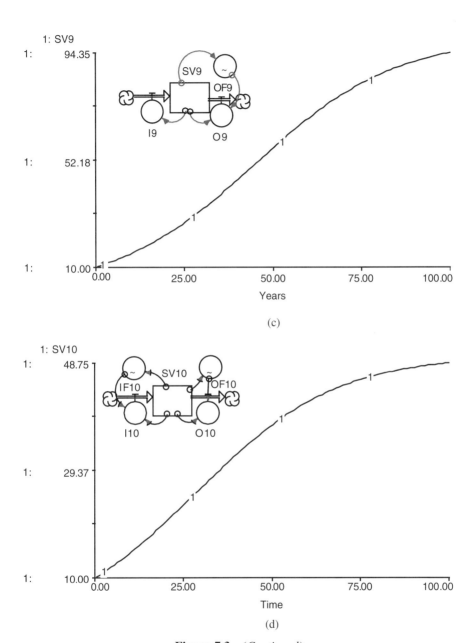

(c)

(d)

Figure 7.3 (*Continued*).

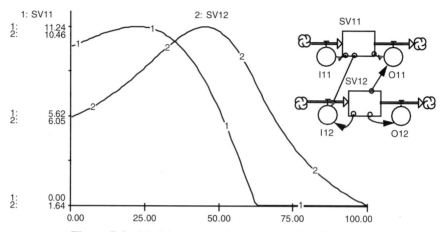

Figure 7.4   Module representing overgrowth and collapse.

7.6   OSCILLATIONS

7.6.1   Self-Generated

This module has the same basic structure as the overgrowth and collapse module, however, the forms of equations controlling flows are different (Figure 7.5a). In this particular example, the inflow of the first state variable is represented as sigmoid growth, the outflow of the second state variable is represented as exponential decline, and both the outflow of the first state variable and the inflow of the second state variable are calculated as the product of the two state variables times a constant. The two state variables oscillate over time as a result of linked positive and negative feedback loops between the level of one state variable and rate of change of the level of the other state variable. More specifically, as the level of the first state variable increases, the inflow of the second state variable increases (positive feedback on the increase of the second state variable), but as the level of the second state variable increases, the outflow of the first state variable increases (negative feedback on the increase of the first state variable). (Note that because even qualitative behavior of this module is sensitive to changes in the values of coefficients, it is difficult to generate stable cycles through trial-and-error adjustments of the equations.)

7.6.2   Externally Generated

This module consists of one state variable, one material transfer that enters the state variable from a source, one material transfer that leaves the state variable to a sink, and one driving variable (Figure 7.5b). The rate of inflow is determined by the driving variable, which, in this example, is calculated as

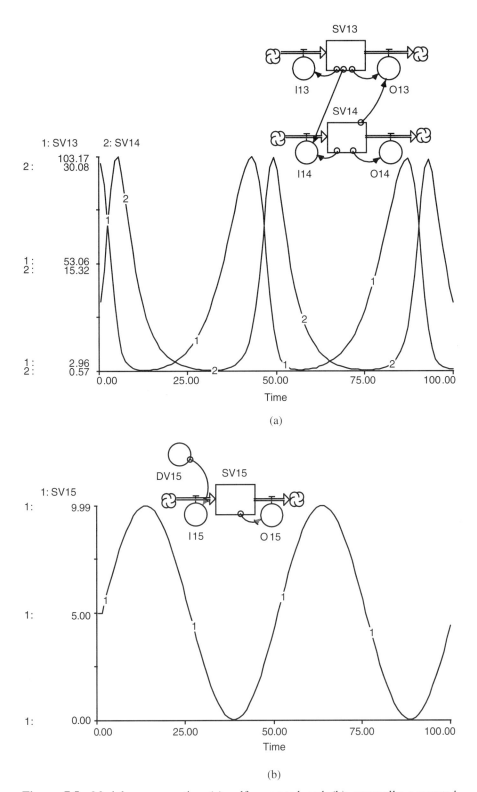

Figure 7.5 Modules representing (a) self-generated and (b) externally generated oscillations.

a sine wave. The rate of outflow is equal to the level of the state variable. Thus, the level of the state variable oscillates over time in direct response to sinusoidal fluctuations of the driving variable.

7.7 TIME LAGS

This module consists of a series of state variables with a material transfer entering the first state variable from a source, a material transfer leaving the last state variable to a sink, and material transfers connecting the first state variable to the second, the second to the third, and the third to the fourth (Figure 7.6). The rate of inflow to the first state variable is determined by a driving variable, which, in this example, is calculated as a sine wave. All outflows are equal to the level of the state variable that they are leaving. The level of each state variable oscillates over time in direct response to sinusoidal fluctuations of the driving variable, however, a one-unit time lag is introduced by each state variable. That is, a given change in the driving variable at time t, which determines inflow to the first state variable during time t to $t + 1$,

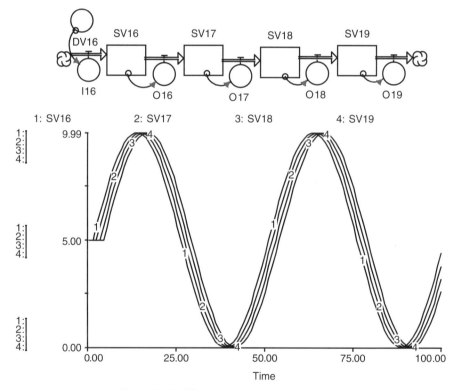

Figure 7.6 Module representing time lags.

is reflected in the level of the first state variable at time $t + 1$, in the level of the second state variable at time $t + 2$, in the level of the third state variable at time $t + 3$, and in the level of the fourth state variable at time $t + 4$.

7.8 MODULE APPLICATIONS

There is an almost endless variety of applications of these modules in ecology and natural resource management—and economics and physics and sociology. In fact, an interesting exercise is to ask a multidisciplinary group of specialists to identify module applications in their particular areas of specialization. The diversity of fundamental processes that exhibit the same general dynamics controlled by the same general processes demonstrates the universality of these modules and the power of the systems perspective on problem solving. For example, just a few applications in basic population and community ecology might include (1) exponential growth, representing population growth in an unlimited environment; (2) sigmoid growth, representing population growth in a limited environment; (3) overgrowth and collapse, representing overgrazing and herbivore population crash; (4) oscillations, representing predator-prey cycles; (5) time lags, representing dynamics of age-structured populations. Rather than providing a long list of specific examples here, we encourage readers to supplement our brief list with examples from their own areas of specialization.

CHAPTER 8

THE MODELING PROCESS IN PRACTICE: ITERATION OF PHASES

8.1 INTRODUCTION

In this chapter, we present a practical adaptation of the theory presented in Part II. The objective is to reflect more accurately the flow of ideas that passes through an experienced modeler's mind during model development and to relate these ideas to corresponding aspects of the theory. The main difference between theory and practice is that we seldom quantify the entire conceptual model before running simulations and evaluating model behavior. Rather, we usually construct a simple "running" model as quickly as possible after formulation of the conceptual model and then expand it through a series of small changes until the model can be used to address the objectives of the modeling project. The rationale for this approach is that we benefit greatly from having a running model as soon as possible because we then can begin learning about the behavior of the system from the model itself. By making each addition to the model as simple as possible, we promote understanding of the relationships within the model that control system behavior and facilitate the identification and correction of errors.

Our practical guide describes three sequential activities in which we develop (1) the preliminary conceptual model, (2) a series of intermediate quantitative models, and (3) the definitive model. We apply the theory (Figure 2.2) in development and evaluation of each model, but relative emphasis of the different theoretical phases changes as our specific objectives change for each successive type of model (Figure 8.1).

Figure 8.1 — Practical guide to simulation-model development

PRELIMINARY CONCEPTUAL MODEL	INTERMEDIATE QUANTITATIVE MODELS			DEFINITIVE MODEL
	first	subsequent	last	

CONCEPTUAL-MODEL FORMULATION

PRELIMINARY CONCEPTUAL MODEL	first	subsequent	last	DEFINITIVE MODEL
$1A_1$ State model objectives	$1A_7$ State model objectives	$1A_{19}$ State model objectives	$1A_{30}$ State model objectives	$1A_{39}$ State model objectives
$2B_2$ Bound the system-of-interest				
$3B_3$ Categorize components within the system-of-interest				
$4B_4$ Identify relationships among components that are of interest				
$5B_5$ Represent the conceptual model	$5B_8$ Represent the conceptual model	$5B_{20}$ Represent the conceptual model		
$6C_6$ Describe expected patterns of model behavior	$6C_9$ Describe expected patterns of model behavior	$6C_{21}$ Describe expected patterns of model behavior	$6C_{31}$ Describe expected patterns of model behavior	$6C_{40}$ Describe expected patterns of model behavior

QUANTITATIVE-MODEL SPECIFICATION

first	subsequent	last	DEFINITIVE MODEL
$1A_{10}$ Select general quantitative structure for the model			
$2B_{11}$ Choose basic time unit for simulations	$2B_{22}$ Choose basic time unit for simulations		
$3C_{12}$ Identify functional forms of model equations	$3C_{23}$ Identify functional forms of model equations	$3C_{32}$ Identify functional forms of model equations	
$4C_{13}$ Estimate parameters of model equations	$4C_{24}$ Estimate parameters of model equations	$4C_{33}$ Estimate parameters of model equations	
$5C_{14}$ Code model equations for the computer	$5C_{25}$ Code model equations for the computer	$5C_{34}$ Code model equations for the computer	
$6D_{15}$ Execute the baseline simulation	$6D_{26}$ Execute the baseline simulation	$6D_{35}$ Execute the baseline simulation	$6D_{41}$ Execute the baseline simulation
			$7E_{42}$ Present model equations

Figure 8.1 Practical guide to simulation-model development describing the various steps within each of three sequential activities in which we develop the preliminary conceptual model, a series of intermediate quantitative models, and the definitive model. Numbers within the body of the table refer to steps within each of the four theoretical phases of systems analysis as presented in Part II. Steps within the same phase that are followed by the same letter in practice are performed simultaneously. Subindexes are used to facilitate cross-referencing with specific points in the text.

MODEL EVALUATION

				MODEL USE
$1A_{16}$ Assess reasonableness of model structure and interpretability of functional relationships within model	$1A_{27}$ Assess reasonableness of model structure and interpretability of functional relationships within model	$1A_{36}$ Assess reasonableness of model structure and interpretability of functional relationships within model		$1A_{45}$ Develop and execute experimental design for simulations
$2B_{17}$ Evaluate correspondence between model behavior and expected patterns of model behavior	$2B_{28}$ Evaluate correspondence between model behavior and expected patterns of model behavior	$2B_{37}$ Evaluate correspondence between model behavior and expected patterns of model behavior		$2B_{46}$ Analyze and interpret simulation results
			$3C_{43}$ Examine correspondence between model predictions and data from real system	$3C_{47}$ Examine additional types of management policies or environmental situations
$4D_{18}$ Determine sensitivity of model predictions to changes in values of important parameters	$4D_{29}$ Determine sensitivity of model predictions to changes in values of important parameters	$4D_{38}$ Determine sensitivity of model predictions to changes in values of important parameters	$4D_{44}$ Determine sensitivity of model predictions to changes in values of important parameters	$4D_{48}$ Communicate simulation results

PLAN FOR QUANTITATIVE MODEL DEVELOPMENT	REVISE PLAN FOR QUANTITATIVE MODEL DEVELOPMENT

Figure 8.1 (Continued).

8.2   PRELIMINARY CONCEPTUAL MODEL

The objective of the preliminary conceptual model is to represent qualitatively all relevant aspects of the system-of-interest as we currently understand them. This involves all of the steps in conceptual-model formulation (Figures 8.1 and 3.1). First, we state the model objectives ($1A_1$). We then bound the system-of-interest ($2B_2$), categorize components ($3B_3$) and identify relationships among components within the system-of-interest ($4B_4$), and represent the conceptual model ($5B_5$). Steps 2 to 5 occur simultaneously as we are drawing and redrawing the box-and-arrow diagram that represents the system-of-interest. Most commonly, this activity is done with paper and pencil (and eraser!) rather than on a computer. We then describe expected patterns of model behavior ($6C_6$). This also is a paper-and-pencil activity that usually involves graphing expected temporal dynamics of key model components and graphically depicting our hypotheses concerning model predictions under different management policies or environmental conditions.

Finally, based on the preliminary conceptual model, we outline a general plan for the quantitative-model development. That is, we identify, in terms of the boxes and arrows in the preliminary conceptual model, each of the intermediate quantitative models that will be constructed en route to obtaining the definitive model. This activity does not correspond to any of the four phases of the theory presented in Part II, because, theoretically, we develop the entire model as a single entity.

8.3   FIRST INTERMEDIATE QUANTITATIVE MODEL

The objective of the first intermediate quantitative model is to construct the simplest model that represents a recognizable, functioning part of the system-of-interest. This involves various steps in conceptual-model formulation, quantitative-model specification, and model evaluation (Figure 8.1). Because we already have bounded the system-of-interest ($2B_2$), categorized components within the system ($3B_3$), and identified relationships among components ($4B_4$) during construction of our general plan for quantitative-model development, conceptual-model formulation only involves stating the specific objectives of this particular model ($1A_7$), representing the conceptual model ($5B_8$), and describing expected patterns of model behavior ($6C_9$). The specific objectives of the first intermediate model and the expected patterns of model behavior necessarily will be different from those identified for the full model, because we are focusing on representation of only one part of the system. Representing the conceptual model consists of extracting from the box-and-arrow diagram of the preliminary conceptual model those boxes and arrows that pertain to the first intermediate quantitative model.

Quantitative-model specification involves the first six of the seven theoretical steps within this phase (Figures 8.1 and 4.1). We first select the general quantitative structure for the model ($1A_{10}$) and then choose the basic time unit for simulations ($2B_{11}$). We then identify functional forms of model equations ($3C_{12}$), estimate parameters of model equations ($4C_{13}$), and code model equations for the computer ($5C_{14}$). After the model is quantified, we execute the baseline simulation ($6D_{15}$).

Steps 3 to 5 usually occur simultaneously, and we should try to complete these steps without losing continuity in our flow of ideas related to model development. Thus, we should minimize time spent analyzing data or searching for additional information. Ideally, we already will have analyzed available information relating to model equations. More commonly, we will feel the need to obtain more information concerning various relationships. If this involves only a brief digression, such as calculating the mean of a series of numbers, looking up an equation in a book that we have at hand, or talking with the specialist across the hall, we usually can perform these activities without losing continuity in model development. However, if the data analysis is lengthy, a literature search is required, or if the specialist is out of town, we should postpone such activities if at all possible until development of the last intermediate model. Often, we can approximate the needed equations with relative confidence based on rough plots of available data or qualitative descriptions of functional relationships.

Obviously, our ability to computerize model equations as they are developed depends primarily on expertise with the simulation program or computer language used. If we need to write original code in what for us is a difficult language, computer coding necessarily will be a separate activity. Thus, a high priority should be placed on choice of a simulation program or computer language that we literally can use, or learn to use, effortlessly.

Model evaluation involves three of the four theoretical steps within this phase (Figures 8.1 and 5.1). We assess the reasonableness of the model structure and the interpretability of the functional relationships within the model ($1A_{16}$), evaluate the correspondence between model behavior and expected patterns of model behavior ($2B_{17}$), and determine the sensitivity of model predictions to changes in the values of important model parameters ($4D_{18}$).

Finally, we review the preliminary conceptual model and our general plan for quantitative-model development and make any modifications that seem appropriate. As we learn more about the system-of-interest from our interactions with the model, we should not be surprised if we need to alter the preliminary conceptual model and/or change our plan for quantitative-model development. We may even modify the objectives of the modeling project.

8.4   SUBSEQUENT INTERMEDIATE QUANTITATIVE MODELS

The objective of subsequent intermediate quantitative models is to expand the first intermediate model through a series of simple changes until we have a quantitative representation of the entire conceptual model. For each successive intermediate model, we follow the same steps in conceptual-model formulation, quantitative-model specification, and model evaluation that were involved for the first intermediate model (Figure 8.1). We also review the preliminary conceptual model and our general plan for quantitative-model development after completion of each subsequent intermediate model.

One noteworthy distinction between the first and subsequent intermediate models is that the degree of complexity involved in quantifying the first intermediate model often is considerably higher. That is, the simplest set of components and relationships that represents a recognizable, functioning part of the system-of-interest by definition (of a system) consists of several interacting components, whereas subsequent additions to the system-of-interest often can be made one component at a time. Other differences are that we usually do not reconsider our choice of the general quantitative structure for subsequent models and as the modeling process continues, it becomes less likely that we will change the basic time unit for simulations.

8.5 LAST INTERMEDIATE QUANTITATIVE MODEL

The objective of the last intermediate quantitative model is to refine those equations that we approximated during model development. That is, we now need to perform the more detailed data analyses that we postponed during development of previous intermediate models and incorporate these results into the model. This involves the same steps in conceptual-model formulation, quantitative-model specification, and model evaluation that we followed for previous intermediate models, except that we do not change representation of the conceptual model nor the basic time unit for simulations (Figure 8.1). We also need not review our general plan for quantitative-model development, because, by definition, the last intermediate model completes the model development.

In theoretical terms, we now have a quantitative version of our original conceptual model that is ready for evaluation before using it to meet our original modeling objectives. In practice, we now have a model that has evolved both conceptually and quantitatively as a result of constant evaluation that is ready for final formal evaluation before using it to meet our (perhaps modified) modeling objectives.

8.6 DEFINITIVE MODEL

The objective of the definitive model is to address the overall objectives of the modeling project. This involves various steps in conceptual-model formulation, quantitative-model specification, model evaluation, and model use (Figure 8.1). Because the definitive model is conceptually identical to the last intermediate model, conceptual-model formulation consists solely of stating model objectives ($1A_{39}$) and describing expected patterns of model behavior ($6C_{40}$). Logically, the objectives and expected patterns of behavior should be those described for the preliminary conceptual model, however, both may have changed somewhat during model development.

Quantitative-model specification involves executing the baseline simulation ($6D_{41}$) and presenting model equations ($7E_{42}$). Although the definitive model is identical quantitatively to the last intermediate model, often a new baseline simulation is required to meet objectives of the definitive model because we need different types of results (tables, graphs) from the model, or, for stochastic models, we need a larger number of replicate simulations.

Model evaluation involves the last two of the four theoretical steps within this phase. We examine correspondence between model predictions and data from the real system ($3C_{43}$), and determine sensitivity of model predictions to changes in values of important model parameters ($4D_{44}$). We may emphasize quantitative comparisons of model predictions with data from the real system or, in some cases, omit them entirely, depending on model objectives and the quantity and quality of real-system data. Often the real-system data that we use in this step are the same as those used to generate expected patterns of model behavior throughout the process of model development. However, we now examine the quantitative correspondence between model predictions and data from the real system within a more formal, rigorous, perhaps statistical context. The emphasis placed on sensitivity analysis also varies, depending on model objectives. However, we almost always conduct a formal sensitivity analysis, whether the emphasis is on understanding relationships among model components per se or on quantifying our level of confidence in model predictions.

Use of the definitive model consists of each of the four theoretical steps in this phase (Figures 8.1 and 6.1). We first develop and execute the experimental design for simulations ($1A_{45}$), and then analyze and interpret simulation results ($2B_{46}$). Next, we usually examine additional types of management policies or environmental situations ($3C_{47}$). Finally, we communicate simulation results ($4D_{48}$). Relative to our initial objectives, the third step is optional. However, almost always we will use the model, perhaps after slight modification, to examine new questions that arise from analysis of simulations run as part of our original experimental design. No fundamental difference exists between the unanticipated questions concerning model behavior that arise at this point and those that arise as we run simulations with the intermediate models. In fact, as should be clear by now, there really is no definitive end to the process of model development. The model continues to evolve as our understanding of the real system evolves and as our specific interests in the system change. But, periodically, for practical purposes, we must temporarily conclude modeling activities and formally communicate our simulation results, a topic to which we will return in Chapter 10.

CHAPTER 9

ANNOTATED EXAMPLE OF MODEL DEVELOPMENT AND USE: SIMULATION OF AQUACULTURE POND MANAGEMENT

9.1 INTRODUCTION

In this chapter, we present a detailed example of simulation-model development and use following the practical guide proposed in the previous chapter (Figure 8.1). After providing some background information on the system-of-interest, which deals with aquaculture pond management, we describe the preliminary conceptual model, a series of intermediate quantitative models, and the definitive model. Development of each model is documented, step by step, and annotated to correspond directly with the scheme presented in Figure 8.1. For example, the "$1A_1$" in Section 9.3 indicates that we are about to begin discussion of the first step of the conceptual-model formulation ($1A$) of the preliminary conceptual model (subindex$_1$). Steps are omitted only when it is obvious what decision was made or action taken. For example, during the quantitative-model specification, the basic time unit for simulations is reevaluated for each intermediate model but is not changed. Thus, we do not present this step for each model. Likewise, during model evaluation, when reasonableness and interpretability of changes to the model are obvious, or when correspondence between model behavior and expected patterns of model behavior is clear, these steps are not presented.

9.2 BACKGROUND INFORMATION ON THE SYSTEM-OF-INTEREST

9.2.1 General Description of the Hypothetical Pond System

The system-of-interest is a hypothetical 1-ha farm pond in the southern United States that is leased from the landowner on a monthly basis at a fixed monthly rate. Each year, the pond manager (lessee) stocks and harvests fish. Harvested fish are sold by bulk weight at a fixed price per unit weight, but individual fish must be heavier than a set weight to be sold legally. Because no fertilizer or artificial feed is added to the pond, stocker fish are obtained free, and there is no cost associated with harvest, the only management cost is the lease fee. The pond manager wishes to investigate the possibility of increasing profit by harvesting a month earlier or later than usual, stocking a month earlier or later, or stocking twice as many fish. The manager has decided that the size of harvest must be changed by at least 10% relative to what is currently harvested to be practically significant within a management framework.

Fish are herbivorous and feed solely on aquatic plants that grow naturally in the pond. No reproduction of fish occurs in the pond; it is strictly a put-and-take operation. Likewise, no natural mortality of fish occurs. Net production of plants is dependent on biomass of plants and water temperature. Consumption of plants by fish is a function of biomass of plants, biomass of fish, and size of individual fish, as well as being temperature-dependent. Fish excretion and respiration also are dependent on biomass of fish, size of individual fish, and water temperature, with excretion dependent on assimilation efficiency of fish as well. Finally, natural mortality of plants is a function of plant biomass.

9.2.2 Specific Information Available on the Pond System

Specific information available on the hypothetical pond system includes (1) information on historical states of the system, (2) information on processes occurring within the system, and (3) information on economic conditions and legal constraints pertaining to pond management.

Information on Historical States of the System. This includes data on the standing crop biomass of plants and fish, and the average weight of individual fish at various times of the year for several years (Table 9.1a). Data also are available on the water temperature recorded at several different locations within the pond on selected dates during a normal year (Table 9.1b). Finally, records indicate that historically, 75 fish, each weighing 0.227 kg, have been stocked on April 15 and harvested on November 15.

Information on Processes Occurring within the System. This includes data on the rate of net production of plants as a function of water temperature (Table 9.2a) and the rate of consumption of plants by fish as a function of water temperature and weight of individual fish (Table 9.2b). It also is known that consumption by fish becomes limited by plant biomass when the plant biomass falls below 20,000 kg/ha and that the consumption rate is reduced by roughly one-half for every 5,000 kg/ha decrease in plant biomass below that point. Finally, it is known that the natural mortality rate of plants is

TABLE 9.1 Data on Historical States of the Pond System Including (a) the Standing Crop Biomass of Plants and Fish, and the Average Weight of Individual Fish on Various Dates during Several Years, and (b) the Water Temperature at Selected Locations within the Pond on Various Dates During a "Normal" Year

(a) Standing Crop Biomass of Plants and Fish, and Average Weight of Individual Fish

Date	Standing Crop Biomass (kg/ha) Plants	Fish	Weight of Individual Fish (kg)	Date	Standing Crop Biomass (kg/ha) Plants	Fish	Weight of Individual Fish (kg)
	1975				1979		
Apr. 15	39,973	17	0.23	Apr. 15	39,973	17	0.23
May 15	39,273	18	0.24	May 15	39,295	20	0.26
Jun. 15	38,534	30	0.40	Jun. 15	38,399	37	0.49
Jul. 15	36,947	60	0.80	Jul. 15	36,207	78	1.03
Aug. 15	34,006	109	1.46	Aug. 15	32,336	141	1.88
Sep. 15	29,925	172	2.29	Sep. 15	27,604	208	2.78
Oct. 15	26,512	216	2.88	Oct. 15	23,919	250	3.33
Nov. 15	24,976	222	2.97	Nov. 15	22,154	258	3.44
	1976				1980		
Apr. 15	39,981	17	0.23	Apr. 15	39,978	17	0.23
May 15	39,259	29	0.39	May 15	39,318	23	0.31
Jun. 15	37,347	67	0.89	Jun. 15	38,084	48	0.64
Jul. 15	32,453	147	1.96	Jul. 15	34,779	107	1.43
Aug. 15	26,227	227	3.03	Aug. 15	29,655	185	2.47
Sep. 15	21,191	267	3.56	Sep. 15	24,608	245	3.27
Oct. 15	17,878	276	3.68	Oct. 15	21,106	273	3.64
Nov. 15	16,212	270	3.60	Nov. 15	19,104	281	3.74
	1977				1981		
Apr. 15	39,976	17	0.23	Apr. 15	39,976	17	0.23
May 15	39,296	21	0.27	May 15	39,306	22	0.30
Jun. 15	38,341	39	0.52	Jun. 15	38,176	45	0.60
Jul. 15	36,006	82	1.09	Jul. 15	35,240	98	1.30
Aug. 15	31,923	148	1.97	Aug. 15	30,504	172	2.29
Sep. 15	27,190	214	2.86	Sep. 15	25,452	236	3.15
Oct. 15	23,630	253	3.38	Oct. 15	21,980	268	3.57
Nov. 15	21,774	262	3.49	Nov. 15	20,058	276	3.67
	1978				1982		
Apr. 15	39,968	17	0.23	Apr. 15	39,968	17	0.23
May 15	39,291	21	0.28	May 15	39,291	21	0.28
Jun. 15	38,348	39	0.52	Jun. 15	38,360	38	0.51
Jul. 15	36,041	81	1.08	Jul. 15	36,090	80	1.06
Aug. 15	31,894	148	2.00	Aug. 15	32,090	145	1.93
Sep. 15	27,078	216	2.88	Sep. 15	27,242	213	2.84
Oct. 15	23,499	254	3.39	Oct. 15	23,659	252	3.37
Nov. 15	21,631	263	3.51	Nov. 15	21,797	262	3.49

TABLE 9.1 (*Continued*)

			(b) Water Temperature								
		Temperature (°C) at Location						Temperature (°C) at Location			
Year	Date	1	2	3	4	5	Year	Date	1	2	3	4	5
1983	Jan. 1	13.9	15.2	16.0	15.2	14.7	1983	Jul. 1	29.7	30.7	29.1	30.8	29.4
	Jan. 15	15.6	14.4	15.1	15.0	14.8		Jul. 15	30.5	30.2	31.1	29.4	28.8
	Feb. 1	15.0	14.5	18.3	13.1	14.3		Aug. 1	31.2	29.5	31.8	28.2	29.3
	Feb. 15	15.4	12.9	13.8	15.1	17.8		Aug. 15	31.8	28.4	28.4	32.4	29.1
	Mar. 1	14.4	14.4	16.7	14.8	14.7		Sep. 1	29.9	29.4	29.9	30.8	30.1
	Mar. 15	16.1	14.5	15.5	13.0	15.7		Sep. 15	28.8	30.0	32.0	29.6	29.5
	Apr. 1	14.9	14.5	14.2	15.4	15.7		Oct. 1	25.1	27.3	26.5	23.0	27.0
	Apr. 15	13.9	13.7	14.1	15.3	17.8		Oct. 15	24.0	21.0	23.6	21.4	22.3
	May 1	21.5	17.6	19.9	17.9	17.6		Nov. 1	17.7	19.1	19.5	17.5	18.5
	May 15	21.0	22.8	19.3	23.3	25.5		Nov. 15	13.4	15.1	14.5	15.5	16.3
	Jun. 1	26.4	26.3	28.1	27.3	24.5		Dec. 1	13.1	13.8	14.9	18.0	14.6
	Jun. 15	29.7	30.9	28.3	30.3	30.6		Dec. 15	15.6	13.9	13.8	17.9	13.6

density-dependent. Although no data are available, experts have suggested that the curve presented in Figure 9.1 is a good approximation of this relationship. There is no direct information available on excretion or respiration of fish in this system. However, fish excretion can be calculated from consumption because assimilation efficiency is known to be 2%. Fish respiration can be represented as a function of the weight of fish and water temperature by the generally applicable empirical relationship

$$VO_2 \text{ (mg } O_2 \text{ respired/g fish-h)} = \beta_0 \, wt^{-0.2} e^{0.07T}$$

where VO_2 is the respiration rate, wt is the live weight of fish in g, T is the water temperature in °C, and β_0 is an empirically derived constant that equals 0.0142.

Information on Economic Conditions and Legal Constraints. The pond is leased from the landowner on a monthly basis for 0.50 dollar/day, harvested fish are sold for 1 dollar/kg, but only fish larger than 3 kg can be sold legally.

Note that the preceding information includes examples of three of the four general types of information mentioned in Chapter 4. Experimental data on the production of plants (Table 9.2a) and on the rate of consumption of plants by fish (Table 9.2b), and observational data on the standing crop biomass (Table 9.1a) and the water temperature in the pond (Table 9.1b) represent quantitative data from direct observation or experimentation with the real system. The equation predicting fish respiration as a function of the weight of fish and water temperature is based on a generally applicable empirical

**TABLE 9.2 Data on Processes Occurring within the Pond System Including
(a) the Net Production Rate of Plants as a Function of Water Temperature and
(b) the Rate of Consumption of Plants by Fish as a Function of Water
Temperature and the Weight of Individual Fish**

(a) Net Production Rate of Plants (g Produced/kg Plant Biomass-Day)

Net Production

Water Temperature (°C)	Rep 1	Rep 2	Rep 3	Rep 4	Rep 5
10	0.225	0.422	0.072	0.358	0.002
15	0.639	0.601	0.578	0.143	0.231
20	0.595	0.353	1.180	0.377	1.555
25	0.814	1.028	1.176	1.223	1.748
30	1.362	2.223	1.612	1.459	1.374
35	2.540	1.436	1.779	2.255	2.009

*(b) Rate of Consumption of Plants by Fish of Different Sizes
(kg Consumed/kg Fish Biomass-Day)*

Weight of Fish (kg)

Water Temperature (°C)	0.227			1.500			3.636		
	Rep 1	Rep 2	Rep 3	Rep 1	Rep 2	Rep 3	Rep 1	Rep 2	Rep 3
15	0.001	0.340	0.387	0.043	0.056	0.243	0.376	0.083	0.086
20	0.730	0.534	1.026	0.360	0.166	0.605	0.132	0.278	0.254
25	2.071	1.270	1.124	0.810	0.710	0.674	0.135	0.816	0.265
30	2.631	1.925	2.284	1.000	1.804	0.718	0.782	0.464	0.553
35	2.631	3.099	2.889	1.402	1.684	1.420	1.053	0.360	1.001

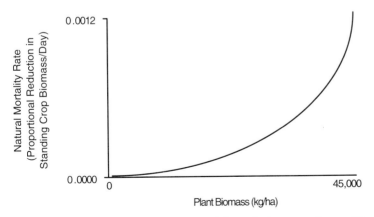

Figure 9.1 Curve based on expert opinion relating natural mortality rate of plants to
plant biomass.

relationship. Density-dependent mortality of plants is postulated by experts (Figure 9.1). Of course, at this point, we have no information based on experimentation with the model itself.

9.3 PRELIMINARY CONCEPTUAL MODEL

9.3.1 Conceptual-Model Formulation

IA, The general objective of the model can be stated quite simply: to determine if any of several alternative stocking and harvesting schemes will yield higher than current profits. Specific questions of interest include the following.

1. What size harvest is expected in a "normal" year under the usual scheme of stocking 75 0.227-kg fish on April 15 and harvesting them on November 15, and what profit is associated with this harvest (this is the baseline situation)?
2. How variable is the harvest (and therefore profit) from year to year under the baseline stocking and harvesting scheme as a result of the inherent variability of the system?
3. Would the size of the harvest and the associated profit be changed by harvesting a month earlier or a month later?
4. Would the size of the harvest and the associated profit be changed by stocking a month earlier or a month later?
5. Would the size of the harvest and the associated profit be changed by stocking twice as many fish?

2B₂–5B₅ Stated simply, we formulate the preliminary conceptual model by "processing" the general description of the pond system and the statement of model objectives through the practical guide to produce the conceptual-model diagram. The manner in which this processing occurs is the most creative part of model development, and thus, unfortunately, is not so simple to describe. The word description that follows attempts to document the authors' thoughts as we formulated the conceptual model; thus, the writing style is rather laborious. We encourage readers to refer frequently to the practical guide to model development (Figure 8.1) so as to remain focused on the general flow of ideas and not become lost in the details. Names of variables appear in capital letters when they refer directly to the conceptual-model diagram that is being developed as we proceed through the following discussion (Figure 9.2).

Based on the general objective of the model profit clearly is the final result of most interest. Profit is calculated based in part on the biomass of fish accumulated on the harvest date, which depends on the net accumulation of fish biomass in the pond since stocking. Therefore, we need to represent fish biomass dynamics. Because fish are herbivorous, their growth depends in part

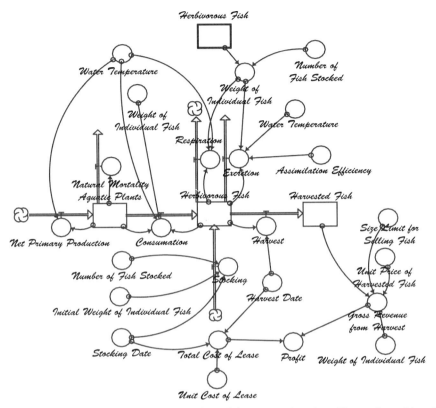

Figure 9.2 Preliminary conceptual model representing the effects of stocking date, harvest date, and stocking density on yield and profit from a hypothetical subtropical aquaculture pond.

on the amount of plant biomass accumulated in the pond at any given time, so we also need to represent plant biomass dynamics. Thus, we might represent biomass of AQUATIC PLANTS, HERBIVOROUS FISH, and HARVESTED FISH as state variables—we are interested in levels of accumulation of these materials within the system—and PROFIT as an auxiliary variable through which the biomass of HARVESTED FISH is converted into dollars at the end of the year (Figure 9.2).

Processes that affect biomass dynamics of AQUATIC PLANTS include NET PRIMARY PRODUCTION, NATURAL MORTALITY, and CONSUMPTION by fish. Processes that affect biomass dynamics of HERBIVOROUS FISH include CONSUMPTION of plants, RESPIRATION, EXCRETION, STOCKING, and HARVEST. Thus, these are material transfers—they represent movement of material into, out of, and within the system.

NET PRIMARY PRODUCTION is a function of biomass of AQUATIC PLANTS and WATER TEMPERATURE, which is a driving variable because it is not affected by any other components in the system (at the level of detail in which we are interested). Thus, information transfers leave WATER TEMPERATURE and AQUATIC PLANTS and enter NET PRIMARY PRODUCTION. NATURAL MORTALITY is a function of biomass of AQUATIC PLANTS and thus receives an information transfer from AQUATIC PLANTS.

CONSUMPTION of AQUATIC PLANTS by HERBIVOROUS FISH is a function of the biomass of AQUATIC PLANTS, the biomass of HERBIVOROUS FISH, and the WEIGHT OF INDIVIDUAL FISH, as well as being dependent on WATER TEMPERATURE. The WEIGHT OF INDIVIDUAL FISH is an auxiliary variable calculated based on the NUMBER OF FISH STOCKED, which is a constant representing the number of fish in the pond because there is no fish mortality, and the biomass of HERBIVOROUS FISH. To calculate CONSUMPTION, we need to know the WEIGHT OF INDIVIDUAL FISH as well as the biomass of HERBIVOROUS FISH and the WATER TEMPERATURE because consumption per unit of fish biomass depends on the WEIGHT OF INDIVIDUAL FISH. Thus, information transfers leave HERBIVOROUS FISH, WEIGHT OF INDIVIDUAL FISH, AQUATIC PLANTS, and WATER TEMPERATURE and enter CONSUMPTION.

Fish EXCRETION and RESPIRATION are dependent on the biomass of HERBIVOROUS FISH, the WEIGHT OF INDIVIDUAL FISH, and the WATER TEMPERATURE, with EXCRETION also dependent on ASSIMILATION EFFICIENCY of fish, which is a constant. Thus, information transfers leave HERBIVOROUS FISH, WEIGHT OF INDIVIDUAL FISH, and WATER TEMPERATURE and enter RESPIRATION; and leave HERBIVOROUS FISH, WEIGHT OF INDIVIDUAL FISH, WATER TEMPERATURE, and ASSIMILATION EFFICIENCY and enter EXCRETION.

STOCKING is calculated based on information transfers from the NUMBER OF FISH STOCKED, the INITIAL WEIGHT OF INDIVIDUAL FISH, which is a constant, and the STOCKING DATE, which also is a constant. HARVEST is calculated based on information transfers from the HERBIVOROUS FISH and the HARVEST DATE, which is a constant. Note that although we will run simulations with different values for the STOCKING DATE, HARVEST DATE, and NUMBER OF FISH STOCKED to address our management questions, during any given simulation these values remain constant.

PROFIT is calculated based on information transfers from the TOTAL COST OF LEASE of the pond and the GROSS REVENUE FROM HARVEST, both of which are auxiliary variables. The TOTAL COST OF LEASE is calculated based on information transfers from the STOCKING DATE and the HARVEST DATE, which determines length of lease, and the UNIT COST OF LEASE, which is a constant. The GROSS REVENUE FROM HARVEST is calculated based on information transfers from HARVESTED FISH, WEIGHT OF INDIVIDUAL FISH, SIZE LIMIT FOR SELLING FISH, which is a constant, and the UNIT PRICE OF HARVESTED FISH, which also is a constant.

Of course, this is not the only possible conceptual model of our system-of-interest, and we can never be sure that it is the best. It does seem reasonable at this point, however, and we will evaluate its usefulness regularly as we proceed with model development.

6C₆ Our expectations concerning patterns of model behavior are based on the same a priori knowledge that we draw on to formulate the conceptual model. We graph information on the historical states of the system (Table 9.1a) to formalize our expectations concerning seasonal changes in the standing crop biomass of plants and fish, and the average weight of individual fish to use as points of reference during model evaluation (Figure 9.3). To ensure that the model provides predictions that allow us to address our questions directly, we represent graphically our hypotheses concerning the relationship of the size of harvest and the associated profit to the six management schemes (Figure 9.4a). We also graphically relate gross revenue from the harvest and the total cost of the lease to the six management schemes (Figure 9.4b), which, together with the graphs of the standing crop biomass of plants and fish, and the average weight of individual fish (Figure 9.3), provide an explanation of how the size of harvest and profit are generated. We hypothesize that stocking a month earlier or harvesting a month later or stocking twice as many fish will increase the size of harvest and profit, whereas stocking a month later or harvesting a month earlier will decrease the harvest and profit, relative to the baseline (Figure 9.4a). Gross revenue from the harvest will exhibit the same trends as the size of harvest, whereas total cost of the lease will increase for early stocking or late harvest, decrease for late stocking or early harvest, and remain unchanged for stocking twice as many fish (Figure 9.4b).

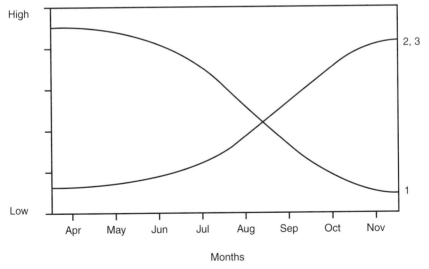

Figure 9.3 Expected patterns of model behavior regarding seasonal changes in (1) the standing crop biomass of plants (kg/ha), (2) herbivorous fish (kg/ha), and (3) the average weight of individual fish (kg) under baseline conditions from April 15 to November 15.

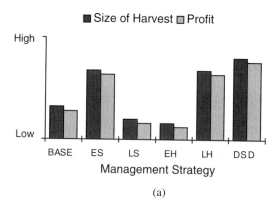

(a)

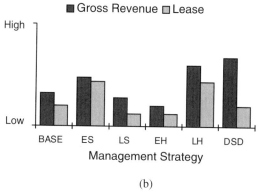

(b)

Figure 9.4 Expected patterns of model behavior regarding (a) the size of harvest in kg/ha and the associated profit in dollars and (b) the gross revenue from the harvest in dollars and the total cost of the lease in dollars under the six management schemes: baseline conditions (BASE), early stocking (ES), late stocking (LS), early harvest (EH), late harvest (LH), and double stocking density (DSD).

9.3.2 Plan for Quantitative-Model Development

Our overall plan for quantifying the model will be to follow the flow of biomass through the system, focusing first on the dynamics of aquatic plants, then on the dynamics of herbivorous fish, and finally on the biomass of harvested fish. In each case, we will begin with the simplest representation possible, describing important material transfers affecting each of these state variables in their simplest forms and ideally adding only one or two material transfers at a time. To further simplify addition of new components and to facilitate understanding of relationships among model components, we often will represent temporarily other system variables as constants. For example, the net primary production and the natural mortality of aquatic plants initially will be represented under conditions of constant water temperature. Once we have evaluated this initial representation, we will represent them under seasonably varying temperature. We will follow the same procedure for the representation of fish respiration and excretion. Likewise, when initially introducing consumption, we will represent biomass of herbivorous fish as a constant, thus focusing only on the effect of consumption on dynamics of aquatic plants. We will postpone the connection of aquatic plants and herbivorous fish via consumption as long as possible, so that we can evaluate first those aspects of the dynamics of each that can be represented without explicit inclusion of their interaction.

Thus, formalizing this general scheme, the first intermediate model will represent net primary production and natural mortality of plants, assuming a constant water temperature. The second intermediate model will add seasonality of water temperature. The third intermediate model will add consumption of plants by fish, assuming a constant biomass of fish. The fourth intermediate model will add fish stocking, assuming a constant biomass of fish after stocking. The fifth intermediate model will allow fish biomass to vary by connecting consumption to fish biomass and adding fish respiration and excretion, assuming a constant water temperature. The sixth intermediate model will add once again the seasonality of water temperature. The seventh intermediate model will add fish harvest. The eighth intermediate model will add the calculations of gross revenue from the harvest, total cost of lease, and profit. Finally, the last intermediate model will refine any equations that were approximated during model development. Thus, our overall plan will include nine intermediate models.

Note that the manner in which we represent a given model component may change from time to time as we proceed with the development of the series of intermediate models. These changes in representation of model components result from changes in the specific objectives of successive intermediate models as we include and evaluate representation of new model components. The specific intermediate models proposed here certainly are not the only possible plan for quantitative-model development. However, arguably, they represent a reasonable application of the principles described in the previous chapter to the problem at hand.

9.4 FIRST INTERMEDIATE QUANTITATIVE MODEL

9.4.1 Conceptual-Model Formulation

1A₇ Recalling our overall plan of following the flow of biomass through the system, the objective of the first intermediate model is to represent the net primary production and the natural mortality of plants and predict the resulting dynamics of standing crop biomass of plants from April 15 through November 15, assuming a constant water temperature.

5B₈ The conceptual model includes a state variable representing the biomass of AQUATIC PLANTS, a material transfer representing NET PRIMARY PRODUC-TION that enters the state variable, and a material transfer representing NAT-URAL MORTALITY that leaves the state variable (Figure 9.5). NET PRIMARY PRODUCTION is a function of the biomass of AQUATIC PLANTS and two aux-iliary variables (NPPRATE and NPPRATE1) relating the rate of NET PRIMARY PRODUCTION to WATER TEMPERATURE, which is in this case a constant. NAT-URAL MORTALITY is a function of biomass of AQUATIC PLANTS and an aux-iliary variable (NMRATE) relating the rate of natural mortality to the biomass of AQUATIC PLANTS.

6C₉ As a point of reference for evaluating model behavior, we will graph expected patterns of seasonal change in the plant biomass. Because we are not yet representing consumption of plants by fish, under constant high water temperature (30°C), we expect a sigmoid increase in plant biomass resulting from increasing rates of primary production during spring and summer and decreasing rates during fall as water temperatures increase and decrease, re-spectively (Figure 9.6).

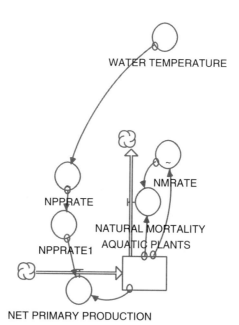

Figure 9.5   Conceptual-model diagram for the first and second intermediate quanti-tative models representing dynamics of standing crop biomass of aquatic plants. Water temperature is represented as a constant for the first intermediate model and as a seasonally varying driving variable for the second intermediate model.

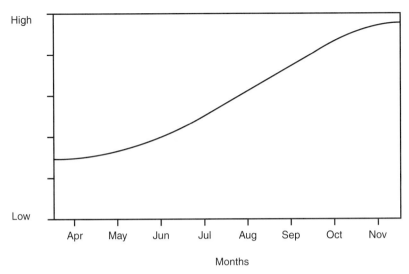

Figure 9.6   Expected patterns of seasonal change in plant biomass (kg/ha) for the first intermediate quantitative model from April 15 to November 15.

9.4.2   Quantitative-Model Specification

1A₁₀ The general quantitative structure of the pond model will consist of a discrete-time compartment-model format, including sets of equations for driving variables, auxiliary variables, material transfers, and state variables. We will specify initial conditions of state variables and values of constants at the beginning of each simulation and solve all equations sequentially in the order indicated before during each time unit.

2B₁₁ We will use 1 day as the basic time unit for simulations. This choice is arbitrary, but certainly is reasonable in view of the four criteria on which to base such decisions suggested in Chapter 4. A time unit of 1 day provides adequate temporal resolution to address our questions of interest, allows us to represent appropriately temporal changes in rates at which processes within the system-of-interest occur, and also facilitates estimation of parameters of model equations in view of temporal resolution of available data. It is also unlikely that computing costs will become a serious concern with $\Delta t = 1$ day in a model of this size because one simulation will consist of roughly 210 days (recall that fish usually are stocked on April 15 and harvested on November 15). One might legitimately argue that $\Delta t = 2$ days or even $\Delta t = 1$ week could have been chosen as the basic time unit. But appropriate representation of temporal changes in process rates within the system might become difficult with Δt much longer than 1 week, and the resolution attained with Δt shorter than 1 day is not needed. Further, energy or biomass flow through individual animals commonly is presented in terms of daily energy budgets.

3C₁₂–5C₁₄ We first focus attention on identifying the functional form, estimating parameters, and writing computer code for the auxiliary variable representing the rate of net primary production (NPPRATE) (Figure 9.5). A plot of available data (Table 9.2a) suggests a linear relationship between the rate of net primary production (g net primary production/kg aquatic plants-day) and water temperature (°C) (Figure 9.7). We will conduct a linear regression analysis on these data later, but for now, we will approximate this relationship graphically with a straight line passing through points (5,0) and (35,2). We will enter this line directly into NPPRATE using a graph. We will create another auxiliary variable (NPPRATE1) in which we divide NPPRATE by 1,000 to convert from g net primary production/kg aquatic plants-day to kg net primary production/kg aquatic plants-day. NET PRIMARY PRODUCTION (kg/ha-day) now can be represented as NPPRATE1 * AQUATIC PLANTS.

We now focus attention on the auxiliary variable representing the rate of natural mortality (NMRATE). Expert opinion suggests an exponential relationship between the rate of natural mortality (proportional reduction in the standing crop biomass/day) and the density of aquatic plants (kg/ha) (Figure 9.1). We will fit an exponential equation to this curve later, but for now we will approximate this relationship graphically with a smooth, roughly exponential curve passing through points (0,0) and (45,000, 0.0012). We will enter this line directly into NMRATE using a graph. NATURAL MORTALITY (kg/ha-day) now can be represented as NMRATE * AQUATIC PLANTS.

Next, we must provide an initial value for biomass of aquatic plants and specify a water temperature, which will remain constant. Because we will begin simulations on April 15 (day of year 105), we initialize AQUATIC PLANTS at 40,000 kg/ha, which approximates observed levels of standing crop

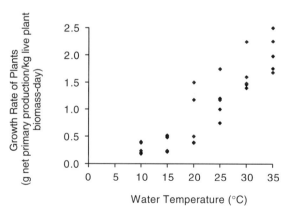

Figure 9.7 Plot of data from Table 9.2a relating the rate of primary production to water temperature.

biomass at this time of year (Table 9.1a). We will set WATER TEMPERA-
TURE = 30°C, which approximates the highest observed water temperatures
(Table 9.1b) and thus should generate maximum rates of plant growth.

Finally, we write the state variable equation to change the level of accumulation of aquatic plant biomass in the system from time t to $t + 1$:

```
AQUATIC PLANTS_{t+1} = AQUATIC PLANTS_t
                     + NET PRIMARY PRODUCTION
                     - NATURAL MORTALITY
```

This completes the quantitative specification of the first intermediate model.
The simulation will run from day of year 105 (April 15) to day of year 319
(November 15).

6D₁₅ The results of the baseline simulation indicating the seasonal dynamics
of AQUATIC PLANTS are presented in Figure 9.8.   C09MOD01

9.4.3 Model Evaluation

1A₁₆ Assessing the reasonableness of the model structure and the interpretability of the functional relationships in view of model objectives, all relationships within the model can be interpreted ecologically based on the basic
principles of ecological energetics and plant biology. Material transfers are
interpretable directly as the net primary production and the natural mortality

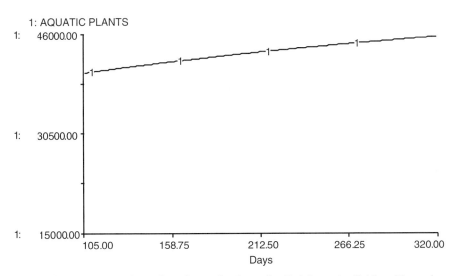

Figure 9.8 Seasonal dynamics of aquatic plants (kg/ha) from April 15 to November
15 predicted under baseline conditions by the first intermediate quantitative model
when water temperature is held constant at 30°C.

of plants. The effect of water temperature on the net primary production represents control of biological processes by physical environmental conditions. The effect of the level of standing crop plant biomass on the natural mortality rate represents density-denpendent mortality due to intraspecific competition for limited resources.

2B$_{17}$ Model behavior corresponds reasonably well with expected seasonal dynamics in plant biomass. Because we are not yet representing consumption of plants by fish, we expected a sigmoid increase in plant biomass under constant high water temperature (30°C) (Figure 9.6). Simulated plant biomass exhibits a monotonic increase, although the expected sigmoidal shape is not evident (Figure 9.8). The rates of net primary production and the natural mortality of plants also appear reasonable.

4D$_{18}$ We will determine the sensitivity of model predictions of the seasonal dynamics of plant biomass to changes in values of water temperature by running a second simulation with WATER TEMPERATURE held constant at 15°C, which approximates the lowest observed winter temperatures (Table 9.1b). We expect a monotonic decrease in plant biomass under this temperature and, indeed, the simulated plant biomass decreases monotonically as expected (Figure 9.9). Once again, the rates of net primary production and natural mortality of plants appear reasonable. Thus, we conclude that the first intermediate model provides an acceptable representation of seasonal dynamics of

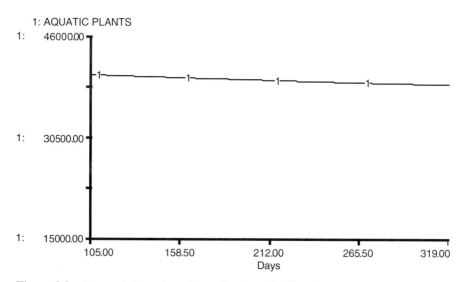

Figure 9.9 Seasonal dynamics of aquatic plants (kg/ha) from April 15 to November 15 predicted by the first intermediate quantitative model when water temperature is held constant at 15°C.

standing crop biomass of plants from April 15 through November 15 under constant water temperatures representative of maximum and minimum temperatures observed in the real system.

9.5 SECOND INTERMEDIATE QUANTITATIVE MODEL

9.5.1 Conceptual-Model Formulation

***1A*₁₉** We simplified the initial introduction of net primary production and natural mortality of plants in the previous model by assuming a constant water temperature. The objective of the second intermediate model is to add seasonality of water temperature and to predict the resulting dynamics of the standing crop biomass of plants from April 15 through November 15.

***5B*₂₀** The conceptual model is the same as the first intermediate model (Figure 9.5), except that we will change WATER TEMPERATURE from a constant to a driving variable.

***6C*₂₁** As for the previous model, we will graph expected patterns of seasonal change in plant biomass. Based on simulation results under constant high and low water temperatures from the previous model, under seasonally varying water temperatures, we expect a slight decrease in plant biomass during spring, a relatively large increase during summer, and another slight decrease during fall (Figure 9.10).

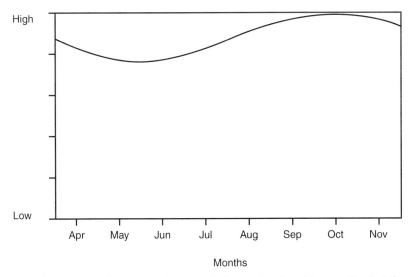

Figure 9.10 Expected patterns of seasonal change in plant biomass (kg/ha) for the second intermediate quantitative model from April 15 to November 15.

9.5.2   Quantitative-Model Specification

2B$_{22}$ We will maintain a 1-day time unit for simulations. Based on our experience with the first intermediate model, 1 day seems to represent appropriately temporal changes in standing crop biomass of aquatic plants, which will provide the basis for the subsequent dynamics of herbivorous fish.

3C$_{23}$–5C$_{25}$ We want to change the functional form of WATER TEMPERATURE from a constant to a seasonally varying driving variable. A plot of available data (Table 9.1b) suggests that water temperature remains relatively constant at approximately 15°C from January through mid-April, increases linearly to about 30°C by mid-June, remains at about 30°C until mid-September, decreases linearly to 15°C by mid-November, and remains at about 15°C for the rest of the year (Figure 9.11). We will conduct a series of piecewise linear regressions on these data later, but for now, we will enter this curve directly into WATER TEMPERATURE using a graph in which WATER TEMPERATURE (°C) is set at (1) 15 for days of year 1 through 105; (2) 15.25 for day 106, 15.50 for day 107, and so on, until reaching 30 on day 165; (3) 30 for days 166 through 258; (4) 29.75 for day 259, 29.50 for day 260, and so on, until reaching 15 on day 317; and (5) 15 for days 319 through 365. This completes the quantitative specification of the second intermediate model. As for the previous model, the baseline simulation will run from day of year 105 (April 15) to day of year 319 (November 15).

6D$_{26}$ The results of the baseline simulation indicating seasonal dynamics of WATER TEMPERATURE and AQUATIC PLANTS are presented in Figure 9.12.   cos

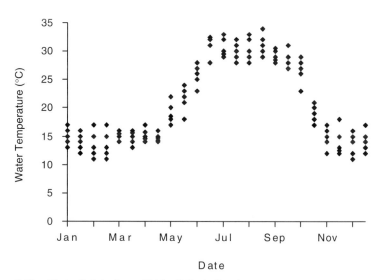

Figure 9.11   Plot of data from Table 9.1b indicating water temperature on various dates during a normal year (1983).

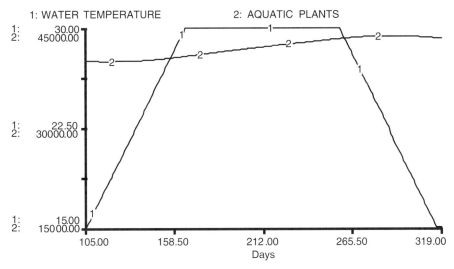

Figure 9.12 Seasonal dynamics of (1) water temperature (°C) and (2) aquatic plants (kg/ha) from April 15 to November 15 predicted under baseline conditions by the second intermediate quantitative model.

9.5.3 Model Evaluation

2B₂₈ Model behavior corresponds reasonably well with expected seasonal dynamics of plant biomass as a result of seasonally varying water temperature. Plant biomass decreases slightly during spring, although the length of the decline is not as long as expected, increases relatively rapidly during summer, and decreases again slightly during fall (Figures 9.12 and 9.10). Seasonal changes in the rates of net primary production and the natural mortality of plants also appear reasonable in terms of their relationship to water temperature and standing crop biomass of plants (Figure 9.1 and Table 9.2). Thus, we conclude that the second intermediate model provides an acceptable representation of the seasonal dynamics of the standing crop biomass of plants from April 15 through November 15 under seasonally varying water temperatures representative of those observed in the real system.

9.6 THIRD INTERMEDIATE QUANTITATIVE MODEL

9.6.1 Conceptual-Model Formulation

1A₁₉ Continuing to follow the flow of biomass through the system, the objective of the third intermediate model is to add the consumption of plants by fish, assuming a constant biomass of fish, and to predict the resulting dynamics of the standing crop biomass of plants from April 15 through November 15. We represent herbivorous fish as a constant to focus our attention on the effect of consumption per se on dynamics of aquatic plants.

5B₂₀ We will add a material transfer representing CONSUMPTION, which leaves the state variable AQUATIC PLANTS, two constants representing WEIGHT OF INDIVIDUAL FISH and total HERBIVOROUS FISH biomass, and an auxiliary variable (CONRATE) relating the rate of consumption to WATER TEMPERATURE, WEIGHT OF INDIVIDUAL FISH, and availability of AQUATIC PLANTS (Figure 9.13).

6C₂₁ As before, we will graph expected patterns of seasonal change in plant biomass. If we hold fish biomass constant at a midseason value of 150 kg/ha (the 75 stocked fish reach 2.0 kg sometime between late July and early September according to Table 9.1a), we expect a monotonic decrease in plant biomass, with the rate of decline more rapid during summer and less rapid during spring and fall (Figure 9.14). This expectation is based on the monotonic decline in observed plant biomass (Table 9.1a), which presumably results from seasonal differences in rates of primary production relative to changes in rates of fish consumption.

9.6.2 Quantitative-Model Specification

3C₂₃–5C₂₅ First, we will choose parameter estimates for the WEIGHT OF INDIVIDUAL FISH and HERBIVOROUS FISH, which in this model are constants.

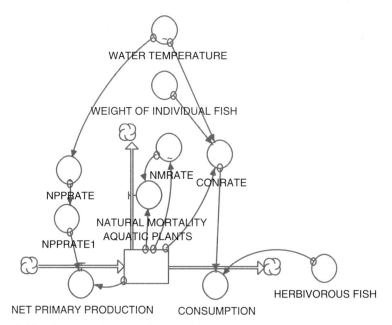

Figure 9.13 Conceptual-model diagram for the third intermediate quantitative model representing dynamics of standing crop biomass of aquatic plants as affected by the consumption of plants by fish, assuming a constant fish biomass and weight of individual fish.

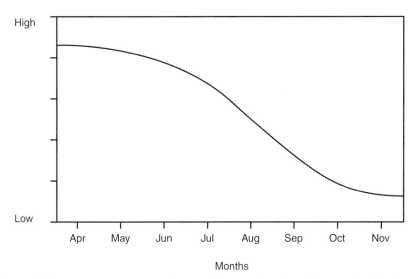

High

Low

Apr   May   Jun   Jul   Aug   Sep   Oct   Nov

Months

Figure 9.14 Expected patterns of seasonal change in plant biomass (kg/ha) for the third intermediate quantitative model from April 15 to November 15.

Because our expected patterns for model evaluation are based on the fish biomass at midseason (150 kg/ha, Table 9.1a) and we know that 75 fish are stocked in a 1-ha pond, we can use 2.0 kg as a representative WEIGHT OF INDIVIDUAL FISH. Thus, HERBIVOROUS FISH will be assigned a value of 150 kg/ha.

Next, we focus attention on identifying the functional form, estimating parameters, and writing computer code for the auxiliary variable (CONRATE) relating rate of consumption to WATER TEMPERATURE, WEIGHT OF INDIVIDUAL FISH, and availability of AQUATIC PLANTS. A plot of available data relating fish consumption in kg of plants consumed per kg of fish biomass per day to water temperature in °C and the weight of individual fish in kg live weight (Table 9.2b) suggests that, for fish of a given size, consumption rate is related linearly to water temperature (Figure 9.15). But the slope of the relationship is steeper for small fish and flatter for large fish. Likewise, a plot of data relating consumption rate at 30°C to fish size suggests a relationship not far from linear (Figure 9.16).

Because the functional form representing the simultaneous effects of the size of fish and water temperature on consumption rate is difficult to visualize, we will analyze these data formally at this time, rather than attempting to approximate the relationship. The fact that both isolated effects appear linear and the fact that there appears to be an interaction between water temperature and size suggest that a linear model including both effects and their interaction is an appropriate functional form.

A multiple linear regression model of the form

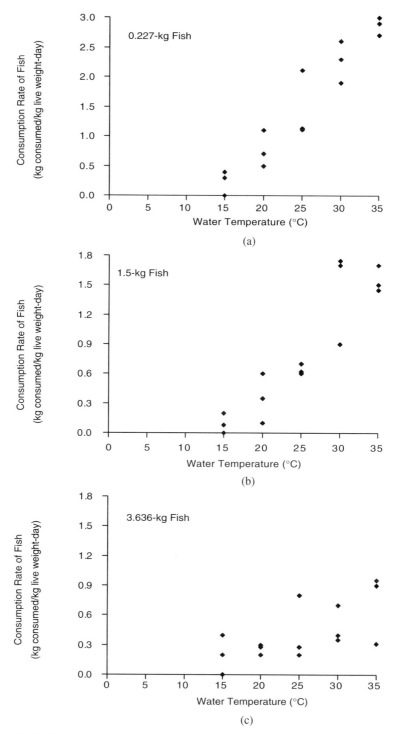

Figure 9.15 Plot of data from Table 9.2b relating fish consumption to water temperature for fish weighing (a) 0.227 kg, (b) 1.5 kg, and (c) 3.636 kg, respectively.

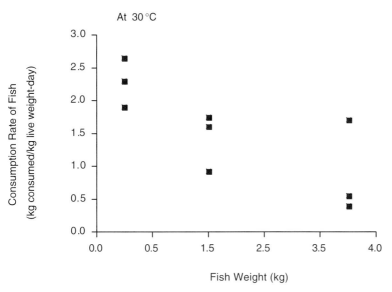

Figure 9.16 Plot of data from Table 9.2b relating fish consumption at a water temperature of 30°C to the weight of fish.

$$Y = \beta_0 + \beta_1 X_1 + \beta_2 X_2 + \beta_3 X_1 X_2 + \epsilon$$

with Y representing the consumption rate of an individual fish, X_1 representing water temperature, X_2 representing individual fish weight, and $X_1 X_2$ representing the interaction of water temperature and fish weight can be fitted to data in Table 9.2b to parameterize the relationship. Parameter estimation through multiple linear regression results in the equation

$$Y = -1.834 + 0.132 X_1 + 0.422 X_2 - 0.029 X_1 X_2$$

The regression equation is significant ($P < 0.0001$) and water temperature, individual fish weight, and their interaction together account for 86% of the variability in consumption rate ($r^2 = 0.86$) (Table 9.3). Thus,

```
CONRATE (kg / kg-day) = -1.834 + 0.132 WATER TEMPERATURE
                      + 0.422 WEIGHT OF INDIVIDUAL FISH
                      - 0.029 (WATER TEMPERATURE *
                               WEIGHT OF INDIVIDUAL FISH)
```

We have represented consumption rate as a function of water temperature and the size of individual fish. This represents the consumption rate when available aquatic plant biomass is not limiting. However, recall that when the plant biomass falls below 20,000 kg/ha, consumption by fish becomes limited by

TABLE 9.3 Results of Simple Linear Regression of the Consumption Rate of Fish (kg Consumed/kg Fish Biomass-Day) on Fish Weight (kg), Water Temperature (°C), and the Interaction of Fish Weight and Water Temperature Based on the Data in Table 9.2b

REGRESSION EQUATION

Fish consumption = $-1.834 + 0.132$ temperature $+ 0.422$ weight -0.029 (temperature $\times$ weight)

($r^2 = 0.86$)

Analysis of Variance					
Source of Variation	Degrees of Freedom	Sum of Squares	Mean Square	F Value	$P > F$
Regression	3	26.205	8.735	85.7	0.0001
Error	41	4.180	0.102		
Total	44	30.385			

Parameter Estimates				
Parameter	Estimate	T for $H_0: B = 0$	$P > T$	Standard Error of Estimate
Intercept	-1.834	-6.483	0.0001	0.283
Temperature	0.132	12.092	0.0001	0.011
Weight	0.422	3.395	0.0015	0.124
Temperature $\times$ Weight	-0.029	-6.052	0.0001	0.005

the availability of plant biomass and the desired consumption rate is reduced by roughly one-half for every 5,000-kg/ha decrease in plant biomass below that point (Section 9.2.2). If we let p represent the proportion of desired consumption actually realized when plant biomass is limiting, p takes the form of an exponentially decreasing function of plant biomass:

$$p = \beta_0 e^{-\beta_1 \text{AQUATIC PLANTS}}$$

or, in this particular case,

$$p = e^{-0.00013863(20,000 - \text{AQUATIC PLANTS})}$$

when AQUATIC PLANTS $< 20,000$ kg/ha (Figure 9.17).

Thus, CONRATE also must depend on the value of AQUATIC PLANTS:

```
IF (AQUATIC PLANTS ≥ 20,000) THEN
CONRATE (kg/kg-day) = -1.834 + 0.132 WATER TEMPERATURE
                      + 0.422 WEIGHT OF INDIVIDUAL FISH
                      - 0.029 (WATER TEMPERATURE *
                      WEIGHT OF INDIVIDUAL FISH)
ELSE
```

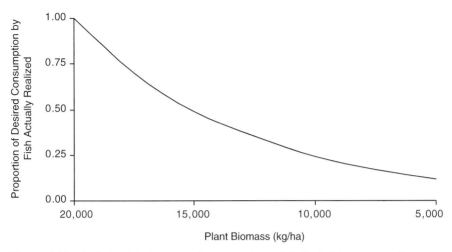

Figure 9.17 Relationship between the proportion of desired fish consumption actually realized and plant biomass.

```
CONRATE (kg / kg-day) = (-1.834 + 0.132 WATER TEMPERATURE
                        + 0.422 WEIGHT OF INDIVIDUAL FISH
                        - 0.029 (WATER TEMPERATURE *
                        WEIGHT OF INDIVIDUAL FISH) *
                        e^(-0.00013863(20,000-AQUATIC PLANTS))
```

CONSUMPTION (kg/ha-day) now can be represented as CONRATE * HERBIVOROUS FISH. This deterministic representation of CONSUMPTION is adequate for our present needs. However, because data (Table 9.2b) suggest that fish consumption per g of fish biomass is not always the same at a given temperature for a given size fish, we will return to these data later to consider a stochastic representation of CONRATE.

This completes the quantitative specification of the third intermediate model. As for the previous model, the baseline simulation will run from day of year 105 (April 15) to day of year 319 (November 15).

6D₂₆ The results of the baseline simulation indicating the seasonal dynamics of AQUATIC PLANTS, HERBIVOROUS FISH, and WEIGHT OF INDIVIDUAL FISH are presented in Figure 9.18.

C09MOD03

9.6.3 Model Evaluation

1A₂₇ Assessing the reasonableness of model structure and the interpretability of functional relationships in view of model objectives, the addition of con-

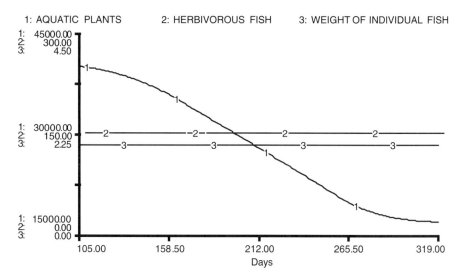

Figure 9.18 Seasonal dynamics of (1) aquatic plants (kg/ha), (2) herbivorous fish (kg/ha), and (3) the weight of individual fish (kg) from April 15 to November 15 predicted under baseline conditions by the third intermediate quantitative model.

sumption of plants by fish as a direct loss of plant biomass seems reasonable based on basic ecological principles concerning trophic relationships. The representation of the consumption of plants by fish as a function of the total fish biomass, size of individual fish, water temperature, and plant biomass is interpretable based on the principles of ecological energetics and foraging ecology. Even though we have held the total fish biomass and the size of individual fish constant, metabolic rates and hence energy requirements and consumption are higher at higher temperatures, which is appropriate for cold-blooded animals such as fish. When plant biomass becomes relatively scarce, the foraging time required to encounter plants will increase and consumption will decrease.

4D₂₉ We will determine the sensitivity of model predictions of the seasonal dynamics of the plant biomass to changes in values of the fish biomass by running two additional simulations with the biomass of HERBIVOROUS FISH constant at (1) near maximum and (2) minimum levels observed—262.5 kg/ha (75 3.5-kg fish) and 17 kg/ha (75 0.227-kg fish), respectively (Table 9.1a). With maximum fish biomass, we expect plant biomass to decrease monotonically at a faster rate than in the baseline simulation (Figure 9.19a). With minimum fish biomass, we expect the plant biomass to follow essentially the same pattern that it does without fish consumption, that is, a slight decrease during spring, a relatively rapid increase during summer, and another slight decrease again during fall (Figure 9.19b).

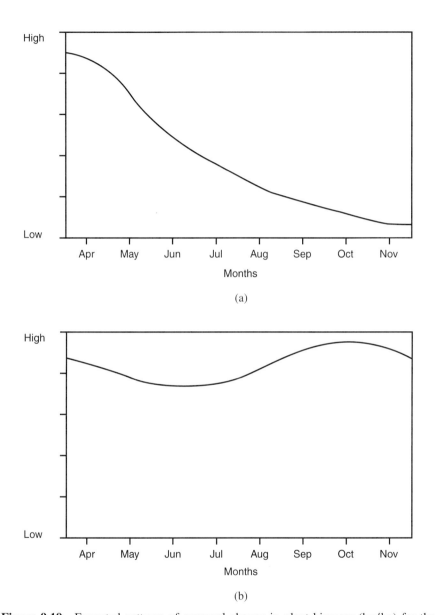

Figure 9.19 Expected patterns of seasonal change in plant biomass (kg/ha) for the third intermediate quantitative model when fish biomass is held constant at near (a) maximum (262.5 kg/ha) and (b) minimum (17 kg/ha) levels from April 15 to November 15.

Simulated plant biomass decreases monotonically with maximum fish bi-omass, but, unexpectedly, at a slower rate than the baseline (Figures 9.18, 9.19a, and 9.20a). Closer examination of simulation results indicates that the slower decline results from the lower consumption rate per unit of body weight of larger fish. For example, 262.5 kg/ha of 3.5-kg fish consume about 146 kg/ha-day during the period in which water temperatures are 30°C, whereas 150 kg/ha of 2.0-kg fish consume about 184 kg/ha-day during the same period.

With minimum fish biomass, simulated plant biomass does not exhibit the expected seasonal fluctuations seen without fish consumption, but, rather, de-clines continuously at an almost imperceptible rate (Figure 9.20b). Closer inspection reveals that net primary production is slightly less than the sum of consumption plus plant mortality throughout the period simulated.

Although sensitivity analysis yielded unexpected results, closer examina-tion of relationships within the model that generated those results provides ecologically reasonable explanations that increase rather than decrease our confidence in the model. This is an example of how difficult it can be to predict system dynamics when the system-of-interest becomes more complex. Thus, we conclude that the third intermediate model provides an acceptable representation of seasonal dynamics of standing crop biomass of plants from April 15 through November 15, assuming a constant biomass of fish, under seasonally varying water temperatures representative of those observed in the real system.

9.7   FOURTH INTERMEDIATE QUANTITATIVE MODEL

9.7.1   Conceptual-Model Formulation

1A₁₉ Having completed initial representation of all the material transfers af-fecting aquatic plants, we now shift our focus to the representation of biomass dynamics of herbivorous fish. The objective of the fourth intermediate model is to add fish stocking, assuming a constant biomass of fish after stocking, and predict the resulting dynamics of the standing crop biomass of plants from April 15 through November 15. Stocking represents the initial flow of fish biomass into the system and sets the stage for subsequent representation of the ecological and physiological processes that generate fish biomass dynamics.

5B₂₀ We will change representation of HERBIVOROUS FISH from a constant to a state variable and add a material transfer entering HERBIVOROUS FISH that represents STOCKING of fish (Figure 9.21). We will not yet connect CON-SUMPTION to HERBIVOROUS FISH. We also will add three constants represent-ing NUMBER OF FISH STOCKED, INITIAL WEIGHT OF INDIVIDUAL FISH, and STOCKING DATE that later will allow us to vary stocking depending on our management plans.

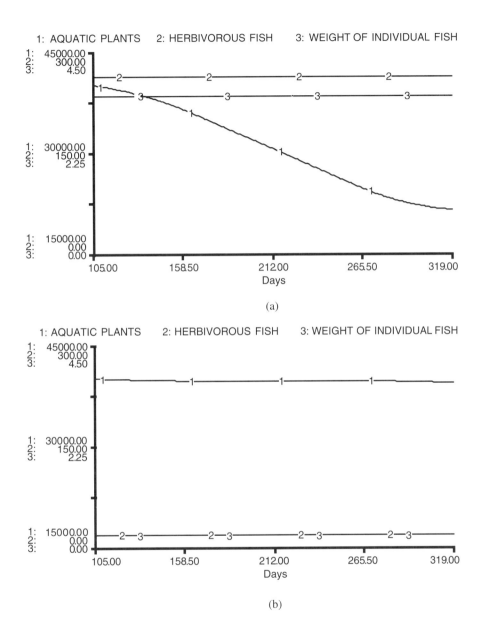

Figure 9.20 Seasonal dynamics of (1) aquatic plants (kg/ha), (2) herbivorous fish (kg/ha), and (3) the weight of individual fish (kg) from April 15 to November 15 predicted by the third intermediate quantitative model when fish biomass is held constant at near (a) maximum (262.5 kg/ha) and (b) minimum (17 kg/ha) levels.

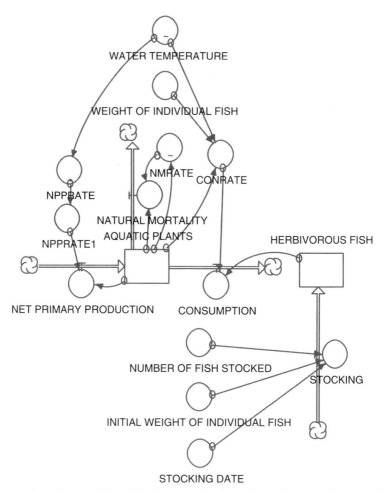

Figure 9.21 Conceptual-model diagram for the fourth intermediate quantitative model representing the dynamics of the standing crop biomass of aquatic plants and the addition of stocked fish.

6C$_{21}$ As before, we will graph expected patterns of seasonal change in plant biomass. If we stock 75 fish, each weighing 2.0 kg on April 15, we expect a monotonic decrease in plant biomass as in the previous model because we are simulating identical conditions (150 kg/ha of fish biomass introduced on day of year 105) (Figure 9.22). The new variables introduced in this model will have no effect on plant biomass dynamics because they will be treated as constants.

9.7.2 Quantitative-Model Specification

3C$_{23}$–5C$_{25}$ First, we will focus attention on parameter estimates for the three constants. We know that historically 75 fish have been stocked on April 15

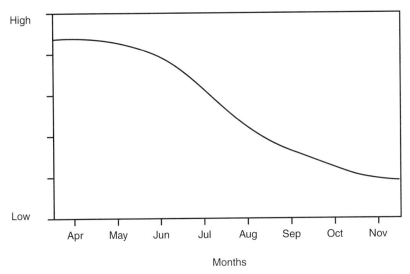

Figure 9.22 Expected patterns of seasonal change in the plant biomass (kg/ha) for the fourth intermediate quantitative model from April 15 to November 15.

(Section 9.2.2), which is the 105th day of the year. For this simulation, we will stock fish weighing 2.0 kg, which is a weight that falls roughly in the middle of the range of weight exhibited by growing fish (0.227 to approximately 3.5 kg, Table 9.1a). Thus, we will assign values of 75, 2.0, and 105 to NUMBER OF FISH STOCKED, INITIAL WEIGHT OF INDIVIDUAL FISH, and STOCKING DATE, respectively.

Because STOCKING is nonzero only on the STOCKING DATE, we will use the following logic to control the material transfer representing stocking of fish:

```
IF (TIME = STOCKING DATE) THEN
STOCKING (kg / ha-day) = INITIAL WEIGHT OF INDIVIDUAL FISH *
                         NUMBER OF FISH STOCKED

ELSE
STOCKING (kg / ha-day) = 0
```

Finally, we write the state variable equation to change the level of accumulation of herbivorous fish biomass in the system from time t to $t + 1$ and specify an initial value for fish biomass at time $t = 0$:

```
HERBIVOROUS FISH_{t+1} = HERBIVOROUS FISH_t+STOCKING
```

and

```
HERBIVOROUS FISH_{t=0}=0
```

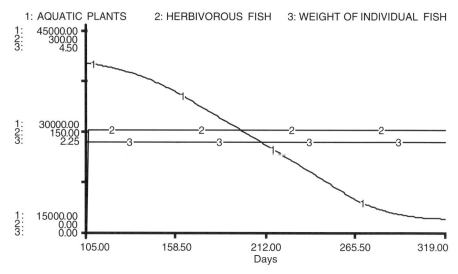

Figure 9.23 Seasonal dynamics of (1) aquatic plants (kg/ha), (2) herbivorous fish (kg/ha), and (3) the weight of individual fish (kg) from April 15 to November 15 predicted under baseline conditions by the fourth intermediate quantitative model.

This completes the quantitative specification of the fourth intermediate model. As for the previous model, the baseline simulation will run from day of year 105 (April 15) to day of year 319 (November 15).

6D₂₆ The results of the baseline simulation indicating seasonal dynamics of AQUATIC PLANTS, HERBIVOROUS FISH, and WEIGHT OF INDIVIDUAL FISH are presented in Figure 9.23.   C09N

9.8 FIFTH INTERMEDIATE QUANTITATIVE MODEL

9.8.1 Conceptual-Model Formulation

1A₁₉. Having represented the initial flow of fish biomass into the system, we now turn to the objective of the fifth intermediate model, which is to allow fish biomass to vary by connecting consumption to fish biomass and adding fish respiration and excretion, assuming a constant water temperature. We will predict the resulting dynamics of the standing crop biomass of plants and fish, and the weight of individual fish from April 15 through November 15. We return to a constant water temperature to simplify evaluation of our representation of respiration and excretion.

5B₂₀ We now will allow CONSUMPTION to enter HERBIVOROUS FISH and will add two material transfers leaving HERBIVOROUS FISH that represent RESPI-

RATION and EXCRETION, respectively (Figure 9.24). We will add a constant representing ASSIMILATION EFFICIENCY and an auxiliary variable (RESRATE) relating the rate of respiration to WATER TEMPERATURE and WEIGHT OF INDIVIDUAL FISH. Finally, we will change WEIGHT OF INDIVIDUAL FISH from a constant to an auxiliary variable depending on the biomass of HERBIVOROUS

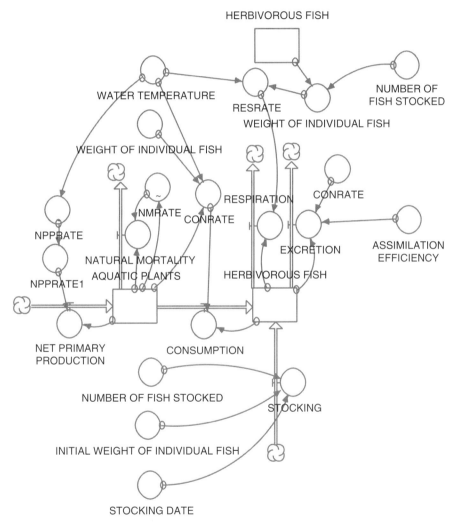

Figure 9.24 Conceptual-model diagram for the fifth and sixth intermediate quantitative models representing the dynamics of the standing crop biomass of aquatic plants and herbivorous fish as affected by the consumption of plants by fish and fish respiration and excretion. Water temperature is represented as a constant for the fifth intermediate model and as a seasonally varying driving variable for the sixth intermediate model.

FISH and NUMBER OF FISH STOCKED, and WATER TEMPERATURE from a driving variable back to a constant.

6C₂₁ We will graph expected patterns of seasonal change in plant biomass, fish biomass, and weight of individual fish. If we stock 75 fish, each weighing 0.227 kg on April 15, and hold water temperature constant at 30°C, we expect a monotonic decrease in plant biomass and a sigmoid increase in both fish biomass and weight of individual fish (Figure 9.25). The expectation for plant biomass is based on baseline simulation results from the previous model in which we held fish biomass constant at a midseason value of 150 kg/ha composed of 75 2.0-kg fish (Figure 9.23). In this simulation, we will begin with a lower biomass composed of smaller fish with a higher consumption rate per unit of body weight and finish with a higher biomass composed of larger fish with a lower consumption rate per unit of body weight. Thus, the net effect on plant biomass should be approximately the same, although there may be seasonal differences in the rate of decrease because water temperature will be constant rather than seasonally variable, as it was in the previous model. The expectation for fish biomass and weight of individual fish, which should parallel each other because the number of fish is constant, is based on basic physiological principles of animal metabolism and growth.

9.8.2 Quantitative-Model Specification

3C₂₃–5C₂₅ First, we will make the necessary changes to the functional forms of WEIGHT OF INDIVIDUAL FISH and WATER TEMPERATURE. Because there is

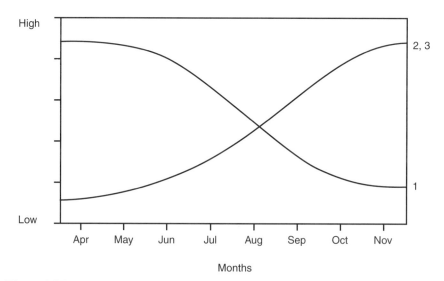

Figure 9.25   Expected patterns of seasonal change in the biomass of (1) aquatic plants (kg/ha), (2) herbivorous fish (kg/ha), and (3) the weight of individual fish (kg) for the fifth intermediate quantitative model from April 15 to November 15.

no mortality of fish in the pond, to allow individual fish weight to change over time, we simply calculate

```
WEIGHT OF INDIVIDUAL FISH (kg) = HERBIVOROUS FISH/
                                 NUMBER OF FISH STOCKED
```

We will set WATER TEMPERATURE constant at 30°C

Next, we will focus attention on identifying the functional form, estimating parameters, and writing computer code for RESPIRATION. We know that fish respiration can be represented as a function of water temperature and weight of individual fish by the generally applicable empirical equation

$$VO_2 = \beta_0\, wt^{-0.2}e^{0.07T}$$

where VO_2 is the respiration rate in mg O_2 respired/g fish-h, wt is the live weight of fish in g, T is the water temperature in °C, and $\beta_0 = 0.0142$ (Section 9.2.2).

We can convert this equation into kg of fish biomass respired per kg of body weight per day (RESRATE) by multiplying the right-hand side of the equation by the following:

1. 3.4 cal/mg O_2 to convert from mg O_2/g-h to cal/g-h
2. 1 kcal/1,000 cal to convert from cal/g-h to kcal/g-h
3. 1 g live wt of fish/1 kcal to convert from kcal/g-h to g/g-h
4. 24 h/day to convert from g/g-h to g/g-day, which is the same as kg/kg-day

Thus,

```
RESRATE (kg/kg-day) = (0.0142 WEIGHT OF INDIVIDUAL FISH⁻⁰·²) *
                      e^(0.07 WATER TEMPERATURE) (3.4)(1/1,000)24
```

or

```
RESRATE (kg/kg-day) = (0.0142 WEIGHT OF INDIVIDUAL FISH⁻⁰·²) *
                      e^(0.07 WATER TEMPERATURE) 0.0816
```

We then multiply by the number of kg/ha of fish in the system to obtain kg/ha respired per day:

```
RESPIRATION (kg/ha-day) = RESRATE*HERBIVOROUS FISH
```

Focusing attention on the functional form of EXCRETION, we know that AS-SIMILATION EFFICIENCY is 2% (Section 9.2.2). Therefore, we know that 98% of CONSUMPTION must be excreted, or

```
ASSIMILATION EFFICIENCY=0.02
```

and

```
EXCRETION (kg/ha-day) = CONRATE * HERBIVOROUS FISH *
                        (1 - ASSIMILATION EFFICIENCY)
```

Finally, we rewrite the state variable equation for HERBIVOROUS FISH to include CONSUMPTION, RESPIRATION, and EXCRETION:

```
HERBIVOROUS FISH(t+1) = HERBIVOROUS FISH(t) + CONSUMPTION +
                        STOCKING - RESPIRATION - EXCRETION
```

This completes the quantitative specification of the fifth intermediate model. As for the previous model, the baseline simulation will run from day of year 105 (April 15) to day of year 319 (November 15).

6D₂₆ The results of the baseline simulation indicating seasonal dynamics of AQUATIC PLANTS, HERBIVOROUS FISH, and WEIGHT OF INDIVIDUAL FISH are presented in Figure 9.26.

C09▮

9.8.3 Model Evaluation

1A₂₇ Assessing the reasonableness of the model structure and the interpretability of the functional relationships in view of model objectives, the representation of fish respiration as a function of the weight of individual fish and water temperature, even though the latter was held constant in this model, is interpretable based on the basic principles of animal physiology. Metabolic rates and hence respiration rates are higher per unit of body weight for smaller animals. Representation of excretion as consumption times (1 − assimilation efficiency) also is interpretable directly in terms of the basic principles of animal physiology.

2B₂₈ Model behavior corresponds well with expected seasonal dynamics. That is, there are only minor seasonal differences in the rate of decrease in the plant biomass compared with the baseline simulation of the previous model (Figures 9.23 and 9.26), which result because water temperature is constant rather than seasonally variable, and fish biomass and weight of individual fish no longer are constants. Both fish biomass and weight of indi-

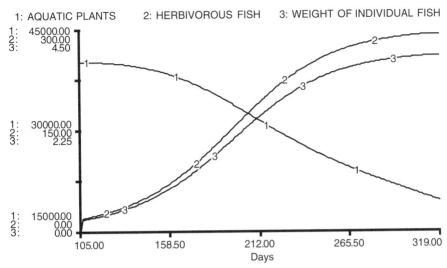

1: AQUATIC PLANTS   2: HERBIVOROUS FISH   3: WEIGHT OF INDIVIDUAL FISH

Figure 9.26 Seasonal dynamics of (1) aquatic plants (kg/ha), (2) herbivorous fish (kg/ha), and (3) the weight of individual fish (kg) from April 15 to November 15 predicted under baseline conditions by the fifth intermediate quantitative model: water temperature is held constant at 30°C.

vidual fish exhibit a sigmoid increase as expected, and the rates of consumption, respiration, and excretion all seem reasonable.

4D₂₉ We will determine the sensitivity of model predictions of the seasonal dynamics of plant biomass, biomass of fish, and weight of individual fish to changes in the values of water temperature by running an additional simulation with WATER TEMPERATURE held constant at 15°C. We are particularly interested in comparing the growth of individual fish under maximum (30°C in baseline simulation) and minimum temperatures.

We expect a monotonic decrease in plant biomass (Figure 9.27). Because both primary production and consumption of plants by fish decrease with decreasing water temperatures, there should be little net change in plant biomass dynamics relative to the baseline simulation. We expect slower sigmoid growth of both fish biomass and weight of individual fish. This expectation is based on results of the baseline simulation and on the temperature dependency of fish consumption, respiration, and excretion. However, it is difficult to predict the net result of plant-fish dynamics under different water temperatures.

Simulated plant biomass decreases monotonically, but, unexpectedly, at a much slower rate than the baseline (Figures 9.26, 9.27, and 9.28). Closer examination of the simulation results indicates that the slower decline is due primarily to the fact that consumption of plants by fish is negligible at 15°C.

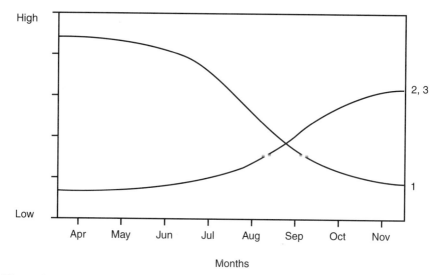

Figure 9.27 Expected patterns of seasonal change in the biomass of (1) aquatic plants (kg/ha), (2) herbivorous fish (kg/ha), and (3) the weight of individual fish (kg) for the fifth intermediate quantitative model when the water temperature is held constant at 15°C from April 15 to November 15.

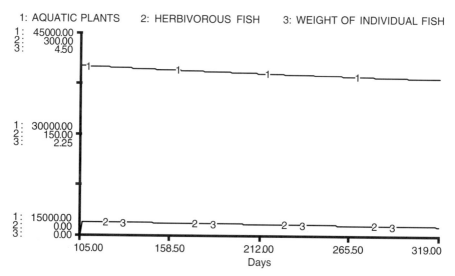

Figure 9.28 Seasonal dynamics of (1) aquatic plants (kg/ha), (2) herbivorous fish (kg/ha), and (3) the weight of individual fish (kg) from April 15 to November 15 predicted by the fifth intermediate quantitative model when the water temperature is held constant at 15°C.

However, even without consumption losses, plant biomass declines because net primary production is always less than plant mortality at 15°C.

Simulated fish biomass and the weight of individual fish both declined rather than exhibiting sigmoidal growth as expected (Figures 9.27 and 9.28). Closer examination of simulation results indicates that this is because respiration plus excretion always exceeds consumption at 15°C.

As before, although the sensitivity analysis yielded unexpected results, closer examination of relationships within the model that generated those results provides ecologically reasonable explanations that increase rather than decrease our confidence in the model. In fact, a more critical analytical look at the various temperature-dependent relationships within the model prior to describing expected patterns of model behavior arguably would have shown us that at such a low temperature, plant and fish biomass are essentially independent of each another and are controlled directly by temperature. Thus, we conclude that the fifth intermediate model provides an acceptable representation of the seasonal dynamics of plant biomass, fish biomass, and weight of individual fish from April 15 through November 15, assuming a constant water temperature.

9.9 SIXTH INTERMEDIATE QUANTITATIVE MODEL

9.9.1 Conceptual-Model Formulation

1A$_{19}$ In the previous model, we simplified the initial introduction of fish respiration and excretion, as well as the initial connection of plants and fish via consumption, by assuming a constant water temperature. The objective of the sixth intermediate model is to add once again seasonality of water temperature and predict the resulting dynamics of the standing crop biomass of plants and fish, and the weight of individual fish from April 15 through November 15.

5B$_{20}$ The conceptual model is the same as the fifth intermediate model (Figure 9.24) except that we will change WATER TEMPERATURE from a constant to a driving variable.

6C$_{21}$ We will graph expected patterns of seasonal change in plant biomass, fish biomass, and weight of individual fish. If we again stock 75 fish, each weighing 0.227 kg on April 15, but now allow water temperature to vary seasonally, we expect essentially the same patterns observed in the baseline simulation of the previous model (in which water temperature was constant at 30°C) (Figure 9.26). That is, a monotonic decrease in plant biomass and a sigmoid increase in both fish biomass and weight of individual fish (Figure 9.29). However, we expect fish biomass and weight of individual fish to increase more slowly due to cooler spring and fall water temperatures, and plant biomass to decrease more slowly due to lower consumption of plants by fish.

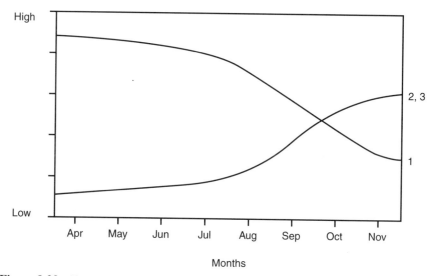

Figure 9.29 Expected patterns of seasonal change in the biomass of (1) aquatic plants (kg/ha), (2) herbivorous fish (kg/ha), and (3) the weight of individual fish (kg) for the sixth intermediate quantitative model from April 15 to November 15.

9.9.2   Quantitative-Model Specification

3C$_{23}$–5C$_{25}$ We will use the same functional form to represent WATER TEMPERATURE that we used in the second, third, and fourth intermediate models. Recall that seasonality of WATER TEMPERATURE was added initially in the second intermediate model, but was deleted temporarily in the fifth intermediate model to allow addition of fish RESPIRATION and EXCRETION under constant WATER TEMPERATURE and thus evaluate more specifically the representation of those processes.

This completes the quantitative specification of the sixth intermediate model. As for the previous model, the baseline simulation will run from day of year 105 (April 15) to day of year 319 (November 15).

6D$_{26}$ The results of the baseline simulation indicating seasonal dynamics of AQUATIC PLANTS, HERBIVOROUS FISH, and WEIGHT OF INDIVIDUAL FISH are presented in Figure 9.30.

C09N

9.9.3   Model Evaluation

2B$_{28}$ Model behavior corresponds well with expected seasonal dynamics, with fish biomass and weight of individual fish increasing more slowly, due to cooler spring and fall water temperatures, and plant biomass decreasing more slowly, due to lower consumption of plants by fish, than in the previous model (in which water temperature was constant at 30°C) (Figures 9.30, 9.29,

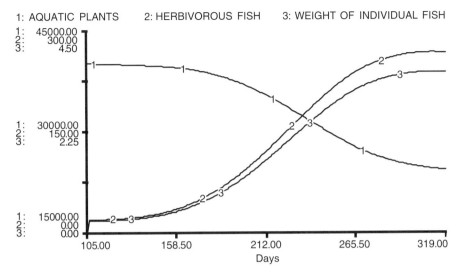

Figure 9.30 Seasonal dynamics of (1) aquatic plants (kg/ha), (2) herbivorous fish (kg/ha), and (3) the weight of individual fish (kg) from April 15 to November 15 predicted under the baseline conditions by the sixth intermediate quantitative model.

and 9.26). Seasonal changes in the rates of consumption, respiration, and excretion also appear reasonable in terms of their relationship to water temperature and weight of individual fish. Thus, we conclude that the sixth intermediate model provides an acceptable representation of the seasonal dynamics of plant biomass, fish biomass, and the weight of individual fish from April 15 through November 15 under seasonally varying water temperatures representative of those observed in the real system.

9.10 SEVENTH INTERMEDIATE QUANTITATIVE MODEL

9.10.1 Conceptual-Model Formulation

1A$_{19}$ To complete the representation of biomass flow through the system, the objective of the seventh intermediate model is to add fish harvest and predict the size of harvest on November 15.

5B$_{20}$ We will add a state variable representing biomass of HARVESTED FISH, a material transfer leaving HERBIVOROUS FISH and entering HARVESTED FISH that represents fish HARVEST, and a constant representing HARVEST DATE (Figure 9.31).

6C$_{21}$ We will graph the expected patterns of seasonal change in plant biomass, fish biomass, and weight of individual fish. If we again stock 75 fish,

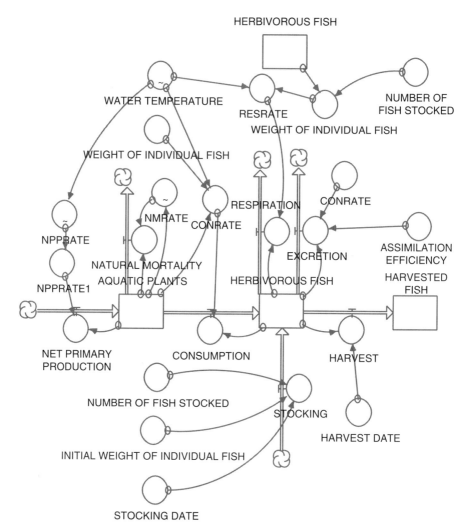

Figure 9.31 Conceptual-model diagram for the seventh intermediate quantitative model representing the dynamics of the standing crop biomass of aquatic plants and herbivorous fish and including the harvest of herbivorous fish.

each weighing 0.227 kg on April 15, we expect exactly the same patterns observed in the baseline simulation of the previous model, that is, a monotonic decrease in plant biomass and a sigmoid increase in both fish biomass and weight of individual fish (Figure 9.32). Of course, all fish biomass will be harvested on November 15.

9.10.2 Quantitative-Model Specification

3C₂₃–5C₂₅ First, we will focus attention on the representation of the constant HARVEST DATE. We know that historically fish have been harvested on No-

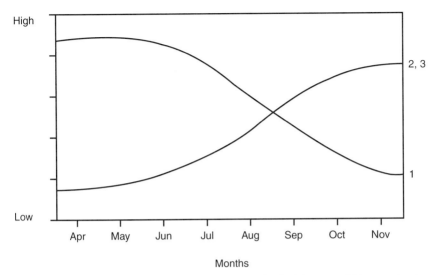

Figure 9.32 Expected patterns of seasonal change in the biomass of (1) aquatic plants (kg/ha), (2) herbivorous fish (kg/ha), and (3) the weight of individual fish (kg) for the seventh intermediate quantitative model from April 15 to November 15.

vember 15 (Section 9.2.2), which is the 319th day of the year. Thus, we will assign a value of 319 to HARVEST DATE.

Because HARVEST is nonzero only on the HARVEST DATE, we will use the following logic to control the material transfer representing fish harvest:

```
IF (TIME = HARVEST DATE) THEN
    HARVEST(kg/ha-day) = HERBIVOROUS FISH
ELSE
    HARVEST(kg/ha-day) = 0
```

Next, we write the state variable equation to change the level of accumulation of harvested biomass in the system from time t to $t + 1$ and specify an initial value for harvested biomass at time $t = 0$:

$$\text{HARVESTED FISH}_{(t+1)} = \text{HARVESTED FISH}_{(t)} + \text{HARVEST}$$

and

$$\text{HARVESTED FISH}_{(t=0)} = 0$$

Finally, we rewrite the state variable equation for HERBIVOROUS FISH to include HARVEST:

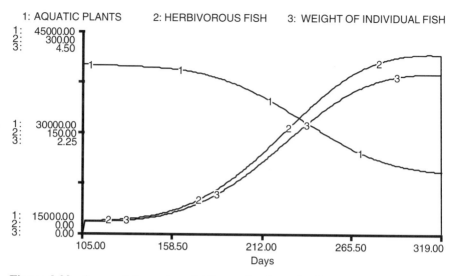

1: AQUATIC PLANTS   2: HERBIVOROUS FISH   3: WEIGHT OF INDIVIDUAL FISH

Figure 9.33 Seasonal dynamics of (1) aquatic plants (kg/ha), (2) herbivorous fish (kg/ha), and (3) the weight of individual fish (kg) from April 15 to November 15 predicted under the baseline conditions by the seventh intermediate quantitative model.

$$
\begin{aligned}
\text{HERBIVOROUS FISH}_{(t+1)} = \ &\text{HERBIVOROUS FISH}_{(t)} + \text{STOCKING} \\
&+ \text{CONSUMPTION} - \text{RESPIRATION} \\
&- \text{EXCRETION} - \text{HARVEST}
\end{aligned}
$$

This completes the quantitative specification of the seventh intermediate model. As for the previous model, the baseline simulation will run from day of year 105 (April 15) to day of year 319 (November 15).

6D₂₆ The results of the baseline simulation indicating seasonal dynamics of AQUATIC PLANTS, HERBIVOROUS FISH, and WEIGHT OF INDIVIDUAL FISH are presented in Figure 9.33.

C09M

9.11   EIGHTH INTERMEDIATE QUANTITATIVE MODEL

9.11.1   Conceptual-Model Formulation

1A₁₉ Having completed the representation of the biomass flow through the system, we now shift our focus to economic aspects of the system. The objective of the eighth intermediate model is to add calculations of gross revenue from the harvest, total cost of lease, and profit, and predict the value of these variables on November 15.

5B$_{20}$ We will add auxiliary variables representing the GROSS REVENUE FROM HARVEST, TOTAL COST OF LEASE, and PROFIT, and constants representing the SIZE LIMIT FOR SELLING FISH, UNIT PRICE OF HARVESTED FISH, and UNIT COST OF LEASE (Figure 9.34).

6C$_{21}$ If we again stock 75 fish, each weighing 0.227 kg, on April 15 and harvest on November 15, we expect exactly the same patterns of seasonal change in plant biomass, fish biomass, and weight of individual fish observed in the baseline simulation of the previous model (Figure 9.33). These new model components do not affect biomass dynamics of plants or fish, but rather

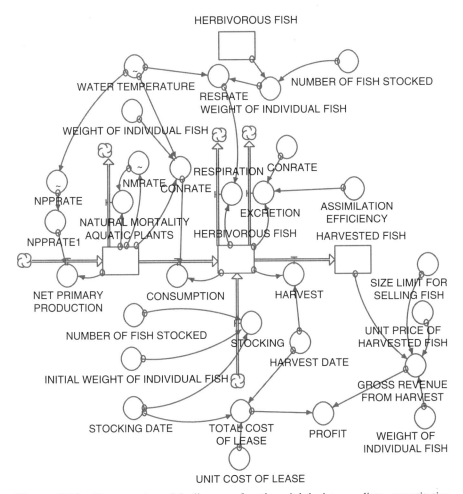

Figure 9.34 Conceptual-model diagram for the eighth intermediate quantitative model representing the addition of economic components including the gross revenue from harvest, total cost of lease, profit, and associated constants.

result from these dynamics. Because we are interested in the values of the new components only at the end of the simulation, we will not graph them.

9.11.2 Quantitative-Model Specification

3C₂₃–5C₂₅ First, we will focus attention on parameter estimates for the three constants. We know that only fish larger than 3 kg can be sold legally, harvested fish can be sold for 1 dollar/kg, and the pond can be leased from the landowner for 0.50 dollar/day (Section 9.2.2). Thus, we will assign values of 3.0, 1.0, and 0.50 to SIZE LIMIT FOR SELLING FISH, UNIT PRICE OF HARVESTED FISH, and UNIT COST OF LEASE, respectively.

We will calculate GROSS REVENUE FROM HARVEST based on the following logic:

```
IF (WEIGHT OF INDIVIDUAL FISH ≥ SIZE LIMIT FOR SELLING FISH) THEN
GROSS REVENUE FROM HARVEST ($) =
                    UNIT PRICE OF HARVESTED FISH * HARVESTED FISH
ELSE
GROSS REVENUE FROM HARVEST ($) = 0
```

We will calculate TOTAL COST OF LEASE ($) as UNIT COST OF LEASE * (HARVEST DATE − STOCKING DATE) and we will calculate PROFIT ($) as GROSS REVENUE FROM HARVEST − TOTAL COST OF LEASE.

This completes the quantitative specification of the eighth intermediate model. As for the previous model, the baseline simulation will run from day of year 105 (April 15) to day of year 319 (November 15).   C09N

9.11.3 Model Evaluation

1A₂₇ Assessing the reasonableness of the model structure in view of model objectives, inclusion of these economic factors as constants, and auxiliary variables connected by information transfers is reasonable because they represent a series of calculations that essentially converts HARVESTED FISH into PROFIT by manipulation of various types of information.

9.12 LAST INTERMEDIATE QUANTITATIVE MODEL

9.12.1 Conceptual-Model Formulation

1A₃₀ We now have a complete representation of our system-of-interest. However, we have approximated several relationships within the model based on a cursory initial evaluation of available data. Thus, the objective of the last intermediate model is to refine our approximate representations of water temperature and rates of net primary production, natural mortality of plants, and consumption of plants by fish. We will compare the resulting dynamics of the standing crop biomass of plants and fish, and the weight of individual fish from April 15 through November 15, as well as predictions of the size of harvest, gross revenue from the harvest, total cost of the lease, and the profit on November 15, with those of the previous intermediate model. We also want to conduct a detailed evaluation of the seasonal dynamics of essential biological processes within the system, including the net primary production, consumption of plants by fish, and fish respiration.

6C₃₁ We will graph expected seasonal changes in plant biomass, fish biomass, and weight of individual fish. If we again stock 75 fish, each weighing 0.227 kg, on April 15 and harvest on November 15, we expect basically the same patterns observed in the baseline simulations of the previous two models, that is, a monotonic decrease in plant biomass and a sigmoid increase in both fish biomass and weight of individual fish (Figures 9.32 and 9.33). However, exact forms of the curves should differ from those of the previous model because we will change representations of some model equations and the curves should no longer be completely smooth because we will introduce random variables into some equations.

9.12.2 Quantitative-Model Specification

3C₃₂–5C₃₄ First, we focus attention on the functional form, parameter estimates, and computer code for WATER TEMPERATURE. Currently, our representation is based on a plot (Figure 9.11) of available data (Table 9.1b) that we have entered directly into the model using a graph. We now conduct a series of five piecewise linear regressions estimating WATER TEMPERATURE as functions (*TEMP*1 through *TIME*5) of day of year (*TIME*) using data from Table 9.1b divided from the following:

1. January 1 (*TIME* = 1) to April 15 (*TIME* = 105)
2. April 16 (*TIME* = 106) to June 15 (*TIME* = 166)
3. June 16 (*TIME* = 167) to September 15 (*TIME* = 258)
4. September 16 (*TIME* = 259) to November 15 (*TIME* = 319)
5. November 16 (*TIME* = 320) to December 31 (*TIME* = 365)

The first regression is not significant ($P > 0.918$) (Table 9.4a), therefore, our best predictor is simply the mean for this time period, or

```
TEMP1=15.015
```

The second regression is significant ($P < 0.0001$) and yields the equation

```
TEMP2=-10.845+0.246 TIME
```

TABLE 9.4 **Results of Simple Linear Regressions of 1983 Water Temperature (°C) in the Pond on the Day of the Year (t) for the Periods (a) January 1 ($t = 1$) to April 15 ($t = 105$), (b) April 16 ($t = 106$) to June 15 ($t = 166$), (c) June 16 ($t = 167$) to September 15 ($t = 258$), (d) September 16 ($t = 259$) to November 15 ($t = 319$), and (e) November 16 ($t = 320$) to December 31 ($t = 365$) Based on the Data in Table 9.1b**

(a) January 1 to April 15

REGRESSION EQUATION

Temperature $= 15.015 - 0.0006t$

$(r^2 = 0.0003)$

Analysis of Variance					
Source of Variation	Degrees of Freedom	Sum of Squares	Mean Square	F Value	$P > F$
Regression	1	0.016	0.016	0.01	0.918
Error	38	55.354	1.457		
Total	39	55.370			

Parameter Estimates				
Parameter	Estimate	T for $H_0: B = 0$	$P > T$	Standard Error of Estimate
Intercept	15.015	42.531	0.0001	0.353
t	−0.0006	−0.102	0.9200	0.006

(b) April 16 to June 15

REGRESSION EQUATION

Temperature $= -10.845 + 0.246t$

$(r^2 = 0.92)$

Analysis of Variance					
Source of Variation	Degrees of Freedom	Sum of Squares	Mean Square	F Value	$P > F$
Regression	1	708.135	708.135	283.7	0.0001
Error	23	57.407	2.496		
Total	24	765.542			

Parameter Estimates				
Parameter	Estimate	T for $H_0: B = 0$	$P > T$	Standard Error of Estimate
Intercept	−10.845	−5.40	0.0001	2.007
t	0.246	16.84	0.0001	0.014

TABLE 9.4 (*Continued*)

(c) June 16 to September 15

REGRESSION EQUATION

Temperature = 29.871 + 0.0006t

(r^2 = 0.0002)

Analysis of Variance

Source of Variation	Degrees of Freedom	Sum of Squares	Mean Square	F Value	$P > F$
Regression	1	0.010	0.010	0.01	0.928
Error	33	40.385	1.224		
Total	34	40.395			

Parameter Estimates

Parameter	Estimate	T for H_0: $B = 0$	$P > T$	Standard Error of Estimate
Intercept	29.871	23.03	0.0001	1.297
t	0.0006	0.091	0.928	0.006

(d) September 16 to November 15

REGRESSION EQUATION

Temperature = 92.846 − 0.244t

(r^2 = 0.95)

Analysis of Variance

Source of Variation	Degrees of Freedom	Sum of Squares	Mean Square	F Value	$P > F$
Regression	1	698.40	698.40	481.98	0.0001
Error	23	33.33	1.449		
Total	24	731.73			

Parameter Estimates

Parameter	Estimate	T for H_0: $B = 0$	$P > T$	Standard Error of Estimate
Intercept	92.846	28.82	0.0001	3.221
t	−0.244	−21.95	0.0001	0.011

TABLE 9.4   (*Continued*)

(e) November 16 to December 31

REGRESSION EQUATION
Temperature $= 14.952 - 0.000t$
$(r^2 = 0.000)$

		Analysis of Variance			
Source of Variation	Degrees of Freedom	Sum of Squares	Mean Square	F Value	$P > F$
Regression	1	0.000	0.000	0.000	0.999
Error	13	32.293	2.484		
Total	14	32.293			

		Parameter Estimates		
Parameter	Estimate	T for H_0: $B = 0$	$P > T$	Standard Error of Estimate
Intercept	14.952	1.39	0.188	10.767
t	-0.0000	-0.000	0.999	0.032

with $r^2 = 0.92$ (Table 9.4b). The third regression is not significant ($P > 0.928$) (Table 9.4c), therefore, our best predictor is the mean for this time period, or

```
TEMP3=29.871
```

The fourth regression is significant ($P < 0.0001$) and yields the equation

```
TEMP4=92.846-0.244 TIME
```

with $r^2 = 0.95$ (Table 9.4d). The fifth regression is not significant ($P > 0.999$) (Table 9.4e), therefore, our best predictor is the mean for this time period, or

```
TEMP5=14.952
```

Thus, WATER TEMPERATURE (°C) is represented by the following logic:

```
IF (TIME≤105) THEN TEMP1
IF (TIME>105) AND (TIME≤166) THEN TEMP2
IF (TIME>166) AND (TIME≤258) THEN TEMP3
IF (TIME>258) AND (TIME≤319) THEN TEMP4
IF (TIME>319) THEN TEMP5
```

Piecewise linear approximations often are useful in quantitatively representing an environmental driving variable such as temperature based on an erratically fluctuating time series of observed values. An alternative approach if the data are not fluctuating too erratically is to fit a single equation to the time series. Sometimes a higher-order polynomial of the form

$$Y = \beta_0 + \beta_1 X_1 + \beta_2 X_2 + \cdots + \beta_n X_n$$

can be used, or general trends in the time series may suggest another particular type of equation. Actually, general trends in our water temperature data (Figure 9.11) suggest that we might have fitted a sine function to this time series. In fact,

```
WATER TEMPERATURE (°C)=21.3+8.9 sin (4.2+(2π(t-1)/364))
```

is a viable alternative to our set of piecewise linear approximations.

We now have a deterministic representation of WATER TEMPERATURE. However, data suggest that water temperature varies from location to location within the pond for any given date. For example, temperatures on April 15 ranged from 13.7°C to 17.8°C from place to place within the pond (Table 9.1b). As described in Chapter 4, one way to represent this inherent randomness explicitly within the model is to generate a normal distribution about each predicted mean value using the mean squared error (MSE) of regression as an unbiased estimate of variance (σ^2). The MSEs of the five water temperature regressions are 1.457, 2.496, 1.224, 1.449, and 2.484, respectively (Table 9.4). Therefore, we represent WATER TEMPERATURE as a stochastic variable by drawing a random variate each day from the appropriate normal distribution using NORMAL (MEAN, STANDARD DEVIATION):

```
TEMP1=NORMAL (15.015, 1.207)
TEMP2=NORMAL (-10.845+0.246 TIME, 1.580)
TEMP3=NORMAL (29.871, 1.106)
TEMP4=NORMAL (92.846-0.244 TIME, 1.204)
TEMP5=NORMAL (14.952, 1.576)
```

Next, we focus attention on NPPRATE. Currently, our representation is based on a plot (Figure 9.7) of available data relating plant growth in g net primary production per kg of live plant biomass per day to water temperature in °C (Table 9.2a) that we have entered directly into the model using a graph. We now conduct a linear regression estimating NPPRATE as a function of water temperature. A simple linear regression model of the form

$$Y = \beta_0 + \beta_1 X + \epsilon$$

with Y representing plant growth, and X representing temperature can be fitted to data in Table 9.2a, which results in the equation

$$Y = -0.604 + 0.073X$$

The regression equation is significant ($P < 0.0001$) and water temperature accounts for 78% of variability in plant growth ($r^2 = 0.78$) (Table 9.5). Because regression predicts plant growth in terms of g net primary production per kg of live plant biomass per day, we must divide this by 1,000 to convert to kg/kg-day, or

```
NPPRATE(g / kg-day)  =  -0.604 + 0.073 * WATER TEMPERATURE
```

and

```
NPPRATE1(kg / kg-day)  =  NPPRATE / 1000
```

We now have a deterministic representation of net primary production. However, data (Table 9.2a) suggest that plant production per kg of live plant biomass is not always the same at a given temperature. Thus, it is appropriate to represent this inherent randomness of plant growth explicitly in the model. As before, we will generate a normal distribution about each mean value predicted by regression using the mean squared error (MSE) as an unbiased estimate of variance. The MSE for regression of plant growth on water temperature is 0.117 (Table 9.5). Therefore, we represent NPPRATE as a sto-

TABLE 9.5   Results of Simple Linear Regression of the Growth Rate of Plants (g Net Primary Production/kg Live Plant Biomass-Day) on Water Temperature (°C) Based on the Data in Table 9.2a

REGRESSION EQUATION
Growth rate = −0.604 + 0.073 temperature
($r^2 = 0.78$)

		Analysis of Variance			
Source of Variation	Degrees of Freedom	Sum of Squares	Mean Square	F Value	$P > F$
Regression	1	11.755	11.755	100.4	0.0001
Error	28	3.280	0.117		
Total	29	15.035			

		Parameter Estimates		
Parameter	Estimate	*T* for H_0: $B = 0$	$P > T$	Standard Error of Estimate
Intercept	−0.604	−3.428	0.0019	0.176
Temperature	0.073	10.017	0.0001	0.0073

chastic variable by drawing a random variate each day from a normal distribution using NORMAL (MEAN, STANDARD DEVIATION):

```
NPPRATE (g/kg-day) = NORMAL (-0.604+0.073 WATER TEMPERATURE,
                            0.342)
NPPRATE 1 (kg/kg-day) = NPPRATE/1000
```

Next, we focus attention on NMRATE. Currently, our representation is based on expert opinion suggesting an exponential relationship between the rate of natural mortality (proportional reduction in standing crop biomass/day) and the density of aquatic plants (kg/ha) (Figure 9.1) that we have entered directly into the model using a graph. We now will fit an exponential equation to this curve. One equation that represents an exponentially increasing curve is

$$Y = \beta_0 e^{\beta_1 X} - 1$$

where β_0 represents the y intercept plus 1, and β_1 controls the degree of curvature, or the rate of increase, of X relative to Y. Because we know the y intercept ($\beta_0 = 0 + 1$) and another point that the curve passes through ($X = 45,000$, $Y = 0.0012$) (Figure 9.1), we can solve the equation $Y = b_0 e^{b_1 X} - 1$ algebraically to obtain $b_1 = 0.00000002665$.

Thus, the parameterized equation passing through points (0, 0) and (45,000, 0.0012) is

$$Y = e^{0.00000002665X} - 1$$

and

```
NMRATE (day⁻¹) = e^(0.00000002665 AQUATIC PLANTS) - 1
```

Next, we focus attention on CONRATE. We already analyzed available data relating fish consumption to water temperature and weight of individual fish (Table 9.2b) to obtain a formal deterministic representation of this relationship during development of the third intermediate model. However, data suggest that fish consumption per g of fish biomass is not always the same at a given temperature for a given size fish. Thus, it is appropriate to represent this inherent randomness of consumption of plants by fish explicitly in the model. As before, we will generate a normal distribution about each mean value predicted by regression using the mean squared error (MSE) as an unbiased estimate of variance. The MSE for regression of fish consumption on water temperature and fish weight is 0.102 (Table 9.3). Therefore, we represent CONRATE as a stochastic variable by drawing a random variate each day from a normal distribution using NORMAL (MEAN, STANDARD DEVIATION):

```
IF (AQUATIC PLANTS > 20,000) THEN
CONRATE (kg / kg-day) = NORMAL (-1.834 + 0.132 WATER
                          TEMPERATURE
                        + 0.422 WEIGHT OF INDIVIDUAL FISH
                        - 0.029 WATER TEMPERATURE *
                        WEIGHT OF INDIVIDUAL FISH, 0.319)
ELSE
CONRATE (kg / kg-day) = NORMAL ((-1.834 + 0.132 WATER
                          TEMPERATURE
                        + 0.422 WEIGHT OF INDIVIDUAL FISH
                        - 0.029 WATER TEMPERTURE *
                        WEIGHT OF INDIVIDUAL FISH) *
```
$e^{(0.00013863 \ (20,000-\text{AQUATIC PLANTS}))}$, 0.319)

This completes the quantitative specification of the last intermediate model. As for the previous model, the baseline simulation will run from day of year 105 (April 15) to day of year 319 (November 15).

6D₃₅ Because we now have a stochastic model, we should run several replicate baseline simulations. We will not calculate formally the number of replicates that we need for statistical analyses of simulation results because we will not perform statistical analyses until we evaluate the definitive model. Rather, we will run a sufficient number of replicates so as to recognize general trends in system dynamics given the inherent variability of the system. In this case, we will run five replicate baseline simulations. The results of the baseline simulations indicating seasonal dynamics of AQUATIC PLANTS, HERBIVOROUS FISH, and WEIGHT OF INDIVIDUAL FISH are presented in Figure 9.35 and the simulated seasonal dynamics of NET PRIMARY PRODUCTION, CONSUMPTION, and RESPIRATION are presented in Figure 9.36.

C09N

9.12.3 Model Evaluation

2B₃₇ Because the model is now complete, we will examine in greater detail the seasonal dynamics of plant and fish biomass and the weight of individual fish, as well as seasonal dynamics of three material transfers that represent essential biological processes within the system: net primary production, consumption of plants by fish, and fish respiration. We will not examine the natural mortality rate of plants because it is a constant proportion of plant biomass nor fish excretion because it always equals the quantity one minus the assimilation efficiency times consumption. (Actually, a similar argument could be made for not presenting results for both fish biomass and weight of individual fish, because the number of fish is constant and therefore fish biomass always equals a constant times the weight of individual fish. However, both results are of particular interest to the pond manager; thus, we have chosen to present both.)

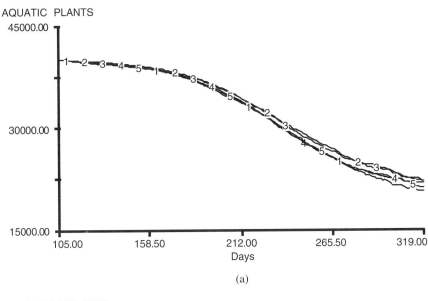

(a)

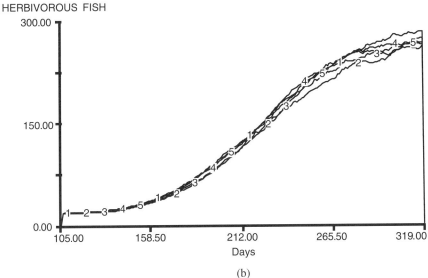

(b)

Figure 9.35   Seasonal dynamics of (a) aquatic plants (kg/ha), (b) herbivorous fish (kg/ha), and (c) the weight of individual fish (kg) from April 15 to November 15 predicted under the baseline conditions by the last intermediate quantitative model. The results of five replicate stochastic simulations are presented.

WEIGHT OF INDIVIDUAL FISH

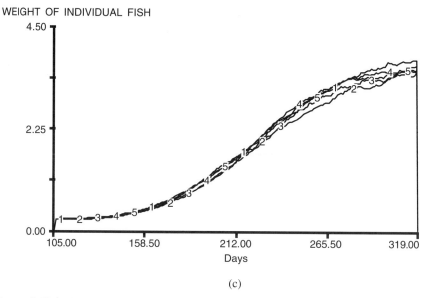

(c)

Figure 9.35   (Continued).

Seasonal dynamics of each biological component seems reasonable in that all maximum and minimum predicted values are within the general ranges of real-system data (Table 9.1a and Figure 9.35), and relative amplitudes and timing of fluctuations are biologically interpretable. Plant biomass decreases monotonically from April through November, with the rate of decrease greater during summer, resulting from increased consumption at warmer water temperatures by an increasing biomass of fish. Fish biomass increases monotonically from April through the early fall, with the rate of increase greater during summer. The weight of individual fish parallels fish biomass, which is expected because the number of fish is constant. Thus, both fish biomass and weight of individual fish exhibit general dynamics consistent with the general dynamics of water temperature; the largest rates of increase in biomass and weight resulting from increased consumption are associated with warmer water temperatures.

Seasonal dynamics of each biological process also seem reasonable in terms of the relative amplitudes and timing of fluctuations (Figure 9.36). Net primary production generally parallels water temperature, increasing from spring to summer and then decreasing into the fall. Primary production is slightly higher at a given water temperature during spring than it is during fall because total plant biomass is higher during spring. Consumption of plants by fish and fish respiration also generally parallel water temperature, increasing from spring to summer and decreasing into the fall. In contrast to plant production, fish consumption and respiration are noticeably higher at a given water temperature during fall than they are during spring because the total biomass of fish is higher during fall.

NET PRIMARY PRODUCTION

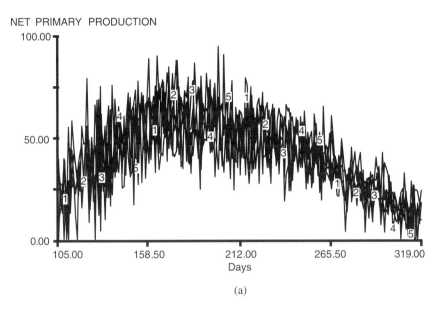

(a)

CONSUMPTION

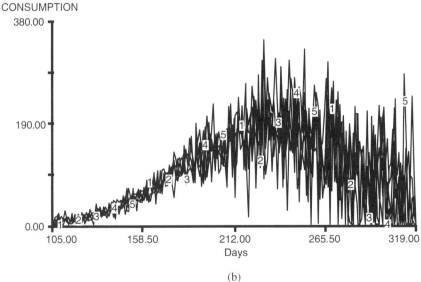

(b)

Figure 9.36 Seasonal dynamics of (a) net primary production (kg/ha-day), (b) consumption of plants by fish (kg/ha-day), and (c) fish respiration (kg/ha-day) from April 15 to November 15 predicted under the baseline conditions by the last intermediate quantitative model. The results of five replicate stochastic simulations are presented.

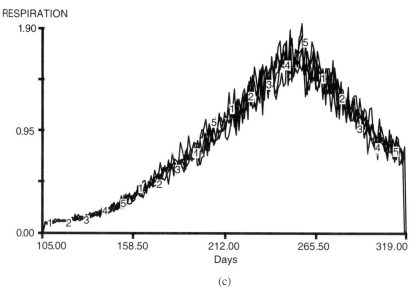

(c)

Figure 9.36   (Continued).

4D₃₈ We will determine the sensitivity of model predictions of the seasonal dynamics of plant biomass, fish biomass, weight of individual fish, net primary production, consumption of plants by fish, and fish respiration to changes in values of water temperature by running two additional simulations in which WATER TEMPERATURE represents unusually hot and unusually cold years, respectively. The objective is to expose inadequacies in the model that may be too subtle to identify when the system is operating close to normal conditions. We will use a deterministic version of the model in which all random variables are assigned their mean values. We will simulate the unusually hot year by adding 4°C and the unusually cold year by subtracting 4°C to WATER TEMPERATURE each day.

As before, seasonal dynamics of each biological component and process seem reasonable and relative amplitudes and timing of fluctuations are biological interpretable (Figures 9.37 and 9.38). During the unusually warm year, the rates of fish consumption and respiration all are higher than normal and the fish biomass and weight of individual fish are higher and the plant biomass lower than normal on November 15. The opposite is true during the unusually cold year, as expected. During the unusually warm year, fish growth slows earlier than normal, although fish grow to a larger size than normal (Figure 9.37c). Further examination shows that this results from restriction of fish consumption because the plant biomass declines below 20,000 kg/ha during fall (Figure 9.37a). Thus, this important negative feedback controlling fish growth, which was not operational under normal conditions, is functioning appropriately.

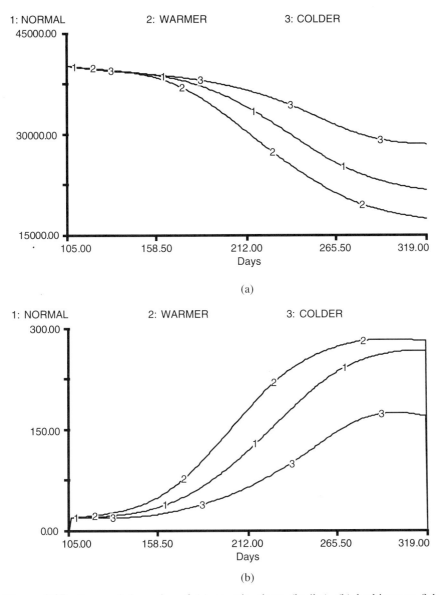

Figure 9.37 Seasonal dynamics of (a) aquatic plants (kg/ha), (b) herbivorous fish (kg/ha), and (c) the weight of individual fish (kg) from April 15 to November 15 predicted by a deterministic version of the last intermediate quantitative model when the water temperature represents (1) baseline conditions, (2) unusually hot (baseline temperatures +4°C), and (3) unusually cold (baseline temperatures −4°C) years.

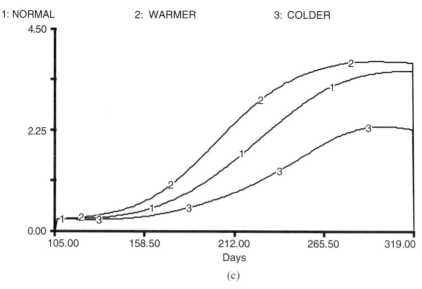

1: NORMAL   2: WARMER   3: COLDER

(c)

Figure 9.37 (Continued).

9.13 DEFINITIVE MODEL

9.13.1 Conceptual-Model Formulation

1A$_{39}$ Objectives of the definitive model are the same as those stated for the preliminary conceptual model (Section 9.3, 1A$_1$).

6C$_{40}$ Likewise, expected patterns of model behavior for the definitive model are the same as those described initially for the preliminary conceptual model (Figures 9.3 and 9.4).

9.13.2 Quantitative-Model Specification

6D$_{41}$ Although the definitive model is quantitatively identical to the last intermediate model, we need to run a new set of baseline simulations because the objectives of the two models are different. During model evaluation, we want to examine some additional types of model results (requiring new graphs) and we probably will need a larger number of replicate simulations for statistical tests comparing model predictions to data from the real system. As before, baseline simulations will run from day of year 105 (April 15) to day of year 319 (November 15).

To determine how many replicate baseline simulations to run, we first run relatively many preliminary baseline simulations to estimate variability of the model results in which we are most interested. Recall that the pond manager

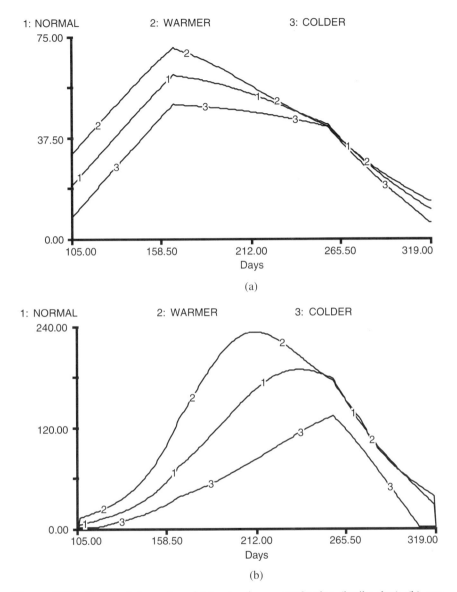

Figure 9.38 Seasonal dynamics of (a) net primary production (kg/ha-day), (b) consumption of plants by fish (kg/ha-day), and (c) fish respiration (kg/ha-day) from April 15 to November 15 predicted by a deterministic version of the last intermediate quantitative model when the water temperature represents (1) baseline conditions, (2) unusually hot (baseline temperatures +4°C), and (3) unusually cold (baseline temperatures −4°C) years.

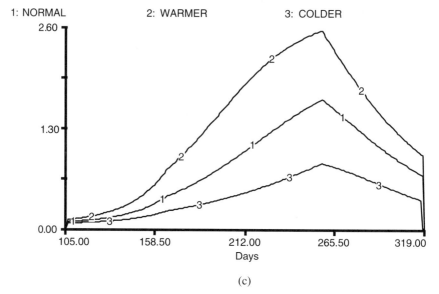

(c)

Figure 9.38   (Continued).

decided that the size of the harvest must change by at least 10% relative to what is usually harvested (baseline) for the change to be important within a management framework (Section 9.2.1). Thus, we will use variability in the biomass of harvested fish to determine the required number of replicate simulations. Figure 9.39 shows the estimated variance of harvested fish biomass under baseline conditions as we increase the number of preliminary simulations used to estimate variance. Each point in Figure 9.39 represents the variance estimated from an independent sample of n replicate stochastic simulations,

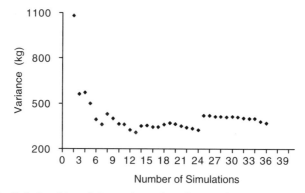

Figure 9.39   Relationship of the estimated variance of the harvested fish biomass under baseline conditions to the number of simulations used to estimate variance.

$$s^2 = \frac{\Sigma X_i^2 - (\Sigma X_i)^2/n}{n-1}$$

where s^2 = estimated variance

X_i = biomass of harvested fish from the ith replicate stochastic simulation

n = number of replicate stochastic simulations used to estimate the variance

Estimates of the variance (σ^2) stabilize at about 380 kg. This is our best estimate of the inherent variability in the biomass of harvested fish.

Next, we specify the magnitude of difference in harvest that we consider practically significant relative to our interests. The mean annual biomass of harvested fish predicted by preliminary baseline simulations is 258 kg. Thus, harvest must change by 25.8 kg, or let us say 25 kg to be practically significant. Suppose the manager would like to show that a true difference of 25 kg in harvest between different management policies is statistically significant at the 95% significance level ($\alpha = 0.05$), with an 80% probability that the difference will be detected if it exists ($P = 0.80$, or type II error $\beta = 0.20$). Then the sample size needed, or number of replicate simulations to run, can be calculated based on the relationship presented in Section 4.7.1.

$$n \geq 2 \left(\frac{\sigma}{\delta}\right)^2 [t_{\alpha,\gamma} + t_{2(1-P),\gamma}]^2$$

where

n = number of samples

σ = true standard deviation, which we estimate as the square root of the estimated variance within samples

δ = smallest true difference that we desire to detect

γ = degrees of freedom of the sample standard deviation with b groups of samples and n samples per group, or $\gamma = b(n-1)$

α = significance level

P = desired probability that a true difference will be found to be significant if it is as small as δ

$t_{\alpha,\gamma}$ and $t_{2(1-P),\gamma}$ = values from a two-tailed t-table with γ degrees of freedom and corresponding to probabilities of α and $2(1-P)$, respectively

In our case, $\sigma^2 = 380$ or $\sigma = 19.49$, $\delta = 25$, $\alpha = 0.05$, and $P = 0.80$. Recall that there are six management schemes, including the baseline, that the manager wishes to compare. If we assume the variablility in the predicted biomass of fish harvested is the same for all six versions of the model, which is the case, and if our initial guess for the correct sample is 10, then

$$\gamma = 6(10 - 1) = 54$$

Thus,

$$10 \geqslant 2 \left(\frac{19.49}{25} \right)^2 t_{0.05,54} + (t_{0.40,54})^2$$

or

$$10 \geqslant 2 \left(\frac{19.49}{25} \right)^2 (2.000 + 0.848)^2$$

and

$$10 \geqslant 9.86$$

and the correct sample size rounded to the nearest whole number is 10.

The results of the 10 stochastic replications of the baseline version of the definitive model are summarized in Table 9.6.

7E₄₂ The equations developed earlier, which collectively describe the pond model, are presented formally in Table 9.7. The initial conditions of the state variables and the values of constants are also presented.

9.13.3 Model Evaluation

3C₄₃ To examine the correspondence between model predictions and observations from the real system, we can use data on the standing crop biomass of plants and fish and the average weight of individual fish (Table 9.1a). These data represent real-world observations that should correspond to model predictions of AQUATIC PLANTS, HERBIVOROUS FISH, and WEIGHT OF INDIVIDUAL FISH, respectively. These are the data on which we have been basing our expected patterns of model behavior throughout model development. However, because they have not been used directly to quantify model equations, they represent an independent data set that can be used to formally evaluate the model. The remaining data on water temperature (Table 9.1b), rate of

TABLE 9.6 Summary of Results of 10 Replicate Stochastic Baseline Simulations of the Definitive Model, including the Biomass of Aquatic Plants and Harvested Fish, Weight of Individual Fish, and Profit on November 15 (Harvest Date)

Replication	Aquatic Plant Biomass (kg/ha)	Harvested Fish Biomass (kg/ha)	Weight of Individual Fish (kg)	Profit (dollars)
1	20,147	275	3.67	168
2	24,482	229	3.05	122
3	22,590	253	3.37	146
4	19,081	281	3.74	173
5	19,511	279	3.72	171
6	21,115	268	3.58	161
7	19,795	278	3.70	170
8	24,032	236	3.14	128
9	19,275	280	3.73	172
10	22,510	255	3.40	147
$\bar{x}$ (± 1 SE)	21,254 (± 637)	263 (± 6)	3.51 (± 0.08)	156 (± 6)

plant growth (Table 9.2a), rate of consumption of plants by fish (Table 9.2b), and on the economic and legal constraints (Section 9.2.2) were used to quantify various model equations and therefore should not be used for the formal quantitative evaluation of the model.

Because the pond model is stochastic, we can make statistical comparisons between the attributes of real-system behavior, for which we have replicated data, and model predictions of these attributes in the set of stochastic baseline simulations. Real-system data on plant biomass, fish biomass, and average weight of individual fish from each replicate sample all are time-series data, that is, we have values for each of these variables at successive points in time. However, we might also think of the data on each variable from each replicate sample as single-value predictions if we concern ourselves only with the value of each variable on the harvest date. Thus, we can base our quantitative comparisons of model predictions and real-system data on analyses of both time-series and single-value predictions.

Comparison of Single-Value Predictions. Analyses of single-value predictions will consist of 3 two-sample *t*-tests comparing baseline model predictions of plant biomass, fish biomass, and the average weight of individual fish on November 15 (harvest date) to real-system data (Table 9.1a). We will determine the number of replicate simulations on which to base our *t*-tests in a manner similar to the way that we determined how many replicate baseline simulations to run in the previous section. Recall that the smallest change in harvested fish biomass between management schemes that has a practical

TABLE 9.7 Equations for the Definitive Model as Represented in STELLA® II (High Performance Systems, Inc., 1994)

☐ AQUATIC_PLANTS(t)=AQUATIC_PLANTS(t-dt)+(NET_PRIMARY_
PRODUCTION-CONSUMPTION-NATURAL_MORTALITY)*dt
 INIT AQUATIC_PLANTS=40000
 DOCUMENT: AQUATIC PLANTS (KG / HA)
 INFLOWS:
  ⌛ NET_PRIMARY_PRODUCTION=NPPRATE1*AQUATIC_PLANTS
  DOCUMENT: NET PRIMARY PRODUCTION (KG / HA-DAY)
OUTFLOWS:
 ⌛ CONSUMPTION=CONRATE*HERBIVOROUS_FISH
 DOCUMENT: CONSUMPTION (KG / HA-DAY)

 ⌛ NATURAL_MORTALITY=NMRATE*AQUATIC_PLANTS
 DOCUMENT: NATURAL MORTALITY (KG / HA-DAY)

☐ HARVESTED_FISH(t)=HARVESTED_FISH(t-dt)+(HARVEST)*dt
INIT HARVESTED_FISH=0
DOCUMENT: HARVESTED FISH (KG / HA)
INFLOWS:
 ⌛ HARVEST=IF(TIME=HARVEST_DATE) THEN HERBIVOROUS_FISH
 ELSE 0
 DOCUMENT: HARVEST (KG / HA-DAY)

☐ HERBIVOROUS_FISH(t)=HERBIVOROUS_FISH(t-dt)+(CONSUMPTION+
STOCKING-HARVEST-RESPIRATION-EXCRETION)*dt
INIT HERBIVOROUS_FISH=0
DOCUMENT: HERBIVOROUS FISH (KG / HA)
INFLOWS:
 ⌛ CONSUMPTION=CONRATE*HERBIVOROUS_FISH
 DOCUMENT: CONSUMPTION (KG / HA-DAY)
 ⌛ STOCKING=IF(TIME=STOCKING_DATE) THEN
 INITIAL_WEIGHT_OF_INDIVIDUAL_FISH*NUMBER_OF_FISH_STOCKED
 ELSE 0
 DOCUMENT: STOCKING (KG / HA-DAY)
 OUTFLOWS:
 ⌛ HARVEST=IF(TIME=HARVEST_DATE) THEN HERBIVOROUS_FISH
 ELSE 0
 DOCUMENT: HARVEST (KG / HA-DAY)
 ⌛ RESPIRATION_RESRATE*HERBIVOROUS_FISH
 DOCUMENT: RESPIRATION (KG / HA-DAY)
 ⌛ EXCRETION=CONRATE*HERBIVOROUS_FISH*(1-ASSIMILATION_
 EFFICIENCY)
 DOCUMENT: EXCRETION (KG / HA-DAY)

○ ASSIMILATION_EFFICIENCY=0.02
 DOCUMENT: CONSTANT-ASSIMILATION EFFICIENCY (PROPORTION)

TABLE 9.7 *(Continued)*

○ CONRATE=IF(AQUATIC_PLANTS>20000) THEN
 NORMAL(-1.834+0.132*WATER_TEMPERATURE+0.422*WEIGHT_OF_
 INDIVIDUAL_FISH-0.029*WATER_TEMPERATURE*WEIGHT_OF_
 INDIVIDUAL_FISH,0.319) ELSE
 NORMAL((-1.834+0.132*WATER_TEMPERATURE+0.422*WEIGHT_OF_
 INDIVIDUAL_FISH-0.029*WATER_TEMPERATURE*WEIGHT_OF_
 INDIVIDUAL_FISH)*EXP(-0.00013863*(20000-AQUATIC_
 PLANTS)),0.319)
 DOCUMENT: AUXILIARY VARIABLE-CONSUMPTION (KG/HA-DAY) PER
 KG/HA OF HERBIVOROUS FISH

○ GROSS_REVENUE_FROM_HARVEST=
 IF(WEIGHT_OF_INDIVIDUAL_FISH>=SIZE_LIMIT_FOR_SELLING_FISH)
 THEN
 UNIT_PRICE_OF_HARVESTED_FISH*HARVESTED_FISH ELSE 0
 DOCUMENT: AUXILIARY VARIABLE-GROSS REVENUE FROM HARVEST ($)

○ HARVEST_DATE=319
 DOCUMENT: CONSTANT-HARVEST DATE (DAY OF YEAR)

○ INITIAL_WEIGHT_OF_INDIVIDUAL_FISH=0.227
 DOCUMENT: CONSTANT-INITIAL WEIGHT OF INDIVIDUAL FISH (KG)

○ NMRATE=EXP(0.00000002665*AQUATIC_PLANTS)-1
 DOCUMENT: AUXILIARY VARIABLE-NATURAL MORTALITY (PROPORTION
 OF AQUATIC PLANTS/DAY)

○ NPPRATE=NORMAL(-0.604+0.073*WATER_TEMPERATURE,0.342)
 DOCUMENT: AUXILIARY VARIABLE-NET PRIMARY PRODUCTION (KG/
 HA-DAY) PER KG/HA OF AQUATIC PLANTS

○ NPPRATE1=NPPRATE/1000

○ NUMBER_OF_FISH_STOCKED=75
 DOCUMENT: CONSTANT-NUMBER OF FISH STOCKED

○ PROFIT=GROSS_REVENUE_FROM_HARVEST-TOTAL_COST_OF_LEASE
 DOCUMENT: AUXILIARY VARIABLE-PROFIT ($)

○ RESRATE=
 (0.0142*WEIGHT_OF_INDIVIDUAL_FISH^-0.2)*EXP(0.07*WATER_
 TEMPERATURE)*0.0816
 DOCUMENT: AUXILIARY VARIABLE-RESPIRATION (KG/HA-DAY) PER
 KG/HA OF HERBIVOROUS FISH

○ SIZE_LIMIT_FOR_SELLING_FISH=3.0
 DOCUMENT: CONSTANT-SIZE LIMIT FOR SELLING FISH (KG)

○ STOCKING_DATE=105
 DOCUMENT: CONSTANT-STOCKING DATE (DAY OF YEAR)

○ TEMP1=NORMAL(15.015,1.207)
 DOCUMENT: DRIVING VARIABLE-WATER TEMPERATURE (DEGREES C)
 FROM DAY OF YEAR 1 TO DAY OF YEAR 105

TABLE 9.7   (*Continued*)

○ TEMP2=NORMAL(-10.845+0.246*TIME,1.580)
   DOCUMENT: DRIVING VARIABLE-WATER TEMPERATURE (DEGREES C)
   FROM DAY OF YEAR 106 TO DAY OF YEAR 165

○ TEMP3=NORMAL(29.871,1.106)
   DOCUMENT: DRIVING VARIABLE-WATER TEMPERATURE (DEGREES C)
   FROM DAY OF YEAR 166 TO DAY OF YEAR 258

○ TEMP4=NORMAL(92.846-0.244*TIME,1.204)
   DOCUMENT: DRIVING VARIABLE-WATER TEMPERATURE (DEGREES C)
   FROM DAY OF YEAR 259 TO DAY OF YEAR 318

○ TEMP5=NORMAL(14.952,1.576)
   DOCUMENT: DRIVING VARIABLE-WATER TEMPERATURE (DEGREES C)
   FROM DAY OF YEAR 319 TO DAY OF YEAR 365

○ TOTAL_COST_OF_LEASE=UNIT_COST_OF_LEASE*(HARVEST_DATE-
   STOCKING_DATE)
   DOCUMENT: AUXILIARY VARIABLE-TOTAL COST OF LEASE ($)

○ UNIT_COST_OF_LEASE=0.50
   DOCUMENT: CONSTANT-UNIT COST OF LEASE ($/DAY)

○ UNIT_PRICE_OF_HARVESTED_FISH=1.00
   DOCUMENT: CONSTANT-UNIT PRICE OF HARVESTED FISH ($/KG)

○ WATER_TEMPERATURE=IF(TIME>319) THEN TEMP5 ELSE IF(TIME>258)
   THEN TEMP4 ELSE
   IF(TIME>166) THEN TEMP3 ELSE IF (TIME>105) THEN TEMP2 ELSE
   TEMP1
   DOCUMENT: AUXILIARY VARIABLE-WATER TEMPERATURE (DEGREES C)

○ WEIGHT_OF_INDIVIDUAL_FISH=HERBIVOROUS_FISH/NUMBER_OF_FISH_
   STOCKED
   DOCUMENT: AUXILIARY VARIABLE-WEIGHT OF INDIVIDUAL FISH (KG)

significance to the pond manager is 25 kg. Also recall that the pond manager wants to show that a true difference of 25 kg in harvest is statistically significant at the 95% confidence level ($\alpha = 0.05$) with an 80% probability that the difference will be detected if it exists ($P = 0.80$, or type II error $\beta = 0.20$). It follows that a difference of less than 25 kg in harvest between baseline model predictions and real-system data is an appropriate criterion for model evaluation. If differences in harvest of less than 25 kg between management schemes are not practically significant, then differences of less than 25 kg in harvest between baseline model predictions and real-system data also should be of no practical significance. Thus, we wish to know how large a sample is needed to show that a true difference of 25 kg in harvest between baseline model predictions and real-system data is statistically significant at the 95% confidence level ($\alpha = 0.05$) with an 80% probability that the difference will be detected if it exists ($P = 0.80$).

We cannot use the general sample size formula presented in the previous section directly in the present situation because the number of samples that we have from the real system is fixed; we have only 8 years of data available (Table 9.1a). However, we can modify the general sample size formula such that we can set n_2 (real system sample size) equal to 8 and solve for the required n_1 (simulation sample size).

$$n_1 \geq \frac{\sigma_1^2}{\delta^2/(t_{\alpha,\gamma} + t_{2(1-P),\gamma})^2 - \sigma_2^2/n_2}$$

where

$\delta = 25$ kg
$\sigma_1^2 = $ variance of model predictions of harvest $= 380$
$\sigma_2^2 = $ variance of real-system data on harvest (Table 9.1a) $= 320$
$\alpha = 0.05$
$P = 0.80$

If we assume that $n_1 = 12$, then

$$\gamma = n_1 + n_2 - 2 \text{ df} = 12 + 8 - 2 = 18 \text{ df}$$

thus

$$n_1 \geq \frac{380}{25^2/(t_{0.05,18} + t_{2(1-0.80),18})^2 - 320/8}$$

and the appropriate number of replicate baseline simulations is 12. We will use predictions of the 10 original replicate baseline simulations (Table 9.6) plus predictions of two additional replicate baseline simulations (Table 9.8) to compare to data from the real system (Table 9.1a) in our 3 two-sample t-tests.

TABLE 9.8 Summary of Results of Two Additional Replicate Stochastic Baseline Simulations of the Definitive Model Run for Use in Model Evaluation, including Biomass of Aquatic Plants and Harvested Fish, and Weight of Individual Fish on November 15 (Harvest Date)

Replication	Aquatic Plant Biomass (kg/ha)	Harvested Fish Biomass (kg/ha)	Weight of Individual Fish (kg)
11	19,316	279	3.72
12	22,587	253	3.38

The results of the 3 two-sample t-tests indicate no statistically significant differences between model predictions of plant biomass, fish biomass, or weight of individual fish on November 15 (harvest date) and estimates based on real-system data (Table 9.9). Thus, based on analyses of single-value outputs, we have no reason to reject the model on the grounds that model predictions do not correspond quantitatively to data from the real system.

Comparison of Time-Series Predictions. Analysis of time-series predictions will consist of quantitatively comparing baseline model predictions of the temporal dynamics of plant biomass, fish biomass, and weight of individual fish to data from the real system (Figure 9.40). Predicted means of plant biomass, fish biomass, and weight of individual fish are all within 5% of the corresponding data means, and confidence intervals (represented in Figure 9.40 as ± 2 standard errors of the mean) about predicted means overlap broadly with confidence intervals about data means. Thus, on average, model predictions of temporal dynamics parallel real-system dynamics closely, and in view of the variation about both model predictions and data from the real system, we can conclude that there are no important differences between predicted and observed values (although we have not conducted formal statistical comparisons of observed and predicted curves). Likewise, variation about predicted means is generally the same as variation about data means. Thus, based on analyses of time-series values, we have no reason to reject the model on the grounds that model predictions do not correspond quantitatively to data from the real system.

4D$_{44}$ We will determine the sensitivity of model predictions of plant biomass, fish biomass, and weight of individual fish on November 15 (harvest date) to changes in values of each of four material transfer rates (NET PRIMARY PRODUCTION, NATURAL MORTALITY, CONSUMPTION, and RESPIRATION) and one constant (ASSIMILATION EFFICIENCY). We will use a deterministic version of the definitive model in which all random variables are assigned their mean values and each of the transfer rates and constant are varied, one at a time, first by +10% and then by -10% of their baseline values. These four transfer rates and constant determine the essential biological dynamics of the pond system.

Examination of the sensitivity of model predictions to changes in other variables or transfer rates certainly is legitimate, but as discussed in Chapter 5, we most often confine our attention to selected variables that seem most interesting. With regard to the pond model, our main interest is in examining model sensitivity, or responsiveness, to changes in the representation of biologically important processes and subsequent evaluation of the soundness of information used to represent those processes.

The results of sensitivity analysis indicate that plant biomass, fish biomass, and weight of individual fish on the harvest date all are relatively sensitive to changes in CONSUMPTION and that fish biomass and the weight of individual

TABLE 9.9   Results of *t*-Tests Comparing Definitive Model Predictions of Biomass of (a) Aquatic Plants, (b) Herbivorous Fish, and (c) Weight of Individual Fish on November 15 (Harvest Date) (from Tables 9.6 and 9.8) and Real-System Estimates (from Table 9.1a)

(a) Plant Biomass

Model Predictions (X_{MP}) of Plant Biomass on November 15 (kg/ha)	Real-System Estimates (X_{RSD}) of Plant Biomass on November 15 (kg/ha)
20,147	24,976
24,482	16,212
22,590	21,774
19,081	21,631
19,511	22,154
21,115	19,104
19,795	20,058
24,032	21,797
19,275	
22,510	
19,316	
22,587	

Degrees of freedom, df = 18
Test statistic, t = 0.238
Significance level, α > 0.05

(b) Fish Biomass

Model Predictions (X_{MP}) of Fish Biomass on November 15 (kg/ha)	Real-System Estimates (X_{RSD}) of Fish Biomass on November 15 (kg/ha)
275	222
229	270
253	262
281	263
279	258
268	281
278	276
236	262
280	
255	
279	
253	

Degrees of freedom, df = 18
Test statistic, t = 0.241
Significance level, α > 0.05

TABLE 9.9   (*Continued*)

(c) Weight of Individual Fish	
Model Predictions (X_{MP}) of Weight of Individual Fish on November 15 (kg)	Real-System Estimates (X_{RSD}) of Weight of Individual Fish on November 15 (kg)
3.67	2.97
3.05	3.60
3.37	3.49
3.74	3.51
3.72	3.44
3.58	3.74
3.70	3.67
3.14	3.49
3.73	
3.40	
3.72	
3.38	

Degrees of freedom, df = 18
Test statistic, t = 1.034
Significance level, $\alpha > 0.05$

fish also are relatively sensitive to changes in ASSIMILATION EFFICIENCY (Table 9.10). Changes in NET PRIMARY PRODUCTION, NATURAL MORTALITY, and RESPIRATION have relatively little effect on plant biomass, fish biomass, or the weight of individual fish.

These results suggest that confidence in the ability of the model to address our original questions rests in large part on the confidence with which we have specified the rate equation representing fish consumption and the confidence that we have in our estimate of assimilation efficiency. The basic rate equation representing fish consumption was developed using multiple linear regression to relate consumption to water temperature and weight of individual fish based on data from the real system. We have relatively high confidence in our representation of this relationship because 86% of variability in observed consumption is accounted for by the regression equation ($r^2 = 0.86$) (Table 9.3). We also added an additional component to the basic consumption equation to represent decreases in desired consumption resulting from shortages of plant biomass, but this additional component affects consumption only at levels of plant biomass (<20,000 kg/ha) lower than those that usually occur in our simulations. However, our confidence in model behavior under conditions resulting in such low levels of plant biomass for extended periods of simulated time must be evaluated in view of our confidence in the representation of this additional relationship. For our present example, we will assume that our confidence in this relationship is high.

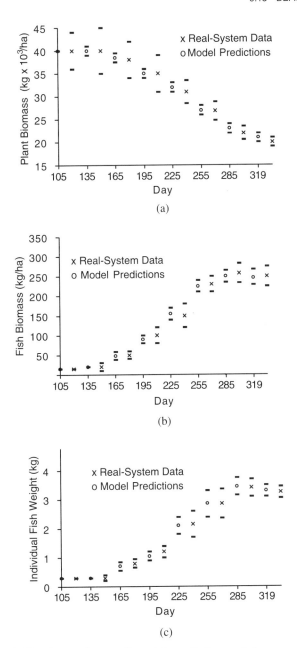

Figure 9.40 Comparisons of model predictions of the seasonal dynamics of (a) aquatic plants (kg $\times$ 10^3/ha), (b) herbivorous fish (kg/ha), and (c) the weight of individual fish (kg) from April 15 to November 15 based on 12 replicate stochastic baseline simulations with real-system data from eight different years (Table 9.1a). Horizontal bars represent ± 2 standard errors of the mean.

TABLE 9.10 Results of Sensitivity Analysis of the Deterministic Version of the Definitive Model Indicating Changes Relative to the Baseline in Biomass of Aquatic Plants, Herbivorous Fish, and Weight of Individual Fish on November 15 (Harvest Date) Resulting from Changes of +10% and −10% in the Indicated Material Transfer Rate or Constant

Material Transfer or Constant Percent Change Relative to Baseline	Plant Biomass		Fish Biomass		Weight of Individual Fish	
	kg/ha	Percent Change Relative to Baseline	kg/ha	Percent Change Relative to Baseline	kg	Percent Change Relative to Baseline
Primary Production						
+10	22,408	+4	265	0	3.53	0
−10	20,684	−4	265	0	3.53	0
Natural Mortality						
+10	20,945	−3	265	0	3.53	0
−10	22,147	+3	265	0	3.53	0
Consumption						
+10	19,525	−10	285	+8	3.81	+8
−10	24,165	+12	234	−13	3.12	−13
Respiration						
+10	21,633	<+1	253	−5	3.38	−4
−10	21,533	<−1	276	+4	3.68	+4
Assimilation Efficiency						
+10	21,590	<+1	286	+8	3.81	+8
−10	22,170	+3	234	−13	3.12	−13

With regard to confidence in our estimate of assimilation efficiency, for our present example, we have stated simply that assimilation efficiency is known to be 2%. We will assume that our confidence in this relationship is high.

9.13.4 Model Use

1A$_{45}$ The experimental design that we will use to address our five original questions (Section 9.3.1, 1A$_1$) will be based on six versions of the model: (1) baseline, (2) early harvest, (3) late harvest, (4) early stocking, (5) late stocking, and (6) double stocking density. Questions 1 and 2 can be addressed by a set of stochastic baseline simulations. Mean harvest and mean profit predicted by the model are the harvest and profit expected in a normal year. Year-to-year variability of harvest and profit are represented by the variances of harvest and profit predicted by the model. Questions 3 and 4 can be addressed by sets of stochastic simulations in which either the beginning (stocking) or ending (harvesting) date of simulated time is either increased or decreased by 30 days relative to the baseline. Question 5 can be addressed by a set of stochastic simulations in which the number of fish stocked is doubled relative to the baseline.

The primary model prediction of interest is profit, although plant and fish biomass and the average weight of individual fish are also of interest. All four will be treated as single-value predictions because we are most interested in their values on the harvest date.

The experimental design for simulations will consist of simulating system behavior under each of the six management policies in which we are interested. Because our model is stochastic, we must also specify the number of replicate simulations of each policy to run. Before executing the baseline simulations, we determined that 10 replicate simulations of each policy are necessary to meet this objective (Section 9.13.2, $6D_{41}$). Thus, our experimental design will consist of 60 simulations: 10 stochastic replicates of each of the 6 different versions of the model. For the baseline situation, we will use the 10 stochastic replicates that we have run already. Results are presented in Table 9.11.   C09MOD09

$2B_{46}$ The results of the analyses of variance indicate statistically significant ($P < 0.0001$) management policy effects on plant biomass, fish biomass, and the weight of individual fish at harvest (Table 9.12). Duncan's Multiple Range Tests (Ott, 1984, p. 376) indicate that the management policy doubling stocking density results in a significantly ($P < 0.05$) lower plant biomass, a significantly ($P < 0.05$) higher fish biomass, and a significantly ($P < 0.05$) lower weight of individual fish than any other policy. Other policies are not significantly ($P > 0.05$) different from each other with regard to biomass of plants or fish, or the weight of individual fish.

We will not conduct analysis of variance on profit because the distribution of profits is extremely nonnormal. Extreme lack of normality in the distribution of profits for some management policies is caused by the legal constraint that fish must be at least 3 kg to be sold. If fish weigh less than 3 kg at harvest, the pond manager obtains no revenue from harvest and still incurs the full cost of the lease. This means that profit is negative and much less than the smallest profit made if fish can be sold, resulting in a discontinuous distribution of profits for any set of stochastic simulations containing some replicates in which fish are at least 3 kg and some replicates in which fish are less than 3 kg at harvest.

TABLE 9.11 Summary of Results of 10 Replicate Stochastic Simulations of the Definitive Model Under Each Management Policy, Including Biomass of Aquatic Plants and Harvested Fish, Weight of Individual Fish, and Profit on Harvest Date

Management Policy	Replication	Aquatic Plant Biomass (kg/ha)	Harvested Fish Biomass (kg/ha)	Weight of Individual Fish (kg)	Profit (dollars)[1]
Baseline	1	20,147	275	3.67	168
	2	24,482	229	3.05	122
	3	22,590	253	3.37	146
	4	19,081	281	3.74	173
	5	19,511	279	3.72	171
	6	21,115	268	3.58	161
	7	19,795	278	3.70	170
	8	24,032	236	3.14	128
	9	19,275	280	3.73	172
	10	22,510	255	3.40	147
	$\bar{x}$ (± 1 SE)	21,254 (± 637)	263 (± 6)	3.51 (± 0.08)	156 (± 6)
Early Stocking (Mar. 15)	1	21,633	256	3.41	133
	2	18,867	277	3.70	154
	3	25,353	206	2.75	−123
	4	21,163	261	3.48	138
	5	22,914	241	3.22	118
	6	24,084	225	3.00	102
	7	22,719	244	3.26	121
	8	22,717	244	3.26	121
	9	21,999	253	3.37	130
	10	20,377	269	3.58	146
	$\bar{x}$ (± 1 SE)	22,183 (± 581)	248 (± 7)	3.30 (± 0.09)	129 (± 5)
Late Stocking (May 15)	1	23,534	251	3.34	158
	2	22,478	262	3.49	170
	3	21,054	274	3.65	181
	4	23,658	249	3.32	156
	5	22,963	257	3.42	164
	6	24,063	244	3.26	152
	7	21,651	269	3.59	177
	8	23,600	250	3.33	157
	9	21,605	269	3.59	177
	10	20,851	276	3.67	183
	$\bar{x}$ (± 1 SE)	22,546 (± 374)	260 (± 4)	3.47 (± 0.05)	168 (± 4)

TABLE 9.11 (*Continued*)

Management Policy	Replication	Aquatic Plant Biomass (kg/ha)	Harvested Fish Biomass (kg/ha)	Weight of Individual Fish (kg)	Profit (dollars)[1]
Early Harvest	1	24,304	244	3.26	152
(Oct. 15)	2	22,314	265	3.53	172
	3	24,311	244	3.26	152
	4	19,691	280	3.73	187
	5	27,259	203	2.70	−92
	6	21,728	269	3.59	177
	7	24,029	248	3.30	155
	8	25,522	229	3.05	136
	9	23,178	257	3.42	164
	10	22,727	261	3.48	169
	$\bar{x}$ (±1 SE)	23,506 (±663)	250 (±7)	3.33 (±0.09)	162 (±5)
Late Harvest	1	17,643	276	3.68	153
(Dec. 15)	2	20,213	263	3.51	141
	3	25,840	192	2.55	−122
	4	17,672	275	3.67	152
	5	21,432	252	3.36	130
	6	20,674	260	3.46	137
	7	22,917	234	3.12	112
	8	21,531	251	3.34	128
	9	22,878	233	3.11	111
	10	21,380	252	3.36	130
	$\bar{x}$ (±1 SE)	21,218 (±773)	249 (±8)	3.32 (±0.10)	133 (±5)
Double Stocking Density					
(150 fish)	1	11,012	360	2.40	−108
	2	8,852	337	2.25	−108
	3	8,337	328	2.19	−108
	4	10,108	353	2.35	−108
	5	8,752	336	2.24	−108
	6	15,299	349	2.32	−108
	7	10,794	359	2.39	−108
	8	10,259	355	2.36	−108
	9	8,163	324	2.16	−108
	10	15,191	350	2.37	−108
	$\bar{x}$ (±1 SE)	10,677 (±824)	345 (±4)	2.30 (±0.03)	—

[1] $\bar{x}$ (±1 SE) for profit does not include negative profits.

TABLE 9.12   Analyses of Variance Comparing Results of the Definitive Model Under Alternative Management Policies with Regard to Biomass of (a) Plants, (b) Harvested Fish, and (c) Weight of Individual Fish on the Harvest Date. Calculations Are Based on Data in Table 9.11

(a) Plant Biomass					

Model Predictions (X) of Plant Biomass (kg/ha) at Harvest

Baseline	Early Stocking	Late Stocking	Early Harvest	Late Harvest	Double Stocking Density
20,147	21,633	23,534	24,304	17,643	11,012
24,482	18,867	22,478	22,314	20,213	8,852
22,590	25,353	21,054	24,311	25,840	8,337
19,081	21,163	23,658	19,691	17,672	10,108
19,511	22,914	22,963	27,259	21,432	8,752
21,115	24,084	24,063	21,728	20,674	15,299
19,795	22,719	21,651	24,029	22,917	10,794
24,032	22,717	23,600	25,522	21,531	10,259
19,275	21,999	21,605	23,178	22,878	8,163
22,510	20,377	20,851	22,727	21,380	15,191

Analysis of Variance Table

Source of Variation	Degrees of Freedom (df)	Sum of Squares (SS)	Mean Square (MS)
Between classes	5	1.1320×10^9	2.2640×10^8
Within classes	54	2.3413×10^8	4.3558×10^6
Total	59	1.3661×10^9	

Test statistic, F = 194.89
Significance level, $\alpha < 0.0001$

(b) Fish Biomass					

Model Predictions (X) of Fish Biomass (kg/ha) at Harvest

Baseline	Early Stocking	Late Stocking	Early Harvest	Late Harvest	Double Stocking Density
275	256	251	244	276	360
229	277	262	265	263	337
253	206	274	244	192	328
281	261	249	280	275	353
279	241	257	203	252	336
268	225	244	269	260	349
278	244	269	248	234	359
236	244	250	229	251	355
280	253	269	257	233	324
255	269	276	261	252	350

TABLE 9.12 *(Continued)*

Analysis of Variance Table

Source of Variation	Degrees of Freedom (df)	Sum of Squares (SS)	Mean Square (MS)
Between classes	5	71,287	14,257
Within classes	54	19,764	366
Total	59	91,051	

Test statistic, F = 38.95
Significance level, $\alpha < 0.0001$

(c) Weight of Individual Fish

Model Predictions (X) of Weight of Individual Fish (kg) at Harvest

Baseline	Early Stocking	Late Stocking	Early Harvest	Late Harvest	Double Stocking Density
3.67	3.41	3.34	3.26	3.68	2.40
3.05	3.70	3.49	3.53	3.51	2.25
3.37	2.75	3.65	3.26	2.55	2.19
3.74	3.48	3.32	3.73	3.67	2.35
3.72	3.22	3.42	2.70	3.36	2.24
3.58	3.00	3.26	3.59	3.46	2.32
3.70	3.26	3.59	3.30	3.12	2.39
3.14	3.26	3.33	3.05	3.34	2.36
3.73	3.58	3.67	3.48	3.36	2.37
3.40	3.37	3.59	3.42	3.11	2.16

Analysis of Variance Table

Source of Variation	Degrees of Freedom (df)	Sum of Squares (SS)	Mean Square (MS)
Between classes	5	10.128	2.0256
Within classes	54	3.329	0.0616
Total	59	13.457	

Test statistic, F = 32.88
Significance level, $\alpha < 0.0001$

Examination of results of our policy-evaluation simulations (Table 9.11) suggests an alternative analysis by which we can compare profit of the different management policies. First, note that there are two essential components of the comparison of profit among policies:

1. the probability that fish will weigh less than 3 kg at harvest, which determines the probabilities of profit and loss (negative profit) in any given year

2. the size of the average profit and average loss for years when fish are at least 3 kg and less than 3 kg, respectively

We can estimate the probabilities of profitable ($\geq$ 3-kg fish) and unprofitable ($<$ 3-kg fish) years for each policy by calculating the proportion of the area under the normal curve representing the distribution of fish weights to the left of 3 kg (Figure 9.41). For example, the proportion of the area under the baseline fish weight distribution curve to the left of 3 kg is about 0.02, or 2%. Under baseline conditions, the pond manager is unable to sell fish 2% of the years. We can estimate the average profit for years when fish are at least 3 kg, as we have done in Table 9.11, by averaging all nonnegative profits for each policy. We can calculate the average loss for years when fish are less than 3 kg by multiplying the unit cost of the lease times the length of the lease.

We now can estimate the mean annual profit for each management policy as the weighted average of the profit from years when fish reach at least 3 kg and from years when fish do not reach at least 3 kg on the harvest date (Table 9.13). For example, the mean annual profit for the baseline policy is $(0.98)(156) + (0.02)(108) = 151$ dollars.

We can now answer the five original questions posed at the beginning of our modeling project. The harvest size expected in a normal year under the usual scheme of stocking 75 0.227-kg fish on April 15 and harvesting them on November 15 is 263 kg, and the profit associated with this harvest is 156 dollars (Table 9.11).

Year-to-year variability in the harvest under normal conditions due to the inherent variability of the system is ± 6 kg, which is the standard error of the mean harvest (Table 9.11). We can depict this variability graphically by generating the distribution of harvest sizes expected under baseline conditions (Figure 9.42). Variability in profit is more difficult to describe since expected profits are not distributed continuously because of losses incurred in years when the average weight of individual fish is less than 3 kg. However, we can predict that the mean annual profit is 151 dollars and that a loss of 108 dollars will be incurred in 2% of the years (Table 9.13).

The size of harvest is not changed significantly by harvesting a month earlier or a month later. Mean harvests are 250 kg and 249 kg under the early and late harvest policies, respectively (Table 9.11), but these are not significantly different from baseline because we did not detect a difference greater than 10% of the mean baseline harvest (at $\alpha = 0.05$ and $P = 0.80$), which is the level of practical significance set by the pond manager. However, the mean annual profit is noticeably lower than the baseline under both early (127 dollars) and late (90 dollars) harvest policies because the probability of fish not reaching 3 kg by harvest is quite high under each policy: 14% under the early and 17% under the late harvest policy (Table 9.13). Early harvest results in a high probability of fish weighing less than 3 kg because of the reduced length of time for growth. Late harvest also results in a high probability of

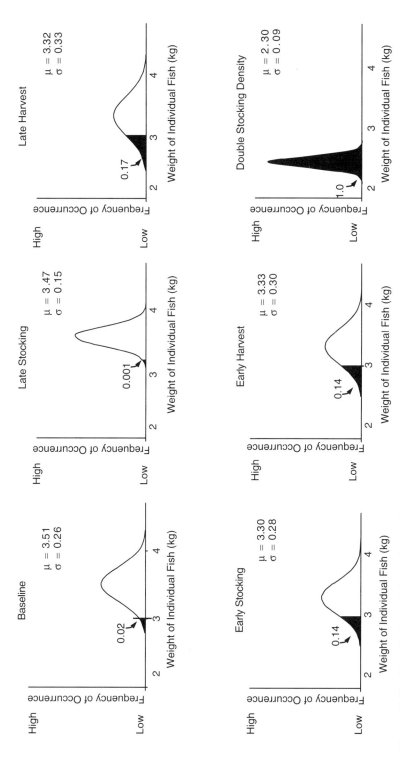

Figure 9.41 Distributions of the weights of individual fish at harvest resulting from 10 replicate stochastic simulations of the definitive model under each management policy. Shaded portions represent the proportion of years that fish weigh < 3 kg on the harvest date.

TABLE 9.13 Summary of Results of 10 Replicate Stochastic Simulations of the Definitive Model Under Each Management Policy Indicating Probability of a Profitable (≥3 kg Fish) Year, Probability of an Unprofitable (<3 kg Fish) Year, Average Profit When Fish Are ≥3 kg, Average Loss When Fish Are <3 kg, and Mean Annual Profit

Management Policy	Profitable Years		Unprofitable Years		Mean Annual Profit ($)
	Probability of Occurrence	Average Profit ($)	Probability of Occurrence	Average Loss ($)	
Baseline	0.98	156	0.02	108	151
Early Stocking (Mar. 15)	0.86	129	0.14	122	94
Late Stocking (May 15)	0.999	168	0.001	92	168
Early Harvest (Oct. 15)	0.86	163	0.14	92	127
Late Harvest (Dec. 15)	0.83	133	0.17	122	90
Double Stocking Density (150 fish)	≈0	—	≈1	108	−108

gathering fish that weigh less than 3 kg because fish actually lose weight as water temperatures decrease during autumn.

The size of the harvest likewise is not changed significantly by stocking a month earlier or a month later. Mean harvests are 248 and 260 kg under the early and late stocking policies, respectively (Table 9.11), but again we did not detect a difference greater than 10% of the mean baseline harvest at $\alpha = 0.05$ and $P = 0.80$. However, mean annual profit is noticeably lower than baseline under the early stocking policy (94 dollars) and is noticeably higher under the late stocking policy (168 dollars) (Table 9.13). Lower profits under the early stocking policy are caused by the 14% chance of fish not reaching 3 kg by harvest. Higher profits under the late stocking policy result because the probability of fish not reaching 3 kg by harvest is essentially zero even

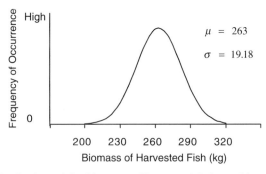

Figure 9.42 Distribution of the biomass of harvested fish resulting from 10 replicate stochastic simulations of the definitive model under baseline conditions.

with the shorter, and therefore less costly, length of the lease. Early stocking results in a high probability of fish weighing less than 3 kg because fish actually lose weight during early spring before water temperatures become favorable for growth. Late stocking and the subsequent reduction in the length of time for growth does not result in a high probability of fish weighing less than 3 kg because the time period lost is one during which water temperatures are too low for substantial growth.

The size of the harvest is increased significantly by doubling the stocking density, but the size of individual fish is decreased significantly. Although the mean size of the harvest is 345 kg, the mean size of individual fish is only 2.30 kg (Table 9.11), which is well below the 3-kg limit for selling fish. Thus, the mean annual profit is −108 dollars and the probability of incurring a loss in any given year is essentially 100% (Table 9.13). Fish weight is low due to competition for plants (food), which are scarce.

We now summarize results in terms that are of most interest to the pond manager. Doubling the stocking density is the only management policy that differs significantly from the baseline in terms of the size of the harvest or the size of individual fish. Unfortunately, the larger harvest under this policy is composed of fish that are too small to sell. Presumably, fish are small due to lack of food because plant biomass at harvest is roughly half of its usual value and well below the 20,000-kg/ha threshold at which availability of plants limits fish growth (Table 9.11). Although other management policies do not produce differences from the baseline in terms of the size of the harvest or the size of individual fish, there are differences in profit due to differences in the length, and therefore cost, of the lease. Both late stocking and early harvest result in somewhat higher profits than the baseline during profitable years (Table 9.11). However, early harvest noticeably increases the probability of incurring a loss because fish fail to reach 3 kg by harvest and hence mean annual profit is less than the baseline (Table 9.13). It appears that of the proposed management alternatives, the only one worthy of serious consideration by the pond manager is the late stocking policy.

3C$_{47}$ The results of initial management policy simulations suggest several additional types of management policies for further examination. In terms of increasing profit, we can (1) reduce the cost of the lease by stocking late or harvesting early or (2) increase revenue by increasing the size of the harvest. The risk we take by reducing the length of the lease is that fish may not have enough time, or enough exposure to warm water temperatures, to grow to 3 kg by harvest. The risk we take by increasing the size of the harvest by increasing stocking density is that fish may not have enough food to reach 3 kg. We might examine the effects on pond dynamics of smaller changes from the baseline in stocking date, harvest date, and stocking density than were represented by our original simulations. The objective is to gain further insight into the response of the pond system to the interplay of these variables and ultimately to see if some new variant of our original management policies is more profitable. We will use the deterministic version of the definitive model to conduct these exploratory simulations (Section 9.12.3, $4D_{38}$).

The results of exploratory simulations in which STOCKING DATE is varied C09 from March 1 (day of year = 60) to June 1 (day of year = 152) while HARVEST DATE and STOCKING DENSITY remain at baseline values are presented in Figure 9.43. Plant biomass remaining at harvest increases exponentially as the stocking date is postponed, but remains above 20,000 kg/ha, the point at which availability of plants begins to limit fish consumption, even when fish are stocked on March 1. Fish biomass and the weight of individual fish at harvest both rise slowly from the March 1 stocking date to the April 22 stocking date (day of year = 112), but decline sharply thereafter. However, the weight of individual fish remains above 3 kg even when fish are stocked on June 1. Profit rises from the March 1 stocking date to the May 15 stocking date (day of year = 135) and then declines.

The results of exploratory simulations in which HARVEST DATE is varied from October 1 (day of year = 274) to December 31 (day of year = 365) while STOCKING DATE and STOCKING DENSITY remain at the baseline values are presented in Figure 9.44. The plant biomass remaining at harvest declines exponentially as the harvest date becomes later, but remains above 20,000 kg/ha even when fish are harvested on December 31. The fish biomass and the weight of individual fish at harvest both rise rapidly from the October 1

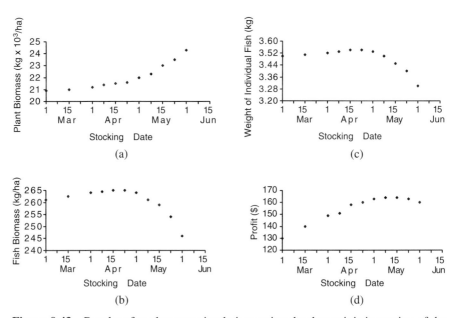

Figure 9.43 Results of exploratory simulations using the deterministic version of the definitive model indicating (a) plant biomass, (b) fish biomass, (c) the weight of individual fish, and (d) profit on the harvest date under different stocking dates.

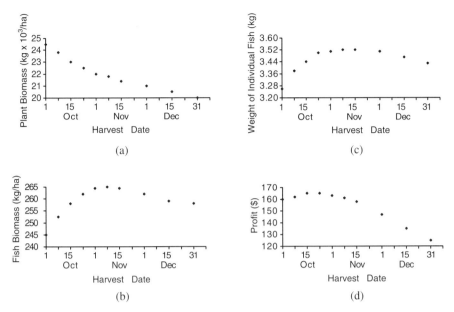

Figure 9.44 Results of exploratory simulations using the deterministic version of the definitive model indicating (a) plant biomass, (b) fish biomass, (c) the weight of individual fish, and (d) profit on different harvest dates.

harvest date to the November 8 harvest date (day of year = 312), but decline thereafter. However, the weight of individual fish remains above 3 kg even when fish are harvested on December 31. Profit rises from the October 1 harvest date to the October 22 harvest date (day of year = 295), but declines thereafter.

The results of exploratory simulations in which STOCKING DENSITY is varied from 50 to 150 fish while STOCKING DATE and HARVEST DATE remain at the baseline values are presented in Figure 9.45. The plant biomass remaining at harvest declines exponentially as stocking density increases and becomes less than 20,000 kg/ha when 85 fish are stocked. The fish biomass at harvest increases as stocking density increases, but the rate of increase decreases markedly at densities above 85 fish. The weight of individual fish remains essentially constant at stocking densities from 50 to 85 fish, but decreases sharply as the stocking density increases above 85 fish. Weight declines below 3 kg at a stocking density of 115 fish. Profit increases up to a stocking density of 110 fish, but at stocking densities above 115 fish, profit is negative.

Based on the results of these exploratory simulations, we might decide to compare formally baseline pond dynamics with dynamics under a new management policy in which we stock 110 fish on May 15 (day of year = 135) and harvest them on October 22 (day of year = 295). STOCKING DATE, HARVEST DATE, and STOCKING DENSITY for the new management policy represent

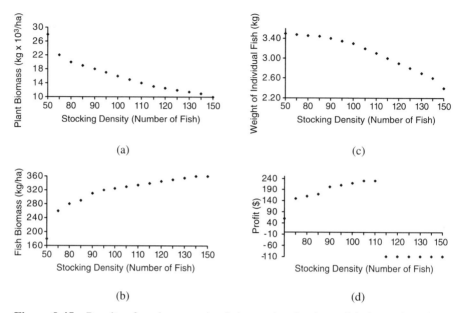

Figure 9.45 Results of exploratory simulations using the deterministic version of the definitive model indicating (a) plant biomass, (b) fish biomass, (c) the weight of individual fish, and (d) profit on the harvest date under different stocking densities.

conditions under which profit curves peaked in Figures 9.43, 9.44, and 9.45, respectively. We will not present results of these analyses here, but rather point out that examination of these results may again raise new questions that we might want to explore using our model.

By this point, the model has become an integral part of our thinking about the pond system. The manner in which our interests in the pond system change will suggest how we might use the model most effectively to pursue these interests. This may involve only minor changes in the model or it may involve major changes requiring collection of new data from the real system to improve the representation of important mechanisms within the model. The ideal relationship between modeling and real-world experimentation is iterative and dynamic.

4D$_{48}$ We will communicate simulation results in the form of an article in a scientific journal, as described in the next chapter.

CHAPTER 10

REPORTING DEVELOPMENT AND USE OF SIMULATION MODELS

Typically, it is awkward to describe development and use of a simulation model within the standard "methods-and-results" format of technical reports and scientific journals. In a sense, the model is both a method and a result. We have found that "overview of the model," "model description," "model evaluation," and "simulation of (objective of project)" are more useful section headings. In what follows, we use this format to write a technical article reporting development and use of the aquaculture pond management project of the previous chapter. No new information is presented, only the style of presentation has been changed. Figure citations appear in a slightly different form than normal to allow direct references to selected figures in the previous chapter.

10.1 EFFECTS OF STOCKING DATE, HARVEST DATE, AND STOCKING DENSITY ON YIELD AND PROFIT FROM A HYPOTHETICAL SUBTROPICAL AQUACULTURE POND: EVALUATION VIA SIMULATION

10.1.1 Abstract

We examine the effect of altering stocking and harvesting dates and stocking density on yield of fish and profit from a hypothetical, 1-ha, subtropical, aquaculture pond using a simulation model. The model consists of an ecological submodel representing biomass dynamics of aquatic plants and herbivorous fish resulting from net primary production and natural mortality of plants, consumption of plants by fish, and fish respiration and excretion and a management submodel representing fish stocking and harvesting and the calculation of profit. Simulated seasonal pond dynamics correspond closely to field observations and there are no significant ($\alpha > 0.05$) differences between mean simulated and observed values of plant biomass, fish biomass, or the weight of individual fish on the harvest date. Simulated pond management schemes representing (1) traditional conditions (stocking 75 0.227-kg fish April 15 and harvesting November 15), (2) harvesting a month earlier and (3) later, (4) stocking a month earlier and (5) later, and (6) doubling the stocking density are significantly different (ANOVA, $\alpha < 0.0001$) with regard to mean values of plant biomass, fish biomass, and the weight of individual fish predicted on the harvest date. Doubling the stocking density results in a significantly (Duncan's Multiple Range, $\alpha < 0.05$) lower biomass of plants, higher biomass of fish, and lower weight of individual fish than any other policy. Late stocking is the only scheme with a higher mean annual profit and a lower probability of an unprofitable year than the traditional scheme. Simulation results suggest that profit could be increased further by finer-scale adjustments about a stocking date of May 15, a harvest date of October 15, and a stocking density of 110 fish/ha.

10.2   INTRODUCTION

Aquaculture is practiced throughout the world using a wide variety of plant and animal species. Typically, the resource species is stocked or confined in owned or leased water, managed to produce the desired yield, harvested, and then sold or otherwise utilized. Thus, aquaculture is essentially aquatic agriculture in that crops are produced through management (Avault, 1980). In less intensively managed aquaculture systems, the principal management variables are the dates on which the resource species is stocked and harvested and the number of organisms stocked. In this paper, we examine the effect of altering stocking and harvesting dates and stocking density on yield of fish and profit from a hypothetical, 1-ha, subtropical, aquaculture pond. More specifically, we determine if annual harvest and the associated profit are changed significantly relative to historical levels by harvesting a month earlier or later, stocking a month earlier or later, or stocking twice as many fish.

10.3   BACKGROUND INFORMATION

Mean water temperature within the pond varies seasonally, with most rapid changes occurring from mid-April to mid-June and from mid-September to mid-October (Table 10.1a). Standing crop biomass of aquatic plants and fish also varies seasonally (Table 10.1b), with net plant production depending on water temperature (Table 10.2a). No data on natural mortality of plants are available, but field observations suggest that mortality can be represented

**TABLE 10.1   Mean (SE) (a) Water Temperature within the Pond on Various
Dates During 1983 (*n* = 5) and (b) Standing Crop Biomass of Plants and Fish,
and Weight of Individual Fish on Various Dates over an 8-Year Period
(1975–1982) (*n* = 8)**

(a) Water Temperature			
Date	Temperature (°C)	Date	Temperature (°C)
Jan. 1	15.00 (0.34)	Jul. 1	29.94 (0.34)
Jan. 15	14.98 (0.20)	Jul. 15	30.00 (0.41)
Feb. 1	15.04 (0.87)	Aug. 1	30.00 (0.66)
Feb. 15	15.00 (0.83)	Aug. 15	30.02 (0.86)
Mar. 1	15.00 (0.43)	Sep. 1	30.02 (0.23)
Mar. 15	14.96 (0.55)	Sep. 15	29.98 (0.54)
Apr. 1	14.94 (0.28)	Oct. 1	25.78 (0.79)
Apr. 15	14.96 (0.76)	Oct. 15	22.46 (0.59)
May 1	18.90 (0.78)	Nov. 1	18.46 (0.38)
May 15	22.38 (1.05)	Nov. 15	14.96 (0.49)
Jun. 1	26.52 (0.60)	Dec. 1	14.88 (0.84)
Jun. 15	29.96 (0.46)	Dec. 15	14.96 (0.82)

(b) Standing Crop Biomass of Plants and Fish and Weight of Individual Fish

Date	Standing Crop Biomass (kg/ha)		Weight of Individual Fish (kg)
	Plants	Fish	
Apr. 15	39,974 (2)	17 (0.0)	0.23 (0.00)
May 15	39,291 (6)	22 (1.2)	0.29 (0.02)
Jun. 15	38,199 (131)	43 (3.9)	0.57 (0.05)
Jul. 15	35,470 (488)	92 (9.3)	1.22 (0.12)
Aug. 15	31,079 (829)	159 (12.5)	2.13 (0.17)
Sep. 15	26,286 (914)	221 (10.0)	2.95 (0.13)
Oct. 15	22,773 (894)	255 (6.7)	3.41 (0.09)
Nov. 15	20,963 (908)	262 (6.3)	3.50 (0.08)

adequately as a function of plant biomass (Figure 9.1). Stocked fish are completely herbivorous and no reproduction or natural mortality of fish occurs in the pond. Consumption of plants by fish depends on water temperature and size of individual fish (Table 10.2b) and availability of plants (Figure 9.17), and 2% of consumed plant biomass is assimilated (unpublished data). Fish respiration also depends on water temperature and size of individual fish and can be represented adequately by an empirical relationship of the general form $\beta_0 W^{\beta_1} e^{\beta_2 WT}$, where W represents fish weight (g), WT represents water temperature (°C), and fish respiration is expressed as mg of O_2 respired per g of fish per h (Neill, personal communication).

The pond manager leases the pond from the landowner on a daily basis for $0.50 per day. Because stocker fish are obtained free and there is no cost associated with either stocking or harvest, the only management cost is the

TABLE 10.2   Mean (SE) (a) Net Production Rate of Plants ($n = 5$) and (b) Rate of Consumption of Plants by Fish of Different Sizes ($n = 3$) as a Function of Water Temperature

(a) Net Production Rate of Plants	
Water Temperature (°C)	Net Production (g Produced/kg Plant Biomass-Day)
10	0.22 (0.08)
15	0.44 (0.10)
20	0.81 (0.24)
25	1.20 (0.16)
30	1.61 (0.16)
35	2.00 (0.19)

(b) Consumption of Plants by Fish of Different Sizes (kg Consumed/kg Fish Biomass-Day)

Water Temperature (°C)	Weight of Fish (kg)		
	0.227	1.500	3.636
15	0.24 (0.12)	0.12 (0.06)	0.18 (0.10)
20	0.76 (0.14)	0.38 (0.13)	0.22 (0.04)
25	1.29 (0.29)	0.73 (0.04)	0.40 (0.21)
30	2.28 (0.20)	1.17 (0.32)	0.60 (0.09)
35	2.87 (0.13)	1.50 (0.09)	0.80 (0.22)

lease fee. Harvested fish are sold to consumers by bulk weight for $1 per kg, but individual fish must be heavier than 3 kg to be sold legally.

Historically, the pond manager has stocked 75 fish, each weighing 0.227 kg, on April 15 and harvested them on November 15. Placing the five alternative stocking and harvesting schemes to be evaluated within a management context, a difference in harvested fish biomass of less than 25 kg is of no practical significance to the pond manager.

10.4   OVERVIEW OF THE MODEL

The model consists of two submodels representing ecological and management aspects, respectively, of the aquaculture system (Figure 10.1). The ecological submodel represents the biomass dynamics of aquatic plants and herbivorous fish that result in the annual yield of harvested fish. Ecological processes represented include net primary production and the natural mortality of plants, consumption of plants by fish, and fish respiration and excretion. Net primary production is a function of water temperature and biomass of aquatic plants. The natural mortality of plants is a density-dependent function of plant biomass. Consumption of plants by fish is a function of biomass of

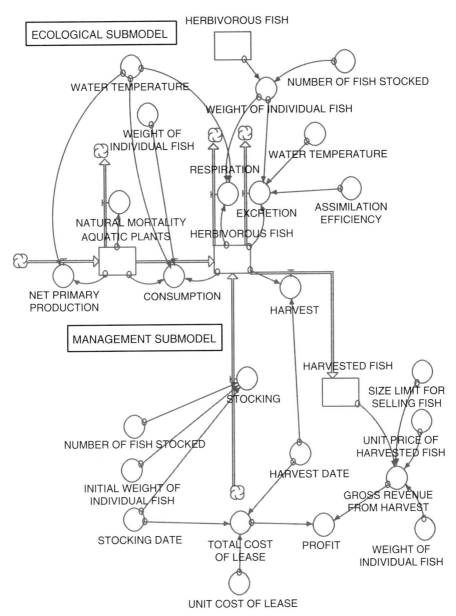

Figure 10.1 Conceptual model representing the effects of stocking date, harvest date, and stocking density on the biomass dynamics of plants and fish and the resulting yield and profit in a hypothetical subtropical aquaculture pond.

plants and fish, water temperature, and weight of individual fish. Fish respiration and excretion are functions of fish biomass, water temperature, and weight of individual fish, with excretion also dependent on assimilation efficiency.

The management submodel represents fish stocking and harvesting and the calculation of profit. Management variables represented include the number of fish stocked, the stocking date, and the harvest date; the initial weight of individual fish at stocking is a constant. Profit is calculated as the difference between the gross revenue from harvest and the total cost of the lease. Gross revenue depends on the biomass of harvested fish, the unit price of harvested fish, and whether the weight of individual fish is greater than the legal size limit for sale. The total cost of the lease depends on the stocking date, the harvest date, and the unit cost of the lease.

10.5 MODEL DESCRIPTION

The model is represented mathematically as a discrete-time, stochastic compartment model based on difference equations with a 1-day time step. Simulations are run using STELLA® II (High Performance Systems, Inc., 1994). Temporal dynamics of state variables representing aquatic plants (AP), herbivorous fish (HF), and harvested fish (HAF) are calculated as

$$AP_{(t+1)} = AP_{(t)} + NPP - NM - CON$$
$$HF_{(t+1)} = HF_{(t)} + FS + CON - RES - EX - FH$$
$$HAF_{(t+1)} = HAF_{(t)} + FH$$

where AP, HF, and HAF are measured in kg/ha, and net primary production (NPP), natural mortality (NM), consumption (CON), fish stocking (FS), fish harvest (FH), respiration (RES), and excretion (EX) are measured in kg/ha-day.

10.5.1 Water Temperature

Linear regressions of water temperature (WT, °C) (Table 10.1a) on day of year (TIME) suggest that general seasonal trends in water temperature can be represented in a piecewise linear fashion: (1) from January 1 (TIME = 1) to April 15 (TIME = 105), WT 15.015 (df = 38, F = 0.01, $P < 0.918$, $r^2 = 0.0003$); (2) from April 15 to June 15 (TIME = 166), WT = $-10.845 + 0.246$ TIME (df = 23, F = 283.7, $P < 0.0001$, $r^2 = 0.92$); (3) from June 15 to September 15 (TIME = 258), WT = 29.871 (df = 33, F = 0.01, $P < 0.928$, $r^2 = 0.0002$); (4) from September 15 to November 15 (TIME = 319), WT = $92.846 - 0.244$ TIME (df = 23, F = 481.98, $P < 0.0001$, $r^2 = 0.954$); and (5) from November 15 to December 31 (TIME = 365), WT = 14.952 (df = 13, F = 0.000, $P < 0.999$, $r^2 = 0.000$).

To represent inherent variability in daily water temperature, each daily value is drawn from a normal distribution generated about the mean predicted by the appropriate previous equation using the mean squared error (MSE) of regression as an unbiased estimate of variance (σ^2). The MSEs of the five water-temperature regressions are 1.457, 2.496, 1.224, 1.449, and 2.484, respectively.

10.5.2 Net Primary Production

Net primary production of plants (g net primary production/kg plant biomass-day) (Table 10.2a) can be represented as a linear function of water temperature (°C): net primary production = $-0.604 + 0.073$ WT (df = 28, F = 100.4, $P < 0.0001$, $r^2 = 0.78$). Thus, net primary production (NPP) can be expressed in kg/ha-day as

```
NPP = (-0.604 + 0.073 WT)/1000) AP
```

To represent inherent variability in daily net primary production, each daily value is drawn from a normal distribution generated about the mean predicted by the previous equation using the MSE of regression (0.117) as an unbiased estimate of variance.

10.5.3 Natural Mortality of Plants

Field observations suggest an exponential relationship between the rate of natural mortality (proportional reduction in standing crop biomass/day) and the density of aquatic plants (AP, kg/ha) (Figure 9.1), thus natural mortality (NM) can be expressed in kg/ha-day as

$$NM = (e^{0.00000002665 \text{ AP}} - 1) \text{ AP}$$

10.5.4 Consumption of Plants by Fish

Assuming that the availability of plant biomass is not limiting, consumption of plants by fish (kg plants consumed/kg fish biomass-day) (Table 10.2b) can be represented as a function of water temperature (°C) and the weight of individual fish (w in kg):

consumption = $-1.834 + 0.132$ WT + 0.422 W − 0.029 WT * W
(df = 41, F = 85.7, $P < 0.0001$, $r^2 = 0.86$)

Thus, consumption (CON) can be expressed in kg/ha-day as

```
CON = (-1.834 + 0.132 WT + 0.422 W - 0.029 WT * W) HF
```

When plant biomass falls below 20,000 kg/ha, consumption by fish becomes limited by availability of plants and desired consumption rate is reduced by roughly one-half for every 5,000 kg/ha decrease in plant biomass below that point (Figure 9.17). Thus, if

$$AP < 20,000$$

$$CON = (-1.834 + 0.132 \ WT + 0.422 \ W - 0.029 \ WT * W) *$$

$$HF * e^{0.00013863 \ (20000-AP)}$$

To represent inherent variability in daily consumption, each daily value is drawn from a normal distribution generated about the mean predicted by the appropriate previous equation using the MSE of regression (0.102) as an unbiased estimate of variance.

10.5.5 Fish Respiration and Excretion

Fish respiration (mg O_2 respired/g fish-h) can be represented as

$$0.0142 \ \text{weight}^{-0.2} \ e^{0.07 \ \text{temperature}}$$

Thus, respiration (RES) in kg biomass respired/kg body weight-day can be expressed as

$$RES = 0.0142 \ W^{-0.2} \ e^{0.07 \ WT} \ 0.0816$$

and in kg/ha-day as

$$RES = 0.0142 \ W^{-0.2} \ e^{0.07 \ WT} \ 0.0816 \ HF$$

Because assimilation efficiency (AE) is 2% for fish of all sizes, excretion (EX) is calculated directly based on the total fish biomass (HF) in kg/ha-day as EX = CON(1 − AE).

10.6 MODEL EVALUATION

10.6.1 Comparison of Simulated and Observed System Dynamics

To evaluate model performance, predictions of temporal dynamics of plant and fish biomass and the weight of individual fish from 12 replicate stochastic simulations representing historical conditions (75 0.227-g fish stocked on April 15 and harvested on November 15, and $AP_{(0)} = 40,000$) were compared with pond data (Table 10.1b). Twelve replications allow detection of a 25-kg difference between simulated and observed fish biomass on the harvest date at $\alpha = 0.05$ (type I error) and $P = 0.80$ (type II error).

The results of t-tests indicate no significant differences between mean simulated and observed values of plant biomass (df $= 18$, $t = 0.238$, $\alpha > 0.05$), fish biomass (df $= 18$, $t = 0.241$, $\alpha > 0.05$), or the weight of individual fish (df $= 18$, $t = 1.304$, $\alpha > 0.05$) on the harvest date and simulated seasonal dynamics of each of these system components corresponded closely to field observations (Figure 9.40). Simulated mean (± 1SE) values for plant and fish biomass and the weight of individual fish on the harvest date were 21,254 (637) kg/ha, 263 (6) kg/ha, and 3.51 (0.08) kg, respectively.

Although no field data are available for direct comparison, mean seasonal dynamics of biological processes explicitly represented in the model also seem reasonable in terms of relative amplitudes and timing of fluctuations (Figure 10.2). Net primary production generally parallels water temperature, increasing from spring to summer and then decreasing during the fall. Primary production is slightly higher at a given water temperature during spring than it is during fall because the total plant biomass is higher during spring. Consumption of plants by fish and fish respiration also generally parallel water temperature, increasing from spring to summer and decreasing into the fall. In contrast to plant production, fish consumption and respiration are noticeably higher at a given water temperature during the fall than they are during the spring because the total biomass of fish is higher during the fall.

10.6.2 Sensitivity Analysis

To further assess the degree of confidence in model predictions, we performed a sensitivity analysis using a deterministic version of the model in which all random variables were assigned their mean values. Analysis consisted of altering, one at a time, the values of net primary production, natural mortality of plants, consumption, respiration, and assimilation efficiency, first by $+10\%$ and then by -10% of their baseline values. These four material transfers and one constant determine the essential biological dynamics of the pond system. Model sensitivity was assessed by examining the effects of the indicated alterations on the predictions of biomass of plants and fish and the weight of individual fish on the harvest date.

The results of sensitivity analysis indicate that predictions of plant and fish biomass and the weight of individual fish on the harvest date all are relatively sensitive to changes in consumption and that fish biomass and the weight of individual fish are also relatively sensitive to changes in assimilation (Table 9.10). Changes in net primary production, natural mortality, and respiration have relatively little effect. Because there is a relatively sound empirical basis for model representations of both consumption (Table 10.2b) and assimilation efficiency (unpublished data), we feel relatively confident in the ability of the model to predict important differences among the alternative management schemes to be evaluated.

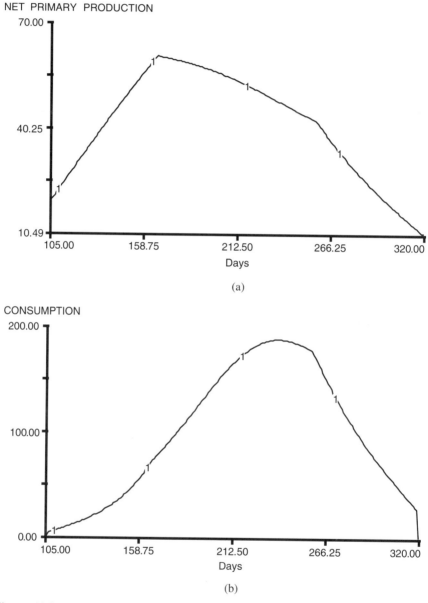

Figure 10.2   Mean ($n = 12$) seasonal dynamics of (a) net primary production (kg/ha-day), (b) consumption of plants by fish (kg/ha-day), and (c) fish respiration (kg/ha-day) from April 15 to November 15 predicted under baseline conditions.

RESPIRATION

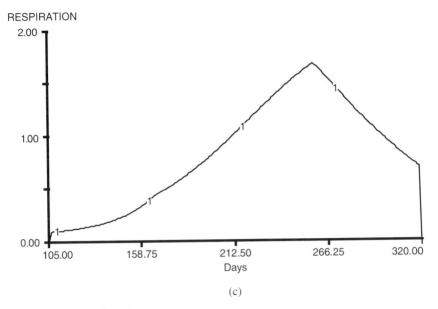

(c)

Figure 10.2   (Continued).

10.7 SIMULATION OF ALTERNATIVE STOCKING AND HARVESTING SCHEMES

To compare the 5 proposed alternative management schemes with the traditional scheme, we ran 6 series of 10 replicate stochastic simulations representing (1) historical conditions, (2) harvesting a month earlier and (3) later, (4) stocking a month earlier and (5) later, and (6) stocking twice as many fish. Ten replications allow detection of a 25-kg difference in predictions of fish biomass on the harvest date at $\alpha = 0.05$ and $P = 0.80$. In addition to examining differences in annual harvest (fish biomass on the harvest date) and the associated profit among the schemes, we also examined plant biomass and the weight of individual fish on the harvest date.

The results of the analysis of variance indicate statistically significant differences among the schemes with regard to mean values of plant biomass (df = 54, F = 52.22, $\alpha < 0.0001$), fish biomass (df = 54, F = 38.95, $\alpha < 0.0001$), and the weight of individual fish (df = 54, F = 32.88, $\alpha < 0.0001$) predicted on the harvest date (Table 10.3). Duncan's Multiple Range Tests indicate that the scheme of doubling stocking density results in a significantly lower biomass of plants (df = 54, $\alpha < 0.05$), a significantly higher biomass of fish (df = 54, $\alpha < 0.05$), and a significantly lower weight of individual fish (df = 54, $\alpha < 0.05$) than any other policy. Other policies are not significantly different from each other with regard to biomass of plants or fish or the weight of individual fish (df = 54, $\alpha > 0.05$).

TABLE 10.3   Simulated Mean (SE) Standing Crop Biomass of Plants and Fish and Weight of Individual Fish on the Harvest Date under Each of Six Management Schemes ($n = 10$)

Management Policy	Plants (kg/ha)	Fish (kg/ha)	Weight of Individual Fish (kg)
Baseline	21,254 (201)	263 (1.9)	3.51 (0.02)
Early Stocking (Mar. 15)	22,183 (184)	248 (2.2)	3.30 (0.03)
Late Stocking (May 15)	22,546 (118)	260 (1.3)	3.47 (0.02)
Early Harvest (Oct. 15)	23,506 (210)	250 (2.2)	3.33 (0.03)
Late Harvest (Dec. 15)	21,218 (244)	249 (2.5)	3.32 (0.03)
Double Stocking Density (150 fish)	10,677 (260)	345 (1.3)	2.30 (0.01)

We did not conduct analysis of variance on profit because the distribution of profits was extremely nonnormal for management schemes under which fish occasionally fail to reach the legal size limit for sale (3 kg). Rather, we calculated a weighted mean annual profit for each scheme based on the probabilities of profitable (fish $\geq$ 3 kg) and unprofitable (fish $<$ 3 kg) years and the average profit or loss during each of these two types of years. Late stocking is the only scheme that results in higher mean annual profit and lower probability of an unprofitable year than the traditional scheme (Table 9.13).

10.8   DISCUSSION

Doubling stocking density is the only management scheme that differs significantly from the traditional scheme in terms of the amount of fish biomass harvested or size of individual fish. Unfortunately, the larger harvest consists of fish that are too small to sell. Fish are small due to the lack of food because the plant biomass at harvest is roughly half of its usual value and well below the 20,000 kg/ha threshold at which availability of plants limits fish growth (Table 10.3).

Although other management schemes do not produce statistically significant differences in the amount of fish biomass harvested or the size of individual fish, there are some interesting management considerations concerning length and timing of the lease that affect profit. Both late stocking and early harvest result in somewhat higher than traditional profits during profitable years (Table 9.13) due to the shorter, less costly lease. However, early harvest noticeably increases the probability of an unprofitable year because fish are removed from the pond during a period when water temperatures still are favorable for growth. In contrast, late stocking does not noticeably increase the probability of an unprofitable year because early spring water temperatures are too low for substantial growth. In fact early stocking results in a high probability of fish weighing less than 3 kg at harvest because fish actually lose weight during early spring before water temperatures become favorable for growth. Similarly, late harvest results in a high probability of fish weighing less than 3 kg at harvest because fish lose weight as water temperatures decrease during autumn.

Clearly, the most promising of the proposed management alternatives is late stocking. However, simulation results suggest finer-scale adjustments of both stocking and harvest dates, to take full advantage of the period during which water temperatures are favorable for fish growth, and stocking density, to more closely match food demands of fish with availability of plant biomass, merit further consideration. Based on normal seasonal fluctuations in water temperature and the resulting dynamics of plant biomass, we suggest a stocking date of May 15, a harvest date of October 22, and a stocking density of 110 fish/ha as a reasonable point of departure for futher studies.

10.9 REFERENCES

Avault, J. W., Jr. 1980. Aquaculture. In R. T. Lackey and L. A. Nielsen (eds.), *Fisheries Management* (New York: John Wiley), pp. 379–411.

High Performance Systems, Inc. 1994, *An Introduction to Systems Thinking* (Hanover, New Hampshire: HPS).

PART IV

APPLICATION OF SIMULATION MODELS IN ECOLOGY

Part IV provides examples of use of simulation models to address a variety of ecological questions at population, community, and individual organism levels of organization. Each example begins with a brief statement of the ecological context and objectives of the model, followed by background information on the system-of-interest, brief descriptions of the model and its use to address the specific questions posed, and ends with suggestions for further use of the model to address related questions. Specific conclusions based on simulation results are presented to demonstrate the manner in which such results can be related directly to model objectives. However, it should be clear that these conclusions have no relevance outside the hypothetical context of the particular example.

Chapter 11 evaluates relative influence of density-independent and density-dependent factors in controlling animal population dynamics under variable environmental conditions. Chapter 12 considers the importance of population age structure and distribution of natality and mortality across age classes in determining population dynamics. Chapter 13 examines the effects of fluctuating environmental conditions on the outcome of interspecific competition. Chapter 14 describes the influence of competition and the frequency of ecological disturbances on community structure. Chapter 15 considers circumstances under which predators control prey populations and vice versa. Chapter 16 examines the trade-offs between increasing the rate of energy intake and reducing the energetic costs of thermoregulation in determining energy balance in homeotherms of different sizes. Because the objective is to provide readers with an opportunity to explore potential uses of models to address different types of ecological questions, few details of model development and evaluation are described and only a few simulation results are presented. Readers can address additional questions of interest using the computerized (STELLA® II) models found in the "nrm" folder on the enclosed CD ROM, which contains documentation defining all variables and units of measure. Names of particular models appear in the right-hand margin of the text.

CHAPTER 11

POPULATION DYNAMICS: EFFECTS OF DENSITY-INDEPENDENT AND DENSITY-DEPENDENT FACTORS

11.1 INTRODUCTION

Population dynamics refers to changes in the number of animals in a population over time. The theory of population dynamics states that populations exhibit exponential growth in an unlimited environment and sigmoidal growth in a limited environment. Under ideal conditions (unlimited resources and ideal physical environmental conditions), natality will exceed mortality and the population will grow exponentially. Population growth may be limited by unfavorable physical environmental conditions, competition for limited resources, or both. Unfavorable physical environmental conditions and competition for limited resources often are thought of as density-independent and density-dependent factors, respectively. The relative importance of density-independent versus density-dependent factors in controlling population dynamics depends on (1) the frequency of occurrence and intensity of unfavorable environmental conditions and (2) the duration and intensity of competition for limited resources.

11.2 MODEL OBJECTIVES

The general objective is to simulate dynamics of a hypothetical animal population to investigate the relative importance of density-independent versus density-dependent factors in controlling population growth. The specific objective is to predict over the next 100 years the impact of periodically occurring years of unfavorable environmental conditions (a density-independent factor) on the dynamics of a hypothetical animal population that normally is controlled by density-dependent factors.

11.3 BACKGROUND INFORMATION ON THE SYSTEM-OF-INTEREST

The system-of-interest consists of a hypothetical animal population in a 1-ha woodlot. The animals depend on favorable environmental conditions during the breeding season for successful reproduction. Conditions are relatively favorable during most years, however, periodically, there are unfavorable years in which no reproduction occurs. Current population size is 100 animals and the population is isolated, that is, there is no immigration or emigration. The population has a maximum annual per capita natality rate of 0.77 (77 individuals born per year per 100 individuals in the population) and a minimum annual per capita mortality rate of 0.70 (70 individuals dying per year per 100 individuals in the population). Relationships of per capita natality to population size during years of favorable environmental conditions and of per capita mortality to population size during all years are presented in Table 11.1 and Table 11.2, respectively.

11.4 MODEL DESCRIPTION

The model represents changes in numbers of animals in the population resulting from natality and mortality (Figure 11.1). Both natality and mortality

Table 11.1   Relative Annual Per Capita Natality Rates of a Hypothetical Animal Population as a Function of Population Size During Years of Favorable Environmental Conditions. Rates Are Presented as Proportions of the Maximum Annual per Capita Natality Rate

Population Size (Number of Individuals)	Relative Annual Natality Rate
<150	1.00
160	0.99
170	0.98
180	0.97
190	0.96
200	0.95
210	0.94
220	0.93
230	0.92
240	0.91
≥250	0.90

Table 11.2   Relative Annual per Capita Mortality Rates of a Hypothetical Animal Population as a Function of Population Size. Rates Are Presented as Proportions of the Minimum Annual per Capita Mortality Rate

Population Size (Number of Individuals)	Relative Annual Mortality Rate
<200	1.00
205	1.01
210	1.02
215	1.03
220	1.04
225	1.05
230	1.06
235	1.07
240	1.08
245	1.09
250	1.10
255	1.15
260	1.20
265	1.25
270	1.30
275	1.35
≥280	1.40

rates are density-dependent, with natality also being dependent on physical environmental conditions.

The baseline simulation, which represents dynamics of the animal popu- C11MOD01
lation under constant favorable environmental conditions, runs from year 1 to year 100 using a time unit of 1 year and the equations in Table 11.3. PHYS ENVIRON is represented as an index with values of 1 and 0 representing years of favorable and unfavorable environmental conditions, respectively. NAT RATE INDEX and MORT RATE INDEX are graphical functions of POP based on data in Table 11.1 and Table 11.2, respectively, that modify maximum and minimum annual per capita natality and mortality, respectively. COUNT is a bookkeeping variable that determines whether unfavorable environmental conditions occur during the present year.

11.5 MODEL USE

To predict the impact of periodically occurring years of unfavorable environmental conditions on the dynamics of the hypothetical animal population over the next 100 years, our experimental design consists of four 100-year simulations representing (1) constant favorable environmental conditions (baseline) and single years of unfavorable environmental conditions occurring at inter-

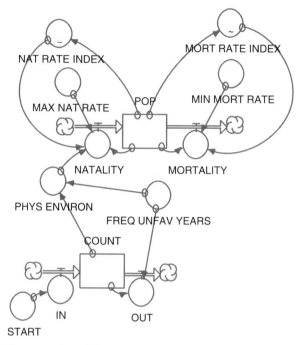

Figure 11.1 Conceptual model representing the effects of density-independent and density-dependent factors on the dynamics of a hypothetical animal population.

vals of (2) 25, (3) 20, and (4) 15 years, respectively. The simulation results indicate that population increases sigmoidally from 100 to a carrying capacity of 215 animals after about 15 years under constant favorable environmental conditions (Figure 11.2). The population can recover to the carrying capacity between the single unfavorable years occurring at 25-year intervals and can recover to a level somewhat below the carrying capacity between the unfavorable years occurring at 20-year intervals, but cannot maintain itself when the unfavorable years occur at 15-year intervals (Figure 11.2).

Regarding the relative importance of density-independent versus density-dependent factors in controlling population growth, the simulation results support the idea that density-dependent factors are more important under favorable, and density-independent factors under unfavorable, environmental conditions. Under favorable conditions, population growth is controlled by density-dependent negative feedback that lowers per capita natality and increases per capita mortality as population size increases. As the frequency of occurrence of unfavorable conditions increases, the duration and intensity of competition for limited resources is lowered and population growth is controlled by the density-independent reduction in natality associated with unfavorable conditions.

We encourage readers to use the model to explore further the relationship between (1) the frequency of occurrence and intensity of unfavorable envi-

Table 11.3   Equations (Baseline Conditions) for the Simulation Model Representing Effects of Density-Independent and Density-Dependent Factors on Dynamics of a Hypothetical Animal Population

---

☐ COUNT(t) = COUNT(t − dt) + (IN − OUT) * dt
  INIT COUNT = 1
  DOCUMENT: COUNTER DETERMINING OCCURRENCE OF UNFAVORABLE
  YEARS
  INFLOWS:
  ⏚ IN = IF(TIME<START) THEN 0 ELSE 1
    OUTFLOWS:
  ⏚ OUT = IF(COUNT=FREQ_UNFAV_YEARS) THEN COUNT ELSE 0

☐ POP(t) = POP(t − dt) + (NATALITY − MORTALITY) * dt
  INIT POP = 100
  DOCUMENT: POPULATION SIZE (ANIMALS / HA)
  INFLOWS:
  ⏚ NATALITY = MAX_NAT_RATE*NAT_RATE_INDEX*PHYS_ENVIRON
    *POP
    DOCUMENT: NATALITY (ANIMALS / HA-YR)
  OUTFLOWS:
  ⏚ MORTALITY = MIN_MORT_RATE*MORT_RATE_INDEX*POP
    DOCUMENT: MORTALITY (ANIMALS / HA-YR)

○ FREQ_UNFAV_YEARS = 999
  DOCUMENT: DRIVING VARIABLE − FREQUENCY OF OCCURRENCE OF
  UNFAVORABLE YEARS
  (NUMBER OF YEARS BETWEEN CONSECUTIVE UNFAVORABLE YEARS)

○ MAX_NAT_RATE = 0.77
  DOCUMENT: CONSTANT − MAXIMUM NATALITY RATE (ANIMALS /
  ANIMAL-YR)

○ MIN_MORT_RATE = 0.7
  DOCUMENT: CONSTANT − MINIMUM MORTALITY RATE (PROPORTION OF
  POPULATION DYING / YR)

○ PHYS_ENVIRON = IF(COUNT=FREQ_UNFAV_YEARS) THEN 0 ELSE 1
  DOCUMENT: AUXILIARY VARIABLE − INDEX ADJUSTING NATALITY
  FOR FAVORABLE AND UNFAVORABLE YEARS (UNITLESS)

○ START = 0

⊘MORT_RATE_INDEX = GRAPH(POP)
  (200, 1.00), (205, 1.01), (210, 1.02), (215, 1.03), (220,
  1.04), (225, 1.05), (230, 1.06), (235, 1.07), (240,
  1.08), (245, 1.09), (250, 1.10)
  DOCUMENT: AUXILIARY VARIABLE − PROPORTIONAL INCREASE IN
  MORTALITY RATE AS POPULATION SIZE INCREASES (UNITLESS)

⊘NAT_RATE_INDEX = GRAPH(POP)
  (150, 1.00), (160, 0.99), (170, 0.98), (180, 0.97), (190,
  0.96), (200, 0.95), (210, 0.94), (220, 0.93), (230,
  0.92), (240, 0.91), (250, 0.9)
  DOCUMENT: AUXILIARY VARIABLE − PROPORTIONAL DECREASE IN
  NATALITY RATE AS POPULATION SIZE INCREASES (UNITLESS)

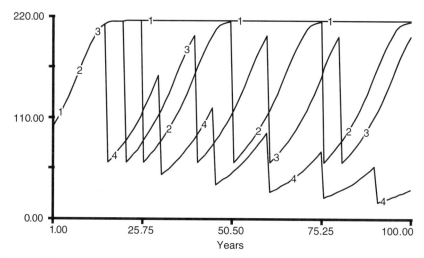

Figure 11.2 Results of four 100-year simulations representing population dynamics (animals/ha) with (1) constant favorable environmental conditions (baseline) and with single years of unfavorable conditions occurring at intervals of (2) 25, (3) 20, and (4) 15 years.

ronmental conditions and (2) the duration and intensity of competition for limited resources in determining the relative importance of density-independent versus density-dependent factors in controlling population dynamics. A variety of relevant situations can be simulated by changing values of PHYS ENVIRON and FREQ UNFAV YEARS, and graphs representing NAT RATE INDEX and MORT RATE INDEX.

CHAPTER 12

POPULATION DYNAMICS: EFFECTS OF AGE-SPECIFIC NATALITY AND MORTALITY

12.1 INTRODUCTION

An important attribute affecting the growth of populations with overlapping generations is their age structure. Natality and mortality usually are distributed unequally across age classes, reflecting age-related, life-history characteristics of the species. Thus, population growth depends in part on the distribution of natality and mortality across age classes, which is a characteristic of the species, and in part on the current distribution of individuals across age classes, which reflects the recent ecological conditions to which the population has been exposed.

12.2 MODEL OBJECTIVES

The general objective is to simulate dynamics of a hypothetical age-structured animal population to investigate the relationship between age-specific, life-history attributes and the potential rate of population growth. The specific objective is to examine the importance of age at the first reproduction in determining the rate of population growth of the hypothetical animal population over the next 50 years.

12.3 BACKGROUND INFORMATION ON THE SYSTEM-OF-INTEREST

The system-of-interest consists of a hypothetical age-structured animal population in a 1-ha woodlot. Natality and mortality rates are age-specific (Table

12.1). The relative effect of population size on per capita rates of natality and mortality is the same for all five age classes, and it is the same as described for the population in the previous example (Tables 11.1 and 11.2). Currently, there are 71, 20, 6, 2, and 1 individuals in age classes 0 through 4, respectively, and the population is isolated, that is, there is no immigration or emigration.

12.4   MODEL DESCRIPTION

The model represents changes in numbers of animals in age classes 0, 1, 2, 3, and 4 within the population resulting from natality and mortality (Figure 12.1). Both natality and mortality rates are age-specific and density-dependent.

The baseline simulation, which represents a population in which natality C12M is distributed across the age classes as indicated in Table 12.1, runs from year 1 to year 50 using a time unit of 1 year and the equations in Table 12.2. MAX NAT RATE 0 through MAX NATE RATE 4 and MIN MORT RATE 0 through MIN MORT RATE 4 are constants based on values presented in Table 12.1. NAT RATE INDEX and MORT RATE INDEX are graphical functions of POP based on data in Table 11.1 and Table 11.2, respectively. TOT REP (Figure 12.1) represents the gross reproductive rate of the population, which is the number of female offspring a female would have if she survived to the end of the last age class, or, for the baseline simulation, $0.75 + 0.80 + 0.90 + 1.00 + 0.80 = 4.25$ (Table 12.1). ADJ TOTAL REP assigns new values to age-specific natality as a function of AGE FIRST REP such as to maintain TOT REP equal to the baseline values.

Table 12.1   Age-Specific Annual per Capita Natality and Mortality Rates of a Hypothetical Animal Population. Table Entries Represent Maximum Natality Rates in Terms of Number of Individuals Born per Individual in the Indicated Age Class per Year, and Minimum Mortality Rates in Terms of Proportion of Individuals Dying in the Indicated Age Class per Year

Age (years)	Maximum Annual Natality Rate (per Capita)	Minimum Annual Mortality Rate (per Capita)
0	0.75	0.7
1	0.80	0.67
2	0.90	0.67
3	1.00	0.67
4	0.80	1.0

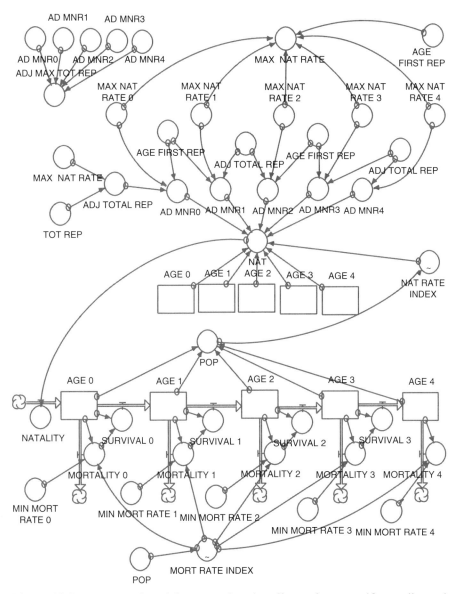

Figure 12.1 Conceptual model representing the effects of age-specific natality and mortality on the dynamics of a hypothetical age-structured animal population.

Table 12.2   Equations (Baseline Conditions) for the Simulation Model Representing Effects of Age-Specific Natality and Mortality on Dynamics of a Hypothetical Age-Structured Animal Population

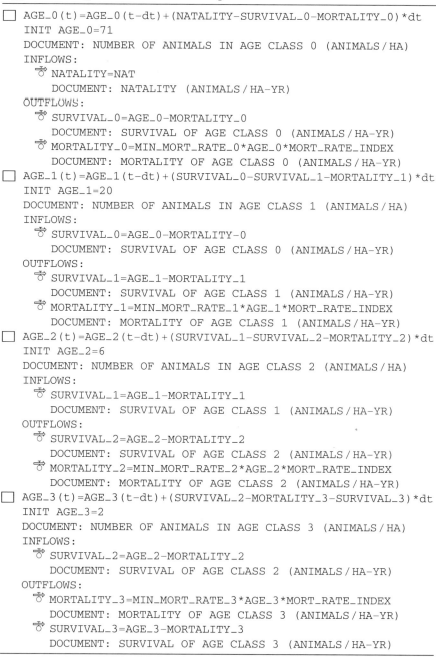

☐ AGE_0(t)=AGE_0(t-dt)+(NATALITY-SURVIVAL_0-MORTALITY_0)*dt
INIT AGE_0=71
DOCUMENT: NUMBER OF ANIMALS IN AGE CLASS 0 (ANIMALS/HA)
INFLOWS:
  NATALITY=NAT
    DOCUMENT: NATALITY (ANIMALS/HA-YR)
OUTFLOWS:
  SURVIVAL_0=AGE_0-MORTALITY_0
    DOCUMENT: SURVIVAL OF AGE CLASS 0 (ANIMALS/HA-YR)
  MORTALITY_0=MIN_MORT_RATE_0*AGE_0*MORT_RATE_INDEX
    DOCUMENT: MORTALITY OF AGE CLASS 0 (ANIMALS/HA-YR)
☐ AGE_1(t)=AGE_1(t-dt)+(SURVIVAL_0-SURVIVAL_1-MORTALITY_1)*dt
INIT AGE_1=20
DOCUMENT: NUMBER OF ANIMALS IN AGE CLASS 1 (ANIMALS/HA)
INFLOWS:
  SURVIVAL_0=AGE_0-MORTALITY-0
    DOCUMENT: SURVIVAL OF AGE CLASS 0 (ANIMALS/HA-YR)
OUTFLOWS:
  SURVIVAL_1=AGE_1-MORTALITY_1
    DOCUMENT: SURVIVAL OF AGE CLASS 1 (ANIMALS/HA-YR)
  MORTALITY_1=MIN_MORT_RATE_1*AGE_1*MORT_RATE_INDEX
    DOCUMENT: MORTALITY OF AGE CLASS 1 (ANIMALS/HA-YR)
☐ AGE_2(t)=AGE_2(t-dt)+(SURVIVAL_1-SURVIVAL_2-MORTALITY_2)*dt
INIT AGE_2=6
DOCUMENT: NUMBER OF ANIMALS IN AGE CLASS 2 (ANIMALS/HA)
INFLOWS:
  SURVIVAL_1=AGE_1-MORTALITY_1
    DOCUMENT: SURVIVAL OF AGE CLASS 1 (ANIMALS/HA-YR)
OUTFLOWS:
  SURVIVAL_2=AGE_2-MORTALITY_2
    DOCUMENT: SURVIVAL OF AGE CLASS 2 (ANIMALS/HA-YR)
  MORTALITY_2=MIN_MORT_RATE_2*AGE_2*MORT_RATE_INDEX
    DOCUMENT: MORTALITY OF AGE CLASS 2 (ANIMALS/HA-YR)
☐ AGE_3(t)=AGE_3(t-dt)+(SURVIVAL_2-MORTALITY_3-SURVIVAL_3)*dt
INIT AGE_3=2
DOCUMENT: NUMBER OF ANIMALS IN AGE CLASS 3 (ANIMALS/HA)
INFLOWS:
  SURVIVAL_2=AGE_2-MORTALITY_2
    DOCUMENT: SURVIVAL OF AGE CLASS 2 (ANIMALS/HA-YR)
OUTFLOWS:
  MORTALITY_3=MIN_MORT_RATE_3*AGE_3*MORT_RATE_INDEX
    DOCUMENT: MORTALITY OF AGE CLASS 3 (ANIMALS/HA-YR)
  SURVIVAL_3=AGE_3-MORTALITY_3
    DOCUMENT: SURVIVAL OF AGE CLASS 3 (ANIMALS/HA-YR)

Table 12.2 (*Continued*)

☐ AGE_4(t)=AGE_4(t-dt)+(SURVIVAL_3-MORTALITY_4)*dt
  INIT AGE_4=1
  DOCUMENT: NUMBER OF ANIMALS IN AGE CLASS 4 (ANIMALS/HA)
  INFLOWS:
    ⇶ SURVIVAL_3=AGE_3-MORTALITY_3
      DOCUMENT: SURVIVAL OF AGE CLASS 3 (ANIMALS/HA-YR)
  OUTFLOWS:
    ⇶ MORTALITY_4=MIN_MORT_RATE_4*AGE_4*MORT_RATE_INDEX
      DOCUMENT: MORTALITY OF AGE CLASS 4 (ANIMAL/HA-YR)
○ ADJ_MAX_TOT_REP=AD_MNR0+AD_MNR1+AD_MNR2+AD_MNR3+AD_MNR4
  DOCUMENT: AUXILIARY VARIABLE-ADJUSTED MAXIMUM NATALITY RATE
  FOR THE POPULATION (ANIMALS/ANIMAL-YR)
○ ADJ_TOTAL_REP=TOT_REP/MAX_NAT_RATE
  DOCUMENT: AUXILIARY VARIABLE-ADJUSTED TOTAL REPRODUCTION
  (ANIMALS/ANIMAL-YR)
○ AD_MNR0=IF(AGE_FIRST_REP>0) THEN 0 ELSE MAX_NAT_RATE_0*ADJ_
  TOTAL_REP
  DOCUMENT: AUXILIARY VARIABLE-ADJUSTED MAXIMUM NATALITY RATE
  FOR AGE CLASS (ANIMALS/ANIMAL-YR)
○ AD_MNR1=IF(AGE_FIRST_REP>1) THEN 0 ELSE MAX_NAT_RATE_1*ADJ_
  TOTAL_REP
  DOCUMENT: AUXILIARY VARIABLE-ADJUSTED MAXIMUM NATALITY RATE
  FOR AGE CLASS (ANIMALS/ANIMAL-YR)
○ AD_MNR2=IF(AGE_FIRST_REP>2) THEN 0 ELSE MAX_NAT_RATE_2*ADJ_
  TOTAL_REP
  DOCUMENT: AUXILIARY VARIABLE-ADJUSTED MAXIMUM NATALITY RATE
  FOR AGE CLASS (ANIMALS/ANIMAL-YR)
○ AD_MNR3=IF(AGE_FIRST_REP>3) THEN 0 ELSE MAX_NAT_RATE_3*ADJ_
  TOTAL_REP
  DOCUMENT: AUXILIARY VARIABLE-ADJUSTED MAXIMUM NATALITY RATE
  FOR AGE CLASS (ANIMALS/ANIMAL-YR)
○ AD_MNR4=MAX_NAT_RATE_4*ADJ_TOTAL_REP
  DOCUMENT: AUXILIARY VARIABLE-ADJUSTED MAXIMUM NATALITY RATE
  FOR AGE CLASS (ANIMALS/ANIMAL-YR)
○ AGE_FIRST_REP=0
  DOCUMENT: CONSTANT-AGE AT FIRST REPRODUCTION (YRS)
○ MAX_NAT_RATE_0=0.75
  DOCUMENT: CONSTANT-MAXIMUM NATALITY RATE OF AGE CLASS 0
  (ANIMALS/ANIMAL-YR)
○ MAX_NAT_RATE_1=0.8
  DOCUMENT: CONSTANT-MAXIMUM NATALITY RATE OF AGE CLASS 1
  (ANIMALS/ANIMAL-YR)
○ MAX_NAT_RATE_2=0.9
  DOCUMENT: CONSTANT-MAXIMUM NATALITY RATE OF AGE CLASS 2
  (ANIMALS/ANIMAL-YR)
○ MAX_NAT_RATE_3=1.0
  DOCUMENT: CONSTANT-MAXIMUM NATALITY RATE OF AGE CLASS 3
  (ANIMALS/ANIMAL-YR)

Table 12.2 (*Continued*)

○ MAX_NAT_RATE_4=0.8
DOCUMENT: CONSTANT-MAXIMUM NATALITY RATE OF AGE CLASS 4
(ANIMALS/ANIMAL-YR)

○ MAX_NAT_RATE=IF(AGE_FIRST_REP=0) THEN
MAX_NAT_RATE_0+MAX_NAT_RATE_1+MAX_NAT_RATE_2+
MAX_NAT_RATE_3+MAX_NAT_RATE_4 ELSE IF(AGE_FIRST_REP=1)THEN
MAX_NAT_RATE_1+MAX_NAT_RATE_2+MAX_NAT_RATE_3+MAX_NAT_RATE_4
ELSE
IF(AGE_FIRST_REP=2) THEN MAX_NAT_RATE_2+MAX_NAT_RATE_3+MAX_
NAT_RATE_4 ELSE
IF(AGE_FIRST_REP=3) THEN MAX_NAT_RATE_3+MAX_NAT_RATE_4 ELSE
MAX_NAT_RATE_4
DOCUMENT: AUXILIARY VARIABLE-MAXIMUM NATALITY RATE OF
POPULATION (ANIMALS/ANIMAL-YR)

○ MIN_MORT_RATE_0=0.7
DOCUMENT: CONSTANT-PROPORTION OF ANIMALS IN AGE CLASS 0
DYING PER YEAR

○ MIN_MORT_RATE_1=0.67
DOCUMENT: CONSTANT-PROPORTION OF ANIMALS IN AGE CLASS 1
DYING PER YEAR

○ MIN_MORT_RATE_2=0.67
DOCUMENT: CONSTANT-PROPORTION OF ANIMALS IN AGE CLASS 2
DYING PER YEAR

○ MIN_MORT_RATE_3=0.67
DOCUMENT: CONSTANT-PROPORTION OF ANIMALS IN AGE CLASS 3
DYING PER YEAR

○ MIN_MORT_RATE_4=1.0
DOCUMENT: CONSTANT-PROPORTION OF ANIMALS IN AGE CLASS 4
DYING PER YEAR

○ NAT=(AD_MNR0*AGE_0+AD_MNR1*AGE_1+AD_MNR2*AGE_2+AD_MNR3*
AGE_3+AD_MNR4*AGE_4)*NAT_RATE_INDEX
DOCUMENT: AUXILIARY VARIABLE-NATALITY (ANIMALS/HA-YR)

○ POP=AGE_0+AGE_1+AGE_2+AGE_3+AGE_4
DOCUMENT: AUXILIARY VARIABLE-POPULATION SIZE (ANIMALS/HA)

○ TOT_REP=4.25
DOCUMENT: TOTAL REPRODUCTION (ANIMALS/ANIMAL-YR)

⊘MORT_RATE_INDEX=GRAPH(POP)
(200, 1.00), (205, 1.01), (210, 1.02), (215, 1.03), (220,
1.04), (225, 1.05), (230, 1.06), (235, 107), (240, 1.08),
(245, 1.09), (250, 1.10)
DOCUMENT: AUXILIARY VARIABLE-PROPORTIONAL INCREASE IN
MORTALITY RATE AS POPULATION SIZE INCREASES (UNITLESS)

⊘NAT_RATE_INDEX=GRAPH(POP)
(150, 1.00), (160, 0.99), (170, 0.98), (180, 0.97), (190,
0.96), (200, 0.95), (210, 0.94), (220, 0.93), (230, 0.92),
(240, 0.91), (250, 0.9)
DOCUMENT: AUXILIARY VARIABLE-PROPORTIONAL DECREASE IN
NATALITY RATE AS POPULATION SIZE INCREASES (UNITLESS)

12.5 MODEL USE

To examine the importance of age at the first reproduction in determining the rate of population growth of the hypothetical animal population over the next 50 years, our experimental design consists of a 50-year baseline simulation using the age-specific natality and mortality rates in Table 12.1 and four series of 50-year simulations in which we postpone age at the first reproduction from age class 0 to age classes 1, 2, 3, and 4, respectively. Within each series, we begin with natality proportionally distributed across the reproductive age classes such as to maintain the baseline gross reproductive rate (TOT REP). Then we determine how much TOT REP would need to increase to maintain the baseline growth rate of the population when the age of first reproduction is postponed sequentially from age 0 to age 4.

Simulation results indicate that with a TOT REP of 4.25 and natality distributed across all five age classes, the population grows to a carrying capacity of almost 230 animals in slightly less than 15 years (Figure 12.2a). When the age at first reproduction is postponed until age class 1, the population decreases exponentially with a TOT REP of 4.25, decreases slightly with a TOT REP of 9, and achieves the baseline rate of growth with a TOT REP between 11 and 12 (Figure 12.2b). When age at the first reproduction is postponed until age class 2, 3, and 4, TOT REPS near 30, 60, and 110, respectively, are required to achieve a growth rate approximately equal to the baseline (Figures 12.2c, 12.2d, 12.2e). Oscillations seen in Figures 12.2d and 12.2e reflect the absence of reproductively active animals in the population while newly recruited cohorts pass through the prereproductive age classes. Thus, simulation results support the importance of age at the first reproduction in determining the rate of population growth.

We encourage readers to use the model to explore further the relationship between age-specific, life-history attributes and the potential rate of population growth. A variety of relevant situations can be simulated by changing values of MAX NAT RATE 0 through MAX NAT RATE 4, NAT RATE INDEX, and MORT RATE INDEX, as well as AGE FIRST REP and TOT REP.

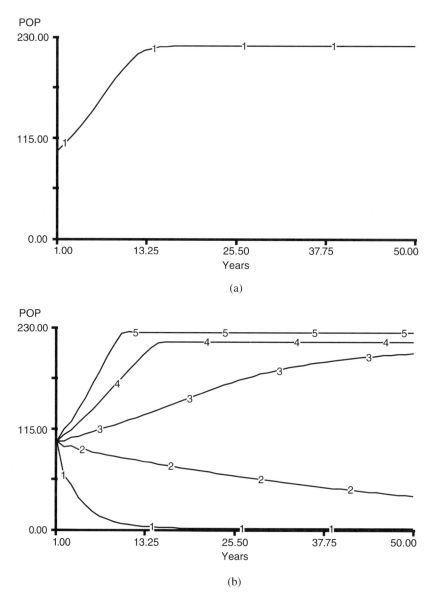

Figure 12.2 Results of sixteen 50-year simulations representing the population dynamics (animals/ha) with (a) age at first reproduction (AFR) equal to 0 (AFR = 0) and total reproduction (TR) equal to 4.25 (TR = 4.25) (baseline); (b) AFR = 1 and (1) TR = 4.25, (2) TR = 9, (3) TR = 10, (4) TR = 11, and (5) TR = 12; (c) AFR = 2 and (1) TR = 4.25, (2) TR = 12, (3) TR = 20, (4) TR = 25, and (5) TR = 30; (d) AFR = 3 and (1) TR = 4.25, (2) TR = 30, (3) TR = 50, (4) TR = 55, and (5) TR = 60; and (e) AFR = 4 and (1) TR = 4.25, (2) TR = 60, (3) TR = 80, (4) TR = 100, and (5) TR = 110.

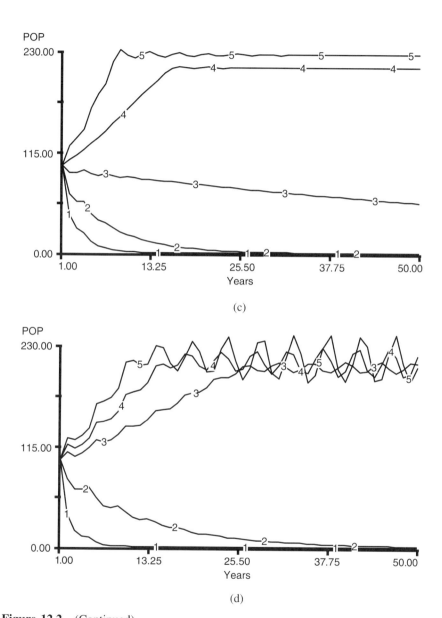

(c)

(d)

Figure 12.2 (Continued).

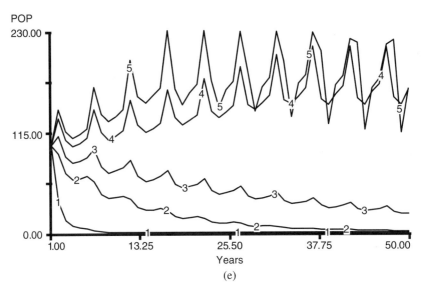

Figure 12.2 (Continued).

CHAPTER 13

INTERSPECIFIC COMPETITION: EFFECTS OF FLUCTUATING ENVIRONMENTAL CONDITIONS

13.1 INTRODUCTION

Interspecific competition occurs when two or more species exploit the same limited resource. The theory of competitive exclusion states that under constant environmental conditions when two species with identical niches compete, the superior competitor will exclude the inferior competitor from the community. However, in a variable environment, competitive superiority may shift from one species to another in such a manner that competing species may coexist indefinitely within the same community. Even under constant environmental conditions, competing species can coexist if prevailing conditions allow a sufficient degree of niche differentiation.

13.2 MODEL OBJECTIVES

The general objective is to simulate population dynamics of two hypothetical competing animal species with each species having the competitive advantage under different environmental conditions. Specific objectives are to predict the effect of (1) prolonged periods of high and low precipitation and (2) periodically fluctuating precipitation levels on the outcome of interspecific competition between these two populations.

13.3 BACKGROUND INFORMATION ON THE SYSTEM-OF-INTEREST

The system-of-interest consists of populations of two hypothetical competing animal species in a 1-ha woodlot. Current population size of each species is

100 animals and the populations are isolated, that is, there is no immigration or emigration. Each population has a maximum annual per capita natality rate of 0.75 (75 individuals born per year per 100 individuals in the population) and a minimum annual per capita mortality rate of 0.70 (70 individuals dying per year per 100 individuals in the population). Relationships of per capita natality and mortality rates to population size in the absence of interspecific competition are the same as those presented in Table 11.1 and Table 11.2, respectively.

Interspecific competition increases per capita mortality of one competing species as a function of population size of the other competing species in a manner similar to the density-dependent effect of intraspecific competition on mortality rates shown in Table 11.2. That is, as the number of individuals in population A increases, this adds to the effective size of population B in terms of calculating per capita mortality rate, and vice versa. However, species A has the competitive advantage during relatively dry years and species B during relatively wet years. Competition coefficients representing the effect of annual precipitation on the relative competitive advantage are presented in Table 13.1. For example, when the annual precipitation is 50 cm, the relative negative impact of an individual of population A on the mortality rate of population B is 1.25 times as great as the relative impact of another individual of population B. Thus, the competition coefficient is 1.25 and the effective size of population B is calculated as (number of individuals in population B) + 1.25(number of individuals in population A). Likewise, when the annual precipitation is 120 cm, the relative negative impact of an individual of population B on the mortality rate of population A is 0.875 times as great as the relative impact of another individual of population A.

Table 13.1   Competition Coefficients Representing Relative Negative Impact of One Interspecific Competitor in Terms of the Negative Impact of One Conspecific Competitor as a Function of Annual Precipitation

Annual Precipitation (cm)	Competition Coefficients	
	Impact of A on B	Impact of B on A
50	1.250	0.000
60	1.125	0.125
70	1.000	0.250
80	0.875	0.375
90	0.750	0.500
100	0.625	0.625
110	0.500	0.750
120	0.375	0.875
130	0.250	1.000
140	0.125	1.125
150	0.000	1.250

13.4 MODEL DESCRIPTION

The model represents the effect of interspecific competition on the population dynamics of two competing species (Figure 13.1). The changes in numbers of animals in each population result from natality and mortality, with both natality and mortality rates being density-dependent. Mortality also is affected by the density of the competing population and the relative competitive advantage, which depends on the amount of annual precipitation.

The baseline simulation, which represents the interspecific competition C13MOD01 with the annual precipitation held constant at 100 cm, runs from year 1 to year 100 using a time unit of 1 year and the equations in Table 13.2. Annual precipitation (PRECIP) can be represented as a constant by specifying the desired number of cm received annually in PPT CONSTANT. Or, annual precipitation can be represented as a sine wave by setting PPT CONSTANT to 999 and specifying the amplitude (PPT AMPLITUDE) and period (PPT PERIOD) of the sine wave. COMP COEF A and COMP COEF B are graphical functions of PRECIP based on data in Table 13.1. NAT RATE INDEX A and NAT RATE INDEX B are graphical functions of POP A and POP B, respectively, based on data in Table 11.1. MORT RATE INDEX A and MORT RATE INDEX B are graphical functions of EFF POP A and EFF POP B, respectively, based on data in Table 11.2 (calculating mortality rate based on the effective population size rather than the population size). NATALITY A and NATALITY B are set equal to zero when POP A and POP B, respectively, fall below 1.0 animal/ha.

13.5 MODEL USE

To predict the effect of prolonged periods of high and low precipitation on the outcome of interspecific competition between the two populations, we run eleven 100-year simulations in which annual precipitation is held constant at 100 cm (baseline), at 90, 80, 70, 60, and 50 cm (favoring population A), and at 110, 120, 130, 140, and 150 cm (favoring population B). The results indicate that the two populations reach the same stable equilibrium under 100 cm of annual precipitation as they have the same competitive effect on each other (Figure 13.2a). As annual precipitation decreases from 100 to 50 cm, population A becomes more abundant and population B decreases until competitive exclusion occurs when annual precipitation is 50 cm (Figure 13.2b). As annual precipitation increases from 100 to 150 cm, population B excludes population A when annual precipitation is 150 cm (Figure 13.2c). Additional simulations indicate that precipitation thresholds are at 53 and 147 cm, with competitive exclusion occurring after 86 years in each case.

To predict the effect of periodically fluctuating precipitation levels on the outcome of interspecific competition between the two populations, we run four 500-year simulations in which annual precipitation fluctuates between 50 and 150 cm as a sine wave with periods of 10, 100, 200, and 250 years, respectively. The results indicate that the two populations reach a dynamic

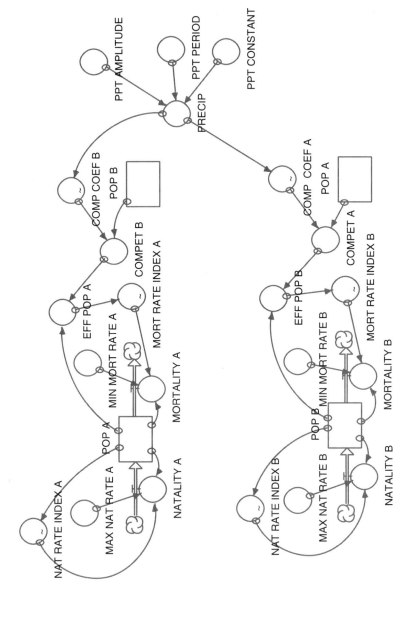

Figure 13.1 Conceptual model representing the population dynamics of two hypothetical species resulting from interspecific competition under fluctuating environmental conditions.

Table 13.2 Equations (Baseline Conditions) for the Simulation Model Representing Population Dynamics of Two Hypothetical Species Resulting from Interspecific Competition

```
☐ POP_A(t)=POP-A(t-dt)+(NATALITY_A-MORTALITY_A)*dt
  INIT POP_A=100
  DOCUMENT: SIZE OF POPULATION A (ANIMALS/HA)
  INFLOWS:
    ⇗ NATALITY_A=IF(POP_A<1.0) THEN 0 ELSE
      MAX_NAT_RATE_A*POP_A*NAT_RATE_INDEX_A
      DOCUMENT: NATALITY OF POPULATION A (ANIMALS/HA-YR)
  OUTFLOWS:
    ⇗ MORTALITY_A=MIN_MORT_RATE_A*POP_A*MORT_RATE_INDEX_A
      DOCUMENT: MORTALITY OF POPULATION A (ANIMALS/HA-YR)
☐ POP_B(t)=POP_B(t-dt)+(NATALITY_B-MORTALITY_B)*dt
  INIT POP_B=100
  DOCUMENT: SIZE OF POPULATION B (ANIMALS/HA)
  INFLOWS:
    ⇗ NATALITY_B=IF(POP_B<1.0) THEN 0 ELSE
      MAX_NAT_RATE_B*POP_B*NAT_RATE_INDEX_B
      DOCUMENT: NATALITY OF POPULATION B (ANIMALS/HA-YR)
  OUTFLOWS:
    ⇗ MORTALITY_B=MIN_MORT_RATE_B*POP_B*MORT_RATE_INDEX_B
      DOCUMENT: MORTALITY OF POPULATION B (ANIMALS/HA-YR)
○ COMPET_A=COMP_COEF_A*POP_A
  DOCUMENT: AUXILIARY VARIABLE-NUMBER OF ANIMALS IN
  POPULATION A REPRESENTED IN TERMS OF ''POPULATION B
  EQUIVALENTS''
○ COMPET_B=COMP_COEF_B*POP_B
  DOCUMENT: AUXILIARY VARIABLE-NUMBER OF ANIMALS OF
  POPULATION B REPRESENTED IN TERMS OF ''POPULATION A
  EQUIVALENTS''
○ EFF_POP_A=POP_A+COMPET_B
  DOCUMENT: AUXILIARY VARIABLE-EFFECTIVE SIZE OF POPULATION A
  (ANIMALS/HA)
○ EFF_POP_B=POP_B+COMPET_A
  DOCUMENT: AUXILIARY VARIABLE-EFFECTIVE SIZE OF POPULATION B
  (ANIMALS/HA)
○ MAX_NAT_RATE_A=0.75
  DOCUMENT: CONSTANT-MAXIMUM NATALITY RATE OF POPULATION A
  (ANIMALS/ANIMAL-YR)
○ MAX_NAT_RATE_B=0.75
  DOCUMENT: CONSTANT-MAXIMUM NATALITY RATE OF POPULATION B
  (ANIMALS/ANIMAL-YR)
○ MIN_MORT_RATE_A=0.7
  DOCUMENT: CONSTANT-MINIMUM MORTALITY RATE OF POPULATION A
  (PROPORTION OF POPULATION A DYING PER YR)
```

Table 13.2 *(Continued)*

○ MIN_MORT_RATE_B=0.7
  DOCUMENT: CONSTANT-MINIMUM MORTALITY RATE OF POPULATION B
  (PROPORTION OF POPULATION B DYING PER YR)

○ PPT_AMPLITUDE=100
  DOCUMENT: DRIVING VARIABLE-AMPLITUDE OF A SINE WAVE
  REPRESENTING PRECIPITATION (CM/YR)-(ONLY FUNCTIONS WHEN
  THE VARIABLE ''PPT CONSTANT'' EQUALS 999)

○ PPT_CONSTANT=100
  DOCUMENT: CONSTANT-CONSTANT PRECIPITATION (CM/YR) (A VALUE
  OF 999 CHANGES REPRESENTATION OF PRECIPITATION TO A SINE
  WAVE CONTROLLED BY THE CONSTANTS ''PPT AMPLITUDE'' AND
  ''PPT PERIOD'')

○ PPT_PERIOD=10
  DOCUMENT: CONSTANT-PERIOD OF A SINE WAVE REPRESENTING
  PRECIPITATION (CM/YR)-(ONLY FUNCTIONS WHEN THE CONSTANT
  ''PPT CONSTANT'' EQUALS 999)

○ PRECIP=IF(PPT_CONSTANT=999) THEN SINWAVE(50,PPT_
  PERIOD)+PPT_AMPLITUDE ELSE PPT_CONSTANT
  DOCUMENT: AUXILIARY VARIABLE-PRECIPITATION (CM/YR)

⊘COMP_COEF_B=GRAPH(PRECIP)
  (50.0, 0.00), (60.0, 0.125), (70.0, 0.25), (80.0, 0.375),
  (90.0, 0.5), (100, 0.625), (110, 0.75), (120, 0.875), (130,
  1.00), (140, 1.13), (150, 1.25)
  DOCUMENT: AUXILIARY VARIABLE-COMPETITION COEFFICIENT
  REPRESENTING THE NEGATIVE EFFECT OF POPULATION B ON
  MORTALITY RATE OF POPULATION A

⊘COMP_COEF_A=GRAPH(PRECIP)
  (50.0, 1.25), (60.0, 1.13), (70.0, 1.00), (80.0, 0.875),
  (90.0, 0.75), (100, 0.625), (110, 0.5), (120, 0.375), (130,
  0.25), (140, 0.125), (150, 0.00)
  DOCUMENT: AUXILIARY VARIABLE-COMPETITION COEFFICIENT
  REPRESENTING THE NEGATIVE EFFECT OF POPULATION A ON
  MORTALITY RATE OF POPULATION B

---

equilibrium when annual precipitation fluctuates with periods between 10 and 200 years, but with a period of 250 years, population A is competitively excluded by population B (Figure 13.3). Population B has the early competitive advantage in all simulations because the annual precipitation first increases from 100 to 150 cm before subsequently decreasing from 150 to 50 cm. With a period of 250 years, population A is excluded by population B before the annual precipitation decreases sufficiently to give population A the competitive advantage. With periods of 200 and 100 years, population A survives, but cannot completely recover from the impact of the early competitive advantage experienced by population B. With a period of 10 years, population A not only recovers from the early disadvantage, but actually gains

Table 13.2 (*Continued*)

⊘MORT_RATE_INDEX_A=GRAPH(EFF_POP_A)
  (200, 1.00), (205, 1.01), (210, 1.02), (215, 1.03), (220,
  1.04), (225, 1.05), (230, 1.06), (235, 1.07), (240, 1.08),
  (245, 1.09), (250, 1.10), (255, 1.15), (260, 1.20), (265,
  1.25), (270, 1.30), (275, 1.35), (280, 1.40), (285, 1.40),
  (290, 1.40), (295, 1.40), (300, 1.40)
  DOCUMENT: AUXILIARY VARIABLE-PROPORTIONAL INCREASE IN
  MORTALITY RATE AS EFFECTIVE SIZE OF POPULATION A INCREASES
  (UNITLESS)
⊘MORT_RATE_INDEX_B=GRAPH(EFF_POP_B)
  (200, 1.00), (205, 1.01), (210, 1.02), (215, 1.03), (220,
  1.04), (225, 1.05), (230, 1.06), (235, 1.07), (240, 1.08),
  (245, 1.09), (250, 1.10), (255, 1.15), (260, 1.20), (265,
  1.25), (270, 1.30), (275, 1.35), (280, 1.40), (285, 1.40),
  (290, 1.40), (295, 1.40), (300, 1.40)
  DOCUMENT: AUXILIARY VARIABLE-PROPORTIONAL INCREASE IN
  MORTALITY RATE AS EFFECTIVE SIZE OF POPULATION B INCREASES
  (UNITLESS)
⊘NAT_RATE_INDEX_A=GRAPH(POP_A)
  (150, 1.00), (160, 0.99), (170, 0.98), (180, 0.97), (190,
  0.96), (200, 0.95), (210, 0.94), (220, 0.93), (230, 0.92),
  (240, 0.91), (250, 0.9)
  DOCUMENT: AUXILIARY VARIABLE-PROPORTIONAL DECREASE IN
  NATALITY RATE AS SIZE OF POPULATION A INCREASES (UNITLESS)
⊘NAT_RATE_INDEX_B=GRAPH(POP_B)
  (150, 1.00), (160, 0.99), (170, 0.98), (180, 0.97), (190,
  0.96), (200, 0.95), (210, 0.94), (220, 0.93), (230, 0.92),
  (240, 0.91), (250, 0.9)
  DOCUMENT: AUXILIARY VARIABLE-PROPORTIONAL DECREASE IN
  NATALITY RATE AS SIZE OF POPULATION B INCREASES (UNITLESS)

the long-term competitive advantage. This results because the net negative effect of intra- and interspecific competition on population B during the low phase of the first precipitation cycle is greater than the net negative impact of competition on population A during the high phase of the first cycle because there are more animals (population A plus population B) during the low phase.

Regarding the effect of environmental conditions on the outcome of interspecific competition, simulation results confirm that even under constant conditions, competing species can coexist if prevailing conditions allow a sufficient reduction in the intensity of competition, that is, a sufficient degree of niche segregation. In a variable environment, competitive superiority may shift from one species to another in such a manner that competing species may coexist indefinitely within the same community.

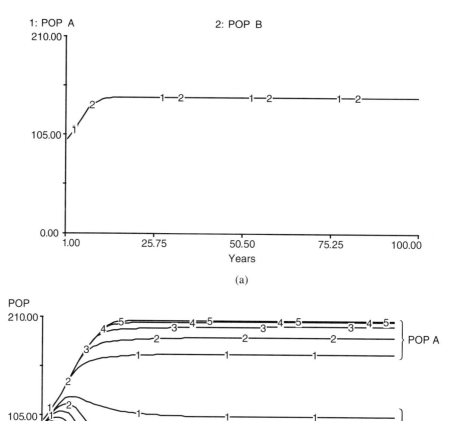

Figure 13.2 Results of eleven 100-year simulations representing interspecific competition (population levels shown as animals/ha) (a) favoring neither population with annual precipitation held constant at 100 cm; (b) favoring population A with precipitation constant at (1) 90 cm, (2) 80 cm, (3) 70 cm, (4) 60 cm, and (5) 50 cm; and (c) favoring population B with precipitation constant at (1) 110 cm, (2) 120 cm, (3) 130 cm, (4) 140 cm, and (5) 150 cm.

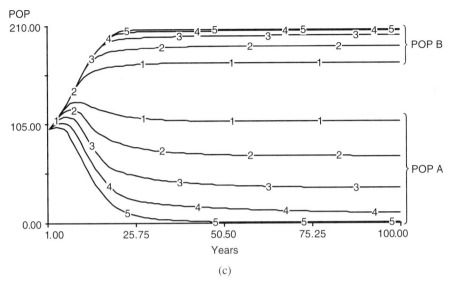

(c)

Figure 13.2 (Continued).

We encourage readers to explore further the effect of fluctuating environmental conditions on the outcome of interspecific competition. For example, one might explore the effect of scenarios in which precipitation initially decreases rather than increases, thus giving population A rather than population B the initial competitive advantage. A variety of relevant situations can be simulated by changing values of PPT AMPLITUDE and PPT PERIOD, and graphs representing COMP COEF A and COMP COEF B.

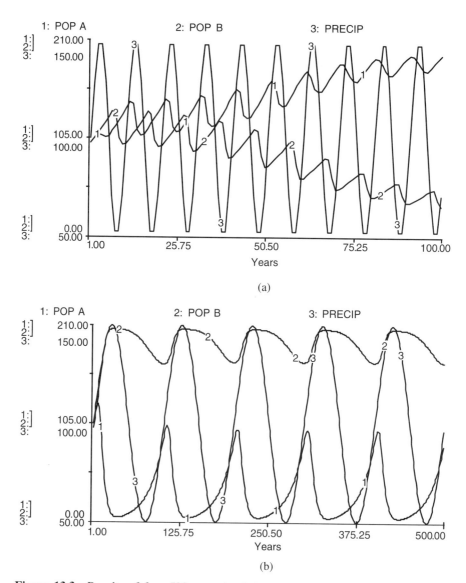

Figure 13.3 Results of four 500-year simulations representing interspecific competition (population levels shown as animals/ha) with annual precipitation fluctuating between 50 and 150 cm as a sine wave with periods of (a) 10, (b) 100, (c) 200, and (d) 250 years.

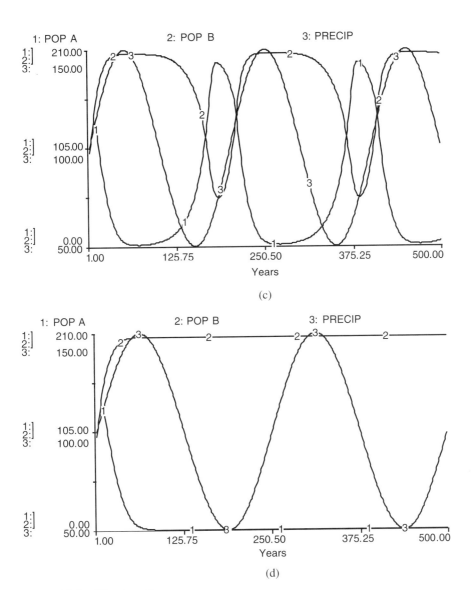

Figure 13.3 (Continued).

CHAPTER 14

COMMUNITY STRUCTURE: EFFECTS OF COMPETITION AND FREQUENCY OF ECOLOGICAL DISTURBANCE

14.1 INTRODUCTION

Among the characteristics theoretically attributed to K-selected species are relatively low reproductive potential and superior competitive ability, whereas r-selected species are characterized as having relatively high reproductive potential and inferior competitive ability. Species composition of a community subject to periodic disturbances (events causing high mortality) is determined by the interaction of interspecific competition, the frequency of disturbance, and the reproductive potential of resident species. Theoretically, in a community containing a mixture of r- and K-selected species, the highest species diversity occurs at intermediate frequencies of disturbance: At low frequencies, r-selected species are competitively excluded, and at high frequencies, K-selected species cannot recover between disturbances.

14.2 MODEL OBJECTIVES

The general objective is to simulate the relationship among interspecific competition, the frequency of disturbance, and the reproductive potential of resident species in determining community structure. The specific objective is to predict the number and type of species (r- versus K-selected) present within the community over 500-year periods with different frequencies of disturbance.

14.3 BACKGROUND INFORMATION ON THE SYSTEM-OF-INTEREST

The system-of-interest consists of a hypothetical ecological community comprised of five animal species, two K-selected and three r-selected, in a 1-ha woodlot. Current population size of each species is 100 animals. The two K-selected species (D and F) have maximum annual per capita natality rates of 0.75 and 0.74, respectively, and both have minimum annual per capita mortality rates of 0.70. The three r-selected species (C, E, and G) also have minimum annual per capita mortality rates of 0.70, but have maximum annual per capita natality rates of 0.85, 0.90, and 0.95, respectively. Relationships of per capita natality and mortality rates to population size for each species are the same as those presented in Tables 11.1 and 11.2. Interspecific competition occurs between populations C and D, E and F, and G and F. In each case, the effect of the superior K-selected competitor on the per capita mortality rate of the inferior r-selected competitor is represented as a competition coefficient affecting effective population size of the inferior competitor in the same manner described in Section 13.3. Competition coefficients representing negative impacts of species D on species C, species F on species E, and species F on species G are 1.28, 4.00, and 3.00, respectively. There is no negative impact of the inferior competitors on the superior competitors. The community is subject to periodic disturbances that cause 90% mortality of all young-of-the-year individuals of both r- and K-selected species but do not affect older individuals.

14.4   MODEL DESCRIPTION

The model represents the effect of interspecific competition and periodic disturbances on population dynamics of five competing species, two K-selected and three r-selected, and the resulting changes in community structure (Figure 14.1). Changes in numbers of animals in each population result from density-dependent natality and mortality. Mortality of r-selected populations also is affected by the density of the competing K-selected populations and the relative competive advantage. Natality, or more strictly speaking, recruitment of the young-of-the-year, is also affected by periodic disturbances to the community.

The baseline simulation, which represents interspecific competition in the absence of disturbances, runs from year 1 to year 500, using a time unit of 1 year and the equations in Table 14.1. FREQ DIST represents the number of years between disturbances and DISTURB is an index that represents the proportional reduction in natality (number of recruits) during years when a disturbance occurs (DISTURB = 1.0 during years without a disturbance). NAT RATE INDEX C through NAT RATE INDEX G are graphical functions of POP C through POP G, respectively, based on data in Table 11.1. MORT RATE INDEX D and MORT RATE INDEX F are graphical functions of POP D and POP F, respectively, and MORT RATE INDEX C, MORT RATE INDEX E, and MORT RATE INDEX G are graphical functions of EFF POP C, EFF POP E, and EFF POP G, respectively, based on data in Table 11.2 (calculating mortality rate based on effective population size rather than population size, as explained in Section

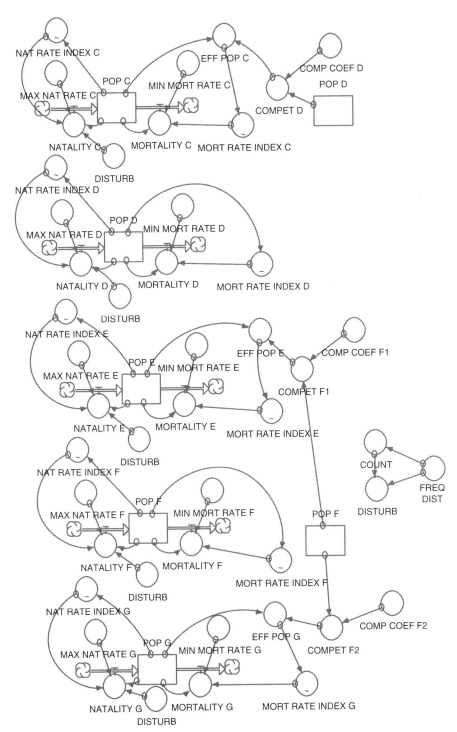

Figure 14.1 Conceptual model representing the effects of competition and frequency of ecological disturbance on community structure.

TABLE 14.1 **Equations (Baseline Conditions) for the Simulation Model Representing Effects of Competition and Frequency of Ecological Disturbance on Community Structure**

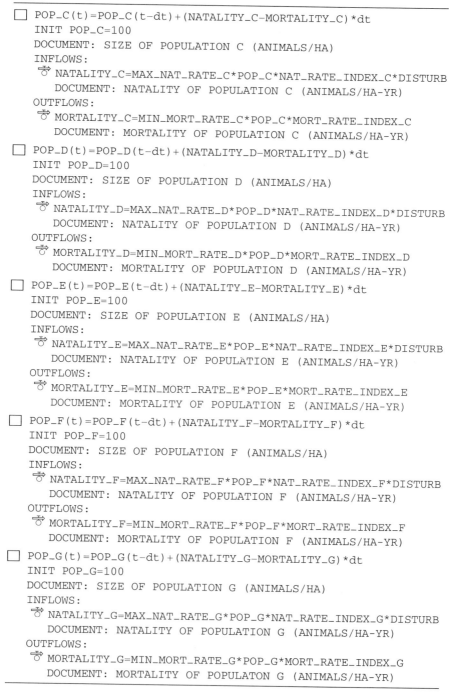

```
☐ POP_C(t)=POP_C(t-dt)+(NATALITY_C-MORTALITY_C)*dt
  INIT POP_C=100
  DOCUMENT: SIZE OF POPULATION C (ANIMALS/HA)
  INFLOWS:
   ⇄ NATALITY_C=MAX_NAT_RATE_C*POP_C*NAT_RATE_INDEX_C*DISTURB
     DOCUMENT: NATALITY OF POPULATION C (ANIMALS/HA-YR)
  OUTFLOWS:
   ⇄ MORTALITY_C=MIN_MORT_RATE_C*POP_C*MORT_RATE_INDEX_C
     DOCUMENT: MORTALITY OF POPULATION C (ANIMALS/HA-YR)
☐ POP_D(t)=POP_D(t-dt)+(NATALITY_D-MORTALITY_D)*dt
  INIT POP_D=100
  DOCUMENT: SIZE OF POPULATION D (ANIMALS/HA)
  INFLOWS:
   ⇄ NATALITY_D=MAX_NAT_RATE_D*POP_D*NAT_RATE_INDEX_D*DISTURB
     DOCUMENT: NATALITY OF POPULATION D (ANIMALS/HA-YR)
  OUTFLOWS:
   ⇄ MORTALITY_D=MIN_MORT_RATE_D*POP_D*MORT_RATE_INDEX_D
     DOCUMENT: MORTALITY OF POPULATION D (ANIMALS/HA-YR)
☐ POP_E(t)=POP_E(t-dt)+(NATALITY_E-MORTALITY_E)*dt
  INIT POP_E=100
  DOCUMENT: SIZE OF POPULATION E (ANIMALS/HA)
  INFLOWS:
   ⇄ NATALITY_E=MAX_NAT_RATE_E*POP_E*NAT_RATE_INDEX_E*DISTURB
     DOCUMENT: NATALITY OF POPULATION E (ANIMALS/HA-YR)
  OUTFLOWS:
   ⇄ MORTALITY_E=MIN_MORT_RATE_E*POP_E*MORT_RATE_INDEX_E
     DOCUMENT: MORTALITY OF POPULATION E (ANIMALS/HA-YR)
☐ POP_F(t)=POP_F(t-dt)+(NATALITY_F-MORTALITY_F)*dt
  INIT POP_F=100
  DOCUMENT: SIZE OF POPULATION F (ANIMALS/HA)
  INFLOWS:
   ⇄ NATALITY_F=MAX_NAT_RATE_F*POP_F*NAT_RATE_INDEX_F*DISTURB
     DOCUMENT: NATALITY OF POPULATION F (ANIMALS/HA-YR)
  OUTFLOWS:
   ⇄ MORTALITY_F=MIN_MORT_RATE_F*POP_F*MORT_RATE_INDEX_F
     DOCUMENT: MORTALITY OF POPULATION F (ANIMALS/HA-YR)
☐ POP_G(t)=POP_G(t-dt)+(NATALITY_G-MORTALITY_G)*dt
  INIT POP_G=100
  DOCUMENT: SIZE OF POPULATION G (ANIMALS/HA)
  INFLOWS:
   ⇄ NATALITY_G=MAX_NAT_RATE_G*POP_G*NAT_RATE_INDEX_G*DISTURB
     DOCUMENT: NATALITY OF POPULATION G (ANIMALS/HA-YR)
  OUTFLOWS:
   ⇄ MORTALITY_G=MIN_MORT_RATE_G*POP_G*MORT_RATE_INDEX_G
     DOCUMENT: MORTALITY OF POPULATON G (ANIMALS/HA-YR)
```

TABLE 14.1 (*Continued*)

○ COMPET_D=COMP_COEF_D*POP_D
  DOCUMENT: AUXILIARY VARIABLE-NUMBER OF ANIMALS OF
  POPULATION D REPRESENTED IN TERMS OF ''POPULATION C
  EQUIVALENTS''

○ COMPET_F1=COMP_COEF_F1*POP_F
  DOCUMENT: AUXILIARY VARIABLE-NUMBER OF ANIMALS OF
  POPULATION F REPRESENTED IN TERMS OF ''POPULATION E
  EQUIVALENTS''

○ COMPET_F2=COMP_COEF_F2*POP_F
  DOCUMENT: AUXILIARY VARIABLE-NUMBER OF ANIMALS OF
  POPULATION F REPRESENTED IN TERMS OF ''POPULATION G
  EQUIVALENTS''

○ COMP_COEF_D=1.28
  DOCUMENT: CONSTANT-COMPETITION COEFFICIENT REPRESENTING THE
  NEGATIVE EFFECT OF POPULATION D ON MORTALITY RATE OF
  POPULATION C

○ COMP_COEF_F1=4
  DOCUMENT: CONSTANT-COMPETITION COEFFICIENT REPRESENTING THE
  NEGATIVE EFFECT OF POPULATION F ON MORTALITY RATE OF
  POPULATION E

○ COMP_COEF_F2=3
  DOCUMENT: CONSTANT-COMPETITION COEFFICIENT REPRESENTING THE
  NEGATIVE EFFECT OF POPULATION F ON MORTALITY RATE OF
  POPULATION G

○ COUNT=COUNTER(1,FREQ_DIST+1)
  DOCUMENT: AUXILIARY VARIABLE-COUNTER DETERMINING TIMING OF
  DISTURBANCES

○ DISTURB=IF(COUNT=FREQ_DIST)
  THEN 0.1 ELSE 1
  DOCUMENT: AUXILIARY VARIABLE-DISTURBANCE-INDEX THAT REDUCES
  NATALITY (REPRESENTING DEATH OF YOUNG-OF-THE-YEAR) DURING
  YEARS WHEN A DISTURBANCE OCCURS (UNITLESS)

○ EFF_POP_C=POP_C+COMPET_D
  DOCUMENT: AUXILIARY VARIABLE-EFFECTIVE SIZE OF POPULATION C
  (ANIMALS/HA)

○ EFF_POP_E=POP_E+COMPET_F1
  DOCUMENT: AUXILIARY VARIABLE-EFFECTIVE SIZE OF POPULATION E
  (ANIMALS/HA)

○ EFF_POP_G=POP_G+COMPET_F2
  DOCUMENT: AUXILIARY VARIABLE-EFFECTIVE SIZE OF POPULATION G
  (ANIMALS/HA)

○ FREQ_DIST=999
  DOCUMENT: CONSTANT-FREQUENCY OF DISTURBANCE (NUMBER OF
  YEARS BETWEEN DISTURBANCES)

○ MAX_NAT_RATE_C=0.85
  DOCUMENT: CONSTANT-MAXIMUM NATALITY RATE OF POPULATION C
  (ANIMALS/ANIMAL-YR)

TABLE 14.1 *(Continued)*

○ MAX_NAT_RATE_D=0.75
DOCUMENT: CONSTANT-MAXIMUM NATALITY RATE OF POPULATION D
(ANIMALS/ANIMAL-YR)

○ MAX_NAT_RATE_E=0.90
DOCUMENT: CONSTANT-MAXIMUM NATALITY RATE OF POPULATION E
(ANIMALS/ANIMAL-YR)

○ MAX_NAT_RATE_F=0.74
DOCUMENT: CONSTANT-MAXIMUM NATALITY RATE OF POPULATION F
(ANIMALS/ANIMAL-YR)

○ MAX_NAT_RATE_G=0.95
DOCUMENT: CONSTANT-MAXIMUM NATALITY RATE OF POPULATION G
(ANIMALS/ANIMAL-YR)

○ MIN_MORT_RATE_C=0.7
DOCUMENT: CONSTANT-MINIMUM MORTALITY RATE OF POPULATION C
(PROPORTION OF POPULATION DYING PER YEAR)

○ MIN_MORT_RATE_D=0.7
DOCUMENT: CONSTANT-MINIMUM MORTALITY RATE OF POPULATION D
(PROPORTION OF POPULATION DYING PER YEAR)

○ MIN_MORT_RATE_E=0.7
DOCUMENT: CONSTANT-MINIMUM MORTALITY RATE OF POPULATION E
(PROPORTION OF POPULATION DYING PER YEAR)

○ MIN_MORT_RATE_F=0.7
DOCUMENT: CONSTANT-MINIMUM MORTALITY RATE OF POPULATION F
(PROPORTION OF POPULATION DYING PER YEAR)

○ MIN_MORT_RATE_G=0.7
DOCUMENT: CONSTANT-MINIMUM MORTALITY RATE OF POPULATION G
(PROPORTION OF POPULATION DYING PER YEAR)

⊘MORT_RATE_INDEX_C=GRAPH(EFF_POP_C)
(200, 1.00), (205, 1.01), (210, 1.02), (215, 1.03), (220,
1.04), (225, 1.05), (230, 1.06), (235, 1.07), (240, 1.08),
(245, 1.09), (250, 1.10), (255, 1.15), (260, 1.20), (265,
1.25), (270, 1.30), (275, 1.35), (280, 1.40), (285, 1.40),
(290, 1.40), (295, 1.40), (300, 1.40)
DOCUMENT: AUXILIARY VARIABLE-PROPORTIONAL INCREASE IN
MORTALITY RATE AS EFFECTIVE SIZE OF POPULATION C INCREASES
(UNITLESS)

⊘MORT_RATE_INDEX_D=GRAPH(POP_D)
(200, 1.00), (205, 1.01), (210, 1.02), (215, 1.03), (220,
1.04), (225, 1.05), (230, 1.06), (235, 1.07), (240, 1.08),
(245, 1.09), (250, 1.10), (255, 1.15), (260, 1.20), (265,
1.25), (270, 1.30), (275, 1.35), (280, 1.40), (285, 1.40),
(290, 1.40), (295, 1.40), (300, 1.40)
DOCUMENT: AUXILIARY VARIABLE-PROPORTIONAL INCREASE IN
MORTALITY RATE AS EFFECTIVE SIZE OF POPULATION D INCREASES
(UNITLESS)

TABLE 14.1 *(Continued)*

⊘MORT_RATE_INDEX_E=GRAPH(EFF_POP_E)
(200, 1.00), (205, 1.01), (210, 1.02), (215, 1.03), (220, 1.04), (225, 1.05), (230, 1.06), (235, 1.07), (240, 1.08), (245, 1.09), (250, 1.10), (255, 1.15), (260, 1.20), (265, 1.25), (270, 1.30), (275, 1.35), (280, 1.40), (285, 1.40), (290, 1.40), (295, 1.40), (300, 1.40)
DOCUMENT: AUXILIARY VARIABLE-PROPORTIONAL INCREASE IN MORTALITY RATE AS EFFECTIVE SIZE OF POPULATION E INCREASES (UNITLESS)

⊘MORT_RATE_INDEX_F=GRAPH(POP_F)
(200, 1.00), (205, 1.01), (210, 1.02), (215, 1.03), (220, 1.04), (225, 1.05), (230, 1.06), (235, 1.07), (240, 1.08), (245, 1.09), (250, 1.10), (255, 1.15), (260, 1.20), (265, 1.25), (270, 1.30), (275, 1.35), (280, 1.40), (285, 1.40), (290, 1.40), (295, 1.40), (300, 1.40)
DOCUMENT: AUXILIARY VARIABLE-PROPORTIONAL INCREASE IN MORTALITY RATE AS EFFECTIVE SIZE OF POPULATION F INCREASES (UNITLESS)

⊘MORT_RATE_INDEX_G=GRAPH(EFF_POP_G)
(200, 1.00), (205, 1.01), (210, 1.02), (215, 1.03), (220, 1.04), (225, 1.05), (230, 1.06), (235, 1.07), (240, 1.08), (245, 1.09), (250, 1.10), (255, 1.15), (260, 1.20), (265, 1.25), (270, 1.30), (275, 1.35), (280, 1.40), (285, 1.40), (290, 1.40), (295, 1.40), (300, 1.40)
DOCUMENT: AUXILIARY VARIABLE-PROPORTIONAL INCREASE IN MORTALITY RATE AS EFFECTIVE SIZE OF POPULATION G INCREASES (UNITLESS)

⊘NAT_RATE_INDEX_C=GRAPH(POP_C)
(150, 1.00), (160, 0.99), (170, 0.98), (180, 0.97), (190, 0.96), (200, 0.95), (210, 0.94), (220, 0.93), (230, 0.92), (240, 0.91), (250, 0.9)
DOCUMENT: AUXILIARY VARIABLE-PROPORTIONAL DECREASE IN NATALITY RATE AS SIZE OF POPULATION C INCREASES (UNITLESS)

⊘NAT_RATE_INDEX_D=GRAPH(POP_D)
(150, 1.00), (160, 0.99), (170, 0.98), (180, 0.97), (190, 0.96), (200, 0.95), (210, 0.94), (220, 0.93), (230, 0.92), (240, 0.91), (250, 0.9)
DOCUMENT: AUXILIARY VARIABLE-PROPORTIONAL DECREASE IN NATALITY RATE AS SIZE OF POPULATION D INCREASES (UNITLESS)

⊘NAT_RATE_INDEX_E=GRAPH(POP_E)
(150, 1.00), (160, 0.99), (170, 0.98), (180, 0.97), (190, 0.96), (200, 0.95), (210, 0.94), (220, 0.93), (230, 0.92), (240, 0.91), (250, 0.9)
DOCUMENT: AUXILIARY VARIABLE-PROPORTIONAL DECREASE IN NATALITY RATE AS SIZE OF POPULATION E INCREASES (UNITLESS)

TABLE 14.1 *(Continued)*

```
⊘NAT_RATE_INDEX_F=GRAPH(POP_F)
   (150, 1.00), (160, 0.99), (170, 0.98), (180, 0.97), (190,
   0.96), (200, 0.95), (210, 0.94), (220, 0.93), (230, 0.92),
   (240, 0.91), (250, 0.9)
   DOCUMENT: AUXILIARY VARIABLE—PROPORTIONAL DECREASE IN
   NATALITY RATE AS SIZE OF POPULATION F INCREASES (UNITLESS)
⊘NAT_RATE_INDEX_G=GRAPH(POP_G)
   (150, 1.00), (160, 0.99), (170, 0.98), (180, 0.97), (190,
   0.96), (200, 0.95), (210, 0.94), (220, 0.93), (230, 0.92),
   (240, 0.91), (250, 0.9)
   DOCUMENT: AUXILIARY VARIABLE—PROPORTIONAL DECREASE IN
   NATALITY RATE AS SIZE OF POPULATION G INCREASES (UNITLESS)
```

13.3). COUNT is a bookkeeping variable that determines whether a disturbance occurs during the present year.

14.5 MODEL USE

To predict the number and type of species (r- or K-selected) present within the community over a 500-year period with different frequencies of disturbance, our experimental design consists of seven 500-year simulations in which there are no disturbances (baseline) and in which disturbances occur every 30, 25, 20, 15, 10, and 5 years, respectively. Simulation results indicate that when there are no disturbances, all three r-selected species are lost from the community, and when disturbances occur every 30 years, two r-selected species are lost, due to competitive exclusion by K-selected species (Figures 14.2a and 14.2b). When disturbances occur every 20, 15, or 10 years, both K-selected species will be eventually lost from the community (Figures 14.2d, 14.2e, and 14.2f), and when disturbances occur every 5 years, all species are lost, because their natality rates are not high enough to allow recovery between disturbances (Figure 14.2g). When disturbances occur every 25 years, four of the five species remain after 500 years, with the abundance of populations of K-selected species reduced by disturbance just before they can competitively exclude two of the r-selected species (Figure 14.2c).

Thus, regarding the effect of interspecific competition, frequency of disturbance, and reproductive potential of resident species on the relative abundance of species, simulation results suggest that in a community containing a mixture of r- and K-selected species, a greater variety of species remain in the community at intermediate frequencies of disturbance. At low frequencies, r-selected species are competitively excluded, and at high frequencies, K-selected species cannot recover between disturbances.

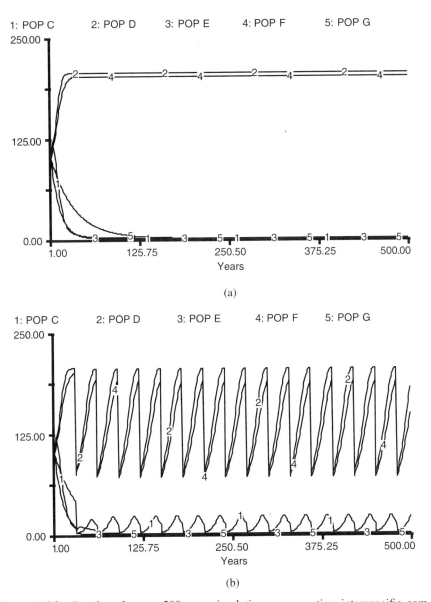

Figure 14.2 Results of seven 500-year simulations representing interspecific competition (population levels shown as animals/ha) in a community with r- (C, E, and G) and K- (D and F) selected species with (a) no ecological disturbances and with disturbances occurring every (b) 30, (c) 25, (d) 20, (e) 15, (f) 10, and (g) 5 years.

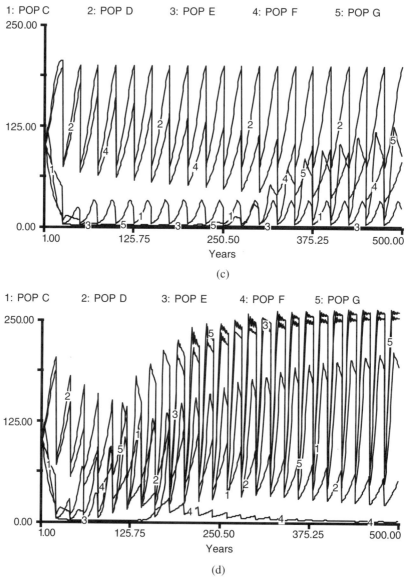

Figure 14.2 (Continued).

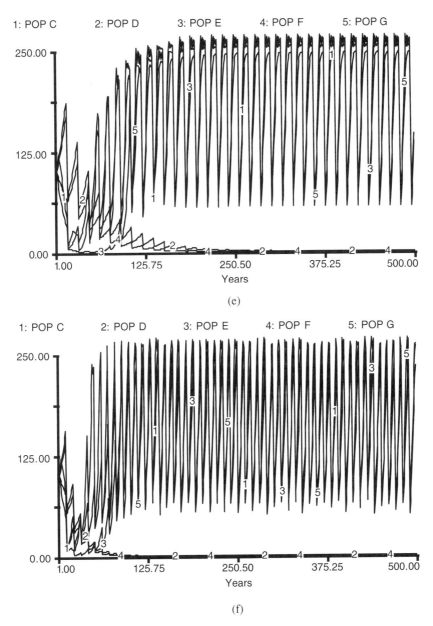

(e)

(f)

Figure 14.2 (Continued).

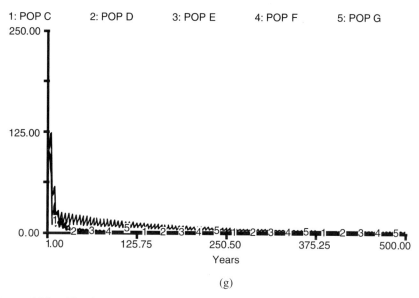

(g)

Figure 14.2   (Continued).

We encourage readers to use the model to explore further the effect of frequency of ecological disturbances on communities composed of different kinds of species. A variety of situations can be simulated by changing values of FREQ DIST, DISTURB, COMP COEF D, COMP COEF F1, COMP COEF F2, and MAX NAT RATE C, MAX NAT RATE E, and MAX NAT RATE G.

CHAPTER 15

PREDATOR-PREY SYSTEMS: EFFECTS OF PREDATOR ON PREY AND PREY ON PREDATOR

15.1 INTRODUCTION

Predation occurs when an individual of one species kills an individual of another species. In theory, population dynamics of predator and prey are completely interdependent, with changes in abundance of one population both caused by and causing changes in the other population. This cause-effect relationship, together with the theorized time lag in response of predator populations to changes in prey abundance, results in the classical predator-prey oscillation, consisting of sinusoidal fluctuations in both populations over time. In practice, the dynamics of both predator and prey populations often depend on ecological factors external to the predator-prey relationship. The circumstances under which predators affect prey population dynamics, and vice versa, depend on such factors as the ability of predators to "switch" to alternate prey and the ability of prey to "escape" numerically from predators due to their higher biotic potential.

15.2 MODEL OBJECTIVES

The general objective is to simulate interactions between one prey population and one predator population to identify circumstances under which predators affect prey population dynamics and vice versa. Specific objectives are to (1) predict environmental conditions under which either prey or predator fails to reach carrying capacity due to the predator-prey interaction and (2) identify periods during predator-prey cycles when one population is affecting dynamics of the other.

15.3   BACKGROUND INFORMATION ON THE SYSTEM-OF-INTEREST

The system-of-interest consists of a hypothetical prey population and a hypothetical predator population in a 1-ha woodlot. Current population sizes are 100 and 20 for prey and predator, respectively, and the populations are isolated, that is, there is no immigration or emigration. Prey have a maximum annual per capita natality rate of 0.77 (77 individuals born per 100 individuals in the population per year), and under normal environmental conditions, the relationship of natality rate to population size is the same as presented in Table 11.1. During unfavorable and favorable environmental conditions, density-dependent realized natality rates fluctuate between -10% and $+5\%$ of the values in Table 11.1. Minimum annual per capita mortality rate in the absence of predation is 0.70 (70 individuals dying per 100 individuals in the population per year) and the relationship of mortality rate to population size is the same as presented in Table 11.2.

Predators have a maximum annual per capita natality rate of 0.37 (37 individuals born per 100 individuals in the population per year) and a minimum annual per capita mortality rate of 0.31 (31 individuals dying per 100 individuals in the population per year). Relationships of per capita natality and mortality rates to population size are presented in Table 15.1 and Table 15.2, respectively.

In addition to the relationships just described, predator natality and prey mortality are also affected by per capita availability of prey to predators.

Table 15.1   Relative Annual per Capita Natality Rates of the Hypothetical Predator Population as a Function of Population Size During Years of Unlimited Prey Availability. Rates Are Presented as Proportions of the Maximum Annual per Capita Natality Rate

Population Size (Number of Individuals)	Relative Annual Natality Rate
<0.01	1.00
5	0.99
10	0.98
15	0.97
20	0.96
25	0.95
30	0.94
35	0.93
40	0.92
45	0.91
≥50	0.90

Table 15.2   Relative Annual per Capita Mortality Rates of the Hypothetical Predator Population as a Function of Population Size. Rates Are Presented as Proportions of the Minimum Annual per Capita Mortality Rate

Population Size (Number of Individuals)	Relative Annual Mortality Rate
<0.01	1.00
5	1.01
10	1.02
15	1.03
20	1.04
25	1.05
30	1.06
35	1.07
40	1.08
45	1.09
≥50	1.10

However, because there is a 12-month time lag between changes in prey abundance and predator responses to these changes, the perceived per capita availability is calculated as the ratio of the number of prey present in the system 12 months earlier to the number of predators currently in the system. Predator natality decreases proportionally as this ratio falls below 5 (Table 15.3). However predators will "switch" to an alternative prey species when

Table 15.3   Proportional Decrease in Relative Annual per Capita Natality Rates of the Hypothetical Predator Population as Perceived per Capita Availability of Prey (Calculated as the Ratio of Number of Prey in the System 12 Months Earlier to Number of Predators Currently in the System) Decreases. Relative Rates Presented in This Table Are Based on Predator Natality Rates Presented in Table 15.1 as Explained in the Text

Perceived per Capita Availability of Prey	Proportional Decrease in Annual Natality Rate
≥5.0	1.00
4.5	0.95
4.0[1]	0.90
3.5	0.85
3.0	0.80
2.5	0.75
2.0	0.70
1.5	0.60
1.0	0.40
0.5	0.20
0.0	0.0

[1]Predators switch to alternative prey species if possible.

perceived per capita availability of the primary prey species falls below 4.0, because there are always other prey species in the community that are at least that abundant. Thus, predator natality potentially is reduced from the maximum per capita rate by two proportions. One proportion represents the general effect of density-dependent, intraspecific competition for all resources except prey (Table 15.1), and the other proportion represents the specific effect of a perceived shortage of prey (Table 15.3).

Prey mortality may increase due to predation when perceived per capita availability of prey to predators increases. As the perceived ratio of prey to predators increases from 4.0 to 5.0, the number of prey at risk to predation increases from 100% to 110% of those that would die within a year due to other natural causes (Table 15.4) and, assuming enough predators are present, predation can increase prey mortality. However, the maximum annual predation rate per predator is 3.75 prey, which establishes an upper limit on the number of prey actually killed by a given number of predators when there is a surplus of prey at risk to predation.

15.4 MODEL DESCRIPTION

The model represents dynamics of a prey and a predator population under different environmental conditions (Figure 15.1). Changes in the numbers of animals in each population result from density-dependent natality and mortality. Prey natality is also affected by environmental conditions. Prey mortality and predator natality are also affected by the perceived ratio of prey to

Table 15.4   Relative Vulnerability of Prey as a Function of Perceived per Capita Availability of Prey (Calculated as the Ratio of Number of Prey in the System 12 Months Earlier to Number of Predators Currently in the System). Index Values Are Relative to the Number of Prey That Would Die within a Year Due to Natural Causes Other Than Predation

Perceived per Capita Availability of Prey	Index of Prey Vulnerability
≥5.0	1.10
4.9	1.09
4.8	1.08
4.7	1.07
4.6	1.06
4.5	1.05
4.4	1.04
4.3	1.03
4.2	1.02
4.1	1.01
≤4.0	1.00

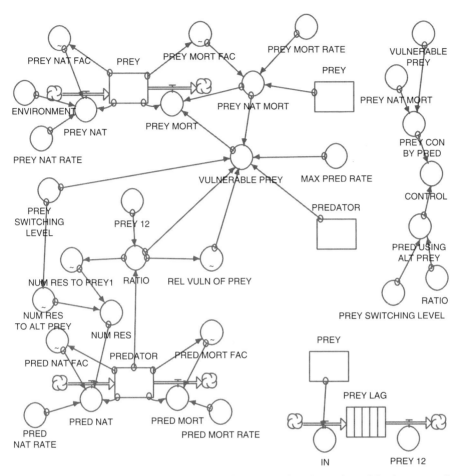

Figure 15.1   Conceptual model representing population dynamics of both prey and predator.

predators, which is the ratio of prey abundance 12 months earlier to current predator abundance.

The baseline simulation, which represents predator-prey dynamics when C15MOD01 environmental conditions are normal with regard to prey natality (ENVIRONMENT = 1.0), runs from month 1 to month 240 using a time unit of 1 month and the equations in Table 15.5. ENVIRONMENT is represented as an index with values ranging from 0.90 to 1.05, representing years ranging from unfavorable to favorable for prey natality. PREY NAT FAC, PREY MORT FAC, PRED NAT FAC, PRED MORT FAC, NUM RESP TO PREY1, and REL VULN OF PREY are graphical functions based on data in Table 11.1 and Table 11.2 and in Table 15.3 through Table 15.5, respectively. PREY SWITCHING LEVEL represents the perceived per capita availability of the primary prey at which the

**Table 15.5 Equations (Baseline Conditions) for the Simulation Model
Representing Effects of Predator on Prey and Prey on Predator**

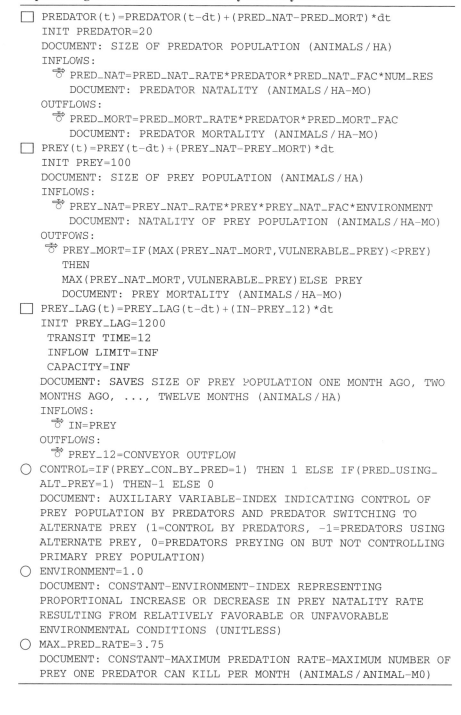

☐ PREDATOR(t)=PREDATOR(t-dt)+(PRED_NAT-PRED_MORT)*dt
  INIT PREDATOR=20
  DOCUMENT: SIZE OF PREDATOR POPULATION (ANIMALS/HA)
  INFLOWS:
    PRED_NAT=PRED_NAT_RATE*PREDATOR*PRED_NAT_FAC*NUM_RES
      DOCUMENT: PREDATOR NATALITY (ANIMALS/HA-MO)
  OUTFLOWS:
    PRED_MORT=PRED_MORT_RATE*PREDATOR*PRED_MORT_FAC
      DOCUMENT: PREDATOR MORTALITY (ANIMALS/HA-MO)
☐ PREY(t)=PREY(t-dt)+(PREY_NAT-PREY_MORT)*dt
  INIT PREY=100
  DOCUMENT: SIZE OF PREY POPULATION (ANIMALS/HA)
  INFLOWS:
    PREY_NAT=PREY_NAT_RATE*PREY*PREY_NAT_FAC*ENVIRONMENT
      DOCUMENT: NATALITY OF PREY POPULATION (ANIMALS/HA-MO)
  OUTFOWS:
    PREY_MORT=IF(MAX(PREY_NAT_MORT,VULNERABLE_PREY)<PREY)
    THEN
    MAX(PREY_NAT_MORT,VULNERABLE_PREY)ELSE PREY
    DOCUMENT: PREY MORTALITY (ANIMALS/HA-MO)
☐ PREY_LAG(t)=PREY_LAG(t-dt)+(IN-PREY_12)*dt
  INIT PREY_LAG=1200
   TRANSIT TIME=12
   INFLOW LIMIT=INF
   CAPACITY=INF
  DOCUMENT: SAVES SIZE OF PREY POPULATION ONE MONTH AGO, TWO
  MONTHS AGO, ..., TWELVE MONTHS (ANIMALS/HA)
  INFLOWS:
    IN=PREY
  OUTFLOWS:
    PREY_12=CONVEYOR OUTFLOW
○ CONTROL=IF(PREY_CON_BY_PRED=1) THEN 1 ELSE IF(PRED_USING_
  ALT_PREY=1) THEN-1 ELSE 0
  DOCUMENT: AUXILIARY VARIABLE-INDEX INDICATING CONTROL OF
  PREY POPULATION BY PREDATORS AND PREDATOR SWITCHING TO
  ALTERNATE PREY (1=CONTROL BY PREDATORS, -1=PREDATORS USING
  ALTERNATE PREY, 0=PREDATORS PREYING ON BUT NOT CONTROLLING
  PRIMARY PREY POPULATION)
○ ENVIRONMENT=1.0
  DOCUMENT: CONSTANT-ENVIRONMENT-INDEX REPRESENTING
  PROPORTIONAL INCREASE OR DECREASE IN PREY NATALITY RATE
  RESULTING FROM RELATIVELY FAVORABLE OR UNFAVORABLE
  ENVIRONMENTAL CONDITIONS (UNITLESS)
○ MAX_PRED_RATE=3.75
  DOCUMENT: CONSTANT-MAXIMUM PREDATION RATE-MAXIMUM NUMBER OF
  PREY ONE PREDATOR CAN KILL PER MONTH (ANIMALS/ANIMAL-M0)

Table 15.5 (*Continued*)

○ NUM_RES=MAX(NUM_RES_TO_PREY1,NUM_RES_TO_ALT_PREY)
DOCUMENT: AUXILIARY VARIABLE-NUMERICAL RESPONSE OF
PREDATORS TO CHANGES IN AVAILABILITY OF PREY-PROPORTIONAL
DECREASE IN PREDATOR NATALITY RATE AS NUMBER OF PREY
AVAILABLE PER PREDATOR DECREASES (UNITLESS)

○ PRED_MORT_RATE=0.31
DOCUMENT: CONSTANT-PREDATOR MORTALITY RATE (PROPORTION OF
POPULATION DYING PER MONTH)

○ PRED_NAT_RATE=0.37
DOCUMENT: CONSTANT-PREDATOR NATALITY RATE (ANIMALS/
ANIMAL-MO)

○ PRED_USING_ALT_PREY=IF(RATIO<PREY_SWITCHING_LEVEL) THEN 1
ELSE 0
DOCUMENT: AUXILIARY VARIABLE-INDEX INDICATING IF PREDATORS
ARE USING ALTERNATE PREY (1=PREDATORS PREYING ON ALTERNATE
PREY, 0=PREDATORS PREYING ON PRIMARY PREY)

○ PREY_CON_BY_PRED=IF(VULNERABLE_PREY>PREY_NAT_MORT) THEN 1
ELSE 0
DOCUMENT: AUXILIARY VARIABLE-PREY CONTROLLED BY
PREDATOR-INDEX INDICATING CONTROL OF PREY POPULATION BY
PREDATORS (1=CONTROL BY PREDATORS, 0=NO CONTROL BY
PREDATORS)

○ PREY_MORT_RATE=0.70
DOCUMENT: CONSTANT-PREY MORTALITY RATE (PROPORTION OF
POPULATION DYING PER MONTH)

○ PREY_NAT_MORT=PREY_MORT_RATE*PREY*PREY_MORT_FAC
DOCUMENT: AUXILIARY VARIABLE-PREY NATURAL MORTALITY
(ANIMALS/HA-MO)

○ PREY_NAT_RATE=0.77
DOCUMENT: CONSTANT-PREY NATALITY RATE (ANIMALS/ANIMAL-MO)

○ PREY_SWITCHING_LEVEL=4
DOCUMENT: CONSTANT-THRESHOLD LEVEL INDICATING NUMBER OF
PRIMARY PREY AVAILABLE PER PREDATOR AT WHICH PREDATOR
SWITCHES TO ALTERNATIVE PREY SPECIES

○ RATIO=IF(PREDATOR=0) THEN 0 ELSE PREY_12/PREDATOR
DOCUMENT: AUXILIARY VARIABLE-RATIO OF NUMBER OF PREY TO
NUMBER OF PREDATORS (UNITLESS)

○ VULNERABLE_PREY=IF(RATIO<PREY_SWITCHING_LEVEL) THEN 0 ELSE
MIN(PREY_NAT_MORT*REL_VULN_OF_PREY,MAX_PRED_RATE*PREDATOR)
DOCUMENT: AUXILIARY VARIABLE-VULNERABLE PREY-NUMBER OF PREY
VULNERABLE TO PREDATION (ANIMALS/HA)

Table 15.5 *(Continued)*

⊘NUM_RES_TO_ALT_PREY=GRAPH(PREY_SWITCHING_LEVEL)
(0.00, 0.00), (0.5, 0.2), (1.00, 0.4), (1.50, 0.6), (2.00,
0.7), (2.50, 0.75), (3.00, 0.8), (3.50, 0.85), (4.00, 0.9),
(4.50, 0.95), (5.00, 1.00)
DOCUMENT: AUXILIARY VARIABLE-NUMERICAL RESPONSE OF PREDATORS
TO CHANGES IN AVAILABILITY OF ALTERNATE PREY-PROPORTIONAL
DECREASE IN PREDATOR NATALITY RATE AS NUMBER OF ALTERNATE
PREY AVAILABLE PER PREDATOR DECREASES (UNITLESS)
⊘NUM_RES_TO_PREY1=GRAPH(RATIO)
(0.00, 0.00), (0.5, 0.2), (1.00, 0.4), (1.50, 0.6), (2.00,
0.7), (2.50, 0.75), (3.00, 0.8), (3.50, 0.85), (4.00, 0.9),
(4.50, 0.95), (5.00, 1.00)
DOCUMENT: AUXILIARY VARIABLE-NUMERICAL RESPONSE OF PREDATORS
TO CHANGES IN AVAILABILITY OF PRIMARY PREY-PROPORTIONAL
DECREASE IN PREDATOR NATALITY RATE AS NUMBER OF PRIMARY PREY
AVAILABLE PER PREDATOR DECREASES (UNITLESS)
⊘PRED_MORT_FAC=GRAPH(PREDATOR)
(0.00, 1.00), (5.00, 1.01), (10.0, 1.02), (15.0, 1.03),
(20.0, 1.04), (25.0, 1.05), (30.0, 1.06), (35.0, 1.07),
(40.0, 1.08), (45.0, 1.09), (50.0, 1.10)
DOCUMENT: AUXILIARY VARIABLE-PREDATOR MORTALITY
FACTOR-PROPORTIONAL INCREASE IN MORTALITY RATE AS SIZE OF
PREDATOR POPULATION INCREASES (UNITLESS)
⊘PRED_NAT_FAC=GRAPH(PREDATOR)
(0.00, 1.00), (5.00, 0.99), (10.0, 0.98), (15.0, 0.97),
(20.0, 0.96), (25.0, 0.95), (30.0, 0.94), (35.0, 0.93),
(40.0, 0.92), (45.0, 0.91), (50.0, 0.9)
DOCUMENT: AUXILIARY VARIABLE-PREDATOR NATALITY
FACTOR-PROPORTIONAL DECREASE IN NATALITY RATE AS SIZE OF
PREDATOR POPULATION INCREASES (UNITLESS)
⊘PREY_MORT_FAC=GRAPH(PREY)
(200, 1.00), (205, 1.01), (210, 1.02), (215, 1.03), (220,
1.04), (225, 1.05), (230, 1.06), (235, 1.07), (240, 1.08),
(245, 1.09), (250, 1.10), (255, 1.15), (260, 1.20), (265,
1.25), (270, 1.30), (275, 1.35), (280, 1.40)
DOCUMENT: AUXILIARY VARIABLE-PREY MORTALITY
FACTOR-PROPORTIONAL INCREASE IN MORTALITY RATE AS SIZE OF
PREY POPULATION INCREASES (UNITLESS)
⊘PREY_NAT_FAC=GRAPH(PREY)
(150, 1.00), (160, 0.99), (170, 0.98), (180, 0.97), (190,
0.96), (200, 0.95), (210, 0.94), (220, 0.93), (230, 0.92),
(240, 0.91), (250, 0.9)
DOCUMENT: AUXILIARY VARIABLE-PREY NATALITY FACTOR-
PROPORTIONAL DECREASE IN NATALITY RATE AS SIZE OF PREY
POPULATION INCREASES (UNITLESS)

Table 15.5 (*Continued*)

⊘REL_VULN_OF_PREY=GRAPH(RATIO)
  (4.00, 1.00), (4.10, 1.01), (4.20, 1.02), (4.30, 1.03),
  (4.40, 1.04), (4.50, 1.05), (4.60, 1.06), (4.70, 1.07),
  (4.80, 1.08), (4.90, 1.09), (5.00, 1.10)
  DOCUMENT: AUXILIARY VARIABLE-FUNCTIONAL RESPONSE OF
  PREDATORS TO CHANGES IN AVAILABLE PREY-PROPORTIONAL INCREASE
  IN NUMBER OF PREY KILLED PER PREDATOR PER MONTH AS NUMBER OF
  PREY AVAILABLE PER PREDATOR INCREASES (UNITLESS)

---

predator will switch to alternative prey. NUM RESP TO ALT PREY is a graphical function numerically identical to NUM RESP TO PREY1, but representing effect of abundance of alternative prey on predator natality. CONTROL is an output variable that indicates periods during which predators are "controlling" prey (CONTROL = 1), during which predators have "switched" to alternative prey (CONTROL = −1), and during which prey have "escaped" from predator control due to rapid reproduction (CONTROL = 0).

15.5 MODEL USE

To predict environmental conditions under which either prey or predator fails to reach the carrying capacity due to their interaction and subsequently identify periods when one population is affecting the dynamics of the other, we first estimate the carrying capacity of each population, assuming it is unaffected by the other. We then compare these results with predictions including prey-predator interaction. Thus, our experimental design consists of three series of 20-year simulations representing population dynamics of (1) the predator with an unlimited source of prey; (2) prey in the absence of predators under five different environmental conditions, ranging from very favorable to very unfavorable for prey natality (ENVIRONMENT = 1.04, 1.02, 1.00 (baseline), 0.95, and 0.90, respectively); and (3) prey and predator interacting under the same five environmental conditions. Simulation results indicate that the carrying capacity for predators with unlimited prey is 44 individuals (Figure 15.2a) and the carrying capacities for prey in the absence of predators range from 228 to 0 for environmental conditions ranging from very favorable to unfavorable for prey natality (Figure 15.2b).

Regarding our first objective, in the presence of each other, both prey and predator reach and maintain their carrying capacity only when environmental conditions are very favorable for prey natality (ENVIRONMENT = 1.04) (Figure 15.3a), although prey also reach the carrying capacity periodically when environmental conditions are normal or slightly favorable (ENVIRONMENT = 1.02 or 1.00) (Figures 15.3b and 15.3c). (We will discuss

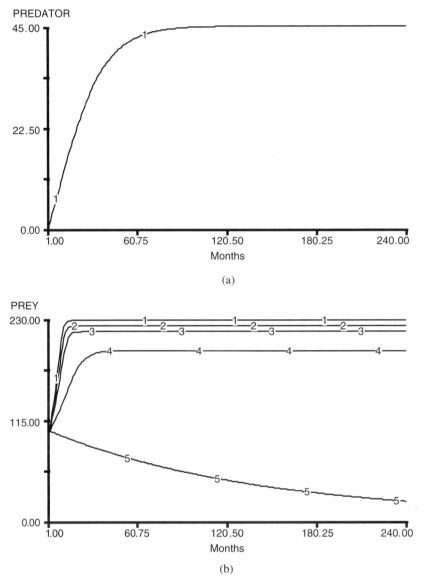

Figure 15.2 Results of six 20-year simulations representing the population dynamics (animals/ha) of (a) the predator with an unlimited source of prey and (b) prey in the absence of predators under five different environmental conditions (ENVIRONMENT is equal to (1) 1.04, (2) 1.02, (3) 1.00, (4) 0.95, and (5) 0.90.

in greater detail predator control of prey when we focus on our second objective). When environmental conditions are unfavorable but not lethal for prey (ENVIRONMENT = 0.95), both prey and predators oscillate below their respective carrying capacities (Figure 15.3d). At ENVIRONMENT = 0.90, prey can no longer maintain a viable population and predators survive by switching to alternative prey species (Figure 15.3e).

With regard to our second objective, simulation results indicate that for this particular predator-prey system, the degree to which one population is affecting dynamics of the other varies from one phase of the cycle to another and also depends on environmental conditions. For example, under environmental conditions slightly unfavorable for prey natality (ENVIRONMENT = 0.95), prey escape from predator control when prey abundance falls to the level at which predators switch to alternative prey (Figure 15.3d). By the time prey abundance has increased back to the level at which predators begin preying on them again, predator abundance has become too low to prevent rapid prey population growth. Thus, prey are not under predator control during the following period of rapid growth. However, as prey population growth is slowed by intraspecific, density-dependent control of natality and mortality, predator abundance is increasing in response to increased prey availability. Eventually, predator abundance increases to a level at which predation causes a decline in prey abundance, which continues until prey abundance again falls to the level at which predators switch to alternative prey. Predator abundance begins to decrease as prey abundance declines to levels that can no longer support such a high predator population and continues to decline until prey once again begin their rapid growth phase.

This basic pattern is seen under normal environmental conditions (ENVIRONMENT = 1.0), although prey abundance never falls to the level at which predators switch to alternative prey (Figure 15.3c). Under very favorable environmental conditions (ENVIRONMENT = 1.04), both predator and prey are under intraspecific, density-dependent population control (Figure 15.3a). When environmental conditions are extremely unfavorable but not lethal for prey (ENVIRONMENT = 0.91), prey natality is not sufficient to escape from predator control and prey abundance is maintained at low levels as predators switch back and forth between the primary and alternative prey (Figure 15.4).

Thus, regarding the circumstances under which predators affect prey population dynamics and vice versa, simulation results suggest that dynamics of both predator and prey populations often depend on ecological factors external to the predator-prey relationship. Such factors include the ability of predators to "switch" to alternate prey and the ability of prey to "escape" from predators due to their higher biotic potential.

We encourage readers to use the model to explore further the interaction of (1) the threshold of prey abundance at which predators switch to alternate

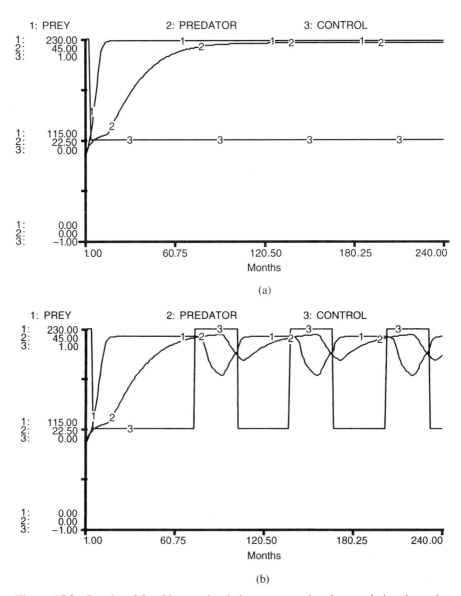

Figure 15.3 Results of five 20-year simulations representing the population dynamics (animals/ha) of predator and prey with ENVIRONMENT equal to (a) 1.04, (b) 1.02, (c) 1.00, (d) 0.95, and (e) 0.90. When CONTROL equals 0 prey have "escaped" from predator control due to rapid reproduction, when CONTROL equals 1 predators are "controlling" prey, and when CONTROL equals −1 predators have "switched" to alternative prey due to low prey abundance.

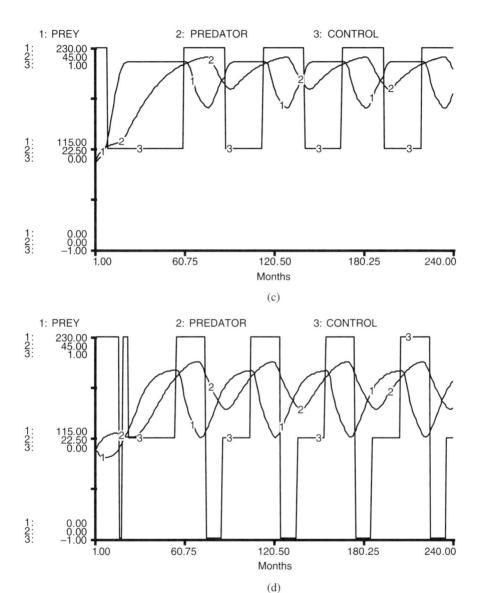

Figure 15.3 (Continued).

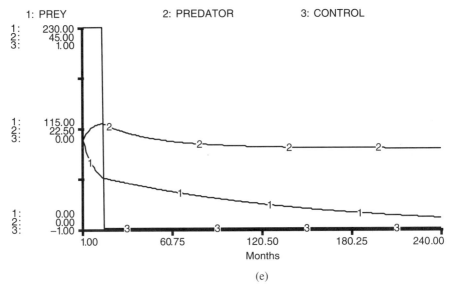

(e)

Figure 15.3 (Continued).

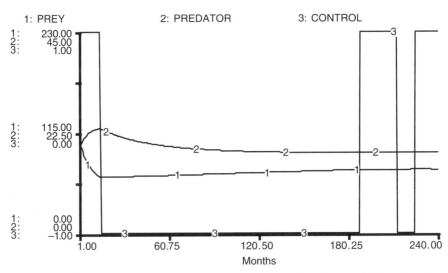

Figure 15.4 Results of a 20-year simulation representing the population dynamics (animals/ha) of predator and prey with ENVIRONMENT equal to 0.91. When CONTROL equals 0 prey have "escaped" from predator control due to rapid reproduction, when CONTROL equals 1 predators are "controlling" prey, and when CONTROL equals −1 predators have "switched" to alternative prey due to low prey abundance.

prey, (2) the maximum predation rate per predator, and (3) the numerical response of predators to changes in prey abundance in terms of the ability of the predator to control prey population dynamics. A variety of relevant situations can be simulated by changing values of PREY SWITCHING LEVEL, MAX PRED RATE, and NUM RES TO PREY1.

CHAPTER 16

ENERGY BALANCE OF HOMEOTHERMS: EFFECTS OF FORAGING AND THERMOREGULATION

16.1 INTRODUCTION

At the level of individual organisms, processes associated with the utilization of energy are among the most important ecologically. For animals, factors affecting the rates of consumption and respiration determine their daily balance of energy, or daily energy budget, which in the short term affects body weight and in the longer term affects reproduction and survival. An important factor influencing daily energy budgets of homeotherms living in cold environments involves the trade-off between remaining in a thermal shelter where food supply is limited versus foraging in a thermally harsh environment where food is more abundant.

16.2 MODEL OBJECTIVES

The general objective of the model is to examine the relative benefit of a thermal shelter to homeotherms as a function of adult body size and environmental temperatures outside the shelter during the coldest period of the year. Specific objectives are to predict energy balance and resulting weight change for homeotherms of different body sizes over a 100-day period during the coldest part of the year (1) in a thermal shelter and (2) foraging outside the shelter exposed to different constant environmental temperatures, and (3) to evaluate scenarios by which these animals might maintain their normal adult body weight during 100-day periods of variable environmental temperatures by altering the allocation of time spent foraging versus in the shelter.

16.3 BACKGROUND INFORMATION ON THE SYSTEM-OF-INTEREST

The system-of-interest consists of a hypothetical adult homeotherm whose winter activity range includes a shelter, in which environmental temperature always is in the thermal neutral zone but food supply is limited, and a foraging area in which food is relatively abundant but environmental temperatures are below the thermal neutral zone. In the shelter, the cost of thermoregulation is zero but consumption is limited to 2.2 weight$^{-0.5}$ kcal per gram of live body weight per day. While foraging outside the shelter, the animal can consume up to 7 weight$^{-0.5}$ kcal per gram of body weight per day but the cost of thermoregulation increases as the environmental temperature decreases below its lower critical temperature of 20°C. The average daily metabolic rate while resting (ADMR) is 2.297 weight$^{-0.5}$ kcal per gram of body weight per day. The additional cost of activity while foraging outside the shelter doubles the ADMR. The additional cost of thermoregulation, which for homeotherms is a function of body size and the difference between lower critical and environmental temperature, is (0.089 weight$^{-0.46}$)(lower critical temperature − environmental temperature) kcal per gram of body weight per day. The daily change in body weight depends on the ratio of consumption/respiration, but the maximum daily weight change, represented as a proportion of normal adult body weight, is 0.025 − 0.00000015 normal body weight for animals weighing up to 100 kg, and 0.01 for heavier animals. Lower lethal body weight is 70% of normal body weight, that is, if the animal loses 30% of its body weight, it will die.

The animal moves between shelter and foraging area depending on a limit on the maximum number of consecutive days it can tolerate in the shelter and its tolerance to environmental temperature in the foraging area. That is, if temperature in the foraging area drops below its tolerance temperature, the animal will enter the shelter and remain there for a fixed number of days, after which it will return to the foraging area due to the limited food resources in the shelter.

16.4 MODEL DESCRIPTION

The model represents energy balance, weight dynamics, and movement of a homeotherm between a thermal shelter and a foraging area (Figure 16.1). The daily energy balance is represented as the ratio of consumption/respiration. Consumption depends on respiration, weight of the animal relative to normal weight, and maximum consumption rate, which depends on whether the animal is in the shelter or outside the shelter. The animal will consume at a rate sufficient to replace respiration costs and regain lost weight as quickly as possible, as constrained by the maximum consumption rate. Respiration depends on the average daily (resting) metabolic rate (ADMR), and, while outside the shelter, additional costs of activity and thermoregulation, with costs

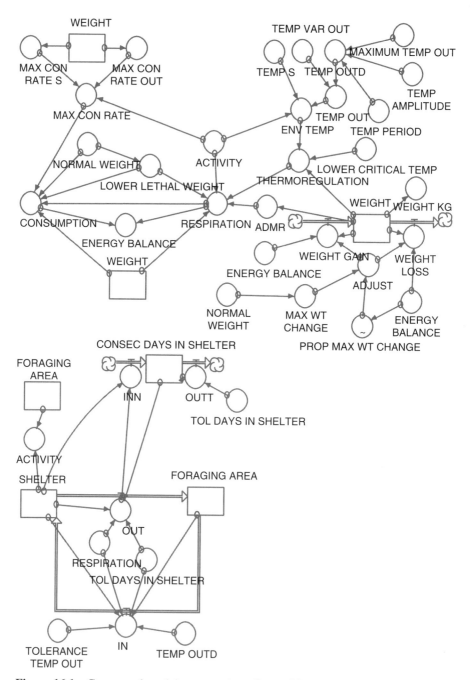

Figure 16.1 Conceptual model representing effects of foraging and thermoregulation on energy balance of homeotherms.

of thermoregulation increasing as environmental temperatures decrease below the lower critical temperature. The daily energy balance is converted into the corresponding proportion of the maximum daily weight change possible, which depends on the normal weight of the animal. Animal movement between the shelter and the foraging area is determined by the number of consecutive days it has spent in the shelter (if it is in the shelter) relative to its tolerance level for consecutive days in the shelter, or environmental temperature in the foraging area (if it is in the foraging area) relative to its tolerance temperature outside the shelter.

The baseline simulation, which represents energy balance for a 10-g homeotherm over a 100-day period in a thermal shelter, runs from day 1 to day 100 using a time unit of 1 day and the equations in Table 16.1. TEMP AMPLITUDE and TEMP PERIOD control the amplitude and periodicity of a sine function representing temperatures outside the shelter (TEMP OUT). TEMP VAR OUT controls the variation of temperature about its mean value. If both TEMP AMPLITUDE and TEMP VAR OUT equal zero, then TEMP OUT is constant at MAXIMUM TEMP OUT. TEMP S represents temperature in the shelter and ACTIVITY adjusts the energetic costs of activity when the animal is outside the shelter. LOWER LETHAL WEIGHT is the minimum body weight at which the animal can survive.

C16MOD01

16.5   MODEL USE

To address our first objective, we will simulate the energy balance and the resulting weight change for homeotherms of different body sizes over a 100-day period in a thermal shelter. The simulation results indicate that animals smaller than 25 kg cannot maintain a body weight above their lower lethal weight for 100 consecutive days in the shelter (Table 16.2). Animals weighing 10, 5, and 2.5 kg can maintain a body weight above the lower lethal limit for 91, 88, and 87 days, respectively, whereas all lighter animals reach their lower lethal weight in 86 days.

To address our second objective, we will simulate the energy balance and the resulting weight change for each of these same homeotherms foraging outside the shelter for 100 days under constant environmental temperatures ranging from their lower critical to their lower lethal temperature. The lower critical temperature is the environmental temperature at which thermoregulation begins (20°C is assumed here), and the lower lethal temperature is the temperature at which the animal loses 30% of its normal body weight in 100 days or less. The simulation results indicate that lower lethal temperatures increase with increasing body weight up to 25 kg and then begin to decrease for heavier animals (Table 16.2). This bimodal response is due to the fact that the advantage of lower costs of thermoregulation per unit of body weight for larger animals is offset by the disadvantage of larger costs of doubling ADMR for activity outside the shelter for animals with normal body weight up to approximately 50 kg.

TABLE 16.1   Equations (Baseline Conditions) for the Simulation Model Representing Effects of Foraging and Thermoregulation on Energy Balance of a Homeotherm

☐ CONSEC_DAYS_IN_SHELTER(t)=CONSEC_DAYS_IN_
SHELTER(t-dt)+(INN-OUTT)*dt
INIT CONSEC_DAYS_IN_SHELTER=0
DOCUMENT: NUMBER OF CONSECUTIVE DAYS THAT THE ANIMAL HAS
BEEN IN THE SHELTER
INFLOWS:
⏚ INN=IF(SHELTER=1) AND(OUT=0) THEN 1 ELSE 0
OUTFLOWS:
⏚ OUTT=IF(CONSEC_DAYS_IN_SHELTER=TOL_DAYS_IN_SHELTER-1)
OR(TOL_DAYS_IN_SHELTER=0) THEN CONSEC_DAYS_IN_SHELTER
ELSE 0

☐ FORAGING_AREA(t)=FORAGING_AREA(t-dt)+(OUT-IN)*dt
INIT FORAGING_AREA=0
DOCUMENT: INDEX REPRESENTING LOCATION OF THE ANIMAL (WITHIN
FORAGING AREA=2, OUTSIDE FORAGING AREA=0)
INFLOWS:
⏚ OUT=IF(RESPIRATION=0) THEN 0 ELSE
IF(CONSEC_DAYS_IN_SHELTER=TOL_DAYS_IN_SHELTER-1) OR
(TOL_DAYS_IN_SHELTER=0) THEN SHELTER ELSE 0
OUTFLOWS:
⏚ IN=(RESPIRATION=0) THEN 0 ELSE IF (TEMP_OUTD<TOLERENCE_
TEMP_OUT) AND(SHELTER=0) AND(TOL_DAYS_IN_SHELTER>0) THEN
FORAGING_AREA ELSE 0

☐ SHELTER(t)=SHELTER(t-dt)+(IN-OUT)*dt
INIT SHELTER=1
DOCUMENT: INDEX REPRESENTING THE LOCATION OF THE ANIMAL
(WITHIN THE SHELTER=1, OUTSIDE THE SHELTER=0)
INFLOWS:
⏚ IN=IF(RESPIRATION=0) THEN 0 ELSE IF(TEMP_OUTD<TOLERANCE_
TEMP_OUT) AND(SHELTER=0) AND(TOL_DAYS_IN_SHELTER>0) THEN
FORAGING_AREA ELSE 0
OUTFLOWS:
⏚ OUT=IF(RESPIRATION=0) THEN 0 ELSE
IF(CONSEC_DAYS_IN_SHELTER=TOL_DAYS_IN_SHELTER-1) OR
(TOL_DAYS_IN_SHELTER=0) THEN SHELTER ELSE 0

☐ WEIGHT(t)=WEIGHT(t-dt)+(WEIGHT_GAIN-WEIGHT_LOSS)*dt
INIT WEIGHT=NORMAL_WEIGHT
DOCUMENT: WEIGHT OF ANIMAL (G)
INFLOWS:
⏚ WEIGHT_GAIN=IF(ENERGY_BALANCE>1) THEN ADJUST*WEIGHT ELSE
0
DOCUMENT: WEIGHT GAIN (G/DAY)
OUTFLOWS:
⏚ WEIGHT_LOSS=IF(ENERGY_BALANCE<1) THEN ADJUST*WEIGHT ELSE
0
DOCUMENT: WEIGHT LOSS (G/DAY)

TABLE 16.1 (*Continued*)

○ ACTIVITY=IF(SHELTER=1) THEN 1 ELSE IF(FORAGING_AREA=1) THEN
2 ELSE 0
DOCUMENT: AUXILIARY VARIABLE-PROPORTIONAL INCREASE IN
AVERAGE DAILY METABOLIC RATE DUE TO ACTIVITY DEPENDING ON
LOCATION OF ANIMAL (UNITLESS)

○ ADJUST=PROP_MAX_WT_CHANGE*MAX_WT_CHANGE
DOCUMENT: AUXILIARY VARIABLE-ACTUAL WEIGHT CHANGE PER DAY
(G)

○ ADMR=2.297*WEIGHT^-0.5
DOCUMENT: AUXILIARY VARIABLE-AVERAGE DAILY METABOLIC
RATE(KCAL/G-DAY)

○ CONSUMPTION=IF(WEIGHT<LOWER_LETHAL_WEIGHT) OR(WEIGHT=LOWER_
LETHAL_WEIGHT) THEN 0 ELSE IF(WEIGHT>NORMAL_WEIGHT)
OR(WEIGHT=NORMAL_WEIGHT) THEN MIN(RESPIRATION,MAX_CON_
RATE*WEIGHT) ELSE MAX_CON_RATE*WEIGHT
DOCUMENT: AUXILIARY VARIABLE-CONSUMPTION (KCAL/DAY)

○ ENERGY_BALANCE=IF(RESPIRATION=0) THEN 1 ELSE CONSUMPTION/
RESPIRATION
DOCUMENT: AUXILIARY VARIABLE-ENERGY BALANCE OF THE ANIMAL
REPRESENTED AS THE RATIO OF CONSUMPTION/RESPIRATION
(UNITLESS)

○ ENV_TEMP=IF(ACTIVITY=1) THEN TEMP_S ELSE TEMP_OUT
DOCUMENT: AUXILIARY VARIABLE-ENVIRONMENTAL TEMPERATURE TO
WHICH THE ANIMAL IS EXPOSED (DEGREES C)

○ LOWER_CRITICAL_TEMP=20
DOCUMENT: CONSTANT-LOWER CRITICAL TEMPERATURE OF ANIMAL
(DEGREES C)

○ LOWER_LETHAL_WEIGHT=NORMAL_WEIGHT*0.7
DOCUMENT: AUXILIARY VARIABLE-LOWER LETHAL WEIGHT (G)

○ MAXIMUM_TEMP_OUT=5
DOCUMENT: CONSTANT-MAXIMUM AMBIENT TEMPERATURE OUTSIDE THE
SHELTER (DEGREES C)

○ MAX_CON_RATE=IF(ACTIVITY=1) THEN MAX_CON_RATE_S ELSE MAX_
CON_RATE_OUT
DOCUMENT: AUXILIARY VARIABLE-MAXIMUM CONSUMPTION RATE
(KCAL/G-DAY)

○ MAX_CON_RATE_OUT=7*WEIGHT^-0.5
DOCUMENT: AUXILIARY VARIABLE-MAXIMUM CONSUMPTION RATE
OUTSIDE THE SHELTER (KCAL/G-DAY)

○ MAX_CON_RATE_S=2.2*WEIGHT^-0.5
DOCUMENT: AUXILIARY VARIABLE-MAXIMUM CONSUMPTION RATE
WITHIN THE SHELTER (KCAL/G-DAY)

○ MAX_WT_CHANGE=MAX(0.025-0.00000015*NORMAL_WEIGHT, 0.01)
DOCUMENT: CONSTANT-NORMAL ADULT BODY WEIGHT (G)

○ NORMAL_WEIGHT=10
DOCUMENT: CONSTANT-NORMAL ADULT BODY WEIGHT (G)

TABLE 16.1   (*Continued*)

○ RESPIRATION=IF(WEIGHT<LOWER_LETHAL_WEIGHT) OR(WEIGHT=LOWER_
LETHAL_WEIGHT) THEN 0 ELSE
(ADMR*ACTIVITY+THERMOREGULATION)*WEIGHT
DOCUMENT: AUXILIARY VARIALE-COST OF RESPIRATION (KCAL/DAY)

○ TEMP_AMPLITUDE=0
DOCUMENT: CONSTANT-AMPLITUDE OF FLUCTUATIONS IN THE SINE
WAVE REPRESENTING AMBIENT TEMPERATURE OUTSIDE THE SHELTER
(UNITLESS)

○ TEMP_OUT-NORMAL(TEMP_OUTD,TEMP_VAR_OUT)
DOCUMENT: AUXILIARY VARIABLE-NORMAL RANDOM VARIATE
REPRESENTING AMBIENT TEMPERATURE OUTSIDE THE SHELTER
(DEGREES C)

○ TEMP_OUTD=(MAXIMUM_TEMP_OUT-TEMP_AMPLITUDE/2)-TEMP_
AMPLITUDE/2*SIN(2*PI*(TIME-TEMP_PERIOD/4)/TEMP_PERIOD)
DOCUMENT: AUXILIARY VARIABLE-MEAN OF THE NORMAL
DISTRIBUTION REPRESENTING AMBIENT TEMPERATURE OUTSIDE THE
SHELTER (DEGREES C)

○ TEMP_PERIOD=100
DOCUMENT: CONSTANT-PERIOD OF FLUCTUATIONS OF THE SINE WAVE
REPRESENTING AMBIENT TEMPERATURE OUTSIDE THE SHELTER
(UNITLESS)

○ TEMP_S=20
DOCUMENT: CONSTANT-AMBIENT TEMPERATURE WITHIN THE SHELTER
(DEGREES C)

○ TEMP_VAR_OUT=0
DOCUMENT: CONSTANT-VARIATION OF THE NORMAL DISTRIBUTION
REPRESENTING AMBIENT TEMPERATURE OUTSIDE THE SHELTER
(DEGREES C)

○ THERMOREGULATION=IF(ENV_TEMP>LOWER_CRITICAL_TEMP) THEN 0
ELSE (0.089*WEIGHT^-0.46)*(LOWER_CRITICAL_TEMP-ENV_TEMP)
DOCUMENT: AUXILIARY VARIABLE-COST OF THERMOREGULATION
(KCAL/G-DAY)

○ TOLERANCE_TEMP_OUT=99
DOCUMENT: CONSTANT-MINIMUM AMBIENT TEMPERATURE OUTSIDE THE
SHELTER THAT THE ANIMAL CAN TOLERATE WITHOUT ENTERING THE
SHELTER (DEGREES C)

○ TOL_DAYS_IN_SHELTER=999
DOCUMENT: CONSTANT-MAXIMUM NUMBER OF CONSECUTIVE DAYS THAT
THE ANIMAL CAN REMAIN IN THE SHELTER

○ WEIGHT_KG=WEIGHT/1000
DOCUMENT: AUXILIARY VARIABLE-CONVERTS WEIGHT IN KILOGRAMS
TO WEIGHT IN GRAMS

⊘ PROP_MAX_WT_CHANGE=GRAPH(ENERGY_BALANCE)
(0.75, 1.00), (0.8, 0.8), (0.85, 0.6), (0.9, 0.4), (0.95,
0.2), (1.00, 0.00), (1.05, 0.2), (1.10, 0.4), (1.15, 0.6),
(1.20, 0.8), (1.25, 1.00)
DOCUMENT: AUXILIARY VARIABLE-PROPORTION OF MAXIMUM POSSIBLE
DAILY WEIGHT CHANGE ACTUALLY REALIZED (UNITLESS)

TABLE 16.2 **Number of Consecutive Days Homeotherms of Different Sizes Can Maintain Body Weight Above the Lower Lethal Weight (70% of Normal Body Weight) in the Thermal Shelter and the Lowest Constant Environmental Temperature Outside the Shelter Under Which Animals Can Maintain Body Weight Above the Lower Lethal Weight for 100 Consecutive Days**

Body Weight (kg)	Consecutive Days in Shelter	Lowest Environmental Temperature (°C)
0.01	86	−7
0.02	86	−6
0.03	86	−6
0.04	86	−6
0.05	86	−5
0.10	86	−5
0.25	86	−4
0.50	86	−3
1.0	86	−2
2.5	87	−2
5.0	88	−1
10.0	91	−1
25.0	100	0
50.0	100	0
75.0	100	0
85.0	100	−1
100.0	100	−2

To address our third objective, we will compare two strategies by which a 25-kg animal allocates time spent foraging versus in the shelter during 100-day periods with variable environmental temperatures. We run five replicate stochastic simulations representing each of four types of winters: (1) mild, predictable; (2) very cold, predictable; (3) mild, unpredictable; and (4) very cold, unpredictable. We will assume that the animal enters the shelter when environmental temperatures in the foraging area are less than or equal to 2°C and then remains in the shelter for either 2 days (strategy A) or 5 days (strategy B) before returning to the foraging area. The simulation results indicate that the animal can regain most of its lost weight by the end of the 100-day period using either strategy during mild, predictable winters (Figure 16.2), but during very cold, predictable winters, the animal can survive (maintain at least 70% of normal body weight) only using strategy B (Figure 16.3). During mild, unpredictable winters, as with predictable winters, there is little noticeable difference between the strategies (Figure 16.4). However, during very cold, unpredictable winters, the superiority of strategy B is much less obvious than during predictable winters (Figure 16.5).

Regarding the relative benefit of a thermal shelter to homeotherms as a function of adult body weight and environmental temperatures outside the

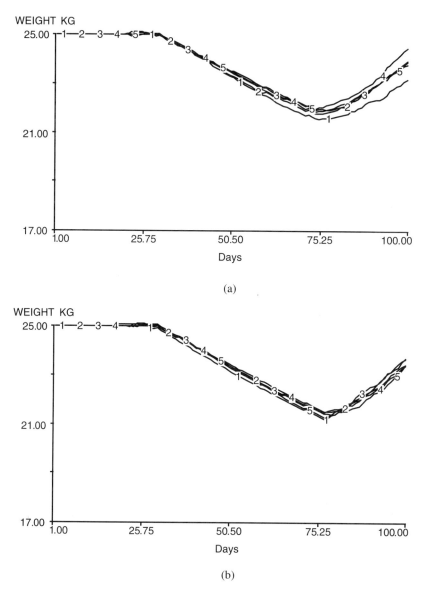

Figure 16.2 Results of two series of five replicate stochastic simulations representing the weight dynamics of a 25-kg homeotherm using (a) strategy A (2 consecutive days in a thermal shelter) and (b) strategy B (5 consecutive days in a shelter) during mild, predictable winters (MAXIMUM TEMP OUT = 5, TEMP PERIOD = 100, TEMP AMPLITUDE = 5, TEMP VAR OUT = 1).

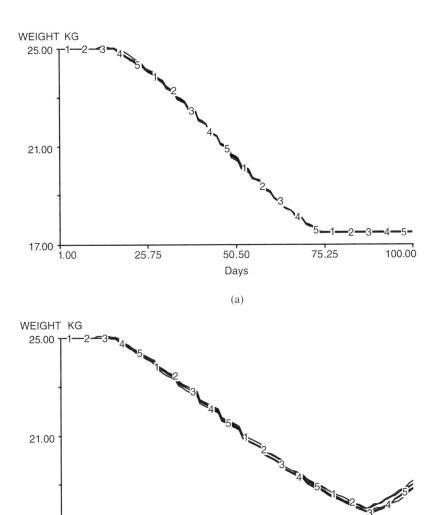

Figure 16.3   Results of two series of five replicate stochastic simulations representing the weight dynamics of a 25-kg homeotherm using (a) strategy A (2 consecutive days in a thermal shelter) and (b) strategy B (5 consecutive days in a shelter) during very cold, predictable winters (MAXIMUM TEMP OUT = 5, TEMP PERIOD = 100, TEMP AMPLITUDE = 15, TEMP VAR OUT = 1).

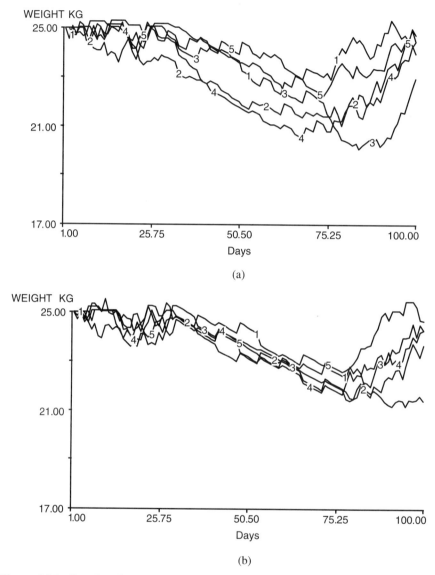

Figure 16.4   Results of two series of five replicate stochastic simulations representing the weight dynamics of a 25-kg homeotherm using (a) strategy A (2 consecutive days in a thermal shelter) and (b) strategy B (5 consecutive days in a shelter) during mild, unpredictable winters (MAXIMUM TEMP OUT = 5, TEMP PERIOD = 100, TEMP AMPLITUDE = 5, TEMP VAR OUT = 10).

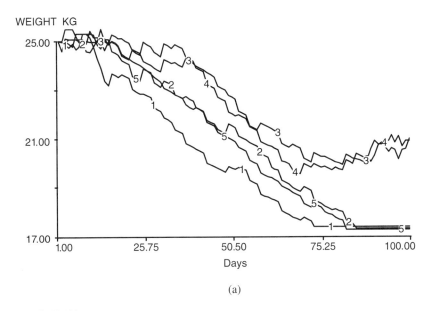

(a)

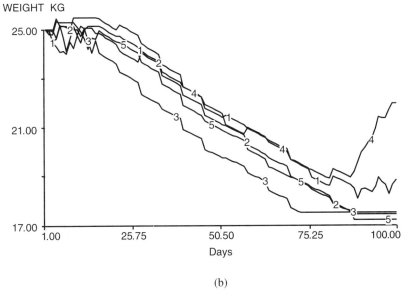

(b)

Figure 16.5 Results of two series of five replicate stochastic simulations representing the weight dynamics of a 25-kg homeotherm using (a) strategy A (2 consecutive days in a thermal shelter) and (b) strategy B (5 consecutive days in a shelter) during very cold, unpredictable winters (MAXIMUM TEMP OUT = 5, TEMP PERIOD = 100, TEMP AMPLITUDE = 15, TEMP VAR OUT = 10).

shelter, the results emphasize the importance of the trade-off between the degree of food limitation in the shelter and the thermoregulatory costs while exposed to cold environmental temperatures.

We encourage readers to use the model to explore further the relative benefits for a 25-kg homeotherm of remaining in a thermal shelter versus foraging where food is more abundant. A variety of additional situations can be simulated by changing values of MAXIMUM TEMP OUT, TOL DAYS IN SHELTER, and TOLERANCE TEMP OUT.

PART V

APPLICATION OF SIMULATION MODELS IN NATURAL RESOURCE MANAGEMENT

Part V provides examples of the use of simulation models to address several hypothetical natural resource management problems within the context of wildlife, fisheries, range, and forest management. Each example begins with a brief statement of the management context and objectives of the model, followed by background information on the system-of-interest, brief descriptions of the model and its use to address the specific questions posed, and ends with suggestions for further use of the model to address related questions. Specific conclusions based on simulation results are presented to demonstrate the manner in which such results can be related directly to model objectives. However, it should be clear that these conclusions have no relevance outside the hypothetical context of the particular example.

Chapter 17 considers the effects of different habitat management schemes on an endangered wildlife species existing as a metapopulation in a fragmented habitat. Chapter 18 examines the influence of alternative harvest regulations on total yield from a fishery to two different user groups. Chapter 19 compares the effects of various stocking densities and frequencies of brush control on rangeland productivity. Chapter 20 evaluates the impacts of different timber harvesting strategies on relative abundance of forest wildlife species. As in the previous part, the objective is to provide readers with an opportunity to explore potential uses of models to address different types of natural resource management questions. Thus, few details of model development and evaluation are described and only a few simulation results are presented. Readers can address additional questions of interest using the computerized (STELLA® II) models found in the "nrm" folder on the enclosed CD ROM, which contain documentation defining all variables and units of measure. Names of particular models appear in the right-hand margin of the text.

CHAPTER 17

WILDLIFE MANAGEMENT: EFFECTS OF HABITAT FRAGMENTATION ON THE MANAGEMENT OF ENDANGERED ANIMAL SPECIES

17.1 INTRODUCTION

One of the central activities in wildlife management is habitat improvement and one of the major causes of decline in wildlife populations is habitat loss. Changing patterns of land use have fragmented the habitat of many animal species such that they exist as semi-isolated subpopulations in remaining patches of suitable habitat connected only by relatively narrow migration corridors. Dynamics of the metapopulation, or group of interconnected subpopulations, depend on both habitat quality within remaining patches and the effectiveness of corridors in permitting movement of animals among patches. In this chapter, we develop a model that simulates effects of different habitat management schemes and land-use decisions on metapopulation dynamics of an animal species endangered by habitat fragmentation.

17.2 MODEL OBJECTIVES

The general objective is to simulate the effect of different habitat management and land-use decisions on population dynamics of an endangered animal species existing as a metapopulation in a fragmented habitat. Specific objectives are to assess the impact on the metapopulation dynamics of (1) habitat improvement via enhancement of breeding habitat in patches and/or protective cover in corridors and (2) further habitat fragmentation via blockage of dispersal corridors.

17.3 BACKGROUND INFORMATION ON THE SYSTEM-OF-INTEREST

The system-of-interest consists of a 500-ha wildlife refuge that supports an endangered animal species with an age-structured population. We are interested in the annual dynamics of this system over the next 200 years. Within the refuge, the species exists as a metapopulation composed of five subpopulation units, one in each of five 50-ha patches of suitable habitat. The patches currently are connected by dispersal corridors, although either of two proposed highways would effectively block animal movement between the northern and southern portions of the refuge, with one of the highways (1) blocking movement between patch B and patch C and the alternative highway (2) blocking movement between patch C and patches D and E (Figure 17.1). That is, all individuals attempting to move through a corridor blocked by a highway would die before reaching the next patch of suitable habitat. Each subpopulation has relatively low rates of natality, mortality, dispersal, and immigration. Sexual maturity is not reached until age class 6 and dispersal occurs only during age class 1. Both natality and dispersal rates are density-dependent, with natality also depending on habitat quality in each patch (Table 17.1). The specific natality rates represented in Table 17.1 apply to current habitat conditions in patch C. Current natality rates in patches A, B, D, and E are 3.0, 2.0, 0.5, and 0.5 times those in patch C, respectively.

Annual mortality rate is 5% for each age class in all patches, however, 50% of all dispersing animals die before reaching one of the other patches of suitable habitat. Surviving dispersers are equally likely to enter any of the

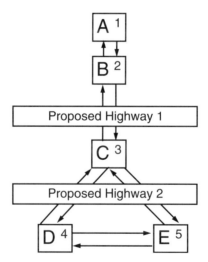

Figure 17.1 Schematic diagram of the wildlife refuge showing habitat patches and migration corridors for a hypothetical endangered animal species and two proposed highway routes.

TABLE 17.1 Rates of Natality (Number of Individuals Born per Individual in Age Class 6 per Year) and Dispersal (Proportion of Individuals in Age Class 1 Dispersing per Year) for the Endangered Animal Species as a Function of Population Density (Number of Individuals per ha). The Specific Natality Rates Presented Apply to Current Habitiat Conditions in Patch C

Population Density	Natality Rate	Dispersal Rate
0	0.075	0.0
10	0.075	0.1
20	0.075	0.2
30	0.07	0.3
40	0.06	0.4
50	0.05	0.5
60	0.04	0.6
70	0.03	0.7
80	0.02	0.8
90	0.01	0.9
100	0.005	1.0

patches connected by a migration corridor with the patch from which they came. Currently, there are 2.92, 2.78, 2.62, 2.48, 2.40, and 47.2 individuals per ha in age classes 1 through 6, respectively, in subpopulations A and B, and 1.95, 1.85, 1.75, 1.65, 1.6, and 31.5 individuals per ha in age classes 1 through 6, respectively, in subpopulations C, D, and E.

The refuge manager wants to stabilize the endangered species population on the refuge, which currently is declining noticeably, and also assess the potential impact of each of the two proposed highways on metapopulation dynamics. To stabilize the population, there are two management alternatives: (1) improve the breeding habitat within patches and (2) improve the protective cover in corridors. However, the relative effectiveness of the two management alternatives may vary, depending on where the highway is constructed. The manager estimates that natality rates can be increased by 10% in each patch by improving the breeding habitat and that mortality rates of dispersers can be reduced to 0 by improving the protective cover in corridors.

17.4 MODEL DESCRIPTION

The model consists of five submodels representing the five subpopulations within the refuge (Figure 17.2). Each submodel represents changes in the number of animals in each age class in the subpopulation resulting from natality (age class 6 only), mortality, dispersal (age class 1 only), and immigration (age class 2 only). Natality and dispersal rates are density-dependent, with natality also affected by habitat management. Mortality rates are constant except for dispersing animals that are exposed to an additional

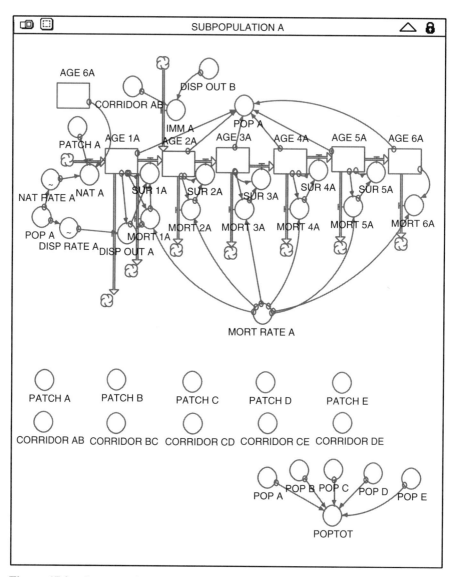

Figure 17.2 Conceptual model representing the effects of habitat fragmentation and habitat management policies on a hypothetical endangered animal species existing as a metapopulation in a wildlife refuge. The metapopulation consists of five subpopulations connected as indicated in Figure 17.1. Only subpopulation A is represented in this figure.

TABLE 17.2   Equations (Baseline Conditions) for the Simulation Model Representing Effects of Habitat Fragmentation and Habitat Management on Population Dynamics of a Hypothetical Endangered Animal Species

SUBPOPULATION A

☐ AGE_1A(t)=AGE_1A(t-dt)+(NAT_A-SUR_1A-MORT_1A-DISP_OUT_A)*dt
INIT AGE_1A=2.92
DOCUMENT: AGE 1A-SIZE OF THE FIRST AGE CLASS IN PATCH A
(ANIMALS/HA)
INFLOWS:
☗ NAT_A=AGE_6A*NAT_RATE_A*PATCH_A
   DOCUMENT: NAT A-NATALITY IN PATCH A (ANIMALS/HA-YR)
OUTFLOWS:
☗ SUR_1A=AGE_1A-MORT_1A-DISP_OUT_A
   DOCUMENT: SUR 1A-SURVIVAL OF ANIMALS IN FIRST AGE CLASS
   (ANIMALS/HA-YR)
☗ MORT_1A=AGE_1A*MORT_RATE_A
   DOCUMENT: MORT 1A-MORTALITY OF ANIMALS IN THE FIRST AGE
   CLASS (ANIMALS/HA-YR)
☗ DISP_OUT_A=(AGE_1A-MORT_1A)*DISP_RATE_A
   DOCUMENT: DISP OUT A-DISPERSAL OF ANIMALS OUT OF PATCH A
   (ANIMALS/HA-YR)

☐ AGE_2A(t)=AGE_2A(t-dt)+(SUR_1A+IMM_A-SUR_2A-MORT_2A)*dt
INIT AGE_2A=2.78
DOCUMENT: AGE 2A-SIZE OF THE SECOND AGE CLASS IN PATCH A
(ANIMALS/HA)
INFLOWS:
☗ SUR_1A=AGE_1A-MORT_1A-DISP_OUT_A
   DOCUMENT: SUR 1A-SURVIVAL OF ANIMALS IN FIRST AGE CLASS
   (ANIMALS/HA-YR)
☗ IMM_A=(DISP_OUT_B/2)*CORRIDOR_AB
   DOCUMENT: IMM A-IMMIGRATION OF ANIMALS INTO PATCH A
   (ANIMALS/HA-YR)
OUTFLOWS:
☗ SUR_2A=AGE_2A-MORT_2A
   DOCUMENT: SUR 2A-SURVIVAL OF ANIMALS IN THE SECOND AGE
   CLASS (ANIMALS/HA-YR)
☗ MORT_2A=AGE_2A*MORT_RATE_A
   DOCUMENT: MORT 2A-MORTALITY OF ANIMALS IN THE SECOND AGE
   CLASS (ANIMALS/HA-YR)

☐ AGE_3A(t)=AGE_3A(t-dt)+(SUR_2A-SUR_3A-MORT_3A)*dt
INIT AGE_3A=2.62
DOCUMENT: AGE 3A-SIZE OF THE THIRD AGE CLASS IN PATCH A
(ANIMALS/HA)

TABLE 17.2 (*Continued*)

```
INFLOWS:
⌛ SUR_2A=AGE_2A-MORT_2A
   DOCUMENT: SUR 2A-SURVIVAL OF ANIMALS IN THE SECOND AGE
   CLASS (ANIMALS/HA-YR)
OUTFLOWS:
⌛ SUR_3A=AGE_3A-MORT_3A
   DOCUMENT: SUR 3A-SURVIVAL OF ANIMALS IN THE THIRD AGE
   CLASS (ANIMALS/HA-YR)
⌛ MORT_3A=AGE_3A*MORT_RATE_A
   DOCUMENT: MORT 3A-MORTALITY OF ANIMALS IN THE THIRD AGE
   CLASS (ANIMALS/HA-YR)
☐ AGE_4A(t)=AGE_4A(t-dt)+(SUR_3A-SUR_4A-MORT_4A)*dt
   INIT AGE_4A=2.48
   DOCUMENT: AGE 4A-SIZE OF THE FOURTH AGE CLASS IN PATCH A
   (ANIMALS/HA)
   INFLOWS:
⌛ SUR_3A=AGE_3A-MORT_3A
   DOCUMENT: SUR 3A-SURVIVAL OF ANIMALS IN THE THIRD AGE
   CLASS (ANIMALS/HA-YR)
OUTFLOWS:
⌛ SUR_4A=AGE_4A-MORT_4A
   DOCUMENT: SUR 4A-SURVIVAL OF ANIMALS IN THE FOURTH AGE
   CLASS (ANIMALS/HA-YR)
⌛ MORT_4A=AGE_4A*MORT_RATE_A
   DOCUMENT: MORT 4A-MORTALITY OF ANIMALS IN THE FOURTH AGE
   CLASS (ANIMALS/HA-YR)
☐ AGE_5A(t)=AGE_5A(t-dt)+(SUR_4A-SUR_5A-MORT_5A)*dt
   INIT AGE_5A=2.4
   DOCUMENT: AGE 5A-SIZE OF THE FIFTH AGE CLASS IN PATCH A
   (ANIMALS/HA)
   INFLOWS:
⌛ SUR_4A=AGE_4A-MORT_4A
   DOCUMENT: SUR 4A-SURVIVAL OF ANIMALS IN THE FOURTH AGE
   CLASS (ANIMALS/HA-YR)
OUTFLOWS:
⌛ SUR_5A=AGE_5A-MORT_5A
   DOCUMENT: SUR 5A-SURVIVAL OF ANIMALS IN THE FIFTH AGE
   CLASS (ANIMALS/HA-YR)
⌛ MORT_5A=AGE_5A*MORT_RATE_A
   DOCUMENT: MORT 5A-MORTALITY OF ANIMALS IN THE FIFTH AGE
   CLASS (ANIMALS/HA-YR)
☐ AGE_6A(t)=AGE_6A(t-dt)+(SUR_5A-MORT_6A)*dt
   INIT AGE_6A=47.2
   DOCUMENT: AGE 6A-SIZE OF THE SIXTH AGE CLASS IN PATCH A
   (ANIMALS/HA)
   INFLOWS:
⌛ SUR_5A=AGE_5A-MORT_5A
   DOCUMENT: SUR 5A-SURVIVAL OF ANIMALS IN THE FIFTH AGE
   CLASS (ANIMALS/HA-YR)
```

TABLE 17.2 (*Continued*)

```
OUTFLOWS:
   MORT_6A=AGE_6A*MORT_RATE_A
      DOCUMENT: MORT 6A-MORTALITY OF ANIMALS IN THE SIXTH AGE
      CLASS (ANIMALS/HA-YR)
○  CORRIDOR_AB=0.5
   DOCUMENT: CONSTANT-INDEX REPRESENTING PROPORTIONAL CHANGE
   IN SURVIVAL OF ANIMALS MOVING FROM PATCH A TO PATCH B
○  CORRIDOR_BC=0.5
   DOCUMENT: CONSTANT-INDEX REPRESENTING PROPORTIONAL CHANGE
   IN SURVIVAL OF ANIMALS MOVING FROM PATCH B TO PATCH C
○  CORRIDOR_CD=0.5
   DOCUMENT: CONSTANT-INDEX REPRESENTING PROPORTIONAL CHANGE
   IN SURVIVAL OF ANIMALS MOVING FROM PATCH C TO PATCH D
○  CORRIDOR_CE=0.5
   DOCUMENT: CONSTANT-INDEX REPRESENTING PROPORTIONAL CHANGE
   IN SURVIVAL OF ANIMALS MOVING FROM PATCH C TO PATCH E
○  CORRIDOR_DE=0.5
   DOCUMENT: CONSTANT-INDEX REPRESENTING PROPORTIONAL CHANGE
   IN SURVIVAL OF ANIMALS MOVING FROM PATCH D TO PATCH E
○  MORT_RATE_A=0.05
   DOCUMENT: CONSTANT-MORT RATE A-PROPORTION OF POPULATION IN
   PATCH A DYING PER YEAR
○  PATCH_A=3.0
   DOCUMENT: CONSTANT-INDEX REPRESENTING PROPORTIONAL CHANGE
   IN NATALITY IN PATCH A RESULTING FROM HABITAT MANAGEMENT IN
   PATCH A
○  PATCH_B=2.0
   DOCUMENT: CONSTANT-INDEX REPRESENTING PROPORTIONAL CHANGE
   IN NATALITY IN PATCH B RESULTING FROM HABITAT MANAGEMENT IN
   PATCH B
○  PATCH_C=1.0
   DOCUMENT: CONSTANT-INDEX REPRESENTING PROPORTIONAL CHANGE
   IN NATALITY IN PATCH C RESULTING FROM HABITAT MANAGEMENT IN
   PATCH C
○  PATCH_D=0.5
   DOCUMENT: CONSTANT-INDEX REPRESENTING PROPORTIONAL CHANGE
   IN NATALITY IN PATCH D RESULTING FROM HABITAT MANAGEMENT IN
   PATCH D
○  PATCH_E=0.5
   DOCUMENT: CONSTANT-INDEX REPRESENTING PROPORTIONAL CHANGE
   IN NATALITY IN PATCH E RESULTING FROM HABITAT MANAGEMENT IN
   PATCH E
```

TABLE 17.2   (*Continued*)

○ POPTOT=POP_A+POP_B+POP_C+POP_D+POP_E

○ POP_A=AGE_1A+AGE_2A+AGE_3A+AGE_4A+AGE_5A+AGE_6A
  DOCUMENT: AUXILIARY VARIABLE-POPULATION SIZE IN PATCH A
  (ANIMALS/HA)

⊘DISP_RATE_A=GRAPH(POP_A)
  (0.00, 0.00), (10.0, 0.1), (20.0, 0.2), (30.0, 0.3),
  (40.0, 0.4), (50.0, 0.5), (60.0, 0.6), (70.0, 0.7),
  (80.0, 0.8), (90.0, 0.9), (100, 1.00)
  DOCUMENT: AUXILIARY VARIABLE-DISP RATE A-PROPORTIONAL
  INCREASE IN DISPERSAL RATE AS POPULATION SIZE INCREASES

⊘NAT_RATE_A=GRAPH(POP_A)
  (0.00, 0.075), (10.0, 0.075), (20.0, 0.075), (30.0, 0.07),
  (40.0, 0.06), (50.0, 0.05), (60.0, 0.04), (70.0, 0.03),
  (80.0, 0.02), (90.0, 0.01), (100, 0.005)
  DOCUMENT: AUXILIARY VARIABLE-NAT RATE A-PROPORTIONAL
  DECREASE IN NATALITY RATE AS POPULATION SIZE INCREASES

---

mortality risk while in the corridor. Immigration depends on the number of animals dispersing from connected patches and the survival rate in the dispersal corridor, which is affected by habitat management.

The baseline simulation, which represents current levels of natality and mortality in patches and dispersal mortality in corridors, runs from year 1 to year 200 using a time unit of 1 year and the equations in Table 17.2. PATCH A through PATCH E and CORRIDOR AB through CORRIDOR DE are indexes representing the relative natality rates in patches (relative to baseline conditions in PATCH C) and survivorship in corridors (proportion of dispersers surviving), respectively. NAT RATE A through NAT RATE E and DISP RATE A through DISP RATE E are graphical functions based on data in Table 17.1. POPTOT represents the total number of animals in the refuge resulting from the dynamics of the five subpopulations.

17.5   MODEL USE

To assess the impact on metapopulation dynamics of habitat improvement via the enhancement of breeding habitat in patches and/or protective cover in corridors, we run four 200-year simulations representing (1) the current situation (current natality and mortality in patches and dispersal mortality in corridors), (2) habitat improvement in all patches (natality increased by 10% in each patch), (3) habitat improvement in all corridors (dispersal mortality reduced to zero), and (4) habitat improvement in all patches and all corridors. The simulation results suggest that improving all patches and corridors stabilizes the metapopulation somewhat below its current level and that improving only corridors stabilizes the metapopulation at a higher level than improving only patches (Figure 17.3a). Under all management schemes, the highest population levels are maintained in patch B, followed by patch A, patch C, and patches D and E (Figures 17.3b to 17.3f). Improving corridors has a noticeably positive effect on subpopulation B, because it is connected to the most productive subpopulation (A).

To assess the impact on metapopulation dynamics of further habitat fragmentation via the blockage of dispersal corridors by each of the proposed highways, we run two additional series of simulations described earlier. However, in one of the series, the migration between habitat patches B and C will be blocked completely to simulate the impact of proposed highway 1, and in the other series, the migration between patches C and D and patches C and E will be blocked completely to simulate impact of proposed highway 2. The simulation results suggest that under either of the proposed highway routes, stabilization of the metapopulation occurs at lower levels than under any of the corresponding management schemes without a highway (Figures 17.3a, 17.4a, and 17.5a). Improving only corridors still stabilizes the metapopulation at a higher level than improving only patches, and the highest subpopulation levels still are maintained in patch B and the lowest levels in patches D and E, under all management schemes (Figures 17.4b to 17.4f and Figures 17.5b to 17.5f). Surprisingly, the proposed highway route (2) that closes two dispersal corridors has less negative impact on the metapopulation than the proposed route (1) that closes one corridor. This is because subpopulation C is close enough to subpopulation A to benefit substantially from immigration from A (through subpopulation B), whereas subpopulations D and E receive relatively little immigration, even when all corridors are open, because they are too far away from the main source of immigrants (subpopulation A).

Regarding the effect of different habitat management and land-use decisions on population dynamics of an endangered animal species existing as a metapopulation in a fragmented habitat, the simulation results suggest that the dynamics of the metapopulation depends on both habitat quality within remaining patches and the effectiveness of corridors in permitting the movement of animals among patches. Results also suggest that the value of dispersal corridors may be difficult to assess. We encourage readers to use the model to explore further the relationship between increased habitat fragmentation via blockage of dispersal corridors and the degree to which natality rates would need to be increased via habitat improvement in patches to maintain each subpopulation. A variety of relevant situations can be simulated by changing values of PATCH A through PATCH E and CORRIDOR AB through CORRIDOR DE. Of particular interest is the impact on metapopulation dynamics if both highways are built or if one of the highway routes is shifted such that it passes between patch A and patch B.

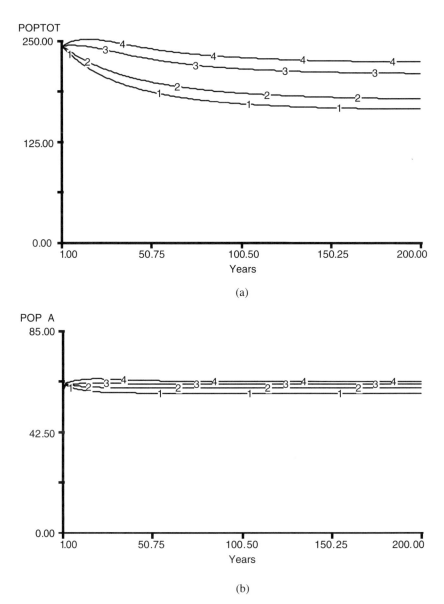

Figure 17.3 Results of four 200-year simulations representing (a) metapopulation dynamics of the endangered animal species (animals/ha) with (1) no habitat improvement (baseline), and habitat improvement in (2) patches only, (3) corridors only, and (4) both patches and corridors. Also presented are the dynamics of subpopulations (b) A, (c) B, (d) C, (e) D, and (f) E under the same four management schemes.

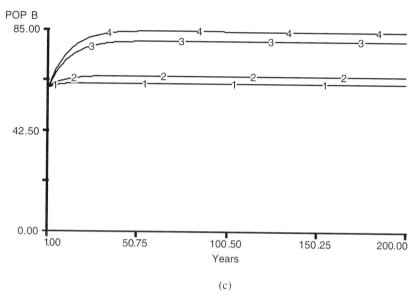

(c)

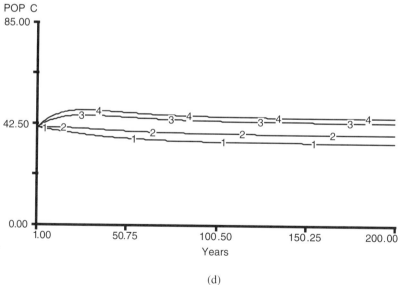

(d)

Figure 17.3   (*Continued*)

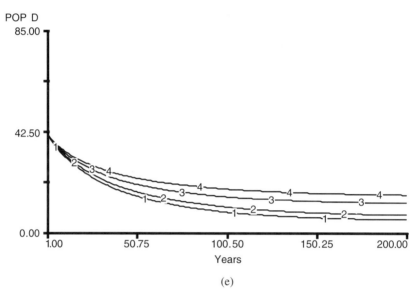

(e)

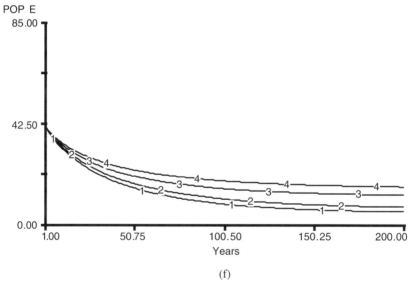

(f)

Figure 17.3 (*Continued*)

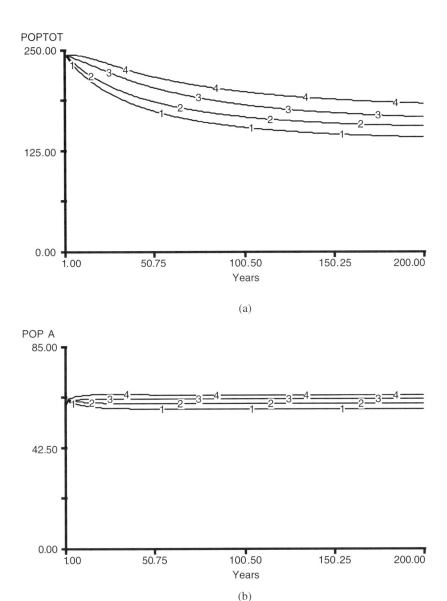

Figure 17.4 Results of four 200-year simulations representing (a) metapopulation dynamics of the endangered animal species (animals/ha), assuming the complete blockage of migration between habitat patches B and C by proposed highway 1, with (1) no habitat improvement (baseline), and habitat improvement in (2) patches only, (3) corridors only, and (4) both patches and corridors. Also presented are the dynamics of subpopulations (b) A, (c) B, (d) C, (e) D, and (f) E under the same four management schemes.

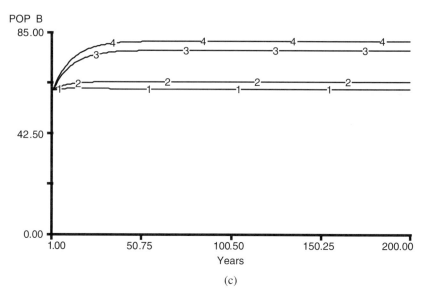

(c)

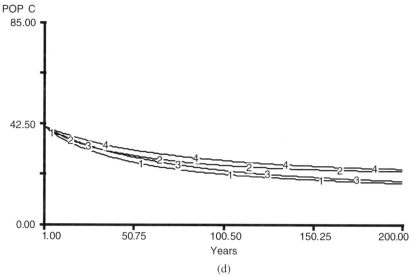

(d)

Figure 17.4 (*Continued*)

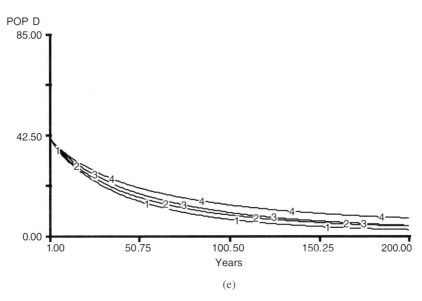

(e)

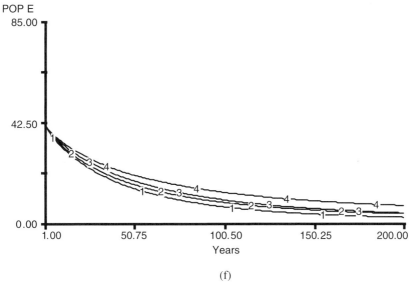

(f)

Figure 17.4 (*Continued*)

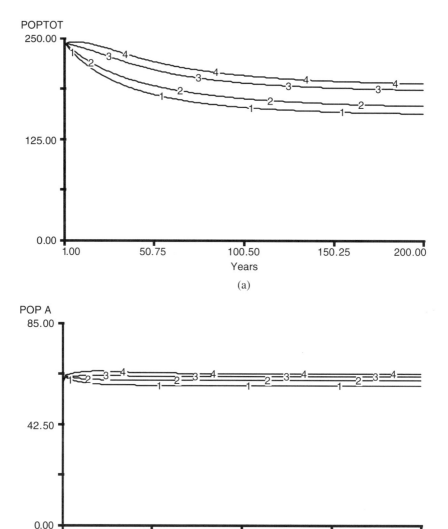

Figure 17.5 Results of four 200-year simulations representing (a) metapopulation dynamics of the endangered animal species (animals/ha), assuming complete blockage of migration between habitat patches C and D and between patches C and E by proposed highway 2, with (1) no habitat improvement, and habitat improvement in (2) patches only, (3) corridors only, and (4) both patches and corridors. Also presented are the dynamics of subpopulations (b) A, (c) B, (d) C, (e) D, and (f) E under the same four management schemes.

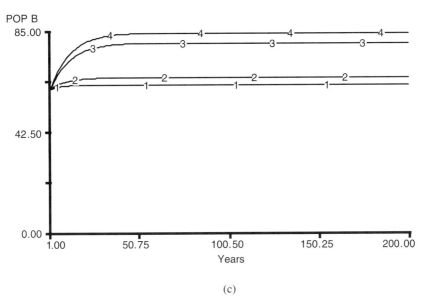

(c)

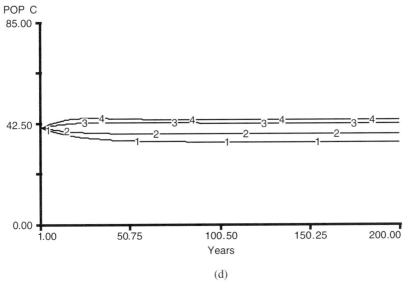

(d)

Figure 17.5 (*Continued*)

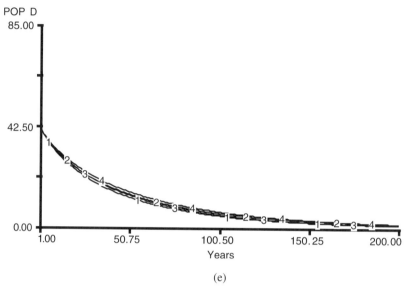

(e)

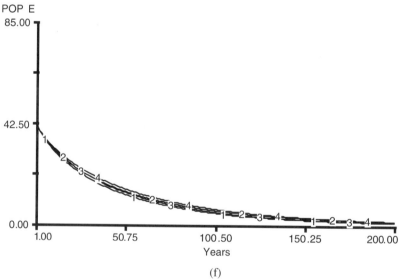

(f)

Figure 17.5   (*Continued*)

CHAPTER 18

FISHERIES MANAGEMENT: EFFECTS OF HARVEST REGULATIONS ON THE BIOMASS YIELD FROM A FISHERY

18.1 INTRODUCTION

One of the central activities in fisheries management is the setting of harvest regulations on populations of recreationally and commercially important species to maintain a sustainable yield. For migratory species, management often is complicated by their movements through different legal jurisdictions and exposure to different user groups. In this chapter, we will develop a model that simulates effects of different harvesting strategies on the yield of biomass of a commercially important migratory species that is subject to two different user groups (bay and ocean fishery).

18.2 MODEL OBJECTIVES

The general objective is to simulate the effect of different harvesting strategies on total harvest from the fishery and profit to each of two different user groups within the fishery. Specific objectives are to examine the effect on harvest and profit of the restriction of fishing effort in (1) the bay fishery and (2) the ocean fishery.

18.3 BACKGROUND INFORMATION ON THE SYSTEM-OF-INTEREST

The system-of-interest consists of a large bay and adjacent ocean waters extending 5 km offshore from which shrimp are harvested commercially. We

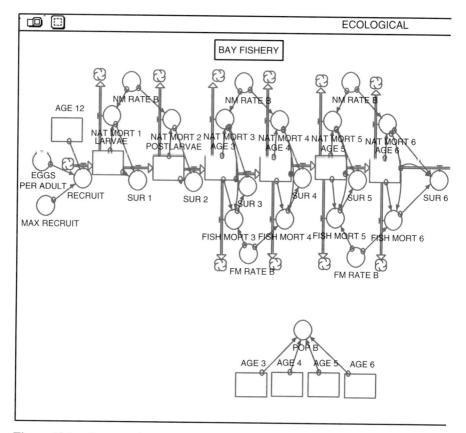

Figure 18.1 Conceptual model representing the effects of harvest regulations on harvest from a shrimp fishery.

are interested in the monthly dynamics of this system over a 10-year period. Shrimp enter the bay as larvae and, after spending a month as larvae, spend another month as postlarvae before becoming susceptible to the bay fishery as small adults. They continue to grow and begin to migrate from the bay toward the ocean, leaving the bay at age 7 months and attaining full size at 12 months of age (Table 18.1).

Spawning begins at 12 months of age and continues throughout life, with approximately 1,000 eggs fertilized each month for each shrimp that has attained 12 months of age. Fertilized eggs are carried by currents into the bay and mature into larvae the same month they are spawned. However, a maximum of 10,000 larvae can be recruited into the bay population during any given month. All shrimp (larvae, postlarvae, and adults) are subject to natural mortality and adults are subject to fishing mortality in both the bay and the ocean. The rate of natural mortality is higher for smaller bay shrimp (35% of the population per month) and is lower for larger ocean shrimp (25% per

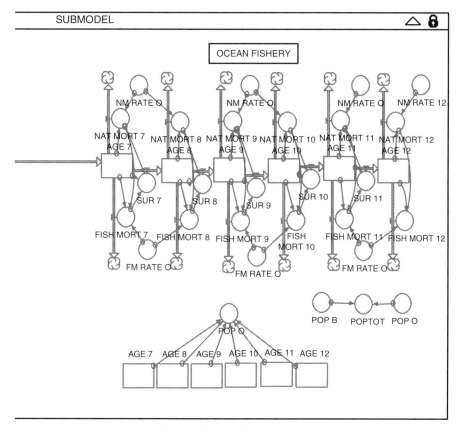

Figure 18.1 (*Continued*)

Table 18.1 Typical Age-Class Distribution in an Unharvested Shrimp Population and Average Weights of Individual Shrimp in Each Age Class

Age (Months)	Number of Shrimp	Weight of Individual Shrimp (g)
1 (larvae)	10,000	—
2 (postlarvae)	6,500	—
3	4,225	20
4	2,746	30
5	1,785	40
6	1,160	50
7	754	80
8	566	120
9	424	160
10	318	200
11	239	230
12	181	250

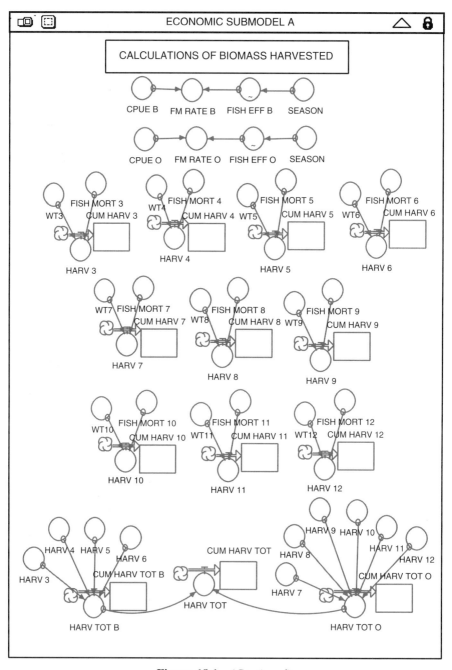

Figure 18.1 (*Continued*)

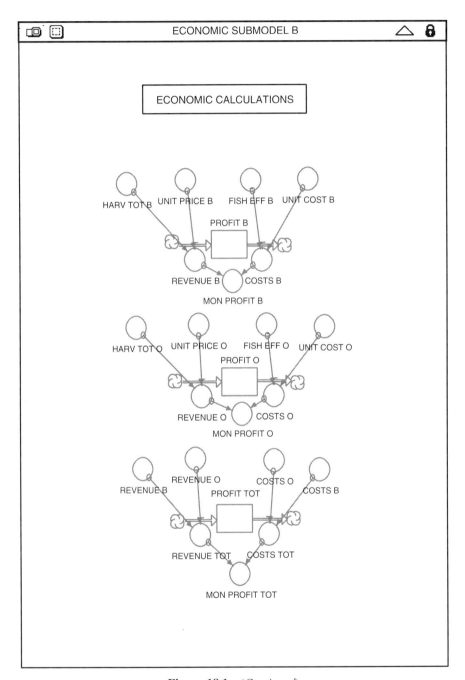

Figure 18.1   (*Continued*)

month) until they spawn, at which time the natural mortality rate increases to 99% per month. The rate of fishing mortality depends on the amount of fishing effort exerted by two distinct groups of fishermen, one group operating only in the bay and the other only in the ocean. The catch per standardized unit of fishing effort is 1.5% of the population in the bay and 1.0% of the population in the ocean. The profit for each group of fishermen depends on the revenue from the harvest and the cost of fishing. The revenue from the harvest depends on the total biomass of the shrimp harvested and the unit price of shrimp, which is lower for the smaller shrimp harvested from the bay ($1/kg) and higher for the larger shrimp harvested from the ocean ($1.5/kg). The cost of fishing depends on the amount of fishing effort and the cost per unit of fishing effort, which is lower for the smaller fishing boats operating in the bay ($250/unit of fishing effort) and higher for the larger fishing boats operating in the ocean ($500/unit of fishing effort).

Currently, fishermen exert 20 units of fishing effort per month in the bay and 30 units per month in the ocean throughout the year. Under these levels of fishing pressure, the fishery has remained profitable, but harvests have been decreasing. The fishery manager wants to achieve a profitable but sustainable harvest by adjusting the amount and perhaps the seasonal distribution of fishing effort in the bay and in the ocean.

18.4   MODEL DESCRIPTION

The model consists of two submodels representing ecology of the resource species and economics of the fishery, respectively (Figure 18.1). The ecological submodel represents changes in the number of animals in each age class resulting from recruitment, natural mortality, and fishing mortality. Growth and migration of animals are represented implicitly by assigning a weight (g) and a location (bay or ocean) to each age class. Recruitment depends on the number of shrimp in age class 12, and the natural and fishing mortality rates depend on whether shrimp are in the bay or ocean. Fishing mortality also depends on the level of fishing effort in the bay and ocean. The economic submodel represents the level of fishing effort, the cost of fishing, the value of the harvest, and the resulting profit in both bay and ocean fisheries.

The baseline simulation, which represents 20 units of fishing effort per C18M month in the bay and 30 units per month in the ocean throughout the year, runs from month 1 to month 120 using a time unit of 1 month and the equations in Table 18.2. FISH EFF B and FISH EFF O are driving variables representing the number units of fishing effort per month in the bay and in the ocean, respectively.

(Text continues on page 320.)

Table 18.2 Equations (Baseline Conditions) for the Simulation Model Representing Effects of Harvest Regulations on Harvest and Profit from a Shrimp Fishery

```
                         ECOLOGICAL SUBMODEL

☐ AGE_10(t)=AGE_10(t-dt)+(SUR_9-SUR_10-FISH_MORT_10-NAT_MORT_
  10)*dt
  INIT AGE_10=318
  DOCUMENT: NUMBER OF AGE CLASS TEN ANIMALS IN THE OCEAN
  INFLOWS:
    SUR_9=AGE_9-NAT_MORT_9-FISH_MORT_9
      DOCUMENT: SURVIVAL OF AGE CLASS NINE ANIMALS
      (ANIMALS/MO)
  OUTFLOWS:
    SUR_10=AGE_10-NAT_MORT_10-FISH_MORT_10
      DOCUMENT: SURVIVAL OF AGE CLASS TEN ANIMALS
      (ANIMALS/MO)
    FISH_MORT_10=(AGE_10-NAT_MORT_10)*FM_RATE_O
      DOCUMENT: FISHING MORTALITY OF AGE CLASS TEN ANIMALS
      (ANIMALS/MO)
    NAT_MORT_10=AGE_10*NM_RATE_O
      DOCUMENT: NATURAL MORTALITY OF AGE CLASS TEN ANIMALS
      (ANIMALS/MO)
☐ AGE_11(t)=AGE_11(t-dt)+(SUR_10-SUR_11-FISH_MORT_11-NAT_
  MORT_11)*dt
  INIT AGE_11=239
  DOCUMENT: NUMBER OF AGE CLASS ELEVEN ANIMALS IN THE OCEAN
  INFLOWS:
    SUR_10=AGE_10-NAT_MORT_10-FISH_MORT_10
      DOCUMENT: SURVIVAL OF AGE CLASS TEN ANIMALS
      (ANIMALS/MO)
  OUTFLOWS:
    SUR_11=AGE_11-NAT_MORT_11-FISH_MORT_11
      DOCUMENT: SURVIVAL OF AGE CLASS ELEVEN ANIMALS
      (ANIMALS/MO)
    FISH_MORT_11=(AGE_11-NAT_MORT_11)*FM_RATE_O
      DOCUMENT: FISHING MORTALITY OF AGE CLASS ELEVEN ANIMALS
      (ANIMALS/MO)
    NAT_MORT_11=AGE_11*NM_RATE_O
      DOCUMENT: NATURAL MORTALITY OF AGE CLASS ELEVEN ANIMALS
      (ANIMALS/MO)
☐ AGE_12(t)=AGE_12(t-dt)+(SUR_11-FISH_MORT_12-NAT_MORT_12)*dt
  INIT AGE_12=181
  DOCUMENT: NUMBER OF AGE CLASS TWELVE ANIMALS IN THE OCEAN
  INFLOWS:
    SUR_11=AGE_11-NAT_MORT_11-FISH_MORT_11
      DOCUMENT: SURVIVAL OF AGE CLASS ELEVEN ANIMALS
      (ANIMALS/MO)
```

Table 18.2   (*Continued*)

```
OUTFLOWS:
   FISH_MORT_12=(AGE_12-NAT_MORT_12)*FM_RATE_O
      DOCUMENT: FISHING MORTALITY OF AGE CLASS TWELVE ANIMALS
      (ANIMALS/MO)
   NAT_MORT_12=AGE_12*NM_RATE_12
      DOCUMENT: NATURAL MORTALITY OF AGE CLASS TWELVE ANIMALS
      (ANIMALS/MO)
AGE_3(t)=AGE_3(t-dt)+(SUR_2-SUR_3-FISH_MORT_3-NAT_
MORT_3)*dt
INIT AGE_3=4225
DOCUMENT: NUMBER OF AGE CLASS THREE AMIMALS IN THE BAY
INFLOWS:
   SUR_2=POSTLARVAE-NAT_MORT_2
      DOCUMENT: SURVIVAL OF POSTLARVAE (ANIMALS/MO)
OUTFLOWS:
   SUR_3=AGE_3-NAT_MORT_3-FISH_MORT_3
      DOCUMENT: SURVIVAL OF AGE CLASS THREE ANIMALS
      (ANIMALS/MO)
   FISH_MORT_3=(AGE_3-NAT_MORT_3)*FM_RATE_B
      DOCUMENT: FISHING MORTALITY OF AGE CLASS THREE ANIMALS
      (ANIMALS/MO)
   NAT_MORT_3=AGE_3*NM_RATE_B
      DOCUMENT: NATURAL MORTALITY OF AGE CLASS THREE ANIMALS
      (ANIMALS/MO)
AGE_4(t)=AGE_4(t-dt)+(SUR_3-SUR_4-FISH_MORT_4-NAT_MORT_
4)*dt
INIT AGE_4=2746
DOCUMENT: NUMBER OF AGE CLASS FOUR ANIMALS IN THE BAY
INFLOWS:
   SUR_3=AGE_3-NAT_MORT_3-FISH_MORT_3
      DOCUMENT: SURVIVAL OF AGE CLASS THREE ANIMALS
      (ANIMALS/MO)
OUTFLOWS:
   SUR_4=AGE_4-NAT_MORT_4-FISH_MORT_4
      DOCUMENT: SURVIVAL OF AGE CLASS FOUR ANIMALS
      (ANIMALS/MO)
   FISH_MORT_4=(AGE_4-NAT_MORT_4)*FM_RATE_B
      DOCUMENT: FISHING MORTALITY OF AGE CLASS FOUR ANIMALS
      (ANIMALS/MO)
   NAT_MORT_4=AGE_4*NM_RATE_B
      DOCUMENT: NATURAL MORTALITY OF AGE CLASS FOUR ANIMALS
      (ANIMALS/MO)
AGE_5(t)=AGE_5(t-dt)+(SUR_4-SUR_5-FISH_MORT_5-NAT_MORT_
5)*dt
INIT AGE_5=1785
DOCUMENT: NUMBER OF AGE CLASS FIVE ANIMALS IN THE BAY
```

Table 18.2   (*Continued*)

```
      INFLOWS:
       ☝ SUR_4=AGE_4-NAT_MORT_4-FISH_MORT_4
          DOCUMENT: SURVIVAL OF AGE CLASS FOUR ANIMALS
          (ANIMALS / MO)
      OUTFLOWS:
       ☝ SUR_5=AGE_5-NAT_MORT_5-FISH_MORT_5
          DOCUMENT: SURVIVAL OF AGE CLASS FIVE ANIMALS
          (ANIMALS / MO)
       ☝ FISH_MORT_5=(AGE_5-NAT_MORT_5)*FM_RATE_B
          DOCUMENT: FISHING MORTALITY OF AGE CLASS FIVE ANIMALS
          (ANIMALS / MO)
       ☝ NAT_MORT_5=AGE_5*NM_RATE_B
          DOCUMENT: NATURAL MORTALITY OF AGE CLASS FIVE ANIMALS
          (ANIMALS / MO)
  □ AGE_6(t)=AGE_6(t-dt)+(SUR_5-FISH_MORT_6-NAT_MORT_6-SUR_
    6)*dt
    INIT AGE_6=1160
    DOCUMENT: NUMBER OF AGE CLASS SIX ANIMALS IN THE BAY
    INFLOWS:
       ☝ SUR_5=AGE_5-NAT_MORT_5-FISH_MORT_5
          DOCUMENT: SURVIVAL OF AGE CLASS FIVE ANIMALS
          (ANIMALS / MO)
      OUTFLOWS:
       ☝ FISH_MORT_6=(AGE_6-NAT_MORT_6)*FM_RATE_B
          DOCUMENT: FISHING MORTALITY OF AGE CLASS SIX ANIMALS
          (ANIMALS / MO)
       ☝ NAT_MORT_6=AGE_6*NM_RATE_B
          DOCUMENT: NATURAL MORTALITY OF AGE CLASS SIX ANIMALS
          (ANIMALS / MO)
       ☝ SUR_6=AGE_6-NAT_MORT_6-FISH_MORT_6
          DOCUMENT: SURVIVAL OF AGE CLASS SIX ANIMALS
          (ANIMALS / MO)
  □ AGE_7(t)=AGE_7(t-dt)+(SUR_6-SUR_7-NAT_MORT_7-FISH_MORT_
    7)*dt
    INIT AGE_7=754
    DOCUMENT: NUMBER OF AGE CLASS SEVEN ANIMALS IN THE OCEAN
    INFLOWS:
       ☝ SUR_6=AGE_6-NAT_MORT_6-FISH_MORT_6
          DOCUMENT: SURVIVAL OF AGE CLASS SIX ANIMALS
          (ANIMALS / MO)
      OUTFLOWS:
       ☝ SUR_7=AGE_7-NAT_MORT_7-FISH_MORT_7
          DOCUMENT: SURVIVAL OF AGE CLASS SEVEN ANIMALS
          (ANIMALS / MO)
       ☝ NAT_MORT_7=AGE_7*NM_RATE_O
          DOCUMENT: NATURAL MORTALITY OF AGE CLASS SEVEN ANIMALS
          (ANIMALS / MO)
       ☝ FISH_MORT_7=(AGE_7-NAT_MORT_7)*FM_RATE_O
          DOCUMENT: FISHING MORTALITY OF AGE CLASS SEVEN ANIMALS
          (ANIMALS / MO)
```

Table 18.2 (*Continued*)

☐ AGE_8(t)=AGE_8(t-dt)+(SUR_7-SUR_8-NAT_MORT_8-FISH_MORT_
8)*dt
INIT AGE_8=566
DOCUMENT: NUMBER OF AGE CLASS EIGHT ANIMALS IN THE OCEAN
INFLOWS:
⏣ SUR_7=AGE_7-NAT_MORT_7-FISH_MORT_7
    DOCUMENT: SURVIVAL OF AGE CLASS SEVEN ANIMALS
    (ANIMALS/MO)
OUTFLOWS:
⏣ SUR_8=AGE_8-NAT_MORT_8-FISH_MORT_8
    DOCUMENT: SURVIVAL OF AGE CLASS EIGHT ANIMALS
    (ANIMALS/MO)
⏣ NAT_MORT_8=AGE_8*NM_RATE_O
    DOCUMENT: NATURAL MORTALITY OF AGE CLASS EIGHT ANIMALS
    (ANIMALS/MO)
⏣ FISH_MORT_8=(AGE_8-NAT_MORT_8)*FM_RATE_O
    DOCUMENT: FISHING MORTALITY OF AGE CLASS EIGHT ANIMALS
    (ANIMALS/MO)
☐ AGE_9(t)=AGE_9(t-dt)+(SUR_8-SUR_9-FISH_MORT_9-NAT_MORT_
9)*dt
INIT AGE_9=424
DOCUMENT: NUMBER OF AGE CLASS NINE ANIMALS IN THE OCEAN
INFLOWS:
⏣ SUR_8=AGE_8-NAT_MORT_8-FISH_MORT_8
    DOCUMENT: SURVIVAL OF AGE CLASS EIGHT ANIMALS
    (ANIMALS/MO)
OUTFLOWS:
⏣ SUR_9=AGE_9-NAT_MORT_9-FISH_MORT_9
    DOCUMENT: SURVIVAL OF AGE CLASS NINE ANIMALS
    (ANIMALS/MO)
⏣ FISH_MORT_9=(AGE_9-NAT_MORT_9)*FM_RATE_O
    DOCUMENT: FISHING MORTALITY OF AGE CLASS NINE ANIMALS
    (ANIMALS/MO)
⏣ NAT_MORT_9=AGE_9*NM_RATE_O
    DOCUMENT: NATURAL MORTALITY OF AGE CLASS NINE ANIMALS
    (ANIMALS/MO)
☐ LARVAE(t)=LARVAE(t-dt)+(RECRUIT-SUR_1-NAT_MORT_1)*dt
INIT LARVAE=10000
DOCUMENT:NUMBER OF LARVAE IN THE BAY
INFLOWS:
⏣ RECRUIT=MIN(AGE_12*EGGS_PER_ADULT,MAX_RECRUIT)
    DOCUMENT: RECRUITMENT OF LARVAE INTO THE BAY (ANIMALS/
    MO)
OUTFLOWS:
⏣ SUR_1=LARVAE-NAT_MORT_1
    DOCUMENT: SURVIVAL OF LARVAE (ANIMALS/MO)
⏣ NAT_MORT_1=LARVAE*NM_RATE_B
    DOCUMENT: NATURAL MORTALITY OF LARVAE (ANIMALS/MO)

Table 18.2   *(Continued)*

☐ POSTLARVAE(t)=POSTLARVAE(t-dt)+(SUR_1-SUR_2-NAT_MORT_2)*dt
    INIT POSTLARVAE=6500
    DOCUMENT: NUMBER OF POSTLARVAE IN THE BAY
    INFLOWS:
      ⚷ SUR_1=LARVAE-NAT_MORT_1
        DOCUMENT: SURVIVAL OF LARVAE (ANIMALS/MO)
    OUTFLOWS:
      ⚷ SUR_2=POSTLARVAE-NAT_MORT_2
        DOCUMENT: SURVIVAL OF POSTLARVAE (ANIMALS/MO)
      ⚷ NAT_MORT_2=POSTLARVAE*NM_RATE_B
        DOCUMENT: NATURAL MORTALITY OF POSTLARVAE (ANIMALS/MO)
○ EGGS_PER_ADULT=1000
    DOCUMENT: CONSTANT-EGGS PER ADULT-NUMBER OF EGGS PER ANIMAL
    IN AGE CLASS 12 PER MONTH
○ MAX_RECRUIT=10000
    DOCUMENT: CONSTANT-MAXIMUM RECRUIT-MAXIMUM NUMBER OF EGGS
    THAT CAN BE RECRUITED AS LARVAE DURING ONE MONTH
○ NM_RATE_12=0.99
    DOCUMENT: CONSTANT-NM RATE 12-NATURAL MORTALITY RATE OF AGE
    CLASS TWELVE ANIMALS (PROPORTION OF AGE CLASS DYING PER
    MONTH)
○ NM_RATE_B=0.35
    DOCUMENT: CONSTANT-NM RATE B-NATURAL MORTALITY RATE IN THE
    BAY (PROPORTION OF POPULATION DYING PER MONTH)
○ NM_RATE_O=0.25
    DOCUMENT: CONSTANT-NM RATE O-NATURAL MORTALITY RATE IN THE
    OCEAN (PROPORTION OF THE POPULATION DYING PER MONTH)
○ POPTOT=POP_B+POP_O
    DOCUMENT: AUXILIARY VARIABLE-POPTOT-TOTAL NUMBER OF ANIMALS
    IN THE BAY PLUS THE OCEAN
○ POP_B=AGE_3+AGE_4+AGE_5+AGE_6
    DOCUMENT: AUXILIARY VARIABLE-POP B-TOTAL NUMBER OF ANIMALS
    IN THE BAY
○ POP_O=AGE_7+AGE_8+AGE_9+AGE_10+AGE_11+AGE_12
    DOCUMENT: AUXILIARY VARIABLE-POP O-TOTAL NUMBER OF ANIMALS
    IN THE OCEAN

ECONOMIC SUBMODEL A

☐ CUM_HARV_10(t)=CUM_HARV_10(t-dt)+(HARV_10)*dt
    INIT CUM_HARV_10=0
    DOCUMENT: CUMULATIVE HARVEST OF AGE CLASS TEN ANIMALS (G)
    INFLOWS:
      ⚷ HARV_10=FISH_MORT_10*WT10
        DOCUMENT: HARVEST OF AGE CLASS TEN ANIMALS (G/MO)
☐ CUM_HARV_11(t)=CUM_HARV_11(t-dt)+(HARV_11)*dt
    INIT CUM_HARV_11=0
    DOCUMENT: CUMULATIVE HARVEST OF AGE CLASS ELEVEN ANIMALS
    (G)
    INFLOWS:

Table 18.2   (*Continued*)

```
⌖ HARV_11=FISH_MORT_11*WT11
   DOCUMENT: HARVEST OF AGE CLASS ELEVEN ANIMALS (G/MO)
☐ CUM_HARV_12(t)=CUM_HARV_12(t-dt)+(HARV_12)*dt
   INIT CUM_HARV_12=0
   DOCUMENT: CUMULATIVE HARVEST OF AGE CLASS TWELVE
   ANIMALS (G)
   INFLOWS:
   ⌖ HARV_12=FISH_MORT_12*WT12
      DOCUMENT: HARVEST OF AGE CLASS TWELVE ANIMALS (G/MO)
☐ CUM_HARV_3(t)=CUM_HARV_3(t-dt)+(HARV_3)*dt
   INIT CUM_HARV_3=0
   DOCUMENT: CUMULATIVE HARVEST OF AGE CLASS THREE ANIMALS (G)
   INFLOWS:
   ⌖ HARV_3=FISH_MORT_3*WT3
      DOCUMENT: HARVEST OF ANIMALS IN AGE CLASS THREE (G/MO)
☐ CUM_HARV_4(t)=CUM_HARV_4(t-dt)+(HARV_4)*dt
   INIT CUM_HARV_4=0
   DOCUMENT: CUMULATIVE HARVEST OF AGE CLASS FOUR ANIMALS (G)
   INFLOWS:
   ⌖ HARV_4=FISH_MORT_4*WT4
      DOCUMENT: HARVEST OF ANIMALS IN AGE CLASS FOUR (G/MO)
☐ CUM_HARV_5(t)=CUM_HARV_5(t-dt)+(HARV_5)*dt
   INIT CUM_HARV_5=0
   DOCUMENT: CUMULATIVE HARVEST OF AGE CLASS FIVE ANIMALS (G)
   INFLOWS:
   ⌖ HARV_5=FISH_MORT_5*WT5
      DOCUMENT: HARVEST OF AGE CLASS FIVE ANIMALS (G/MO)
☐ CUM_HARV_6(t)=CUM_HARV_6(t-dt)+(HARV_6)*dt
   INIT CUM_HARV_6=0
   DOCUMENT: CUMULATIVE HARVEST OF AGE CLASS SIX ANIMALS (G)
   INFLOWS:
   ⌖ HARV_6=FISH_MORT_6*WT6
      DOCUMENT: HARVEST OF AGE CLASS SIX ANIMALS (G/MO)
☐ CUM_HARV_7(t)=CUM_HARV_7(t-dt)+(HARV_7)*dt
   INIT CUM_HARV_7=0
   DOCUMENT: CUMULATIVE HARVEST OF AGE CLASS SEVEN ANIMALS (G)
   INFLOWS:
   ⌖ HARV_7=FISH_MORT_7*WT7
      DOCUMENT: HARVEST OF AGE CLASS SEVEN ANIMALS (G/MO)
☐ CUM_HARV_8(t)=CUM_HARV_8(t-dt)+(HARV_8)*dt
   INIT CUM_HARV_8=0
   DOCUMENT: CUMULATIVE HARVEST OF AGE CLASS EIGHT ANIMALS (G)
   INFLOWS:
   ⌖ HARV_8=FISH_MORT_8*WT8
      DOCUMENT: HARVEST OF AGE CLASS EIGHT ANIMALS (G/MO)
☐ CUM_HARV_9(t)=CUM_HARV_9(t-dt)+(HARV_9)*dt
   INIT CUM_HARV_9=0
   DOCUMENT: CUMULATIVE HARVEST OF AGE CLASS NINE ANIMALS (G)
   INFLOWS:
```

Table 18.2 (*Continued*)

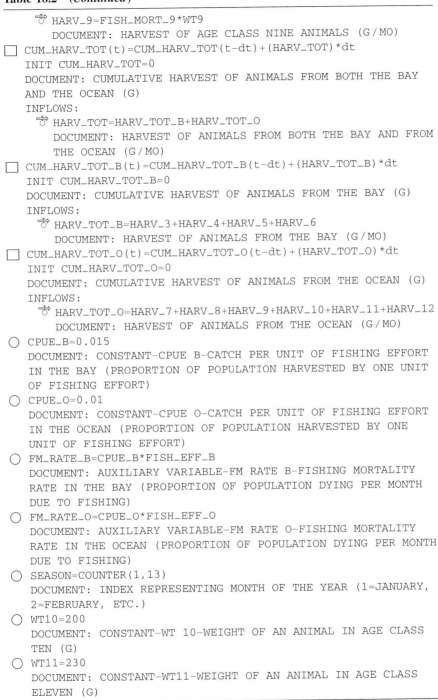

☞ HARV_9=FISH_MORT_9*WT9
 DOCUMENT: HARVEST OF AGE CLASS NINE ANIMALS (G/MO)
☐ CUM_HARV_TOT(t)=CUM_HARV_TOT(t-dt)+(HARV_TOT)*dt
 INIT CUM_HARV_TOT=0
 DOCUMENT: CUMULATIVE HARVEST OF ANIMALS FROM BOTH THE BAY
 AND THE OCEAN (G)
 INFLOWS:
  ☞ HARV_TOT=HARV_TOT_B+HARV_TOT_O
   DOCUMENT: HARVEST OF ANIMALS FROM BOTH THE BAY AND FROM
   THE OCEAN (G/MO)
☐ CUM_HARV_TOT_B(t)=CUM_HARV_TOT_B(t-dt)+(HARV_TOT_B)*dt
 INIT CUM_HARV_TOT_B=0
 DOCUMENT: CUMULATIVE HARVEST OF ANIMALS FROM THE BAY (G)
 INFLOWS:
  ☞ HARV_TOT_B=HARV_3+HARV_4+HARV_5+HARV_6
   DOCUMENT: HARVEST OF ANIMALS FROM THE BAY (G/MO)
☐ CUM_HARV_TOT_O(t)=CUM_HARV_TOT_O(t-dt)+(HARV_TOT_O)*dt
 INIT CUM_HARV_TOT_O=0
 DOCUMENT: CUMULATIVE HARVEST OF ANIMALS FROM THE OCEAN (G)
 INFLOWS:
  ☞ HARV_TOT_O=HARV_7+HARV_8+HARV_9+HARV_10+HARV_11+HARV_12
   DOCUMENT: HARVEST OF ANIMALS FROM THE OCEAN (G/MO)
○ CPUE_B=0.015
 DOCUMENT: CONSTANT-CPUE B-CATCH PER UNIT OF FISHING EFFORT
 IN THE BAY (PROPORTION OF POPULATION HARVESTED BY ONE UNIT
 OF FISHING EFFORT)
○ CPUE_O=0.01
 DOCUMENT: CONSTANT-CPUE O-CATCH PER UNIT OF FISHING EFFORT
 IN THE OCEAN (PROPORTION OF POPULATION HARVESTED BY ONE
 UNIT OF FISHING EFFORT)
○ FM_RATE_B=CPUE_B*FISH_EFF_B
 DOCUMENT: AUXILIARY VARIABLE-FM RATE B-FISHING MORTALITY
 RATE IN THE BAY (PROPORTION OF POPULATION DYING PER MONTH
 DUE TO FISHING)
○ FM_RATE_O=CPUE_O*FISH_EFF_O
 DOCUMENT: AUXILIARY VARIABLE-FM RATE O-FISHING MORTALITY
 RATE IN THE OCEAN (PROPORTION OF POPULATION DYING PER MONTH
 DUE TO FISHING)
○ SEASON=COUNTER(1,13)
 DOCUMENT: INDEX REPRESENTING MONTH OF THE YEAR (1=JANUARY,
 2=FEBRUARY, ETC.)
○ WT10=200
 DOCUMENT: CONSTANT-WT 10-WEIGHT OF AN ANIMAL IN AGE CLASS
 TEN (G)
○ WT11=230
 DOCUMENT: CONSTANT-WT11-WEIGHT OF AN ANIMAL IN AGE CLASS
 ELEVEN (G)

Table 18.2 *(Continued)*

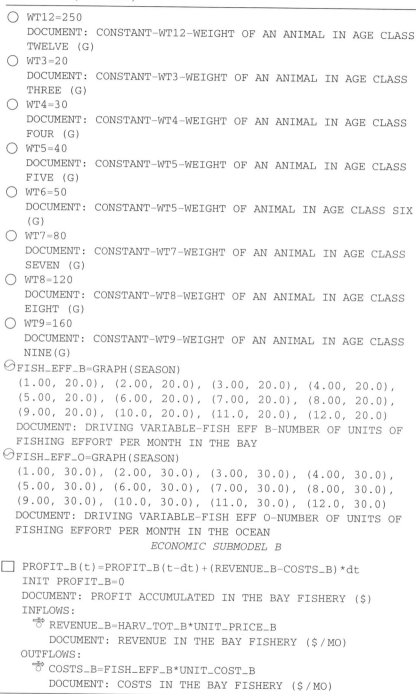

○ WT12=250
  DOCUMENT: CONSTANT-WT12-WEIGHT OF AN ANIMAL IN AGE CLASS
  TWELVE (G)
○ WT3=20
  DOCUMENT: CONSTANT-WT3-WEIGHT OF AN ANIMAL IN AGE CLASS
  THREE (G)
○ WT4=30
  DOCUMENT: CONSTANT-WT4-WEIGHT OF AN ANIMAL IN AGE CLASS
  FOUR (G)
○ WT5=40
  DOCUMENT: CONSTANT-WT5-WEIGHT OF AN ANIMAL IN AGE CLASS
  FIVE (G)
○ WT6=50
  DOCUMENT: CONSTANT-WT5-WEIGHT OF ANIMAL IN AGE CLASS SIX
  (G)
○ WT7=80
  DOCUMENT: CONSTANT-WT7-WEIGHT OF AN ANIMAL IN AGE CLASS
  SEVEN (G)
○ WT8=120
  DOCUMENT: CONSTANT-WT8-WEIGHT OF AN ANIMAL IN AGE CLASS
  EIGHT (G)
○ WT9=160
  DOCUMENT: CONSTANT-WT9-WEIGHT OF AN ANIMAL IN AGE CLASS
  NINE(G)
⊘FISH_EFF_B=GRAPH(SEASON)
  (1.00, 20.0), (2.00, 20.0), (3.00, 20.0), (4.00, 20.0),
  (5.00, 20.0), (6.00, 20.0), (7.00, 20.0), (8.00, 20.0),
  (9.00, 20.0), (10.0, 20.0), (11.0, 20.0), (12.0, 20.0)
  DOCUMENT: DRIVING VARIABLE-FISH EFF B-NUMBER OF UNITS OF
  FISHING EFFORT PER MONTH IN THE BAY
⊘FISH_EFF_O=GRAPH(SEASON)
  (1.00, 30.0), (2.00, 30.0), (3.00, 30.0), (4.00, 30.0),
  (5.00, 30.0), (6.00, 30.0), (7.00, 30.0), (8.00, 30.0),
  (9.00, 30.0), (10.0, 30.0), (11.0, 30.0), (12.0, 30.0)
  DOCUMENT: DRIVING VARIABLE-FISH EFF O-NUMBER OF UNITS OF
  FISHING EFFORT PER MONTH IN THE OCEAN
                    ECONOMIC SUBMODEL B

☐ PROFIT_B(t)=PROFIT_B(t-dt)+(REVENUE_B-COSTS_B)*dt
  INIT PROFIT_B=0
  DOCUMENT: PROFIT ACCUMULATED IN THE BAY FISHERY ($)
  INFLOWS:
    ⏣ REVENUE_B=HARV_TOT_B*UNIT_PRICE_B
      DOCUMENT: REVENUE IN THE BAY FISHERY ($/MO)
  OUTFLOWS:
    ⏣ COSTS_B=FISH_EFF_B*UNIT_COST_B
      DOCUMENT: COSTS IN THE BAY FISHERY ($/MO)

Table 18.2   (*Continued*)

☐ PROFIT_O(t)=PROFIT_O(t-dt)+(REVENUE_O-COSTS_O)*dt
  INIT PROFIT_O=0
  DOCUMENT: PROFIT ACCUMULATED IN THE OCEAN FISHERY ($)
  INFLOWS:
    ⌖ REVENUE_O=HARV_TOT_O*UNIT_PRICE_O
      DOCUMENT: REVENUE IN THE OCEAN FISHERY ($/MO)
  OUTFLOWS:
    ⌖ COSTS_O=FISH_EFF_O*UNIT_COST_O
      DOCUMENT: COSTS IN THE OCEAN FISHERY ($/MO)
☐ PROFIT_TOT(t)=PROFIT_TOT(t-dt)+(REVENUE_TOT-COSTS_TOT)*dt
  INIT PROFIT_TOT=0
  DOCUMENT: PROFIT ACCUMULATED IN BOTH THE BAY AND THE OCEAN
  FISHERIES ($)
  INFLOWS:
    ⌖ REVENUE_TOT=REVENUE_B+REVENUE_O
      DOCUMENT: REVENUE IN THE FISHERY ($/MO)
  OUTFLOWS:
    ⌖ COSTS_TOT=COSTS_B+COSTS_O
      DOCUMENT: COSTS IN THE FISHERY ($/MO)
○ MON_PROFIT_B=REVENUE_B-COSTS_B
  DOCUMENT: AUXILIARY VARIABLE-MON PROFIT B-MONTHLY PROFIT IN
  THE BAY FISHERY ($)
○ MON_PROFIT_O=REVENUE_O-COSTS_O
  DOCUMENT: AUXILIARY VARIABLE-MON PROFIT O-MONTHLY PROFIT IN
  THE OCEAN FISHERY ($)
○ MON_PROFIT_TOT=REVENUE_TOT-COSTS_TOT
  DOCUMENT: AUXILIARY VARIABLE-MON PROFIT TOT-MONTHLY PROFIT
  IN THE FISHERY ($)
○ UNIT_COST_B=250
  DOCUMENT: CONSTANT-UNIT COST B-COST OF ONE UNIT OF FISHING
  EFFORT IN THE BAY ($/UNIT EFFORT)
○ UNIT_COST_O=500
  DOCUMENT: CONSTANT-UNIT COST O-COST OF ONE UNIT OF FISHING
  EFFORT IN THE OCEAN ($/UNIT EFFORT)
○ UNIT_PRICE_B=1
  DOCUMENT: CONSTANT-UNIT PRICE B-UNIT PRICE OF ANIMALS
  HARVESTED FROM THE BAY ($/KG)
○ UNIT_PRICE_O=1.5
  DOCUMENT: CONSTANT-UNIT PRICE O-UNIT PRICE OF ANIMALS
  HARVESTED FROM THE OCEAN ($/KG)

18.5   MODEL USE

To examine the effect on harvest and profit of (1) the restriction of fishing effort in the bay fishery and (2) the restriction of fishing effort in the ocean fishery, we run two series of 10-year simulations in which we reduce the fishing effort relative to current levels (20 and 30 units per month in the bay and ocean, respectively) in (1) the bay and (2) the ocean until harvests become sustainable. Simulation results indicate that under current conditions, the total harvest from the fishery decreases rapidly over the next several years, with the total profit accumulated from the fishery beginning to decline within 5 years (Figure 18.2). The ocean fishery begins to lose money within 2 years, whereas the bay fishery remains profitable for roughly 6 years and subsequently incurs smaller losses than the ocean fishery. If the fishing effort is maintained at 30 units per month in the ocean, the effort in the bay must be reduced to 16 units per month to achieve a sustainable harvest (Figure 18.3a). The bay fishery remains profitable over the next decade at all simulated levels of bay fishing effort except 20 units per month (Figure 18.3b), whereas the ocean fishery remains profitable only when the bay effort is reduced to 16 units per month (Figure 18.3c). If the fishing effort is maintained at 20 units per month in the bay, the effort in the ocean must be reduced to 25 units per month to achieve a sustainable harvest (Figure 18.4a). The bay fishery remains profitable over the next decade at all simulated levels of the ocean fishing

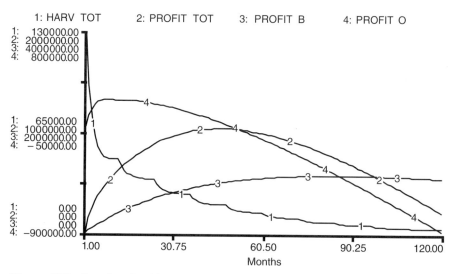

Figure 18.2   Results of a 10-year simulation representing (1) total harvest (kg) and (2) profit ($) from both bay and ocean fisheries, and profit from the (3) bay and (4) ocean sectors of the fishery under current conditions of 20 units of fishing effort per month in the bay and 30 units of effort in the ocean.

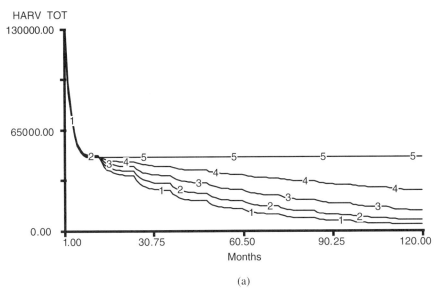

(a)

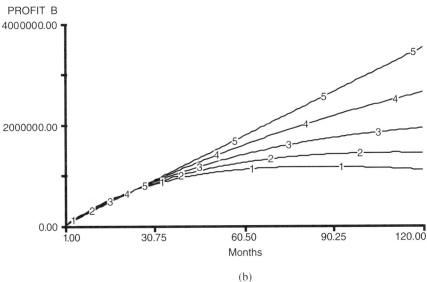

(b)

Figure 18.3 Results of five 10-year simulations representing (a) total harvest (kg) from both bay and ocean fisheries, and profit ($) from the (b) bay and (c) ocean sectors of the fishery with 30 units of fishing effort per month in the ocean and (1) 20, (2) 19, (3) 18, (4) 17, and (5) 16 units of effort in the bay.

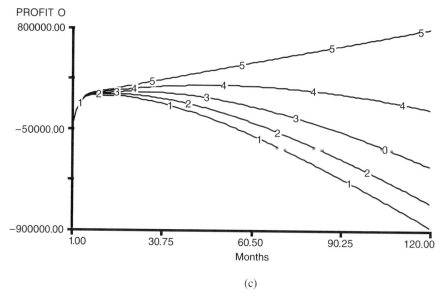

(c)

Figure 18.3   (*Continued*)

effort except 30 units per month (Figure 18.4b), whereas the ocean fishery remains profitable only when the ocean effort is reduced to 25 units per month (Figure 18.4c).

Regarding the effect of different harvesting strategies on the total harvest from the fishery and the profit to each of two different user groups within the fishery, the simulation results suggest that management efforts should be focused on reducing the fishing effort in the bay if a management goal is to maintain viable fisheries in both the bay and the ocean. One potential management problem is that bay fishermen may not see the need to restrict effort. However, our simulations suggest that long before shrimp populations decline to a level that no longer supports a profitable bay fishery, the ocean fishery will be bankrupt and the resource severely depleted (Figure 18.2.).

We encourage readers to use the model to examine the effect on harvest and profit of various seasonal closures of the bay and/or ocean fisheries. A variety of relevant situations can be simulated by changing values of FISH EFF B and FISH EFF O.

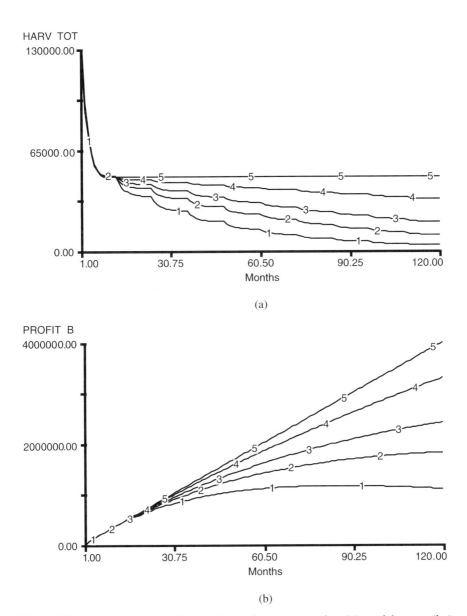

(a)

(b)

Figure 18.4 Results of five 10-year simulations representing (a) total harvest (kg) from both bay and ocean fisheries, and profit ($) from the (b) bay and (c) ocean sectors of the fishery with 20 units effort per month in the bay and (1) 30, (2) 28, (3) 27, (4) 26, and (5) 25 units of effort in the ocean.

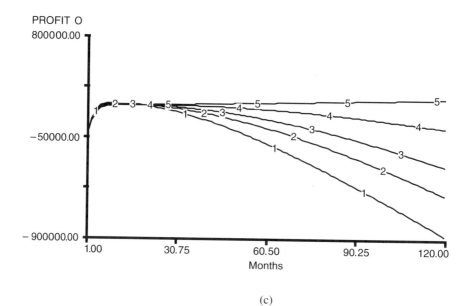

(c)

Figure 18.4 (*Continued*)

CHAPTER 19

RANGELAND MANAGEMENT: EFFECTS OF STOCKING DENSITY AND FREQUENCY OF BRUSH CONTROL ON RANGELAND PRODUCTIVITY

19.1 INTRODUCTION

Among the central activities of range management throughout the world are the adjustment of grazing pressure of domestic livestock and the control of woody vegetation (brush) to provide a high yield of meat products without overexploiting forage resources. In this chapter, we develop a model that simulates the effects of different stocking densities of livestock and the frequency of brush control on rangeland productivity.

19.2 MODEL OBJECTIVES

The general objective is to simulate forage production in a rangeland ecosystem under different cattle stocking densities and frequencies of brush control. Specific objectives are (1) to identify combinations of stocking densities and frequencies of burning that result in sustainable forage production, and (2) to evaluate the influence of the month of burning on the effectiveness of brush control.

19.3 BACKGROUND INFORMATION ON THE SYSTEM-OF-INTEREST

The system-of-interest consists of a 250-ha cattle ranch containing a mixture of herbaceous (live and standing dead grass) and woody (brush) vegetation. We are interested in the monthly dynamics of this system over a 50-year period. The proportion of grass and brush varies both seasonally and from year to year, depending on the amount of precipitation, grazing pressure, and the frequency of burning to control brush. Precipitation during the growing season averages 73 cm and is distributed as indicated in Table 19.1. During periods of drought, which usually occur once per decade and last for 2 or 3 years, the total growing season precipitation is reduced by 50%, but the seasonal distribution of precipitation is not changed.

The maximum rate of the aboveground net primary production of grass is 54 kg per ha per month per cm of growing season precipitation, but this rate decreases with increasing canopy cover of brush (Table 19.2). The senescence rate of live grass is 80% per month, with 70% remaining in the field as standing dead and 10% lost from the system. The rate of decomposition of dead grass is 3% per month, except during the first month of the growing season (March), when all standing dead grass accumulated over the winter is decomposed.

The rate of increase in the canopy cover of brush depends on precipitation and is density-dependent. Density-dependent rates of increase during months of normal precipitation are presented in Table 19.3. These rates increase or decrease proportionally with monthly precipitation above or below normal levels. For example, if precipitation is one-half the normal level, the rate of increase in canopy cover of brush is reduced by one-half. Brush accumulates until it is burned, with the proportional reduction in canopy cover resulting from fire depending on the amount of fine fuel (live plus dead grass) present at the time of the fire (Table 19.4). All live and dead grass is burned when a fire occurs.

Each cow requires 340 kg of grass per month. To meet this requirement, cattle first consume all available live grass and then all available dead grass. The availability of live and dead grass depends on the current standing crop biomass of live and dead grass, respectively (Table 19.5).

Currently (in January), there are 270 kg/ha of live grass, 2,200 kg/ha of dead grass, 1% canopy cover of brush, and 0.2 cow/ha in the system. The

Table 19.1   Mean Monthly Precipitation During the Growing Season

Month	Precipitation (cm)
March	3.0
April	10.0
May	10.0
June	10.0
July	8.0
August	7.0
September	10.0
October	7.0
November	5.0
December	3.0

Table 19.2   Relative Rate of Aboveground Net Primary Production (NPP) of Grass as a Function of Current Canopy Cover of Brush

Canopy Cover of Brush (%)	Relative NPP Rate of Grass (Proportion of Maximum Rate)
≤20	1.00
30	0.80
40	0.60
50	0.40
60	0.25
70	0.15
80	0.10
90	0.05
100	0.00

ranch manager wants to maintain the highest cattle stocking density that is sustainable by forage resources while using the lowest burning frequency. Each month, the manager can adjust the size of the herd and decide whether to burn brush.

19.4   MODEL DESCRIPTION

The model represents dynamics of production and loss of brush and live and dead grass (Figure 19.1). Production of brush is density-dependent and depends on precipitation. Brush is lost only through burning, with the proportion of brush burned depending on the amount of fine fuel (live plus dead grass)

Table 19.3   Proportional Increase per Month in Canopy Cover of Brush During Months of Normal Precipitation as a Function of Current Canopy Cover of Brush

Canopy Cover of Brush (%)	Proportional Increase in Canopy Cover of Brush
<1	0.040
8	0.036
16	0.032
24	0.028
32	0.024
40	0.020
48	0.016
56	0.012
64	0.008
72	0.004
80	0.000

Table 19.4 Proportional Reduction of Canopy Cover of Brush Resulting from Fire as a Function of Aboveground Standing Crop Biomass of Fine Fuel (Live Plus Dead Grass) Present at the Time of the Fire

Standing Crop Biomass of Fine Fuel (kg/ha)	Proportional Reduction of Canopy Cover of Brush
≤300	0.00
600	0.10
900	0.20
1,200	0.40
1,500	0.60
1,800	0.75
2,100	0.85
2,400	0.90
2,700	0.95
3,000	0.95

available. Production of live grass depends on the amount of precipitation and the amount of brush. Live grass senesces to become dead grass, both live and dead grass are lost through burning and grazing, and dead grass also is lost through decomposition. Grazing losses depend on the number of cattle and the relative availability of live and dead grass.

The baseline simulation, which represents normal precipitation and a stock- c19mc ing density of 0.2 cow per ha, runs from year 1 to year 50 using a time unit of 1 month and the equations in Table 19.6. REL ANN PPT is an index representing the proportion of normal precipitation received each year. MONTHLY PPT, PROP MAX G PROD, NPP RATE B, and PROP BRUSH BURNED are graphical functions based on the data in Tables 19.1 through 19.4, respectively. L GRASS AVAIL and D GRASS AVAIL are graphical functions based on the data in Table 19.5.

Table 19.5 Availability of Live or Dead Grass to Cattle as a Function of Current Standing Crop Biomass of Live or Dead Grass

Standing Crop Biomass of Live or Dead Grass (kg/ha)	Proportion of Standing Crop of Live or Dead Grass Available to Cattle
0	0.000
100	0.755
200	0.825
300	0.885
400	0.935
500	0.990
600	1.000

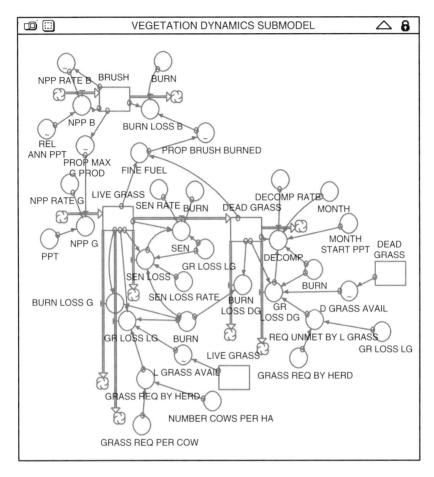

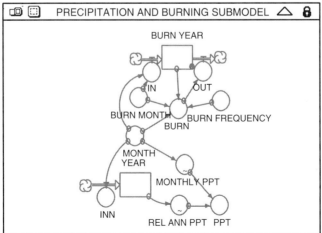

Figure 19.1 Conceptual model representing the effects of stocking density and frequency of brush control on rangeland productivity.

Table 19.6   Equations (Baseline Conditions) for the Simulation Model Representing Effects of Stocking Density and Frequency of Brush Control on Rangeland Productivity

PRECIPITATION AND BURNING SUBMODEL

☐ BURN_YEAR(t)=BURN_YEAR(t-dt)+(IN-OUT)*dt
INIT BURN_YEAR=1
DOCUMENT: INDEX INDICATING YEAR TO BURN
INFLOWS:
    ⌵ IN if(MONTH=BURN MONTH) then 1 else 0
OUTFLOWS:
    ⌵ OUT=if(BURN=1) then BURN_YEAR else 0
☐ YEAR(t)=YEAR(t-dt)+(INN)*dt
INIT YEAR=1
DOCUMENT: INDEX REPRESENTING THE CURRENT YEAR OF THE
SIMULATION
INFLOWS:
    ⌵ INN=if(MONTH=12) then 1 else 0
○ BURN=if(MONTH=BURN_MONTH) and(BURN_YEAR=BURN_FREQUENCY)
then 1 else 0
DOCUMENT: AUXILIARY VARIABLE-INDEX INDICATING WHEN TO BURN
(1=BURN, 0=DO NOT BURN)
○ BURN_FREQUENCY=5
DOCUMENT: CONSTANT-BURN FREQUENCY (NUMBER OF YEARS BETWEEN
BURNS)
○ BURN_MONTH=2
DOCUMENT: CONSTANT-BURN MONTH (INDEX INDICATING MONTH TO
BURN, 1=JANUARY, 2=FEBRUARY, ETC.)
○ MONTH=COUNTER(1,13)
DOCUMENT: INDEX REPRESENTING MONTH OF THE YEAR (1=JANUARY,
2=FEBRUARY, ETC.)
○ PPT=MONTHLY_PPT*REL_ANN_PPT
DOCUMENT: AUXILIARY VARIABLE-MONTHLY PRECIPITATION (CM)
⊘MONTHLY_PPT=GRAPH(MONTH)
(1.00, 0.00), (2.00, 0.00), (3.00, 3.00), (4.00, 10.0),
(5.00, 10.0), (6.00, 10.0), (7.00, 8.00), (8.00, 7.00),
(9.00, 10.0), (10.0, 7.00), (11.0, 5.00), (12.0, 3.00)
DOCUMENT: DRIVING VARIABLE-MONTHLY PRECIPITATION DISTRIBUTED
ACROSS THE MONTHS DURING A NORMAL YEAR (CM)
⊘REL_ANN_PPT=GRAPH(YEAR)
(1.00, 1.00), (2.00, 1.00), (3.00, 1.00), (4.00, 1.00),
(5.00, 1.00), (6.00, 1.00), (7.00, 1.00), (8.00, 1.00),
(9.00, 1.00), (10.0, 1.00), (11.0, 1.00), (12.0, 1.00),
(13.0, 1.00), (14.0, 1.00), (15.0, 1.00), (16.0, 1.00),
(17.0, 1.00), (18.0, 1.00), (19.0, 1.00), (20.0, 1.00),
(21.0, 1.00), (22.0, 1.00), (23.0, 1.00), (24.0, 1.00),

Table 19.6 (*Continued*)

(25.0, 1.00), (26.0, 1.00), (27.0, 1.00), (28.0, 1.00),
(29.0, 1.00), (30.0, 1.00), (31.0, 1.00), (32.0, 1.00),
(33.0, 1.00), (34.0, 1.00), (35.0, 1.00), (36.0, 1.00),
(37.0, 1.00), (38.0, 1.00), (39.0, 1.00), (40.0, 1.00),
(41.0, 1.00), (42.0, 1.00), (43.0, 1.00), (44.0, 1.00),
(45.0, 1.00), (46.0, 1.00), (47.0, 1.00), (48.0, 1.00),
(49.0, 1.00), (50.0, 1.00)
DOCUMENT: DRIVING VARIABLE–RELATIVE ANNUAL PRECIPITATION
ACROSS THE YEARS OF THE SIMULATION (PROPORTION OF NORMAL
ANNUAL PRECIPITATION)

VEGETATION DYNAMICS SUBMODEL

☐ BRUSH(t)=BRUSH(t-dt)+(NPP_B-BURN_LOSS_B)*dt
  INIT BRUSH=1
  DOCUMENT: BRUSH–PERCENT CANOPY COVER
  INFLOWS:
    ⌀ NPP_B=NPP_RATE_B*BRUSH*REL_ANN_PPT
      DOCUMENT: NET PRIMARY PRODUCTION OF BRUSH–(INCREASE IN
      PERCENT CANOPY COVER PER MONTH)
  OUTFLOWS:
    ⌀ BURN_LOSS_B=if(BURN=1) then PROP_BRUSH_BURNED*BRUSH
      else 0
      DOCUMENT: BURNING LOSS OF BRUSH (DECREASE IN PERCENT
      CANOPY COVER PER MONTH)
☐ DEAD_GRASS(t)=DEAD_GRASS(t-dt)+(SEN-DECOMP-BURN_LOSS_DG-GR_
  LOSS_DG)*dt
  INIT DEAD_GRASS=2200
  DOCUMENT: DEAD GRASS–STANDING CROP OF ABOVEGROUND BIOMASS
  (KG / HA)
  INFLOWS:
    ⌀ SEN=IF(BURN=1) THEN 0 ELSE SEN_RATE*(LIVE_GRASS-GR_
      LOSS_LG-SEN_LOSS)
      DOCUMENT: SENESCENCE OF LIVE GRASS TO DEAD GRASS (KG/
      HA-MO)
  OUTFLOWS:
    ⌀ DECOMP=if(BURN=1) then 0 else if(MONTH=MONTH_START_PPT)
      then DEAD_GRASS-GR_LOSS_DG else DECOMP_RATE*(DEAD_
      GRASS-GR_LOSS_DG)
      DOCUMENT: DECOMPOSITION OF DEAD GRASS (KG / HA-MO)

Table 19.6 (*Continued*)

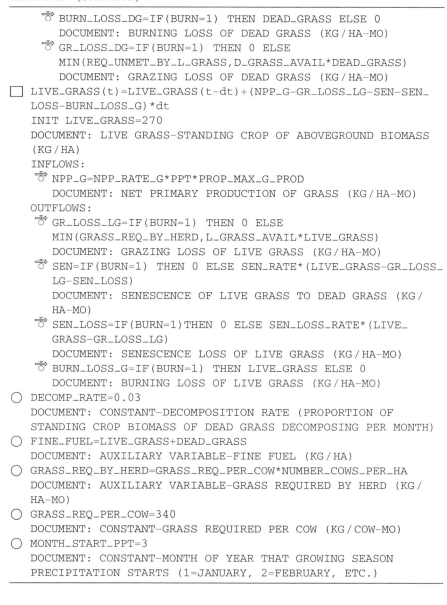

```
BURN_LOSS_DG=IF(BURN=1) THEN DEAD_GRASS ELSE 0
   DOCUMENT: BURNING LOSS OF DEAD GRASS (KG/HA-MO)
GR_LOSS_DG=IF(BURN=1) THEN 0 ELSE
   MIN(REQ_UNMET_BY_L_GRASS,D_GRASS_AVAIL*DEAD_GRASS)
   DOCUMENT: GRAZING LOSS OF DEAD GRASS (KG/HA-MO)
LIVE_GRASS(t)=LIVE_GRASS(t-dt)+(NPP_G-GR_LOSS_LG-SEN-SEN_
LOSS-BURN_LOSS_G)*dt
INIT LIVE_GRASS=270
DOCUMENT: LIVE GRASS-STANDING CROP OF ABOVEGROUND BIOMASS
(KG/HA)
INFLOWS:
NPP_G=NPP_RATE_G*PPT*PROP_MAX_G_PROD
   DOCUMENT: NET PRIMARY PRODUCTION OF GRASS (KG/HA-MO)
OUTFLOWS:
GR_LOSS_LG=IF(BURN=1) THEN 0 ELSE
   MIN(GRASS_REQ_BY_HERD,L_GRASS_AVAIL*LIVE_GRASS)
   DOCUMENT: GRAZING LOSS OF LIVE GRASS (KG/HA-MO)
SEN=IF(BURN=1) THEN 0 ELSE SEN_RATE*(LIVE_GRASS-GR_LOSS_
   LG-SEN_LOSS)
   DOCUMENT: SENESCENCE OF LIVE GRASS TO DEAD GRASS (KG/
   HA-MO)
SEN_LOSS=IF(BURN=1)THEN 0 ELSE SEN_LOSS_RATE*(LIVE_
   GRASS-GR_LOSS_LG)
   DOCUMENT: SENESCENCE LOSS OF LIVE GRASS (KG/HA-MO)
BURN_LOSS_G=IF(BURN=1) THEN LIVE_GRASS ELSE 0
   DOCUMENT: BURNING LOSS OF LIVE GRASS (KG/HA-MO)
DECOMP_RATE=0.03
DOCUMENT: CONSTANT-DECOMPOSITION RATE (PROPORTION OF
STANDING CROP BIOMASS OF DEAD GRASS DECOMPOSING PER MONTH)
FINE_FUEL=LIVE_GRASS+DEAD_GRASS
DOCUMENT: AUXILIARY VARIABLE-FINE FUEL (KG/HA)
GRASS_REQ_BY_HERD=GRASS_REQ_PER_COW*NUMBER_COWS_PER_HA
DOCUMENT: AUXILIARY VARIABLE-GRASS REQUIRED BY HERD (KG/
HA-MO)
GRASS_REQ_PER_COW=340
DOCUMENT: CONSTANT-GRASS REQUIRED PER COW (KG/COW-MO)
MONTH_START_PPT=3
DOCUMENT: CONSTANT-MONTH OF YEAR THAT GROWING SEASON
PRECIPITATION STARTS (1=JANUARY, 2=FEBRUARY, ETC.)
```

Table 19.6 (*Continued*)

○ NPP_RATE_G=54
DOCUMENT: CONSTANT-NET PRIMARY PRODUCTION RATE OF GRASS (KG
/HA-CM PPT)

○ NUMBER_COWS_PER_HA=0.2
DOCUMENT: CONSTANT-NUMBER OF COWS PER HECTARE

○ REQ_UNMET_BY_L_GRASS=GRASS_REQ_BY_HERD-GR_LOSS_LG
DOCUMENT: AUXILIARY VARIABLE-REQUIREMENT UNMET BY LIVE
GRASS (KG/HA-MO)

○ SEN_LOSS_RATE=0.10
DOCUMENT: CONSTANT-SENESCENCE LOSS RATE (PROPORTION OF
STANDING CROP BIOMASS OF LIVE GRASS LOST FROM SYSTEM PER
MONTH)

○ SEN_RATE=0.70
DOCUMENT: CONSTANT-SENESCENCE RATE (PROPORTION OF STANDING
CROP BIOMASS OF LIVE GRASS BECOMING DEAD GRASS PER MONTH)

⊘ D_GRASS_AVAIL=GRAPH(DEAD_GRASS)
(0.00, 0.00), (100, 0.755), (200, 0.825), (300, 0.885),
(400, 0.935), (500, 0.99), (600, 1.00), (700, 1.00), (800,
1.00), (900, 1.00), (1000, 1.00)
DOCUMENT: AUXILIARY VARIABLE-DEAD GRASS AVAILABLE
(PROPORTION OF STANDING CROP BIOMASS OF DEAD GRASS AVAILABLE
TO COWS)

⊘ L_GRASS_AVAIL=GRAPH(LIVE_GRASS)
(0.00, 0.00), (100, 0.755), (200, 0.825), (300, 0.885),
(400, 0.935), (500, 0.99), (600, 1.00), (700, 1.00), (800,
1.00), (900, 1.00), (1000, 1.00)
DOCUMENT: AUXILIARY VARIABLE-LIVE GRASS AVAILABLE
(PROPORTION OF STANDING CROP BIOMASS OF LIVE GRASS AVAILABLE
TO COWS)

⊘ NPP_RATE_B=GRAPH(BRUSH)
(0.00, 0.04), (8.00, 0.036), (16.0, 0.032), (24.0, 0.028),
(32.0, 0.024), (40.0, 0.02), (48.0, 0.016), (56.0, 0.012),
(64.0, 0.008), (72.0, 0.004), (80.0, 0.00)
DOCUMENT: AUXILIARY VARIABLE-NET PRIMARY PRODUCTION RATE OF
BRUSH (INCREASE IN PERCENT CANOPY COVER PER PERCENTAGE POINT
OF CURRENT CANOPY COVER PER MONTH)

⊘ PROP_BRUSH_BURNED=GRAPH(FINE_FUEL)
(0.00, 0.00), (300, 0.00), (600, 0.1), (900, 0.2), (1200,
0.4), (1500, 0.6), (1800, 0.75), (2100, 0.85), (2400, 0.9),
(2700, 0.95), (3000, 0.95)
DOCUMENT: AUXILIARY VARIABLE-PROPORTION OF BRUSH BURNED
(INDEX REPRESENTING PROPORTION OF BRUSH BURNED AS A FUNCTION
OF BIOMASS OF FINE FUEL AVAILABLE)

Table 19.6 (*Continued*)

⊘ PROP_MAX_G_PROD=GRAPH(BRUSH)
  (0.00, 1.00), (10.0, 1.00), (20.0, 1.00), (30.0, 0.8),
  (40.0, 0.6), (50.0, 0.4), (60.0, 0.25), (70.0, 0.15), (80.0,
  0.1), (90.0, 0.05), (100, 0.00)
DOCUMENT: AUXILIARY VARIABLE-PROPORTION OF MAXIMUM GRASS
PRODUCTION (INDEX REPRESENTING PROPORTION OF MAXIMUM GRASS
PRODUCTION REALIZED AS A FUNCTION OF AMOUNT OF CANOPY COVER
OF BRUSH)

BOOKKEEPING SUBMODEL

☐ ANNUAL_PPT(t)=ANNUAL_PPT(t-dt)+(INP-OUTP)*dt
INIT ANNUAL_PPT=0
DOCUMENT: ANNUAL PRECIPITATION-ACCUMULATION OF MONTHLY
PRECIPITATION DURING ONE YEAR
INFLOWS:
  ⇶ INP=PPT
OUTFLOWS:
  ⇶ OUTP=if(MONTH=1) then ANNUAL_PPT else 0
☐ ANN_FOR_PROD(t)=ANN_FOR_PROD(t-dt)+(INF-OUTF)*dt
INIT ANN_FOR_PROD=0
DOCUMENT: ANNUAL FORAGE PRODUCTION-ACCUMULATION OF MONTHLY
NET PRIMARY PRODUCTION OF GRASS DURING ONE YEAR
INFLOWS:
  ⇶ INF=NPP_G
OUTFLOWS:
  ⇶ OUTF=if(MONTH=1) then ANN_FOR_PROD else 0

19.5 MODEL USE

To identify combinations of stocking densities and frequencies of burning that result in sustainable forage production, we run seven series of 50-year simulations representing periods without drought and stocking densities of 0.2 (baseline), 0.3, 0.4, 0.5, 0.6, 0.7, and 0.8 cow per ha. At each stocking density, we begin with the burning frequency that resulted in sustainable forage production at the previous stocking density and successively shorten the interval between burns by 1 year until forage production is sustained for the entire 50 years. All burns occur during February. Simulation results indicate that at stocking densities of 0.2, 0.3, 0.4, 0.5, 0.6, and 0.7 cow per ha, burns must occur every 5, 4, 3, 3, 2, and 1 years, respectively, to sustain forage production, whereas at 0.8 cow per ha, forage production cannot be sustained even with annual burns (Figure 19.2).

To evaluate the influence of the month of burning on the effectiveness of brush control, we run seven additional 50-year simulations in which all burns occur in February, March, April, January, December, November, and October,

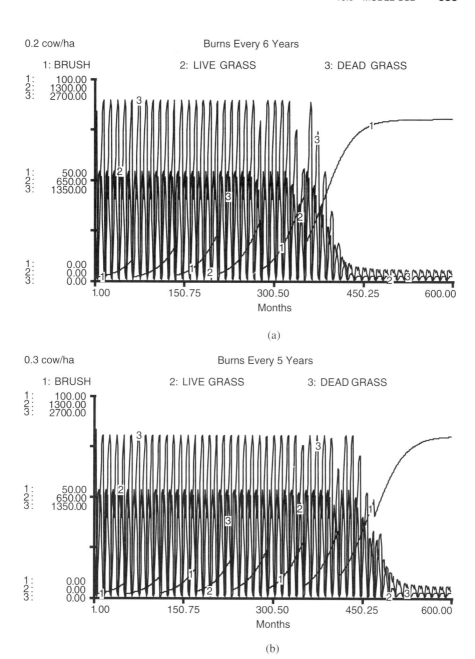

Figure 19.2 Results of 50-year simulations representing the dynamics of canopy cover of (1) brush (%), and standing crop biomass (kg/ha) of (2) live grass, and (3) dead grass with normal precipitation and the indicated stocking densities and frequencies of brush control.

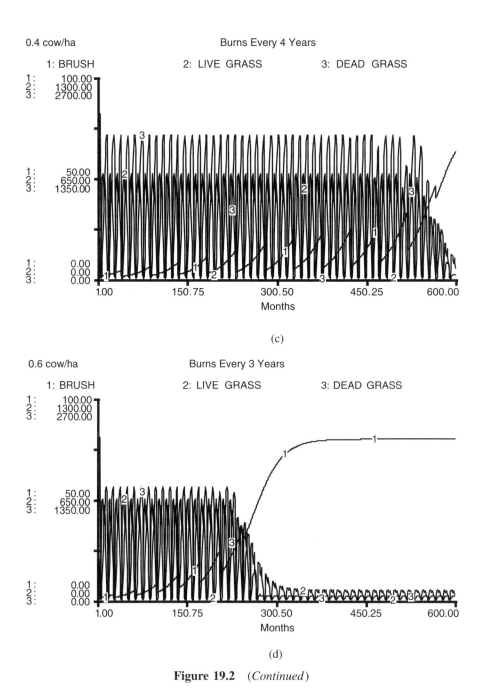

(c)

(d)

Figure 19.2 (*Continued*)

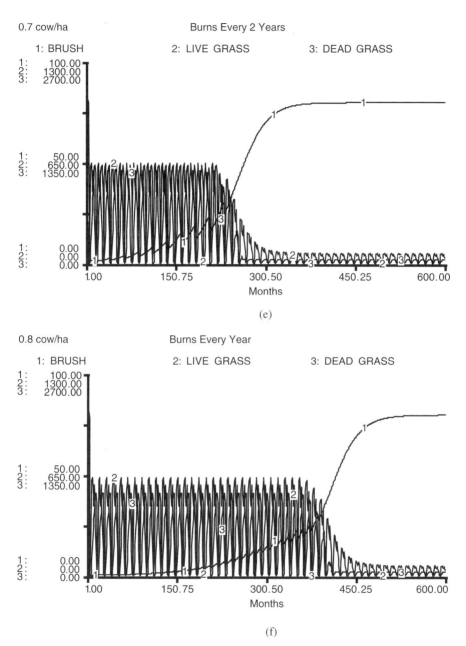

0.7 cow/ha   Burns Every 2 Years

1: BRUSH   2: LIVE GRASS   3: DEAD GRASS

(e)

0.8 cow/ha   Burns Every Year

1: BRUSH   2: LIVE GRASS   3: DEAD GRASS

(f)

Figure 19.2   (*Continued*)

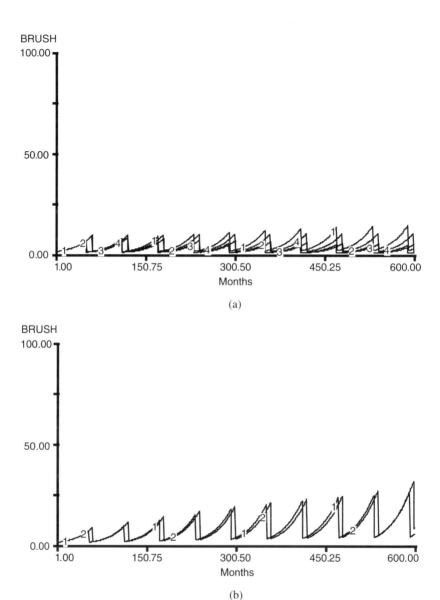

Figure 19.3 Results of seven 50-year simulations representing the dynamics of canopy cover of brush (%) with normal precipitation, a stocking density of 0.2 cow per ha, and brush control every 5 years during (a) (1) February, (2) January, (3) December, and (4) November; (b) (1) March and (2) October; and (c) April.

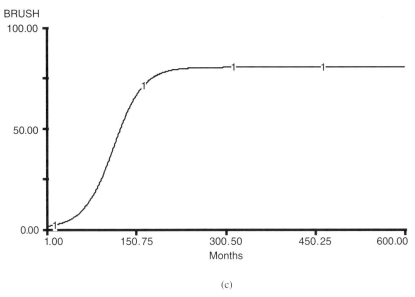

Figure 19.3   (*Continued*)

respectively. All simulations represent periods without drought, a stocking density of 0.2 cow per ha, and a burning frequency of once every 5 years. The simulation results indicate that November through February burns control brush most efficiently (Figure 19.3a), with burns during March and October being noticeably less efficient (Figure 19.3b), and April burns failing to control brush at all (Figure 19.3c).

Regarding forage production in rangeland ecosystems under different cattle stocking densities and frequencies of brush control, the simulation results suggest that during periods without drought, forage production can be sustained at higher cattle stocking densities by increasing the frequency of burning. However, there is a threshold level of brush encroachment, immediately preceded by a marked decrease in availability of fine fuel (live and standing dead grass), beyond which further encroachment cannot be prevented by burning. Availability of fine fuel depends on grazing losses to cattle and the rate of net primary production, which is affected by the current level of canopy cover of brush. Thus, there is a potentially delicate balance between stocking density and the frequency of burning that maintains a sufficient quantity of fine fuel and permits effective brush control via burning.

We encourage readers to use the model to examine the effect of drought on sustainability of forage production under different combinations of stocking densities and frequencies of burning. A variety of relevant situations can be simulated by changing values of REL ANN PPT, NUMBER COWS PER HA, BURN FREQUENCY, and BURN MONTH.

CHAPTER 20

FOREST MANAGEMENT: EFFECTS OF TIMBER HARVEST ON THE RELATIVE ABUNDANCE OF WILDLIFE SPECIES

20.1 INTRODUCTION

One of the central activities in forest management is the adjustment of harvesting schedules to provide sustainable yield of timber while minimizing the negative impact on other forest resources such as wildlife. In this chapter, we develop a model that simulates the effects of different harvesting strategies on timber production and the relative abundance of wildlife species.

20.2 MODEL OBJECTIVES

The general objective is to simulate the effect of different harvesting strategies on the sustainability of timber production and the abundance of wildlife species in a forest ecosystem. Specific objectives are to examine the manner in which (1) the length of the cutting cycle and (2) the size and spatial pattern of clear-cuts interact to affect the yield of tree biomass and the relative abundance of wildlife species with different sizes of activity ranges.

20.3 BACKGROUND INFORMATION ON THE SYSTEM-OF-INTEREST

The system-of-interest consists of a recently isolated 16-km² tract of forest containing three important wildlife species that is to be managed for timber production by clear-cutting (Figure 20.1). We are interested in the annual dynamics of this system over a 200-year period. The rates of increase in tree

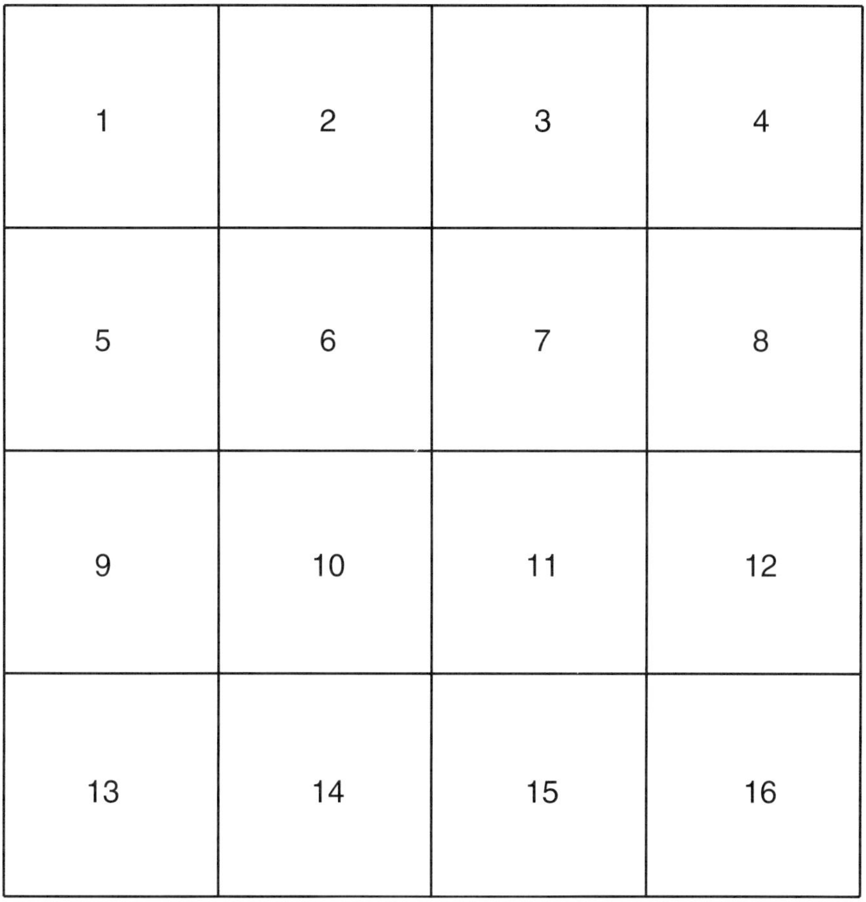

1	2	3	4
5	6	7	8
9	10	11	12
13	14	15	16

Figure 20.1 Schematic diagram of the 16-km^2 forest showing the numbering system identifying sixteen 1-km^2 blocks.

biomass for managed forests in this region and the expected timber yields under different cutting cycles are summarized in Tables 20.1 and 20.2, respectively.

Habitat suitability for each of the three wildlife species depends on the amount and distribution of tree biomass within the forest. The three species have the same natality rates, which are density-dependent and not affected directly by tree biomass (Table 20.3). However, the species differ in the size of their activity ranges and the local mortality rates depend directly on the amount of tree biomass available within the activity ranges of individual animals (Table 20.4).

Currently, there are 30×10^3 metric tons per km^2 of tree biomass and 500 individuals per km^2 of each wildlife species distributed evenly throughout the

TABLE 20.1 Rates of Increase in Tree Biomass for Managed Forests in the Region Represented as the Proportional Annual Increase in Aboveground Standing Crop Biomass

Aboveground Standing Crop Biomass (Metric Tons $\times$ 10^3/km^2)	Proportional Annual Increase
<0.03	0.20
3	0.18
6	0.16
9	0.14
12	0.12
15	0.10
18	0.08
21	0.06
24	0.04
27	0.02
30	0.0

TABLE 20.2 Expected Yields from Managed Forests in the Region Represented as the Total Yield of Tree Biomass at the Time of Harvest and as Average Annual Yield, Using the Indicated Cutting Cycles

Cutting Cycle (Years)	Total Yield at Harvest (Metric Tons $\times$ 10^3/km^2)	Average Annual Yield (Metric Tons/km^2-yr)
20	0.9	0.04
25	2.2	0.09
30	5.1	0.17
35	10.4	0.30
40	17.6	0.44
45	24.0	0.53
50	27.7	0.55
55	29.2	0.53
60	29.7	0.50
65	29.9	0.46
70	30.0	0.43
75	30.0	0.40
80	30.0	0.38
85	30.0	0.35
90	30.0	0.33
95	30.0	0.32
100	30.0	0.30

TABLE 20.3 Annual per Capita Natality Rates of Wildlife Species A, B, and C as a Function of Densities of Conspecifics within the 1-km² Block of Forest in which Their Activity Range Is Centered

Density of Conspecifics (Number/km²)	Annual Natality Rate (per Capita)
≤350	0.100
400	0.050
450	0.040
500	0.025

forest. However, because the land surrounding the forest was converted recently from forest to a variety of other land uses, none of which provides suitable habitat for the three wildlife species, animal densities near the newly created border are in transition as they adjust to the recent reduction in available tree biomass.

The proposed management scheme involves a 50-year moratorium on timber harvesting followed by clear-cutting the entire forest on a 50-year cutting cycle, with 0.03×10^3 metric tons per km² of seedlings planted the year after each harvest. However, the forest manager wants to evaluate alternative harvest schemes in terms of the timber yield and the impact on the three wildlife species. In particular, the manager is interested in adjusting the length of the cutting cycle and the size and shape of the clearcuts.

20.4 MODEL DESCRIPTION

The model consists of 16 modules, each representing a 1-km² block of forest. Each module consists of four submodels representing changes in tree biomass and in the numbers of animals belonging to species A, B, and C, respectively (Figure 20.2). The growth rate of trees from planting to harvest is density-dependent. For each wildlife species, the natality rate is density-dependent and the mortality rate depends on the amount of tree biomass available to individual animals whose activity range is centered in the given 1-km² block of forest. The tree biomass available to individual animals includes the biomass within their home block of forest and the proportion of biomass in adjacent blocks that falls within their activity ranges, with the latter being a constant for each species.

The baseline simulation, in which the entire forest is clear-cut using a cutting cycle of 50 years, runs from year 0 to year 200 using a time unit of 1 year and the equations in Table 20.5. GROWTH RATE, NAT RATE (A, B, and C), and MORT RATE (A, B, and C) are graphical functions based on information in Tables 20.1, 20.3, and 20.4, respectively. CUTTING CYCLE represents the number of years between successive harvests. START 1 through START 16 are

C20MOD01

TABLE 20.4   Annual per Capita Mortality Rates of Wildlife Species A, B, and C as a Function of Amount of Tree Biomass Available within Activity Ranges of Individual Animals

Species A (Size of Activity Range = 1 km²)	
Tree Biomass Available within Activity Range of Individuals (Metric Tons × 10³)	Annual Mortality Rate (per Capita)
0	0.175
3	0.165
6	0.150
9	0.125
12	0.100
15	0.080
18	0.065
21	0.050
24	0.040
27	0.030
30	0.025
Species B (Size of Activity Range = 5 km²)	
0	0.200
15	0.175
30	0.150
45	0.125
60	0.100
75	0.080
90	0.065
105	0.050
120	0.040
135	0.030
150	0.025
Species C (Size of Activity Range = 9 km²)	
≤81	0.200
108	0.175
135	0.150
162	0.125
189	0.100
216	0.075
243	0.050
270	0.025

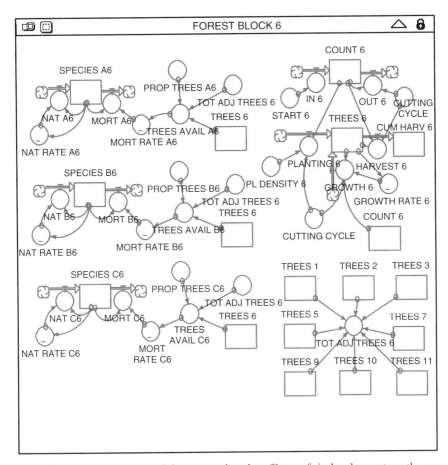

Figure 20.2   Conceptual model representing the effects of timber harvest on the sustainability of timber production and the relative abundance of wildlife species. The forest is represented as sixteen submodels representing the sixteen 1-km² blocks shown in Figure 20.1, only one of which is shown in this figure.

bookkeeping variables that determine the first year that trees are harvested in the corresponding block of forest. COUNT 1 through COUNT 16 are bookkeeping variables that determine subsequent years in which trees are harvested in the corresponding block of forest.

20.5 MODEL USE

To examine the manner in which the length of cutting cycle affects the sustainability of timber production and relative abundance of wildlife species with different sizes of activity ranges, we run three simulations in which the

**TABLE 20.5 Equations (Baseline Conditions) for the Simulation Model
Representing Effects of Timber Harvest on Sustainability of Timber Production
and Relative Abundance of Wildlife Species**

FOREST BLOCK 6

☐ COUNT_6(t)=COUNT_6(t-dt)+(IN_6-OUT_6)*dt
INIT COUNT_6=0
INFLOWS:
　⏾ IN_6=if(time<START_6) then 0 else 1
OUTFLOWS:
　⏾ OUT_6=if(COUNT_6=CUTTING_CYCLE) then COUNT_6 else 0

☐ CUM_HARV_6(t)=CUM_HARV_6(t-dt)+(HARVEST_6)*dt
INIT CUM_HARV_6=0
INFLOWS:
　⏾ HARVEST_6=if(COUNT_6=CUTTING_CYCLE) then TREES_6 else 0

☐ SPECIES_A6(t)=SPECIES_A6(t-dt)+(NAT_A6-MORT_A6)*dt
INIT SPECIES_A6=500
INFLOWS:
　⏾ NAT_A6=SPECIES_A6*NAT_RATE_A6
OUTFLOWS:
　⏾ MORT_A6=SPECIES_A6*MORT_RATE_A6

☐ SPECIES_B6(t)=SPECIES_B6(t-dt)+(NAT_B6-MORT_B6)*dt
INIT SPECIES_B6=500
INFLOWS:
　⏾ NAT_B6=SPECIES_B6*NAT_RATE_B6
OUTFLOWS:
　⏾ MORT_B6=SPECIES_B6*MORT_RATE_B6

☐ SPECIES_C6(t)=SPECIES_C6(t-dt)+(NAT_C6-MORT_C6)*dt
INIT SPECIES_C6=500
INFLOWS:
　⏾ NAT_C6=SPECIES_C6*NAT_RATE_C6
OUTFLOWS:
　⏾ MORT_C6=SPECIES_C6*MORT_RATE_C6

☐ TREES_6(t)=TREES_6(t-dt)+(PLANTING_6+GROWTH_6-HARVEST_6)*dt
INIT TREES_6=30
INFLOWS:
　⏾ PLANTING_6=if(COUNT_6=CUTTING_CYCLE) then PL_DENSITY_6
　　else 0
　⏾ GROWTH_6=if(COUNT_6=CUTTING_CYCLE) then 0 else GROWTH_
　　RATE_6*TREES_6
OUTFLOWS:
　⏾ HARVEST_6=if(COUNT_6=CUTTING_CYCLE) then TREES_6 else 0

○ PL_DENSITY_6=0.03
○ PROP_TREES_A6=0
○ PROP_TREES_B6=0.5
○ PROP_TREES_C6=1

TABLE 20.5   (*Continued*)

○ START_6=0

○ TOT_ADJ_TREES_6=TREES_1+TREES_2+TREES_3+TREES_5+TREES_7+TREES_9+TREES_10+TREES_11

○ TREES_AVAIL_A6=TREES_6+(TOT_ADJ_TREES_6*PROP_TREES_A6)

○ TREES_AVAIL_B6=TREES_6+(TOT_ADJ_TREES_6*PROP_TREES_B6)

○ TREES_AVAIL_C6=TREES_6+(TOT_ADJ_TREES_6*PROP_TREES_C6)

⊘GROWTH_RATE_6=GRAPH(TREES_6)
  (0.00, 0.2), (3.00, 0.18), (6.00, 0.16), (9.00, 0.14),
  (12.0, 0.12), (15.0, 0.1), (18.0, 0.08), (21.0, 0.06),
  (24.0, 0.04), (27.0, 0.02), (30.0, 0.00)

⊘MORT_RATE_A6=GRAPH(TREES_AVAIL_A6)
  (0.00, 0.175), (3.00, 0.165), (6.00, 0.15), (9.00, 0.125),
  (12.0, 0.1), (15.0, 0.08), (18.0, 0.065), (21.0, 0.05),
  (24.0, 0.04), (27.0, 0.03), (30.0, 0.025)

⊘MORT_RATE_B6=GRAPH(TREES_AVAIL_B6)
  (0.00, 0.02), (15.0, 0.175), (30.0, 0.15), (45.0, 0.125),
  (60.0, 0.1), (75.0, 0.08), (90.0, 0.065), (105, 0.05),
  (120, 0.04), (135, 0.03), (150, 0.025)

⊘MORT_RATE_C6=GRAPH(TREES_AVAIL_C6)
  (0.00, 0.02), (27.0, 0.2), (54.0, 0.2), (81.0, 0.2), (108,
  0.175), (135, 0.15), (162, 0.125), (189, 0.1), (216,
  0.075), (243, 0.05), (270, 0.025)

⊘NAT_RATE_A6=GRAPH(SPECIES_A6)
  (0.00, 0.1), (50.0, 0.1), (100, 0.1), (150, 0.1), (200,
  0.1), (250, 0.1), (300, 0.1), (350, 0.1), (400, 0.05),
  (450, 0.04), (500, 0.025)

⊘NAT_RATE_B6=GRAPH(SPECIES_B6)
  (0.00, 0.1), (50.0, 0.1), (100, 0.1), (150, 0.1), (200,
  0.1), (250, 0.1), (300, 0.1), (350, 0.1), (400, 0.05),
  (450, 0.04), (500, 0.025)

⊘NAT_RATE_C6=GRAPH(SPECIES_C6)
  (0.00, 0.1), (50.0, 0.1), (100, 0.1), (150, 0.1), (200,
  0.1), (250, 0.1), (300, 0.1), (350, 0.1), (400, 0.05),
  (450, 0.04), (500, 0.025)

entire forest is clear-cut using cutting cycles of 50 (baseline), 80, and 100 years, respectively. In each case, we simulate four consecutive cutting cycles, with the initial harvest moratorium being equal to the length of the cutting cycle. The simulation results indicate that populations of all three wildlife species decline drastically under the 50-year cutting cycle (Figure 20.3a). As the length of the cutting cycle is increased, population declines become some-

TABLE 20.5 (*Continued*)

MANAGEMENT VARIABLES

○ CUTTING_CYCLE=50

SPECIES A

○ SPECIES_A=SPECIES_A1+SPECIES_A2+SPECIES_A3+SPECIES_
A4+SPECIES_A5+SPECIES_A6+SPECIES_A7+SPECIES_A8+SPECIES_
A9+SPECIES_A10+SPECIES_A11+SPECIES_A12+SPECIES_A13+SPECIES_
A14+SPECIES_A15+SPECIES_A16

SPECIES B

○ SPECIES_B=SPECIES_B1+SPECIES_B2+SPECIES_B3+SPECIES_
B4+SPECIES_B5+SPECIES_B6+SPECIES_B7+SPECIES_B8+SPECIES_
B9+SPECIES_B10+SPECIES_B11+SPECIES_B12+SPECIES_B13+SPECIES_
B14+SPECIES_B15+SPECIES_B16

SPECIES C

○ SPECIES_C=SPECIES_C1+SPECIES_C2+SPECIES_C3+SPECIES_
C4+SPECIES_C5+SPECIES_C6+SPECIES_C7+SPECIES_C8+SPECIES_
C9+SPECIES_C10+SPECIES_C11+SPECIES_C12+SPECIES_C13+SPECIES_
C14+SPECIES_C15+SPECIES_C16

---

what less drastic, but species B and C cannot maintain viable (nondecreasing) populations even with a 100-year cutting cycle (Figures 20.3b and 20.3c). Species A can maintain a viable population only when the cutting cycle is lengthened to at least 80 years (Figure 20.3b). The simulated average annual timber harvest (CUMHARV/number of years simulated) falls from 6.8 to 4.5 to 3.6 metric tons $\times$ 10^3/km^2 as the cutting cycle is lengthened from 50 to 80 to 100 years (Figure 20.3). Thus, viable wildlife populations cannot be maintained if the entire forest is clear-cut, even if the cutting cycle is lengthened far beyond the point where the average annual timber harvests begin to decline noticeably.

To examine the manner in which the size and spatial pattern of clear-cuts interact to affect the sustainability of timber production and the relative abundance of wildlife species with different sizes of activity ranges, we run a set of simulations representing a variety of sizes and spatial patterns of clear-cuts, with the only restrictions being (1) to observe the initial 50-year harvest moratorium and (2) to maintain a 50-year cutting cycle within each 1-km^2 block of forest. Examples of simulated management schemes include (1) dividing the forest in half (blocks 1–8 and 9–16, Figure 20.1) and harvesting the second half 10, 20, or 30, and so on, years after the first half; (2) dividing the forest in quarters (blocks 1, 2, 5, 6; 3, 4, 7, 8; 9, 10, 13, 14; and 11, 12,

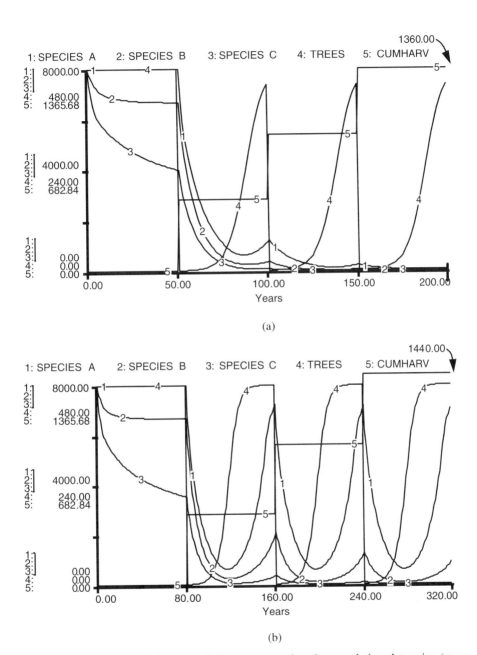

Figure 20.3 Results of three simulations representing the population dynamics (animals/16 km²) of wildlife species (1) A, (2) B, and (3) C, (4) standing crop biomass of trees (metric tons × 10³/km²), and (5) the cumulative timber harvest (metric tons × 10³/km²) during four consecutive cutting cycles of (a) 50, (b) 80, and (c) 100 years.

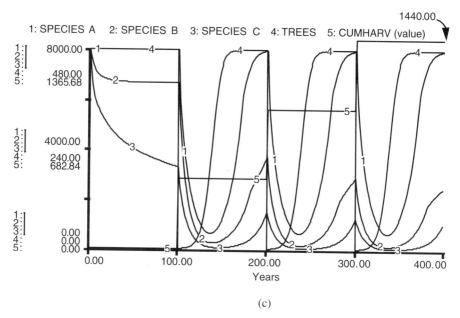

Figure 20.3 (*Continued*)

15, 16) and, moving clockwise around the forest, lagging the harvest of each quarter 10, 20, or 30, and so on, years after the previous quarter; and (3) leaving an unharvested central portion (blocks 6, 7, 10, 11) and harvesting the remaining four corners of the forest (blocks 1, 2, 5; 3, 4, 8; 12, 15, 16; and 9, 13, 14) and, moving clockwise around the forest, lagging the harvest of each corner by 12 (or 13) years after the previous corner. By using this last scheme (time-lagged perimeter harvest, Figure 20.4), the simulated average annual timber harvest (CUMHARV/200 years) is 5.1 metric tons × 10^3/km² and wildlife species A and B, but not C, can maintain viable populations (Figure 20.5), although the distribution of each species is essentially confined to the unharvested center of the forest by year 100 (Figure 20.6).

Thus, regarding the effect of different harvesting strategies on the sustainability of timber production and the relative abundance of wildlife in this hypothetical forest ecosystem, the simulation results suggest that it will be difficult, if not impossible, to maintain a reasonable timber harvest without losing the three wildlife species if the entire forest is harvested, even if different portions of the forest are harvested at different times. If a 4-km² central portion is not harvested, the two species with smaller activity ranges (A and B) can survive, but the species with the largest activity range (C) cannot survive.

We encourage readers to use the model to explore further the effect of different sizes and spatial patterns of clear-cuts on the relative abundance of the three wildlife species. A variety of relevant situations can be simulated by changing values of CUTTING CYCLE and START 1 through START 16.

1	2	3	4
fh 50	fh 50	fh 62	fh 62
5	6	7	8
fh 50	no cut	no cut	fh 62
9	10	11	12
fh 87	no cut	no cut	fh 75
13	14	15	16
fh 87	fh 87	fh 75	fh 75

Figure 20.4 Schematic diagram representing the time-lagged perimeter harvest in which a central portion (blocks 6, 7, 10, 11) is not harvested and the remaining four corners (blocks 1, 2, 5; 3, 4, 8; 12, 15, 16; and 9, 13, 14) are harvested moving clockwise around the forest, lagging the harvest of each corner by 12 (or 13) years after the previous corner. A 50-year cutting cycle is used within each individual block; the year of the first harvest is indicated by fh.

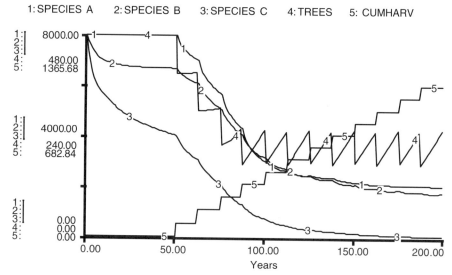

Figure 20.5 Results of a 200-year simulation representing the population dynamics (animals/16 km²) of wildlife species (1) A, (2) B, and (3) C, (4) standing crop biomass of trees (metric tons × 10³/km²), and (5) the cumulative timber harvest (metric tons × 10³/km²) during the time-lagged perimeter harvest described in Figure 20.4.

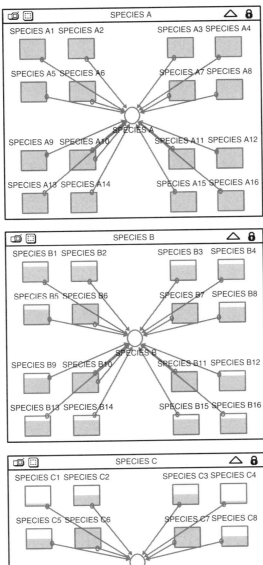

(a)

Figure 20.6 Results of a 200-year simulation representing the relative abundance of wildlife species A, B, and C in each of the 16 blocks of forest after (a) 50, (b) 100, (c) 150, and (d) 200 years under the time-lagged perimeter harvest described in Figure 20.4 (completely shaded areas indicate maximum abundance).

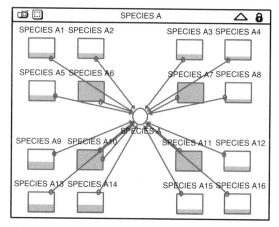

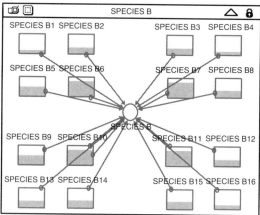

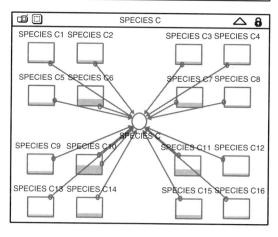

(b)

Figure 20.6 (*Continued*)

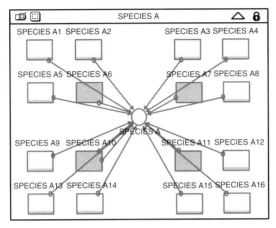

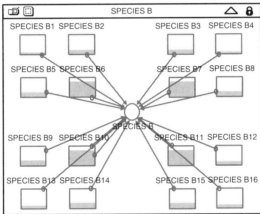

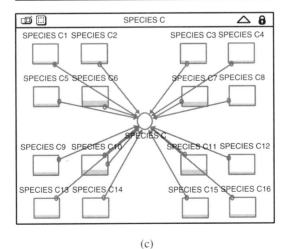

(c)

Figure 20.6   (*Continued*)

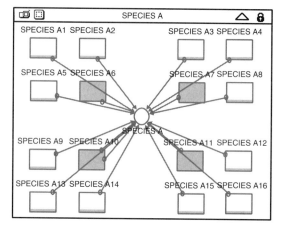

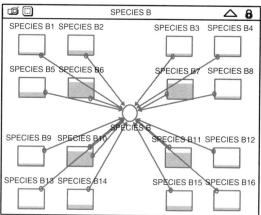

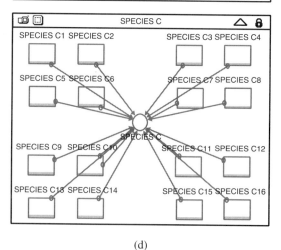

(d)

Figure 20.6 (*Continued*)

CHAPTER 21

REFLECTIONS

In closing, we would like to offer a few reflections within a historical context regarding the acceptance and use of systems analysis and simulation in ecology and natural resource management. Given the compelling arguments for use of the systems approach when dealing with complex problems and the obvious complexity of many ecological and natural resource systems, it seems surprising that we have been so reluctant to promote the systems perspective in ecological research and natural resource management. Although the current climate is favorable for promotion of holistic approaches to problem solving, three decades after the introduction of systems concepts in ecology, the development and use of ecological models is still surrounded by considerable misunderstanding and skepticism.

Historical roots of this misunderstanding can be found in the false expectations and subsequent perceived failures of initial ecological modeling efforts. Early ecological modeling projects focused on the model as an end product capable of correctly predicting the dynamics of complex systems, rather than emphasizing the modeling process as a powerful means of integrating available information in a dynamic, useful way. As a consequence, the inability of these models to provide accurate predictions of system behavior was viewed as a failure of the systems approach, even though substantial advances in our understanding of important ecological processes were achieved. The fact that some early ecological modeling projects, notably those conducted during the late 1960s and early 1970s as part of the International Biological Program, were well funded heightened prior expectations and inflamed subsequent criticisms. However, the real problem was not with ecological models or modeling, but with the false expectations held by modelers and critics alike.

This early skepticism has been nurtured over the years by the recurring misuse of ecological models. Often, use of sophisticated quantitative techniques has been overemphasized while the philosophical basis for their application has been ignored and the ecological interpretation of model results has been contrived. Often, models have been labeled "ecological" solely because the point of departure for their mathematical derivation is an equation recognized by ecologists—the never-ending series of extensions of the Lotka-Volterra equations is an example. Thus, the criticism that ecological modelers construct models for the sake of modeling, or that they use complicated models as a substitute for critical thinking is in part well founded. But, again, the real problem is not with ecological models or modeling, but with the failure of some practitioners to develop and use their models within an appropriate context.

Recent interest in the use of advanced computer technologies in natural resource management has been accompanied by a variety of ecologically oriented courses and training programs in geographic information systems, remote sensing and automated data processing, as well as simulation. Such training commonly emphasizes technical aspects of these methodologies, which is an obvious prerequisite for their effective use. As ecologists and natural resource managers, we are interested in these powerful technologies because we are interested in studying and managing complex natural systems. This is a clear, although implicit, manifestation of interest in the systems approach to problem solving. However, technical training should not be confused with or substituted for formal exposure to the basic philosophy and principles of systems analysis.

In terms of opportunities to promote use of systems analysis and simulation in ecology and natural resource management, the current climate is in several respects similar to that of three decades ago. We are interested in systems problems, but have not yet taken full advantage of systems principles in addressing these questions. Natural resource managers are striving to consider explicitly the complex dynamics of natural resource systems to manage for multiple use by different user groups and to assess long-term impacts of environmental contamination. Ecologists are focusing on a variety of questions that require explicit integration of hierarchically nested ecological systems with different temporal and spatial scales, with particular emphasis on the effect of spatial heterogeneity on temporal dynamics.

Convincing arguments that were presented eloquently three decades ago provide the rationale for use of the basic principles of general systems theory to represent structure and function of complex ecological systems (Patten, 1971; Watt, 1968; VanDyne, 1969). The challenge today is to draw on our cumulative practical experience to present more realistic expectations of the use of systems analysis and simulation in ecology and natural resource management, and to provide wider access to appropriate systems training within an ecological context.

REFERENCES

Cochran, W. G., and G. M. Cox. 1957. *Experimental Design.* New York: John Wiley.

Daniel, C., and F. S. Wood. 1971. *Fitting Equations to Data.* New York: John Wiley.

Forrester, J. W. 1961. *Industrial Dynamics.* Cambridge, Mass: The MIT Press.

Gold, H. J. 1977. *Mathematical Modeling of Biological Systems: An Introductory Guidebook.* New York: John Wiley.

Grant, W. E. 1986. *Systems Analysis and Simulation in Wildlife and Fisheries Sciences.* New York: John Wiley.

Hastings, N. A. J., and J. B. Peacock. 1975. *Statistical Distributions.* London: Butterworth.

High Performance Systems, Inc. 1994. *STELLA® II Technical Documentation.* Hanover, New Hampshire: High Performance Systems, Inc.

Holling, C. S. 1978. *Adaptive Environmental Assessment and Management.* New York: John Wiley.

Innis, G. S. 1979. A spiral approach to ecosystem simulation, I. In G. S. Innis and R. V. O'Neill (eds.), *Systems Analysis of Ecosystems.* Burtonsville, Md.: International Cooperative Publishing House.

Jeffers, J. N. R. 1978. *An Introduction to Systems Analysis: With Ecological Applications.* Baltimore: University Park Press.

Johnson, N. I., and S. Kotz. 1969. *Discrete Distributions.* Boston: Houghton Mifflin.

Kitching, R. L. 1983. *Systems Ecology: An Introduction to Ecological Modelling.* St. Lucia, Queensland: University of Queensland Press.

Law, A. M., and W. D. Kelton. 1982. *Simulation and Analysis.* New York: McGraw-Hill.

Ott, L. 1984. *An Introduction to Statistical Methods and Data Analysis.* Boston: Duxbury.

Patten, B. C. 1971. A primer for ecological modeling and simulation with analog and digital computers. In B. C. Patten (ed.), *Systems Analysis and Simulation in Ecology,* Vol. 1. New York: Academic Press.

Rohlf, F. J., and R. R. Sokal. 1969. *Statistical Tables.* San Francisco: W. H. Freeman.

Rykiel, E. J., Jr. 1996. Testing ecological models: The meaning of validation. *Ecological Modelling* 90:229–244.

Smith, F. E. 1973. Analysis of ecosystems. In D. E. Reichle (ed.), *Analysis of Temperate Forest Ecosystems.* New York: Springer-Verlag.

Snedecor, G. W., and W. G. Cochran. 1967. *Statistical Methods.* Ames: Iowa State University Press.

Sokal, R. R., and F. J. Rohlf. 1969. *Biometry.* San Francisco: W. H. Freeman.

Spain, J. D. 1982. *BASIC Microcomputer Models in Biology.* Reading, Mass.: Addison-Wesley.

Starfield, A. M., and A. L. Bleloch. 1986. *Building Models for Conservation and Wildlife Management.* New York: Macmillan.

Steinhorst, R. K. 1979. Parameter identifiability, validation, and sensitivity analysis of large system models. In G. S. Innis and R. V. O'Neill (eds.), *Systems Analysis of Ecosystems.* Burtonsville, Md.: International Cooperative Publishing House.

Van Dyne, G. M. 1969. *The Ecosystem Concept in Natural Resource Management.* New York: Academic Press.

von Bertalanffy, L. 1969. *General Systems Theory: Foundations, Development, Applications.* New York: George Braziller.

Watt, K. E. F. 1968. *Ecology and Resource Management.* New York: McGraw-Hill.

Weinberg, G. M. 1975. *An Introduction to General Systems Thinking.* New York: John Wiley.

ABOUT THE CD-ROM

INTRODUCTION

The enclosed CD-ROM contains fully operational versions of all of the simulation models to which we refer in the book. You can modify and run these models to reproduce any of the simulation results that we report in the text. You also can make any additional modifications that you like, or, erase our model completely and construct your own. We encourage you to do the latter, drawing on the basic principles of systems analysis and simulation that we present in the text. (Please note that you will not be able to save any of the modifications that you make using the Run-time version of STELLA®II included on the CD-ROM. That is, your modifications will disappear when you close the model.)

The model names on the CD-ROM correspond to the model names indicated in the right-hand margin of the text close to the point where we first refer to simulation results from the indicated model. For example, C04MOD01 and C04MOD02 are the first and second models, respectively, in Chapter 4, which we reference on pages 60 and 63, respectively. A list of the models, including brief descriptions, follows. (Note that we have not included the qualitative, conceptual models presented in Chapter 3.)

Model Name	Brief Description
C01MOD01	Water diversion upstream from a wildlife refuge
C02MOD01	Weight fluctuation of an animal
C04MOD01	Weight fluctuation of an animal (deterministic)
C04MOD02	Weight fluctuation of an animal (stochastic)
C07MOD01	Modules for representing common system dynamics

Model Name	Brief Description
C09MOD01	First intermediate aquaculture model
C09MOD02	Second intermediate aquaculture model
C09MOD03	Third intermediate aquaculture model
C09MOD04	Fourth intermediate aquaculture model
C09MOD05	Fifth intermediate aquaculture model
C09MOD06	Sixth intermediate aquaculture model
C09MOD07	Seventh intermediate aquaculture model
C09MOD08	Eighth intermediate aquaculture model
C09MOD09	Last interm. and definitive stochastic aquaculture models
C09MOD10	Last interm. and definitive deterministic aquaculture models
C11MOD01	Population dynamics: Density-dependent effects
C12MOD01	Population dynamics: Age-specific natality and mortality
C13MOD01	Inter-specific competition in fluctuating environments
C14MOD01	Community structure with competition and disturbance
C15MOD01	Predator-prey relationships
C16MOD01	Energy balance of a homeotherm
C17MOD01	Wildlife management: Habitat fragmentation
C18MOD01	Fisheries management: Harvest regulations
C19MOD01	Rangeland management: Brush control
C20MOD01	Forest management: Timber harvest and wildlife

MINIMUM SYSTEM REQUIREMENTS

Windows System Requirements

- 486 computer
- 8 MB RAM
- 6 MB free disk space
- CD-ROM drive

Macintosh System Requirements

- System 6.0.4 or higher
- 8 MB RAM
- 6 MB free disk space
- CD-ROM drive

INSTALLATION INSTRUCTIONS

Windows Version:

1. **Prepare for installation.**
   - Exit all applications, except for Windows.
   - Make sure that you have at least 6 MB of free space on your hard disk.

2. **Launch the STELLA® II Run-time & NRM installer.**
   - Insert the CD into the CD-ROM drive.
     Choose Run from the File menu in the Program Manager (from the Start button in Windows 95).
   - Type: **d:\setup** in the command line, where "d" is the letter for your CD-ROM drive.
   - Click **OK.**
   - Wait while the Installer application loads.
     The Setup screen will appear, showing a pre-defined installation directory (stella2r).
   - Click the **OK** button in the Setup screen.

3. **Wrap up the installation.**
   - Wait while installation take place.
   - When installation is complete, eject the CD.

The **STELLA® II** 3.0.7 Run-time application will be found in the "STELLA® II & NRM" group in the Program Manager (Windows 3.1) or in the Programs menu (Windows 95). The application (stella2.exe) will be located in the stella2r directory in File Manager; the models will be located in the nrm subdirectory within the stella2r directory.

Macintosh Version:

1. **Prepare for installation.**
   - Quit all applications.
   - Make sure that you have at least 6 MB of free space on your hard disk.

2. **Launch the installer.**
   - Insert the CD into the CD-ROM drive.

- Double click the Installer icon.
  *The **STELLA**® **II** Screen will appear.*

3. **Begin installation to your hard disk.**
   - Click **Continue** on the **STELLA**® **II** screen.
   - From the "Select destination folder" window, select the destination on your hard disk where you would like to install the program.
     A folder named "STELLA® II and NRM" will be automatically created for you in the location you choose.
   - Click the **Install into** button located at the bottom of the "Select destination folder" window.

4. **Wrap up the installation.**
   - Wait while installation takes place.
   - When installation is complete, click the **Quit** button.
   - Eject the CD.

The **STELLA**® **II** 3.0.6 Run-time application and the models will be found in the "STELLA® II and NRM" folder.

TECHNICAL SUPPORT

For technical support with the **STELLA**® **II** Run-time software or to purchase a full version of the **STELLA**® software, call (603) 643-9636, fax (603) 643-9502, or e-mail support@hps-inc.com.

HIGH PERFORMANCE SYSTEMS, INC. SOFTWARE LICENSE AGREEMENT

Before opening this diskette envelope, please review the following terms and conditions of this Agreement carefully. This is a legal agreement between you and High Performance Systems, Inc. The terms of this Agreement govern your use of this software. Opening this diskette envelope or use of the enclosed materials will constitute your acceptance of the terms and conditions of this Agreement.

1. Grant of License.
In consideration of payment of the license fee, which is part of the price you paid for this software package (referred to in this Agreement as the "Software"), High Performance Systems, Inc., as Licensor, grants to you, as Licensee, a non-exclusive right to use and display this copy of the Software on a single computer (i.e., a single CPU) only at one location at any time. To "use" the Software means that the Software is either loaded in the temporary memory (i.e., RAM) of a computer or installed on the permanent memory of a computer (i.e. hard disk, CD ROM, etc.). You may use at one time as many copies of the Software as you have licenses for. You may install the Software on a common storage device shared by multiple computers, provided that if you have more computers having access to the common storage device than the number of licensed copies of the Software, you must have some software mechanism which locks-out any concurrent users in excess of the number of licensed copies of the Software (an additional license is not needed for the one copy of Software stored on the common storage device accessed by multiple computers).

2. Ownership of Software
As Licensee, you own the magnetic or other physical media on which the Software is originally or subsequently recorded or fixed, but High Performance Systems, Inc. retains title and ownership of the Software, both as originally recorded and all subsequent copies made of the Software regardless of the form or media in or on which the original or copies may exist. This license is not a sale of the original Software or any copy.

3. Copy Restrictions
The Software and the accompanying written materials are protected by U.S. Copyright laws. Unauthorized copying of the Software, including Software that has been modified, merged, or included with other software or of the original written material is expressly forbidden. You may be held legally responsible for any copyright infringement that is caused or encouraged by your failure to abide by the terms of this Agreement. Subject to these restrictions, you may make one (1) copy of the Software solely for back-up purposes provided such back-up copy contains the same proprietary notices as appear in this Software.

4. Use Restrictions
As the Licensee, you may physically transfer the Software from one computer to another provided that the Software is used on only one computer at a time. You may not distribute copies of the Software or the accompanying written materials to others. You may not modify, adapt, translate, reverse engineer, decompile, disassemble, or create derivative works based on the Software. You may not modify, adapt, translate or create derivative works based on the written materials without the prior written consent of High Performance Systems, Inc.

5. Transfer Restrictions.
This Software is licensed to only you, the Licensee, and may not be transferred to anyone else without the prior written consent of High Performance Systems, Inc. Any authorized transferee of the Software shall be bound by the terms and conditions of this Agreement. In no event may you transfer, assign, rent, lease, sell or otherwise dispose of the Software on a temporary or permanent basis except as expressly provided herein.

6. Termination.
This license is effective until terminated. This license will terminate automatically without notice from High Performance Systems, Inc. if you fail to comply with any provision of this license.

Upon termination you shall destroy the written materials and all copies of the Software, including modified copies, if any.

7. Update Policy.
High Performance Systems, Inc. may create from time to time, updated versions of the Software. At its option, High Performance Systems, Inc. will make such updates available to Licensee and transferees who have returned the Registration Card which accompanies this software package.

8. Disclaimer of Warranty and Limited Warranty.
THE SOFTWARE AND ACCOMPANYING WRITTEN MATERIALS ARE PROVIDED "AS IS" WITHOUT WARRANTY OF ANY KIND, EXPRESS OR IMPLIED OF ANY KIND, AND HIGH PERFORMANCE SYSTEMS, INC. SPECIFICALLY DISCLAIMS THE WARRANTIES OF FITNESS FOR A PARTICULAR PURPOSE AND MERCHANTABILITY.

However, High Performance Systems, Inc. warrants to the original Licensee that the disk(s) on which the Software is recorded is free from defects in materials and workmanship under normal use and service for a period of ninety (90) days from the date of delivery as evidenced by a copy of the receipt of purchase. Further, High Performance Systems, Inc. hereby limits the duration of any implied warranty(ies) on the disk to the period stated above. Some jurisdictions may not allow limitations on duration of an implied warranty, so the above limitation may not apply to you.

THE ABOVE ARE THE ONLY WARRANTIES OF ANY KIND, EITHER EXPRESS OR IMPLIED, THAT ARE MADE BY HIGH PERFORMANCE SYSTEMS, INC. ON THE SOFTWARE. NO ORAL OR WRITTEN INFOR-MATION OR ADVICE GIVEN BY HIGH PERFORMANCE SYSTEMS, INC., ITS DEALERS, DISTRIBUTORS, AGENTS OR EMPLOYEES SHALL CREATE A WARRANTY OR IN ANY WAY INCREASE THE SCOPE OF THIS WARRANTY, AND YOU MAY NOT RELY UPON SUCH INFORMATION OR ADVICE. THIS WAR-RANTY GIVES YOU SPECIFIC LEGAL RIGHTS. YOU MAY HAVE OTHER RIGHTS, WHICH VARY AC-CORDING TO JURISDICTION.

9. Limitations of Remedies.
NEITHER HIGH PERFORMANCE SYSTEMS, INC. NOR ANYONE ELSE WHO HAS BEEN INVOLVED IN THE CREATION, PRODUCTION OR DELIVERY OF THE SOFTWARE SHALL BE LIABLE FOR ANY DIRECT, INDIRECT, CONSEQUENTIAL, OR INCIDENTAL DAMAGE (INCLUDING DAMAGE FOR LOSS OF BUSINESS PROFIT, BUSINESS INTERRUPTION, LOSS OF DATA, AND THE LIKE) ARISING OUT OF THE USE OF OR INABILITY TO USE THE SOFTWARE EVEN IF HIGH PERFORMANCE SYSTEMS, INC. HAS BEEN ADVISED OF THE POSSIBILITY OF SUCH DAMAGE. AS SOME JURISDICTION MAY NOT ALLOW THE EXCLUSION OR LIMITATION OF LIABILITY FOR CONSEQUENTIAL OR INCIDENTAL DAMAGE.

High Performance Systems', Inc. entire liability and your exclusive remedy as to the disk(s) shall be replacement of the defective disk. If failure of any disk has resulted from accident, abuse or misapplication, High Performance Systems, Inc. shall have responsibility to replace the disk. Any replacement disk will be warranted for the remainder of the original warranty period or thirty (30) days, whichever is longer.

10. Miscellaneous.
This Agreement shall be governed by the laws of the State of New Hampshire and you agree to submit to personal jurisdiction in the State of New Hampshire. This Agreement constitutes the complete and exclusive statement of the terms of the Agreement between you and High Perform-ance Systems, Inc. It supersedes and replaces any previous written or oral agreements and com-munications relating to this Software. If for any reason a court of competent jurisdiction finds any provision of this Agreement, or portion thereof, to be unenforceable, that provision of the Agreement shall be enforced to the maximum extent permissible so as to effect the intent of the parties, and the remainder of this Agreement shall continue in full force and effect.

CUSTOMER NOTE: IF THIS BOOK IS ACCOMPANIED BY SOFTWARE, PLEASE READ THE FOLLOWING BEFORE OPENING THE PACKAGE

This software contains files to help you utilize the models described in the accompanying book. By opening the package, you are agreeing to be bound by the following agreement:

This software product is protected by copyright and all rights are reserved by the author, John Wiley & Sons, Inc., or their licensors. You are licensed to use this software on a single computer. Copying the software to another medium or format for use on a single computer does not violate the U.S. Copyright Law. Copying the software for any other purpose is a violation of the U.S. Copyright Law.

This software product is sold as is without warranty of any kind, either express or implied, including but not limited to the implied warranty of merchantability and fitness for a particular purpose. Neither Wiley nor its dealers or distributors assumes any liability for any alleged or actual damages arising from the use of or the inability to use this software. (Some states do not allow the exclusion of implied warranties, so the exclusion may not apply to you.)

INDEX